Word® 6 for Windows™
SmartStart

JEAN S. INSINGA

MIDDLESEX COMMUNITY-TECHNICAL COLLEGE

Word 6 for Windows SmartStart

Copyright © 1995 by Que® Corporation.

All rights reserved. Printed in the United States of America. No part of this book may be used or reproduced in any form or by any means, or stored in a database or retrieval system, without prior written permission of the publisher except in the case of brief quotations embodied in critical articles and reviews. Making copies of any part of this book for any purpose other than your own personal use is a violation of United States copyright laws. For information, address Que College, Macmillan Computer Publishing, 201 W. 103rd Street, Indianapolis, IN 46290.

Library of Congress Catalog No.: 94-68005

ISBN: 1-56529-796-2

This book is sold *as is,* without warranty of any kind, either express or implied, respecting the contents of this book, including but not limited to implied warranties for the book's quality, performance, merchantability, or fitness for any particular purpose. Neither Que Corporation nor its dealers or distributors shall be liable to the purchaser or any other person or entity with respect to any liability, loss, or damage caused or alleged to be caused directly or indirectly by this book.

98 97 96 95   4 3 2 1

Interpretation of the printing code: the rightmost double-digit number is the year of the book's printing; the rightmost single-digit number, the number of the book's printing. For example, a printing code of 94-1 shows that the first printing of the book occurred in 1994.

Screens reproduced in this book were created using Collage Plus from Inner Media, Inc., Hollis, NH.

Word 6 for Windows SmartStart is based on Microsoft Word for Windows Version 6.0.

Publisher: David P. Ewing

Associate Publisher: Paul Boger

Book Designer: Paula Carroll

Production Team: Steve Adams, Dan Caparo, Lisa Daugherty, Mike Dietsch, Karen Dodson, Beth Lewis, Bobbi Satterfield

Indexer: Greg Eldred

About the Author

Jean S. Insinga is Professor of Information Systems and Accounting at Middlesex Community-Technical College. She has an extensive background in computer programming and application software fields. She is also the author of *Accounting in Lotus Made Easy, WordPerfect 5.1 SmartStart, dBASE IV SmartStart,* and *dBASE IV First Run,* published by Que College, and *The Prentice Hall Computerized Accounting Practice Sets.* Jean has earned B.S. and M.S. degrees from Central Connecticut State University. She also holds a C.A.I.S. (Computer Applications Information Systems) certificate from the University of New Haven.

Composed in *Stone Serif* and *MCPdigital* by Que Corporation

Trademark Acknowledgments

All terms mentioned in this book that are known to be trademarks or service marks have been appropriately capitalized. Que cannot attest to the accuracy of this information. Use of a term in this book should not be regarded as affecting the validity of any trademark or service mark.

Microsoft is a registered trademark and Windows is a trademark of Microsoft Corporation.

Lotus and 1-2-3 are registered trademarks of Lotus Development Corporation.

Acknowledgments

Que College is grateful for the assistance provided by the following reviewers: Samantha Penrod, Purdue University Calumet; Debbie Drewien, College of Southern Idaho; and Karen Mitchell, Kibler Corporation. And thank you to our technical editor, Michele Reader, College of DuPage.

Publishing Manager
Chris Katsaropoulos

Series Editor
Mary-Terese Cozzola

Managing Editor
Sheila B. Cunningham

Senior Editor
Jeannine Freudenberger

Production Editors
Barb Colter
Sally Yuska

Editorial Coordinator
Elizabeth D. Brown

Preface

Que College is the educational publishing imprint of Macmillan Computer Publishing, the world's leading computer book publisher. Macmillan Computer Publishing books have taught over 20 million people how to be productive with their computers.

This expertise in producing high-quality computer tutorial and reference books is evident in every Que College title we publish. The same tried and true authoring and product development process that makes Macmillan Computer Publishing books bestsellers is used to ensure that every Que College textbook has the most accurate and most up-to-date information. Experienced and respected college instructors write and review every manuscript to provide class-tested pedagogy. Quality-assurance editors check every keystroke and command in Que College books to ensure that instructions are clear and precise.

Above all, Macmillan Computer Publishing and, in turn, Que College, have years of experience in meeting the learning demands of computer users in business and at home. This "real-world" experience means that Que College textbooks help students understand how the skills they learn will be applied and why these skills are important.

A Smart Start to Learning Word

Word 6 for Windows SmartStart provides a hands-on approach to one of the most popular word processing programs available. The design of the text is flexible enough to meet a wide variety of needs. This text can introduce a student to word processing, or it can supplement a student's previous learning. The abundant step-by-step, hands-on tutorials allow the student to learn independently or within a large lab setting.

Prior to presenting the step-by-step tutorials, *Word 6 for Windows SmartStart* explains the purpose and practical use of each software feature. Within this context, students quickly learn how to use the software. The explanations and abundance of tutorials enable students to remember how to apply the particular skill and to transfer their knowledge easily to other software applications. This approach ensures that students will use their skills in a practical manner.

Organization

Word 6 for Windows SmartStart uses a logical, simple-to-complex organization. Features that are easy to use and understand are presented first. The student can quickly master basic features and develop a framework for learning more complicated features. In addition, software features that students can use to improve efficiency as they are learning are introduced very early in the text.

Each chapter contains many hands-on tutorials, tables, and screen illustrations to facilitate learning. Learning objectives are listed after the introduction and then repeated at the appropriate points within the chapter. Each chapter ends with a summary to help the student absorb and remember the chapter skills. The end-of-chapter exercises include objective questions and hands-on projects to help students check and apply their skills.

Distinctive Features

Word 6 for Windows SmartStart provides many distinctive features to ensure students success, including the following:

- For convenience and easy reference, key terms are defined in the margin where a new term is first used.

- Each tutorial consists of concise, clear steps. These steps are highlighted in the book design for ease of use and later reference.

- Notes, tips, shortcuts, cautions, and other helpful hints provide additional information to enhance learning.

- "If you have problems..." sections act as a teaching assistant in the lab by anticipating where common student errors occur and offering practical assistance.

- A special chapter on increasing productivity is included to help students use the software to increase their efficiency.

- Each project is realistic and designed to appeal to a wide variety of business skills and interests.

- The numerous end-of-chapter exercises focus on developing and applying critical thinking skills—not on rote memorization.

- Continuing projects are provided throughout the text. The continuing projects help learners "pull the pieces together."

- A command reference of shortcut keys is included for convenience.

- A glossary is provided.

- An alphabetical index helps users quickly locate information.

To the Student:

Although this SmartStart provides a step-by-step approach, it is much more than a button-pushing book. In response to your requests, we have included a short explanation of the purpose for each software feature. Our focus is on teaching you to use the software effectively rather than on simply listing the software's features. We want to make certain that you remember how to apply your knowledge of Word 6 for Windows long after you have taken this course.

You will not spend a great deal of time simply typing documents. We have provided your instructor with a data disk containing example information for many of the hands-on projects. You can then spend your time completing interesting projects with real-life scenarios.

To the Instructor:

As a result of your feedback, this SmartStart includes several improvements over previous books in the SmartStart series. The number of screen illustrations has been increased to help students move through the steps more quickly. The number of skills-checking exercises has been increased; this SmartStart has twice as many end-of-chapter questions and projects as previous SmartStarts. These new end-of-chapter exercises do not test rote memorization; they do reinforce practical knowledge. Each chapter has enough end-of-chapter exercises to ensure that all objectives have been fully addressed.

The instructor's manual includes a Curriculum Guide to help you plan class sessions and assignments. Each chapter in the instructor's manual contains teaching tips, answers to "Checking Your Skills" questions, transparency masters, and test questions and answers. The manual also offers advice on what to teach when time is short or when the students have a specific need. Additional project ideas and suggestions also are included.

Look for the following additional SmartStarts:

Access 2 for Windows SmartStart	1-56529-874-8
BASIC SmartStart	1-56529-402-5
dBASE IV SmartStart	1-56529-251-0
Excel 5 for Windows SmartStart	1-56529-794-6
Lotus 1-2-3 SmartStart (covers 2.4 and below)	1-56529-245-6
Lotus for Windows SmartStart	1-56529-404-1
MS-DOS SmartStart	1-56529-249-9
Novell NetWare SmartStart	1-56529-411-4
Paradox for Windows SmartStart	1-56529-405-X
Personal Computing SmartStart	1-56529-455-6
Quattro Pro for Windows 1.0 SmartStart	1-56529-409-2
Windows 3.1 SmartStart	1-56529-203-0
WordPerfect 5.1 SmartStart	1-56529-246-4
WordPerfect 6 SmartStart	1-56529-407-6
WordPerfect for Windows SmartStart	1-56529-403-3
Works for DOS SmartStart	1-56529-396-7
Works for Windows SmartStart	1-56529-394-0

For more information call:

1-800-428-5331

Contents at a Glance

Introduction 1

1 Getting Started 5

2 Editing a Document 35

3 Checking Your Work 77

4 Managing and Printing Files 101

5 Enhancing the Text in a Document 121

6 Formatting a Paragraph 147

7 Formatting a Page 197

8 Designing Tables in a Document 233

9 Merging Files 267

10 Increasing Your Productivity 299

A Working with Windows 341

Index 357

Table of Contents

Introduction 1
An Overview of Word for Windows 6.0 Features 1
    How This Book Is Organized 2
    Conventions Used in This Book 3

1 Getting Started 5
Objectives 5
Objective 1: Recognize the Word for Windows Environment 5
    Standard Toolbar 7
    Formatting Toolbar 7
    Horizontal Ruler 7
    Text Area 7
    Scroll Bars 7
    Status Bar 8
    Style Area 9
Objective 2: Work with Toolbars 9
    Choosing from the Standard Toolbar 15
Objective 3: Create a New Document 16
    Identifying the Text Area 18
    Understanding Word Wrap 18
    Typing Text in a Document 19
Objective 4: Save a Document 20
    Choosing the Save or Save As Command 21
Objective 5: Print a Document 21
Objective 6: Access Help 22
    Using the Index 26
    Using Context-Sensitive Help 26
    Getting Help about a Command 26
    Getting Help about a Dialog Box 27
Objective 7: Close Word 27
Chapter Summary 27
Checking Your Skills 28
    True/False Questions 28
    Multiple-Choice Questions 28
    Fill-in-the-Blank Questions 30

Applying Your Skills 31
    Review Exercises 31
        Exercise 1: Changing Toolbars 31
        Exercise 2: Creating MEDICAL.DOC 31
        Exercise 3: Creating and Saving a Document 32
        Exercise 4: Using the Standard Toolbar to Create a Document 32
        Exercise 5: Using the Formatting Toolbar 32
    Continuing Projects 33
        Project 1: Practice in Using Word 33
        Project 2: Federal Department Store 33
        Project 3: Real Entertainment Corporation 33

2 Editing a Document   35

Objectives 35
Objective 1: Open an Existing Document 35
    Opening a Recently Used Document 36
Objective 2: Move Around in a Document 37
    Using the Mouse to Move the Insertion Point 37
    Using the Keyboard to Move the Insertion Point 39
    Moving to a Specific Location 40
Objective 3: Use AutoCorrect to Prevent Mistakes 41
    Changing the AutoCorrect List of Errors 43
Objective 4: Use Basic Editing Features 44
    Understanding Insert and Overtype Modes 44
    Inserting Blank Lines 44
    Displaying Nonprinting Characters 45
    Selecting Text 46
        Being Careful with Paragraph Marks 47
        Selecting Text with the Mouse 47
        Using the Keyboard to Select Text 48
        Extending a Selection 49
        Deleting with Shortcut Keys 50
    Moving, Copying, and Deleting Text 50
    The Clipboard 52
    Undoing Your Mistakes 58
    Using Undo 58
    Using the Edit Menu to Undo and Redo Actions 60
    Repeating an Action 60
Objective 5: Work with More than One Document 61
    Working with Different Documents on the Same Screen 62
    Displaying Documents in Different Views 64
    Changing between Views 64

Deciding Which View to Use	65
Using Full Screen View	67

Chapter Summary 68
Checking Your Skills 68
    True/False Questions 68
    Multiple-Choice Questions 69
    Fill-in-the-Blank Questions 71
Applying Your Skills 72
    Review Exercises 72
        Exercise 1: Adding Text to FIRST.DOC 72
        Exercise 2: Using Help to Learn More about Magnification 72
        Exercise 3: Changing Views 72
        Exercise 4: Editing Text 72
        Exercise 5: Copying Text 73
    Continuing Projects 73
        Project 1: Practice in Using Word 73
        Project 2: Federal Department Store 74
        Project 3: Real Entertainment Corporation 74

3 Checking Your Work   77

Objectives 77
Objective 1: Check Your Spelling 77
    Detecting and Correcting Unrecognized Words 78
    Working with Custom Dictionaries 79
        Choosing Other Spelling Options 83
Objective 2: Use the Thesaurus 83
Objective 3: Check Your Grammar 85
Objective 4: Find and Replace Text 88
    Narrowing the Search 89
    Replacing Text, Special Characters, or Formatting 92
Chapter Summary 94
Checking Your Skills 94
    True/False Questions 94
    Multiple-Choice Questions 95
    Fill-in-the-Blank Questions 97
Applying Your Skills 97
    Review Exercises 97
        Exercise 1: Using Find and Spelling Checker 97
        Exercise 2: Using Find, Replace, and Spelling Checker 98
        Exercise 3: Using the Grammar Checker and the Thesaurus 98
        Exercise 4: Using the Spelling Checker and Grammar Checker ..98
        Exercise 5: Using Find, Replace, and Spelling Checker 98

Continuing Projects 98
    Project 1: Practice in Using Word 98
    Project 2: Federal Department Store 99
    Project 3: Real Entertainment Corporation 99

4 Managing and Printing Files   101

Objectives 101
Objective 1: Use Summary Information 101
    Creating Summary Information 102
    Viewing Document Statistics 103
Objective 2: Find Files 104
    Finding Files with Find File 104
Objective 3: Compare Versions of the Same Document 107
Objective 4: Insert Files from Word and Other Programs 108
Objective 5: Print a Document 109
    Selecting a Printer 110
    Printing an Entire Active Document 111
    Printing Selected Pages of the Active Document 111
    Selecting Printing Options 112
    Printing Special Information 113
    Printing to a File 114
Chapter Summary 114
Checking Your Skills 115
    True/False Questions 115
    Multiple-Choice Questions 115
    Fill-in-the-Blank Questions 117
Applying Your Skills 118
    Review Exercises 118
        Exercise 1: Using Summary Information 118
        Exercise 2: Using Find Files 118
        Exercise 3: Printing Files 119
        Exercise 4: Adding Text to BUTTON.DOC 119
    Continuing Projects 119
        Project 1: Practice in Using Word 119
        Project 2: Federal Department Store 119
        Project 3: Real Entertainment Corporation 120

5 Enhancing the Text in a Document   121

Objectives 121
Overview of Formatting 121
Objective 1: Change Fonts and Font Sizes 122
Objective 2: Improve the Appearance of Text 129

Objective 3: Change Character Spacing 133
Objective 4: Set and Restore the Default Character Format 135
Objective 5: Remove and Copy Character Formatting 137
    Removing Character Formatting 138
Chapter Summary 140
Checking Your Skills 140
    True/False Questions 140
    Multiple-Choice Questions 140
    Fill-in-the-Blank Questions 142
Applying Your Skills 143
    Review Exercises 143
        Exercise 1: Applying Font Styles 143
        Exercise 2: Changing Fonts in FIRST.DOC 143
        Exercise 3: Changing Fonts in SCHEDULE.DOC 144
        Exercise 4: Changing Font Sizes and Copying Formatting 144
        Exercise 5: Applying Font Styles and Sizes 144
    Continuing Projects 144
        Project 1: Practice in Using Word 144
        Project 2: Federal Department Store 145
        Project 3: Real Entertainment Corporation 145

6 Formatting a Paragraph — 147

Objectives 147
An Overview of Paragraph Formatting 147
Objective 1: Set the Unit of Measurement 149
Objective 2: Set Tab Positions and Tab Alignment 151
Objective 3: Indent Paragraphs 155
    Using the Formatting Toolbar to Change Indentation 155
    Using the Keyboard to Indent Paragraphs 156
    Using the Paragraph Dialog Box to Indent Paragraphs 160
Objective 4: Align Paragraphs 161
    Using the Formatting Toolbar to Set Paragraph Alignment 162
    Using the Keyboard to Set Paragraph Alignment 163
Objective 5: Use Automatic Hyphenation 164
    Using Hyphens in a Document 164
Objective 6: Control Line Spacing 168
    Using the Keyboard to Set Line Spacing within Paragraphs 168
    Setting the Space Between Paragraphs 169
    Using the Paragraph Dialog Box Text Flow Options 170
Objective 7: Remove and Repeat Paragraph Formatting 171

Objective 8: Apply Borders and Shading to Paragraphs 172
    Adding Borders to Paragraphs 172
    Using the Paragraph Borders and Shading Dialog Box 174
    Creating Borders and Shading with the Shading Toolbar 175
Objective 9: Create Bulleted and Numbered Lists 176
Objective 10: Create an Outline 178
    Changing the Level of Headings 183
Chapter Summary 189
Checking Your Skills 190
    True/False Questions 190
    Multiple-Choice Questions 190
    Fill-In-the-Blank Questions 193
Applying Your Skills 193
    Review Exercises 193
        Exercise 1: Indenting Paragraphs 193
        Exercise 2: Using Custom Tabs 193
        Exercise 3: Centering a Paragraph 194
        Exercise 4: Creating a Bulleted List 194
        Exercise 5: Applying Borders and Shading 194
    Continuing Projects 194
        Project 1: Practice in Using Word 194
        Project 2: Federal Department Store 195
        Project 3: Real Entertainment Corporation 196

7 Formatting a Page   197

Objectives 197
Objective 1: Set Margins 198
Objective 2: Choose Paper Size and Orientation 201
Objective 3: Choose a Paper Source 202
Objective 4: Control Pagination 203
    Setting Page Breaks 203
    Repaginating a Document 204
    Numbering Pages 205
Objective 5: Create Headers and Footers 207
    Editing Headers and Footers 212
Objective 6: Divide a Document into Sections 212
    Deleting a Section Break 214
    Assigning Formats to Sections 214
Objective 7: Divide Pages into Columns 215
    Setting the Column Format 216
    Changing Column Widths and Spacing 219
    Setting Up Columns with Exact Measurements 219

Placing Lines between Columns 220
Balancing Column Lengths 220
Objective 8: Import Pictures 220
Linking a Picture File 222
Objective 9: Achieve Special Text Effects 222
Chapter Summary 226
Checking Your Skills 226
True/False Questions 226
Multiple-Choice Questions 227
Fill-in-the-Blank Questions 229
Applying Your Skills 229
Review Exercises 229
Exercise 1: Formatting FIRST.DOC 229
Exercise 2: Formatting SCHEDULE.DOC 230
Exercise 3: Formatting MEDICAL.DOC 230
Exercise 4: Formatting GUIDELINE.DOC 230
Exercise 5: Formatting STEP2.DOC 230
Continuing Projects 231
Project 1: Practice Using Word 231
Project 2: Federal Department Store 231
Project 3: Real Entertainment Corporation 231

8 Designing Tables in a Document — 233

Objectives 233
Objective 1: Recognize When to Use Tables 234
Objective 2: Create Side-by-Side Columns and Tables 234
Objective 3: Enter Data in a Table 237
Entering Records in a Table 238
Objective 4: Select Cells, Columns, and Rows 240
Objective 5: Move between Cells 242
Objective 6: Change Column Widths and Row Heights 242
Changing Row Heights 245
Objective 7: Insert and Delete Columns, Rows, and Cells 246
Deleting Columns, Rows, and Cells 248
Objective 8: Move Columns, Rows, and Cells 249
Objective 9: Edit Text in a Table 251
Objective 10: Add Borders and Shading 253
Adding Borders and Shading Manually 254
Objective 11: Calculate Values 254
Multiplying Numbers 257
Chapter Summary 258

Checking Your Skills 258
   True/False Questions 258
   Multiple-Choice Questions 259
   Fill-in-the-Blank Questions 261
Applying Your Skills 262
   Review Exercises 262
      Exercise 1: Creating a Two-Column Table 262
      Exercise 2: Creating a Three-Column Table 262
      Exercise 3: Inserting a Table in MEDICAL.DOC 262
      Exercise 4: Inserting a Table in FONTS.DOC 263
      Exercise 5: Inserting a Table into GUIDELINE.DOC 263
   Continuing Projects 264
      Project 1: Practice in Using Word 264
      Project 2: Federal Department Store 264
      Project 3: Real Entertainment Corporation 264

9 Merging Files   267

Objectives 267
Objective 1: Understand the Basic Merge Procedure 267
Objective 2: Create a Main Document 268
   Creating a Main Document for a Form Letter 268
   Creating a Main Document for Labels 270
Objective 3: Create or Open a Data Source 271
   Creating a New Data Source 272
   Opening an Existing Data Source 277
Objective 4: Insert Merge Fields in the Main Document 278
   Inserting Merge Fields for Envelopes 280
Objective 5: Merge the Data and Document 286
   Merging Form Letters, Envelopes, or Labels 287
   Merging with Toolbar Shortcuts 288
Objective 6: Use Other Merging Features 288
   Checking the Merge for Errors 288
   Merging Only Certain Records 289
   Sorting Data before Merging 291
Chapter Summary 291
Checking Your Skills 292
   True/False Questions 292
   Multiple-Choice Questions 292
   Fill-in-the-Blank Questions 294
Applying Your Skills 295
   Review Exercises 295
      Exercise 1: Creating a Main Document 295

Exercise 2: Creating a Data Source	295
Exercise 3: Merging	296
Exercise 4: Create a Main Label Document	296
Exercise 5: Merging	296
Continuing Projects	296
Project 1: Preparing a Mail Merge	296
Project 2: Federal Department Store	296
Project 3: Real Entertainment Corporation	296

10 Increasing Your Productivity — 299

Objectives	299
Overview of Templates, Styles, and Style Sheets	299
Objective 1: Work with Styles and Style Sheets	301
Applying Styles in a Normal Template	301
Applying a Style	302
Expanding the List of Style Names	304
Examining Styles	308
Modifying a Style	310
Specifying the Style for a Following Paragraph	314
Objective 2: Use AutoFormat	315
Objective 3: Use Wizards	316
Objective 4: Use AutoText	318
Inserting an AutoText Entry	320
Objective 5: Install Word Macros	324
Objective 6: Record Macros	326
Objective 7: Run Macros	328
Running Macros from the Macro Dialog Box	328
Assigning Macros to Shortcut Keys	329
Objective 8: Rename and Delete Macros	333
Chapter Summary	334
Checking Your Skills	334
True/False Questions	334
Multiple-Choice Questions	335
Fill-in-the-Blank Questions	337
Applying Your Skills	338
Review Exercises	338
Exercise 1: Applying Styles	338
Exercise 2: Using AutoFormat and AutoText	338
Exercise 3: Using the Calendar Wizard	338
Exercise 4: Using Agenda Wizard	338
Exercise 5: Using AutoFormat	338
Continuing Projects	338

Project 1: Practice Using Word 338
Project 2: Federal Department Store 339
Project 3: Real Entertainment Corporation 339

A Working with Windows — 341

Objective 1: Start Windows 341
    Starting Windows 341
Objective 2: Use a Mouse in Windows 342
Objective 3: Understand the Windows Desktop 343
    The Title Bar 343
    Menus 344
    Dialog Boxes 345
    Buttons 345
Objective 4: Understand the Program Manager 345
Objective 5: Get Help 346
    Displaying Help for a Topic 347
    Closing the Help Window 347
Objective 6: Get Comfortable with Windows 347
    Opening a Window 348
    Changing the Active Window 348
    Resizing a Window 349
    Moving a Window 350
    Maximizing a Window 351
    Minimizing a Window 352
    Restoring a Window 352
    Arranging the Windows on Your Desktop 353
    Closing a Window 354
Objective 7: Exit Windows 355

Index — 357

Introduction

An Overview of Word for Windows 6.0 Features

Windows
The capitalized *Windows* refers to Microsoft Windows version 3.1, the operating environment under which Word runs. The lowercase *window* or *windows* refers to the active portion of your screen.

Word for Windows 6.0 is a word processing program that meets the needs of people in a variety of industries and professions. Word easily supports basic word processing features such as enhancing text with underlined, boldface, or italic type and checking for spelling errors. Word also supports far more sophisticated features used in creating, editing, and publishing documents—features such as automating work by using macros and AutoText building tables and outlines and handling graphics. Word now includes many features you expect to find only in high end desktop publishing applications.

The following list summarizes Word For Windows features you can use to save time and increase productivity:

- You can see on-screen all text in the font and size you have chosen by using WYSIWYG (what-you-see-is-what-you-get).

- You can use many different fonts and font sizes, and add emphasis by choosing boldface or italic type. You can define paragraph styles and apply them throughout a document.

- You can easily move text by dragging it with the mouse.

Macro
A stored list of commands recorded or defined by the user. When retrieved, macros replay the command to accomplish a task such as changing directories.

- You can automate repetitive work by using *macros* and *templates*.

- You can create tables of contents for multipart documents.

- You can import pictures from Word's library of clip art or other sources.

- You can easily create headers and footers.

- You can create newspaper-style columns that start anywhere on a page. You can have different numbers of columns within a document and even on a single page.

Template
A pattern for a document. A template contains all the features that are common among all documents of one type.

- You can print some pages of a document in portrait orientation (vertically) and others in landscape orientation (horizontally).

- You can enhance pages with borders and shading.

- You can choose to display one or more toolbars, each of which provides instant access to commands and provides shortcut methods of performing various tasks. From a toolbar, for example, you can number lists or create bulleted entries, cut and paste text, open or save existing documents, and start new documents. You can customize toolbars to suit your particular needs.

- Word has a Spelling Checker, a Thesaurus, and a Grammar Checker.
- A Preview feature enables you to check the contents of a document before you open it, making file management easier.

In the pages that follow, you will find step-by-step instructions for using most of these capabilities. This Word upgrade makes the application a very versatile document generator; its capabilities enable you to achieve professional—and useful—results.

How This Book Is Organized

Word 6 for Windows SmartStart shows you how to use the word processing program Microsoft Word for Windows Version 6.0.

Chapter 1, "Getting Started," introduces the Word for Windows environment, as well as the general features of a word processing program.

Chapter 2, "Editing a Document," shows how to open and make changes to an existing document.

Chapter 3, "Checking Your Work," covers the features Word provides for checking documents and making changes to the text.

Chapter 4, "Managing and Printing Files," presents methods for managing files—procedures for opening, deleting, copying, and printing more than one document.

Chapter 5, "Enhancing the Text in a Document," shows how to improve the appearance of a document by changing the character formatting.

Chapter 6, "Formatting a Paragraph," illustrates paragraph-formatting options such as indenting text, double-spacing text, setting up tables using tabs within a document, and aligning text.

Chapter 7, "Formatting a Page," shows how to format pages, to set margins, paper size, and orientation; use page numbering and insert page breaks; create headers and footers; format sections; work with columns; import pictures; and use special text effects.

Chapter 8, "Designing Tables in a Document," presents how to create tables or side-by-side paragraphs within your documents, and how to edit and format tables.

Chapter 9, "Merging Files," introduces the powerful and time-saving Mail Merge Helper, which guides users through the process of linking a document file with a type of database file.

Chapter 10, "Increasing Your Productivity," explains how to use several other features for automating the repetitive aspects of your work—the Styles, Wizard, AutoText, and Macros features.

Appendix A, "Working with Windows," is a reference for using Windows 3.1.

Conventions Used in This Book

The conventions used in this book have been established to help you learn to use Word 6 quickly and easily. As much as possible, the conventions correspond with those used in the Word 6 program and documentation.

In this book, selecting means highlighting text or an option, and choosing means executing a command from a menu or a dialog box.

The keys you press and the text you type appear in **boldfaced second-color** type in the numbered steps and projects and in **boldfaced** type elsewhere. Key combinations are joined by a plus sign: Shift+F5 in numbered steps and Shift+F5 elsewhere.

The key combination Shift+F5 indicates that you are to press and hold down Shift while you press and release F5. The key combination Shift, F5 indicates that you are to press and release Shift, and then press F5.

File names and directory names are written in all capital letters. Options, commands, menu names, and dialog box names are capitalized like headlines.

On-screen prompts and messages are in a `special typeface`.

CHAPTER 1
Getting Started

Document
A file containing the work created by a program.

In this chapter, you learn simple yet essential aspects of working in Word for Windows 6.0. People often want to jump right into a new program and work on a sophisticated project. You will find, however, that you can gain proficiency much quicker when you know the basics. Therefore, you start by learning the Word for Windows environment, which includes buttons and toolbars, as well as the general features of a word processing program—word wrap, saving, printing, and so on. These basic techniques provide the necessary foundation for you to work effectively and efficiently on *documents* in Word.

This chapter also introduces you to the Word Help feature, a valuable tool for anyone working in Word.

Objectives

By the time you finish this chapter, you will have learned to

1. Recognize the Word for Windows Environment
2. Work with Toolbars
3. Create a New Document
4. Save a Document
5. Print a Document
6. Access Help
7. Close Word

Objective 1: Recognize the Word for Windows Environment

Word 6 for Windows is a user-friendly program once you become familiar with the environment. The program has the same general features as other Windows applications.

Starting Word

To begin the program from within Windows, follow these steps:

❶ Double-click the Word icon. The opening Word logo appears for a moment, and then the Tip of the Day displays (see figure 1.1).

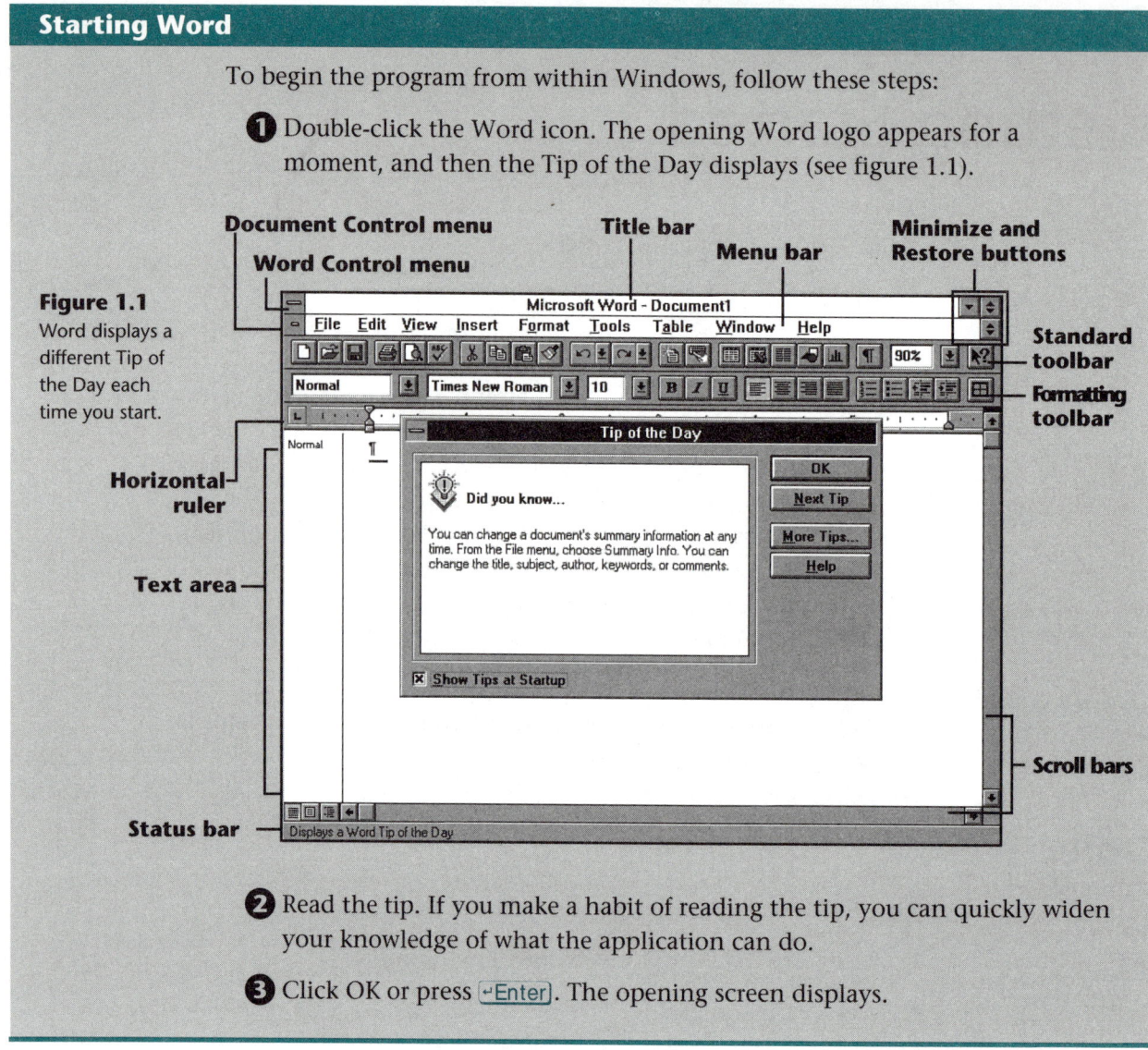

Figure 1.1
Word displays a different Tip of the Day each time you start.

❷ Read the tip. If you make a habit of reading the tip, you can quickly widen your knowledge of what the application can do.

❸ Click OK or press [←Enter]. The opening screen displays.

Note: *Word provides you with two ways of confirming a selection—by clicking OK or by pressing* [←Enter]. *From this point on, this book uses* choose OK *to refer to these methods of confirmation.*

Default
A choice Word makes unless you choose something different.

The screen in figure 1.1 is what you see the first time Word runs after you have installed it. In this screen, Word is maximized so that it occupies the entire screen, and the new document also is maximized so that it occupies as much space as possible. Don't be surprised if your screen isn't quite the same as this one. You can change the way Word looks in many ways by changing the setup *defaults*. If you choose not to display the tip of the day, for example, only the Word screen will appear.

Note: *The Word windows used in the figures in this book vary to demonstrate that the windows can be changed to accommodate the preferences of the user or the requirements of the word processing project.*

When you start Word, the application opens a new document titled Document1. You will want to save this document with a more appropriate name when you begin working.

You can open many Word documents at one time, each in its own window (Chapter 2 tells you how to switch to other documents). Word numbers additional new documents sequentially—Document2, Document3, and so on. When you exit and then restart Word, it starts with Document1 again.

As you can tell from figure 1.1, Word has many of the same features that Windows has. In this section, you learn about the unique components of the opening Word screen—two toolbars, the horizontal ruler, the text area, two scroll bars, the status bar, and the style area.

Standard Toolbar

The first toolbar, the Standard toolbar, is just below the menu bar. This toolbar contains a row of buttons that provide shortcuts to Word menu commands as well as some other features. The Standard toolbar is described in more detail later in this chapter.

Formatting Toolbar

Select
To highlight or mark text by dragging the mouse so that you can perform an operation on the text.

The Formatting toolbar, just below the Standard toolbar, also provides shortcuts to menu commands. You can use it to make *selected* text boldface, underlined, or italic; to control paragraph alignment; to control indentation; and to create borders around sections of text. You also can use this toolbar to select fonts, font sizes, and paragraph styles. The Formatting toolbar is covered in more detail in Chapter 5.

Horizontal Ruler

The horizontal ruler, just below the Formatting toolbar, provides convenient ways to change margins, adjust indents, and change the width of newspaper-style and table columns. The horizontal ruler is covered in more detail in Chapter 6.

Text Area

Insertion point
A flashing vertical bar on-screen that indicates where Word will place text or an object.

Just below the horizontal ruler is the text area, where you type text and insert tables and graphics. A flashing vertical bar—the *insertion point*—appears in the upper left corner of the text area. The insertion point indicates where text will appear when you begin to type. A horizontal bar marks the end of the document.

Scroll Bars

Scroll
Moving the text on-screen vertically or horizontally.

At the bottom and right side of the screen are the horizontal and vertical scroll bars. If you point to the arrow at the right end of the horizontal scroll bar and press the mouse button, the text on-screen *scrolls* to the right. The arrow at the left end scrolls to the left. You can use the buttons at the top and bottom of the vertical scroll bar to scroll up or down, just as you can in Windows.

8   Getting Started

The Word scroll bars have features that differ from the Windows scroll bar, however.

- The *split box,* a small black box just above the arrow at the top of the vertical scroll bar, splits the current window into two panes so that you can see two parts of the same document simultaneously.

- The three buttons at the left end of the horizontal scroll bar provide different views of your document—Normal, Page Layout, and Outline.

Status Bar

The bottom line of the window is the status bar, which displays information about the page in which the insertion point is positioned, about the highlighted command, or about the toolbar button to which you are pointing (see figure 1.2).

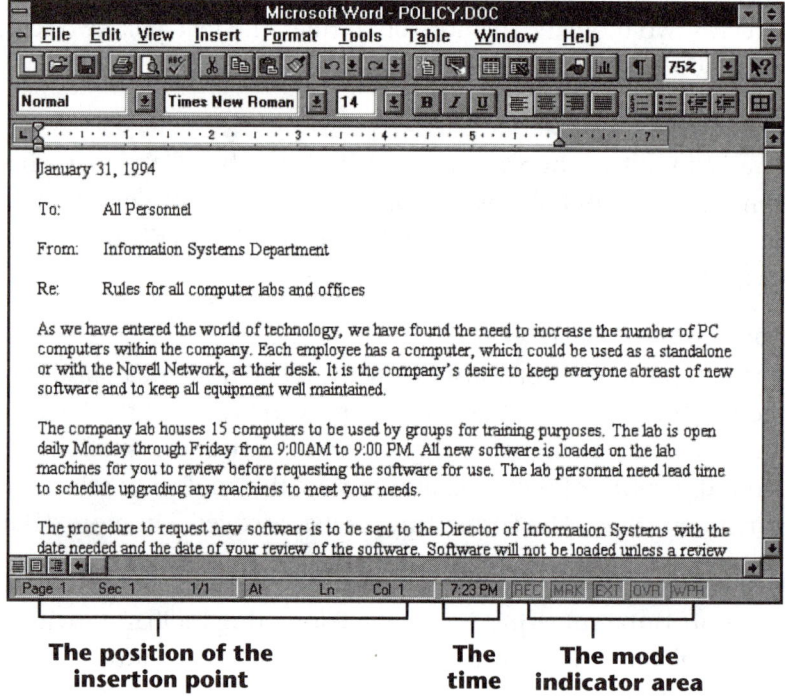

Figure 1.2
In this figure, the first part of the status bar indicates that the insertion point is on page 1 in section 1 of the document, and that the page is page 1 of 1.

The second part shows the insertion point position measured in inches from the top edge of the page (including the top margin), together with the line and column position.

The third part indicates the time of day.

The fourth part of the status bar contains five buttons, all of which are dimmed when you start Word. Each button represents an aspect (or mode) of the way Word works. Double-click any of these buttons to activate or deactivate them. When a button is active, the three letters are black; when a button is inactive, the letters are gray. The five buttons on the status bar are the following:

- REC starts the macro recorder, as explained in Chapter 10.
- MRK marks revisions, as explained in Chapter 2.
- EXT turns on Extend Selection. This is covered in Chapter 2.
- OVR selects Word's Overtype mode, as explained in Chapter 2. When OVR is not selected, Word is in the Insert mode.
- WPH displays Help messages to assist WordPerfect users.

The status bar changes when you perform certain actions. If you point to one of the buttons in a toolbar, the status bar displays a message indicating what will happen when you click that button. When you open a menu, the information in the status bar changes to a summary of the function of the highlighted menu item.

Style Area

Style
A combination of character and paragraph formatting that you save as a collection in a file called a style sheet.

You may see a vertical line close to the left edge of the text area. The space to the left of this line is the style area. Word assigns a *style* to each paragraph you type. The style area, which you can choose to display or not, shows the style name for each paragraph. Chapter 10 provides information on styles and on displaying style names.

These Word features—the Standard and Formatting toolbars, the horizontal ruler, the text area, the horizontal and vertical scroll bars, the status bar, and the style area—make your word processing tasks easier.

Objective 2: Work with Toolbars

When you first start Word, the screen displays the Standard and Formatting toolbars. To use Word efficiently, you should become familiar with the functions accessible from these toolbars; they save keystrokes or extra mouse movement so that you don't have to use the pull-down menus.

In addition to the Standard and Formatting toolbars, Word has several others you can display to help you with specific tasks. The information that follows applies to all the toolbars in Word.

Using Toolbars

Most users find that using the Word toolbars makes working in Word easy and increases efficiency. To start the Spelling Checker, for example, you can click the **T**ools menu and then click the **S**pelling command, or you can use the Standard toolbar, just below the menu bar. To use the Standard toolbar, follow these steps:

❶ Position the mouse pointer on the button that has ABC and a check mark on it, but don't click. A yellow flag—known as a ToolTip—displays the button's name (see figure 1.3).

(continues)

Using Toolbars (continued)

Figure 1.3
Hold the mouse pointer on a toolbar button or list box to display a ToolTip that gives the object's name.

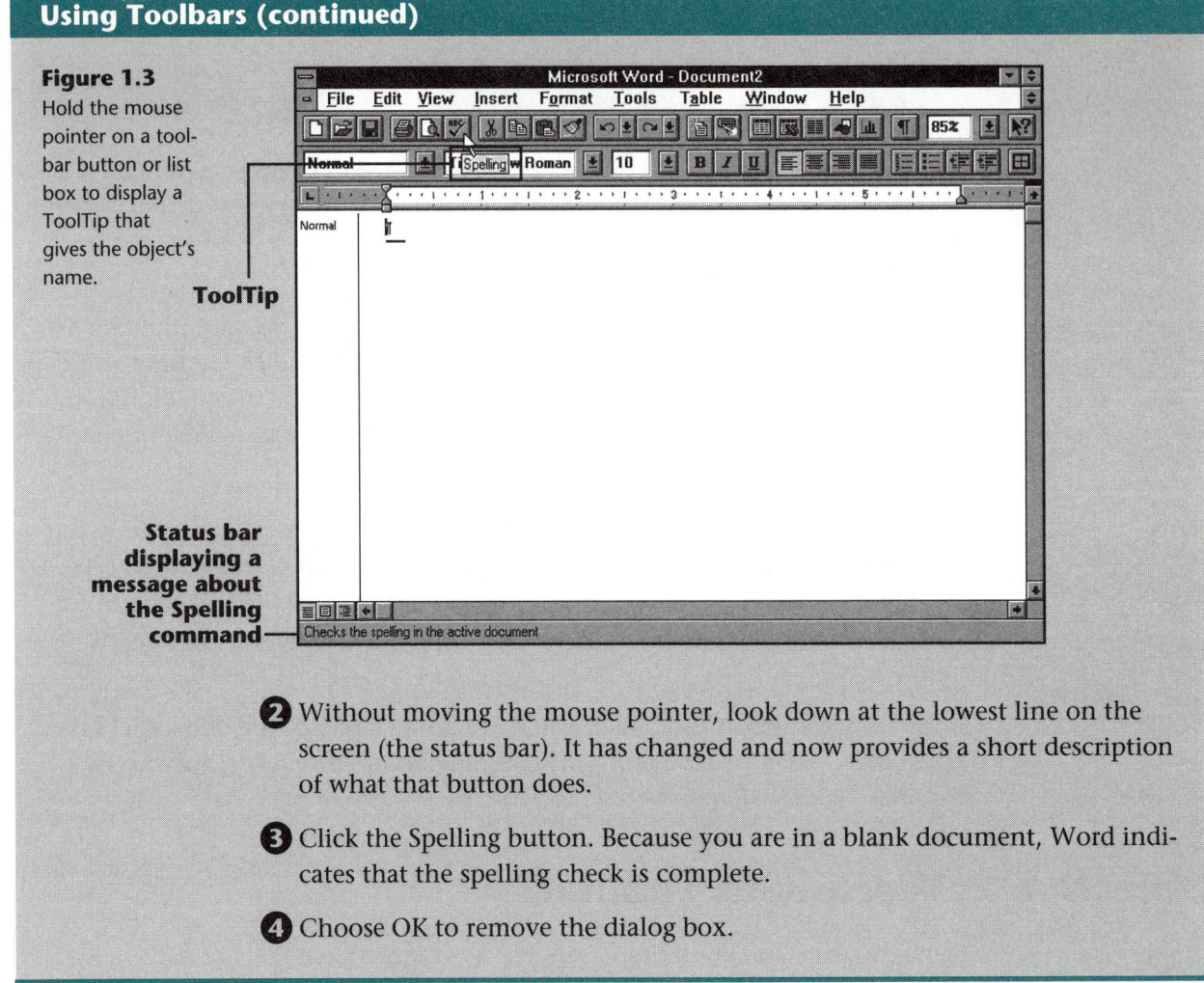

ToolTip

Status bar displaying a message about the Spelling command

❷ Without moving the mouse pointer, look down at the lowest line on the screen (the status bar). It has changed and now provides a short description of what that button does.

❸ Click the Spelling button. Because you are in a blank document, Word indicates that the spelling check is complete.

❹ Choose OK to remove the dialog box.

The Standard and Formatting toolbars in figure 1.1 are shown in their normal position, shape, and size, as they appear when you first start Word. With your document on-screen, you can change the shape and position of the toolbar. Changing the position and shape of the toolbar can give more vertical or horizontal workspace on-screen.

Changing the Position and Shape of a Toolbar

You can change the position and shape of a toolbar. To change the Standard toolbar, follow these steps:

❶ Point to the Standard toolbar, anywhere between two buttons but not on a button.

❷ Double-click the left mouse button. The toolbar immediately changes shape and moves into the text area. Notice that the toolbar now has a title bar of its own (see figure 1.4).

When a toolbar is in the rectangular format, it is known as a floating toolbar because you can move it anywhere on-screen.

Figure 1.4
The Standard toolbar is shown here in the rectangular format.

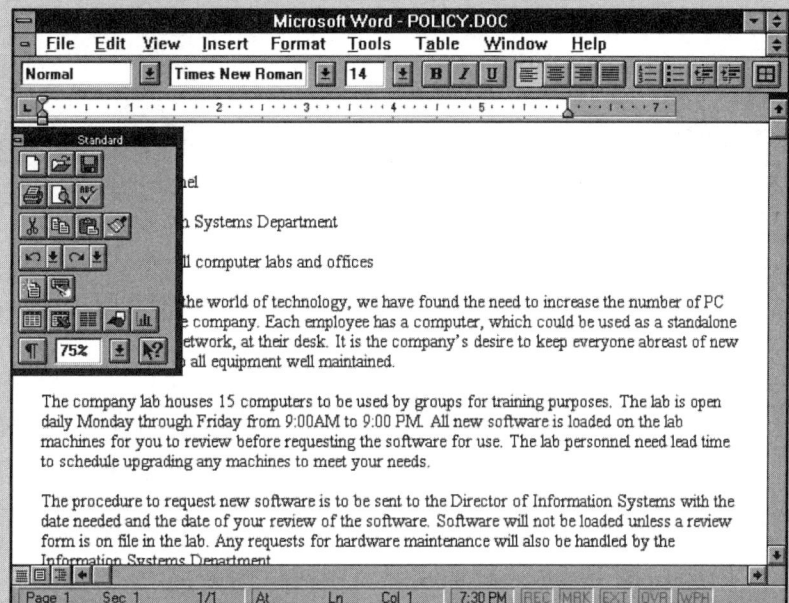

③ Point to the toolbar's title bar, press the left mouse button, and drag the pointer to move the toolbar to wherever you want it to be.

④ To change the shape of the toolbar, position the pointer on one of the toolbar borders.

⑤ When the pointer changes to a double-headed arrow, hold down the left mouse button, and drag the toolbar up, down, and over (see figure 1.5).

Figure 1.5
When the pointer is in the correct position, it changes to a double-headed arrow.

The double-headed arrow

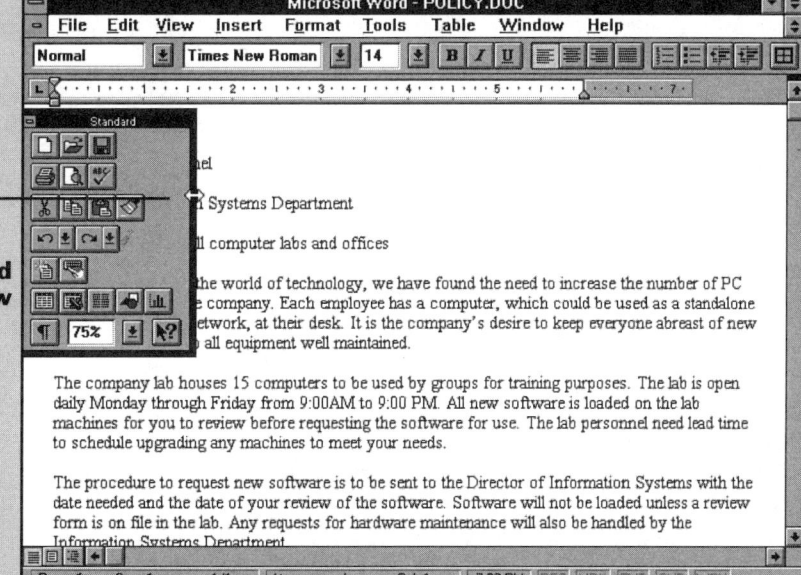

⑤ Point to a space between buttons, and double-click. The toolbar then returns to its initial position and shape.

In addition to changing the position and shape of a toolbar, you can change the size of its buttons. You can display the toolbar with the buttons shown in previous illustrations or with large buttons.

Changing the Size of the Toolbar Buttons

To change from displaying small toolbar buttons to large buttons, follow these steps:

1 Point anywhere on a toolbar, and click the right mouse button.

A menu with the Toolbar option near the bottom appears (see figure 1.6).

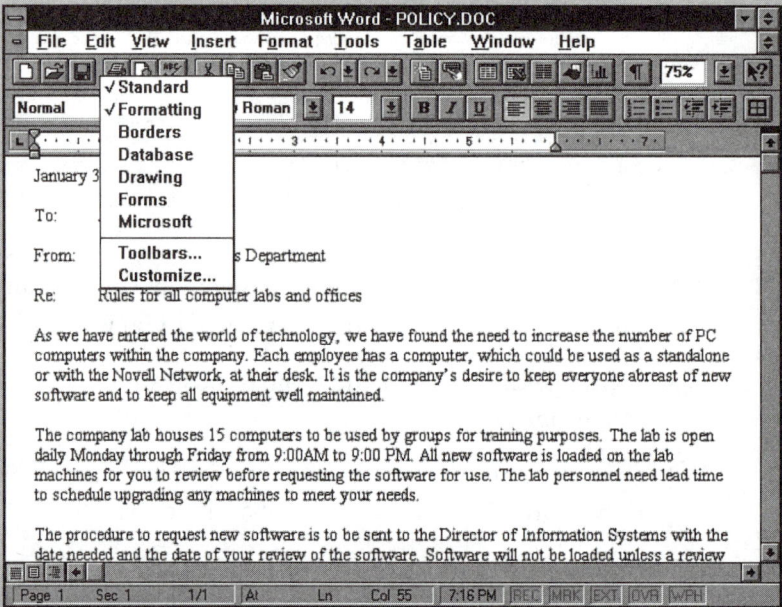

Figure 1.6
Use the menu to choose to display toolbars.

Note: *When you point to a toolbar and click the right mouse button, you see a shortcut menu. Shortcut menus are mentioned throughout this book.*

2 Using the left mouse button, click Toolbars to display the Toolbars dialog box (see figure 1.7).

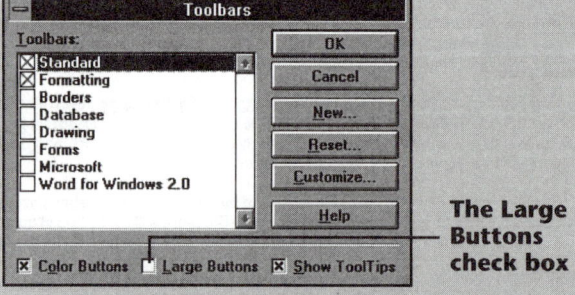

Figure 1.7
Use the Large Buttons check box at the bottom of the Toolbars dialog box to choose between small and large buttons.

❸ Click the Large Buttons check box until an X is in the box, indicating that the Large Buttons option is selected.

❹ Choose OK to confirm that you want large buttons (see figure 1.8).

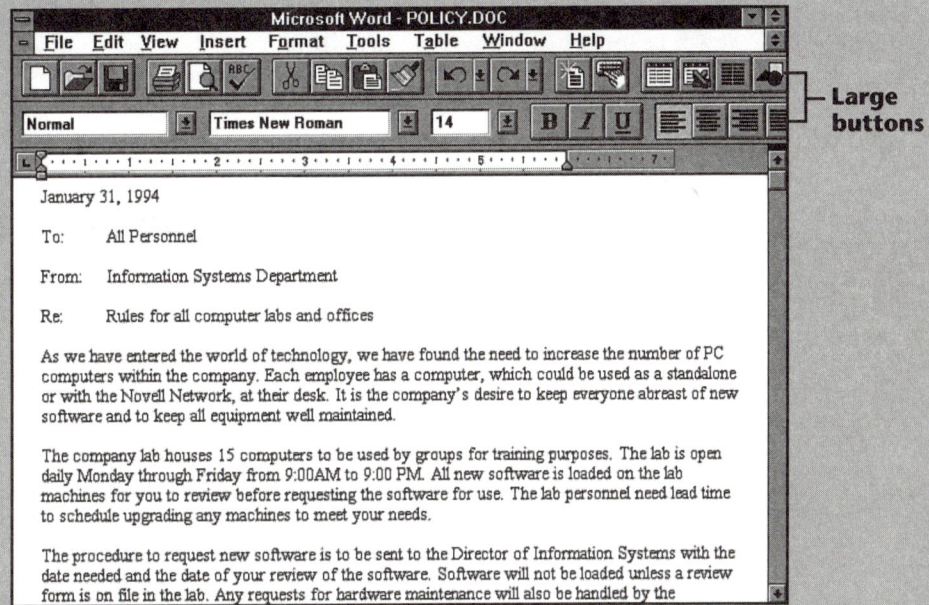

Figure 1.8
Now Word displays large buttons on both the Standard and Formatting toolbars.

Note: *You cannot have one toolbar with small buttons and another with large buttons.*

❺ To display small buttons, repeat the preceding steps until step 3.

❻ Click the Large Buttons check box until the box is empty.

❼ Choose OK to confirm that the toolbars display small buttons.

Large buttons are easier to see but take up a considerable amount of valuable screen space. In the case of a toolbar with many buttons, such as the Standard toolbar, you do not see all the buttons when the toolbar is in its initial position and large buttons are selected. If large buttons are used, it is best to customize the toolbar with buttons commonly used or to display the toolbar vertically to the left or right of the screen.

Displaying Other Toolbars

When you were changing from displaying small to large buttons, you opened the Toolbars dialog box, which contained a list of eight toolbars with check boxes next to them. The Standard and Formatting check boxes were checked, showing that those toolbars were displayed. To display another toolbar, follow these steps:

(continues)

Displaying Other Toolbars (continued)

❶ Point anywhere on a toolbar, and click the right mouse button. A menu with the Toolbar option near the bottom appears.

❷ Click the Toolbar option, and the Toolbar dialog box appears.

❸ Point to the Drawing check box, and click the mouse button to place an x in the box.

The Drawing toolbar appears on-screen (see figure 1.9).

Figure 1.9
The Drawing toolbar appears above the status bar.

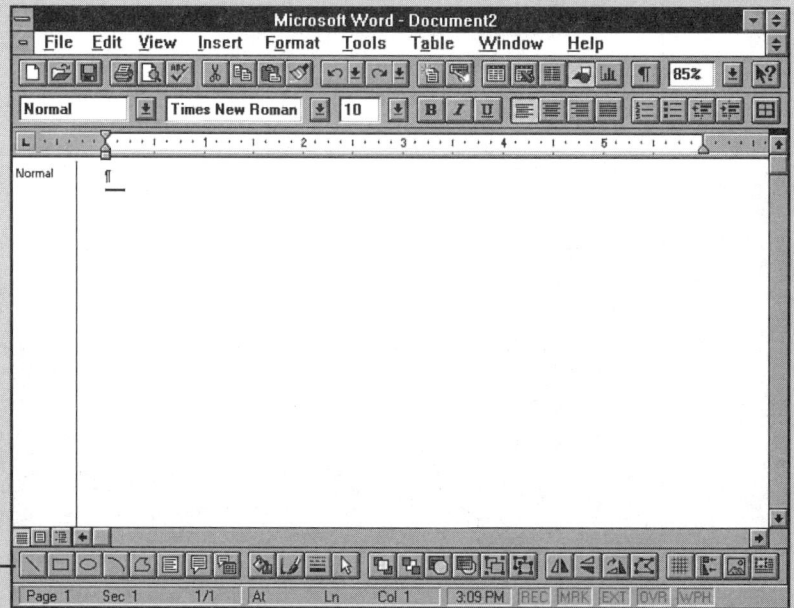

Drawing toolbar

❹ To remove the toolbar, point anywhere on the toolbar, and click the right mouse button.

❺ Click the Toolbar option.

Note: *When the Toolbar dialog box opens, notice the check boxes at the bottom of the box for turning off colored buttons and ToolTips. (If you have a monochrome screen, you might find buttons easier to see if you turn off Colored Buttons).*

❻ Click the Drawing check box until no x is in the box.

❼ Choose OK to confirm that the Drawing toolbar is not displayed.

Tip

Word has an even quicker way to choose to display toolbars. When you right-click a toolbar and the menu appears, click the name of the toolbar you want to display until a check appears beside the name. To remove the toolbar, click the name on the menu until the check is no longer there.

Choosing from the Standard Toolbar

The Standard toolbar is one that you probably will use frequently in your word processing. Table 1.1 gives additional information about the Standard toolbar.

Template
The basic design of a document.

Note: *Many of the descriptions in Table 1.2 refer to documents and* templates, *terms that occur frequently in this book. Think of a document as what you will print on paper. Think of a template as the basic design of a document. What Word calls the Normal template is essentially a blank piece of paper.*

Table 1.1	Standard Toolbar Buttons	
Button	**Name**	**Effect**
	New	Creates a new document based on the Normal template.
	Open	Opens an existing document or template (previously saved as a file on disk).
	Save	Saves the active document or template by writing it to a disk.
	Print	Prints the active document.
	Print Preview	Displays entire pages as they will be printed.
	Spelling	Checks the spelling in the active document.
	Cut	Cuts the highlighted text to the Clipboard, deleting it from your document. The Clipboard is where you can temporarily keep information to copy to another location.
	Copy	Copies the highlighted text to the Clipboard (leaving it in your document).
	Paste	Inserts the contents of the Clipboard into the current document at the insertion point.
	Format Painter	Copies the format of selected text to other text.
	Undo	Reverses some actions (you cannot reverse all actions).
	Redo	Reverses a previously undone action.
	AutoFormat	Automatically formats a document.
	Insert AutoText	Automatically inserts an AutoText entry into a document at the insertion point.
	Insert Table	Inserts a table at the insertion point.
	Insert Microsoft Excel Worksheet	Inserts an Excel worksheet.
	Columns	Changes the column format of selected sections.

(continues)

Table 1.1 Continued

Button	Name	Effect
	Drawing	Shows or hides the Drawing toolbar.
	Insert Chart	Inserts a Microsoft Graph object at the insertion point.
	Show/Hide	Shows or hides all nonprinting characters.
	Zoom Control	Changes the magnification of what is shown in the text area.
	Help	Accesses Help about commands, toolbar buttons, and dialog boxes. Also provides information about paragraph and character formatting.

Although most items in the Standard toolbar are ordinary buttons, three have arrow buttons you can click to open a drop-down list box that shows options from which you can choose. Clicking the down arrow next to the Undo button, for example, displays a list box that shows your previous editing actions (see figure 1.10).

Figure 1.10
Use the Undo list box to choose which previous action you want to undo.

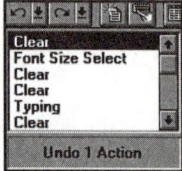

Just click the action in the list. You can use the vertical scroll bar at the right to scroll back through many previous actions.

Similarly, after you have undone one or more actions, you can open the Redo list box and click the undo action you want to reverse.

Zoom Control is also different. This part of the toolbar indicates the present on-screen magnification of your document. You can use the Zoom Control button (the down arrow beside the percentage box) to choose a different magnification from a list box or to enter the magnification you want.

Objective 3: Create a New Document

You can begin typing text as soon as you start Word. The document which appears on-screen, Document1, is based on a template called NORMAL.DOT. This template provides basic settings established by Word. The Normal template includes the following settings:

- The Times New Roman font at 10-point size
- Left and right margins of 1.25 inches

- Top and bottom margins of 1 inch
- Single-spaced paragraphs aligned flush with the left margin
- Tab stops set every half-inch

Note: *These are the settings when you first install Word. You can change any of them, as explained in Chapter 5.*

Word contains several templates, each with different settings, and you can create additional templates of your own. If you base your documents on templates, you do not have to define basic settings each time you start a new document because Word uses the settings in the template as a guideline for formatting the document. You can change the settings before you start typing or at any time while you are typing.

You should create a separate template for each type of document you use frequently.

You can create a new document by choosing a command from a menu or a button from the Standard toolbar.

Creating a New Document

To create a new document by using a menu command, follow these steps:

1. From the File menu, choose the New command to display the New dialog box (see figure 1.11).

2. Choose OK to open a new document based on the Normal template. Word gives the temporary name Document2 to the new document (see figure 1.12).

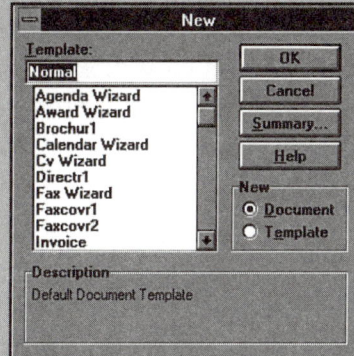

Figure 1.11 By default, the Normal template is selected. Notice that the Description box under the list of templates provides a brief description of the selected template.

(continues)

Creating a New Document (continued)

Figure 1.12
Word displays a new document and titles it DocumentX (the number depends on how many documents you have opened during this Word session).

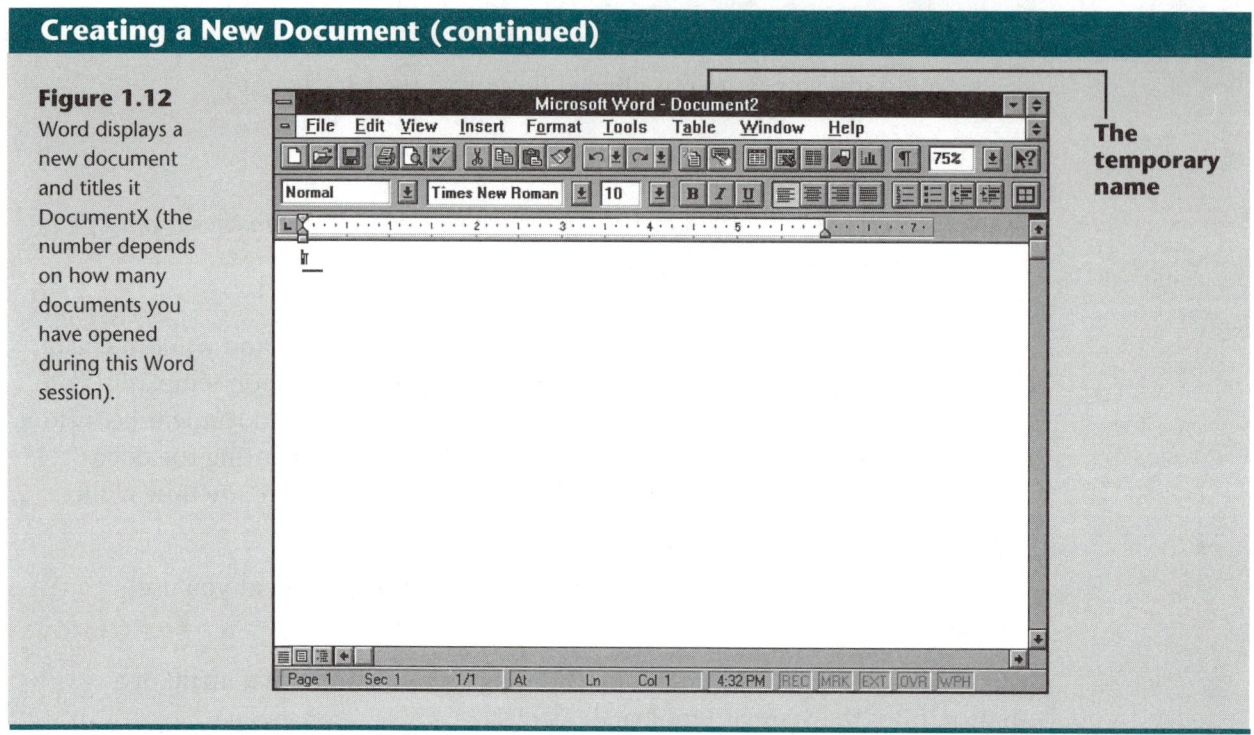

The temporary name

Note: *You also can begin a new document by clicking the New button in the Standard toolbar. When you use the New button, Word automatically uses the Normal document template. To use a different template, you can change its template (as explained in Chapter 10), or you can start the document by using the New command.*

Identifying the Text Area

The insertion point, the flashing vertical bar in the text area of the document, marks the place where text you type is inserted into a document. In a new document, the insertion point appears in the upper left corner of the text area. When you type, text appears immediately to the left of the insertion point, and the insertion point moves to the right. You can move the insertion point by using the keyboard or the mouse, but you cannot move the insertion point beyond the last character in a document.

The short horizontal line in the text area marks the last line in a document. In a new document, this line occurs immediately under the first line because the document contains no text.

Understanding Word Wrap

Word wrap
A Word feature that automatically moves a complete word to the beginning of a new line whenever text overflows the right margin.

Characters you type normally start at the left end of a line and progressively fill the line. As you near the right margin, if the word you type is too long to fit on the line, Word places all the characters of that word at the left end of the next line. This feature, known as *word wrap,* makes it unnecessary for you to press the *carriage return* key (usually ⏎Enter on computer keyboards) at the end of a line. Word wrap keeps your text within the margins and keeps all the characters of individual words together.

In fact, it is very important that you do *not* press [↵Enter] at the end of each line, since that would insert unnecessary editing codes. Only press [↵Enter] when you want to make sure that the next character is placed on a new line, such as at the end of a paragraph or after each item in a list.

Typing Text in a Document

Typing text in a word processing program is much faster and easier than writing on paper or using a typewriter; with a word processing program, you can make changes quickly. If you change your mind about the structure of a sentence or the organization of a paragraph, you can easily insert, delete, or move text.

Entering Text in the New Document

Enter the following text. Be sure to use the word wrap feature. Don't worry about typos at this time; just type the document.

January 31, 1994

To: All Personnel

From: Information Systems Department

Re: Rules for all computer labs and offices

As we have entered the world of technology, we have found the need to increase the number of PC computers within the company. Each employee has a computer, which could be used as a standalone or with the Novell Network, at their desk. It is the company's desire to keep everyone abreast of new software and to keep all equipment well maintained.

The company lab houses 15 computers to be used by groups for training purposes. The lab is open daily Monday through Friday from 9:00AM to 9:00 PM. All new software is loaded on the lab machines for you to review before requesting the software for use. The lab personnel need lead time to schedule upgrading any machines to meet your needs.

The procedure to request new software is to be sent to the Director of Information Systems with the date needed and the date of your review of the software. Software will not be loaded unless a review form is on file in the lab. Any requests for hardware maintenance will also be handled by the Information Systems Department.

(continues)

Entering Text in the New Document (continued)

If you have questions or concerns about the new procedure, please feel free tocontact the Information Systems Department at extension 5350. We look forward to working with each one of you.

Complete the next exercise before you leave the Word program.

Objective 4: Save a Document

After creating a document, it is important to save the document to disk for future use. You can save documents by choosing a command from the **F**ile menu or choosing a button in the Standard toolbar. The **F**ile menu has three commands for saving documents:

- Save
- Save As
- Save All

In the Standard toolbar, choose the Save button—the third button from the left—to save your document.

Saving a New Document

To save a new document (using default options), click the Save button in the Standard toolbar or follow these steps:

1 From the **F**ile menu, choose Save **A**s to display the Save As dialog box (see figure 1.13).

Figure 1.13
Use the Save As dialog box to assign a file name to your document and to specify the disk drive and directory to which you want to save it.

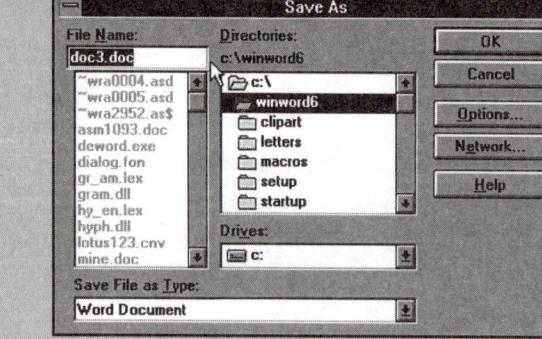

② In the File Name text box, indicated by the pointer in the preceding illustration, type **POLICY**. (The name of the document can be up to eight characters.) The name you type replaces the temporary name (Document1, for example) assigned by Word. Word automatically adds DOC as the file name extension.

③ To save the document to a different drive, open the Drives drop-down list box and click the letter corresponding to the drive you want to use. If your data drive is drive A, click A; if your data drive is drive B, click B.

To choose a different directory, double-click the single letter at the top of the Directories list to display a list of all the first-level directories. Then click the name of the directory you want to use.

To save the document to the current disk drive and directory, choose OK. (Other options are described later.)

④ If the Summary Info dialog box appears (this is an option that may not be activated on your computer), you can type a title, subject, key words, and comments for the document.

The Save As dialog box always appears when you save a new document, whether you choose the Save button from the Standard toolbar or choose **S**ave or Save **A**s from the **F**ile menu. This dialog box specifies what format and to what disk and directory a document is saved.

Choosing the Save or Save As Command

The Save **A**s command provides choices that the **S**ave command does not; you can specify the drive and directory where you want to store the document, the document type, and the access rights of other users. When you need to change these options, choose the Save **A**s command from the **F**ile menu.

If you don't need to change the file name, drive, directory, file format, or access rights, choose the **S**ave command from the **F**ile menu or click the Save button on the toolbar.

Note: *If you choose the Exit command from the File menu when you have multiple documents open, Word prompts you to save any unsaved changes to each document before you exit the program.*

Objective 5: Print a Document

Before you print a document, you should choose the Print Pre**v**iew command from the **F**ile menu to check a reduced version of the document layout. Or you may want to use the Normal view to see the character and formatting information.

After you check the layout and formatting, you can use either of two methods to print the active document:

22 Getting Started

> **Caution**
> When you click the Print button, you cannot change any settings in the Print dialog box.

- Click the Print button in the Standard toolbar, which immediately sends the document to the printer.
- Choose the Print command from the File menu. This method enables you to make several choices about how the document should be printed, as described in the following steps.

Printing the New Document

To print the active POLICY document by choosing the **P**rint command, follow these steps:

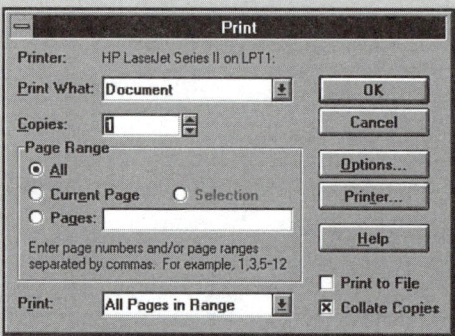

Figure 1.14
Use the Print dialog box to set printing options.

1. From the **F**ile menu, choose the **P**rint command. Word opens the Print dialog box, in which you can make some choices about printing (see figure 1.14).

2. Click the down arrow beside the **P**rint What list box. The options Document, Summary Info, Annotations, Styles, AutoText Entries, or Key Assignments appear.

3. Click the down arrow again to select the option Document.

4. Make sure that the Copies list box is set to 1.

5. After you make sure that all the other options are correct, choose OK to print the POLICY document.

Objective 6: Access Help

> **Select**
> The action you take to identify the text you want to affect or the command you want to use.

The Help feature in Word and many other Windows applications is a very sophisticated information system. You can use Word's extensive Help feature in four ways:

- By activating general Help
- By accessing context-sensitive Help
- By accessing Help before selecting a command
- By clicking the Help button in a dialog box

Activating General Help

As you type a document or make changes to a document, you may find a feature that you do not fully understand; you may need more information on it. By selecting general Help, you can access Help on a specific list of topics displayed.

To activate Help in Word, follow these steps:

❶ Click the **H**elp option on the menu bar to open the menu (see figure 1.15).

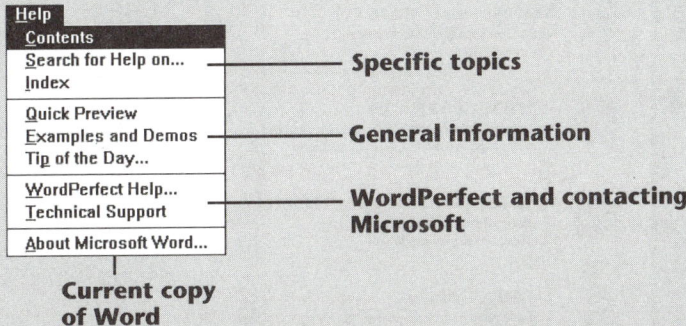

Figure 1.15
The Help menu has four sections.

The first section provides three ways you can find information about specific topics. The second provides more general information. The third gives useful information about using Word if you are familiar with WordPerfect and tells you how to contact Microsoft; the fourth provides information about the copy of Word you are using.

❷ Choose **C**ontents. Word displays a window for selections in topics such as Using Word, Examples and Demos, Reference Information, Programming with Microsoft Word, and Technical Support.

❸ Close the Help window.

Becoming familiar with the Help menu and its options will assist you in using Word more efficiently. In the following exercises, you use the Contents, Search, and Index options to access Help.

Activating The Word Help Contents

To activate the Word Help Contents in the open POLICY.DOC, follow these steps:

❶ Place the insertion point on the first character of paragraph one of POLICY.DOC.

❷ Choose **C**ontents from the general **H**elp menu, and you arrive at a window titled Word Help Contents (see figure 1.16).

(continues)

Activating The Word Help Contents (continued)

Figure 1.16
Click any of the subjects in the Word Help Contents window to access a more detailed breakdown of that subject.

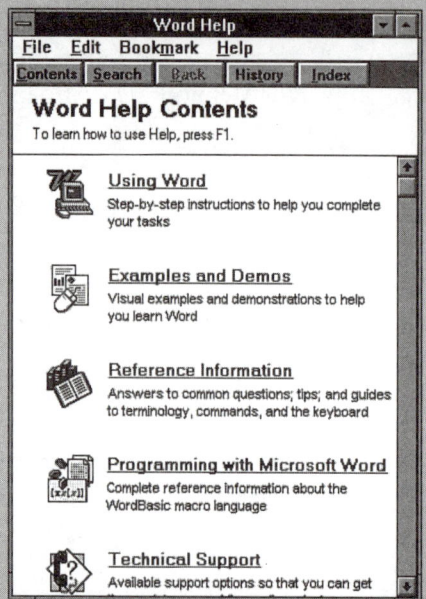

3 Choose Examples and Demos.

Depending on the subjects you choose, you will see more detailed lists. Each time you see a list, choose one of the subject titles.

4 When you are finished using the Word Help Contents, choose Close to leave each opened window.

5 Open the **F**ile menu at the top of the Help window, and choose E**x**it.

Tip

You also can close the Word Help Contents window by clicking in the opened POLICY.DOC.

Sometimes you want help on a particular topic. Help has an option for initiating this type of search.

Activating the Search For Help On

To activate the Search for Help On dialog box, follow these steps:

1 Choose **H**elp.

2 Choose **S**earch For Help On. The Search dialog box appears. In it, you can type a subject or use the scroll bars to select the subject with which you want help (see figure 1.17).

Figure 1.17
The Search Dialog Box.

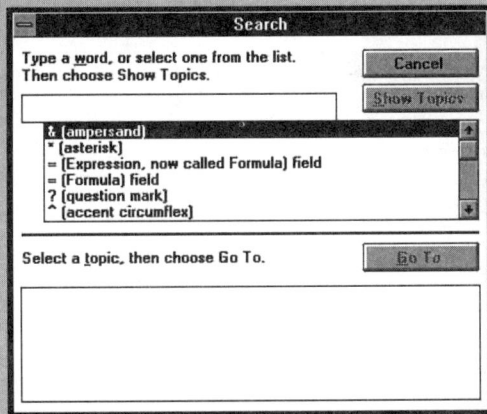

3 Type **Header** in the text box.

4 Click the Show Topics button. A list of topics appears in the Search dialog box (see figure 1.18).

Figure 1.18
When you click **S**how Topics, the lower part of the Search dialog box shows a list of topics related to headers.

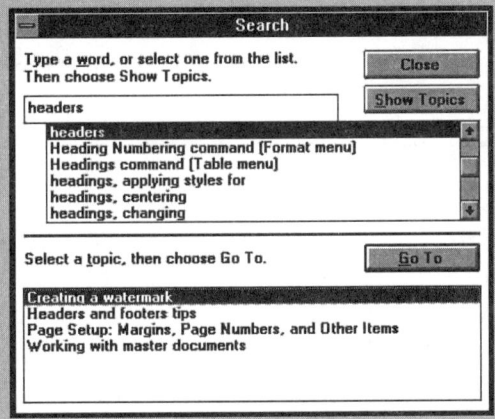

5 Double-click the topic Headers and Footer Tip.

or

Click the topic Creating a Watermark, and then click the Go To button (see figure 1.19).

(continues)

Activating the Search For Help On (continued)

Figure 1.19
Word displays tips about headers and footers.

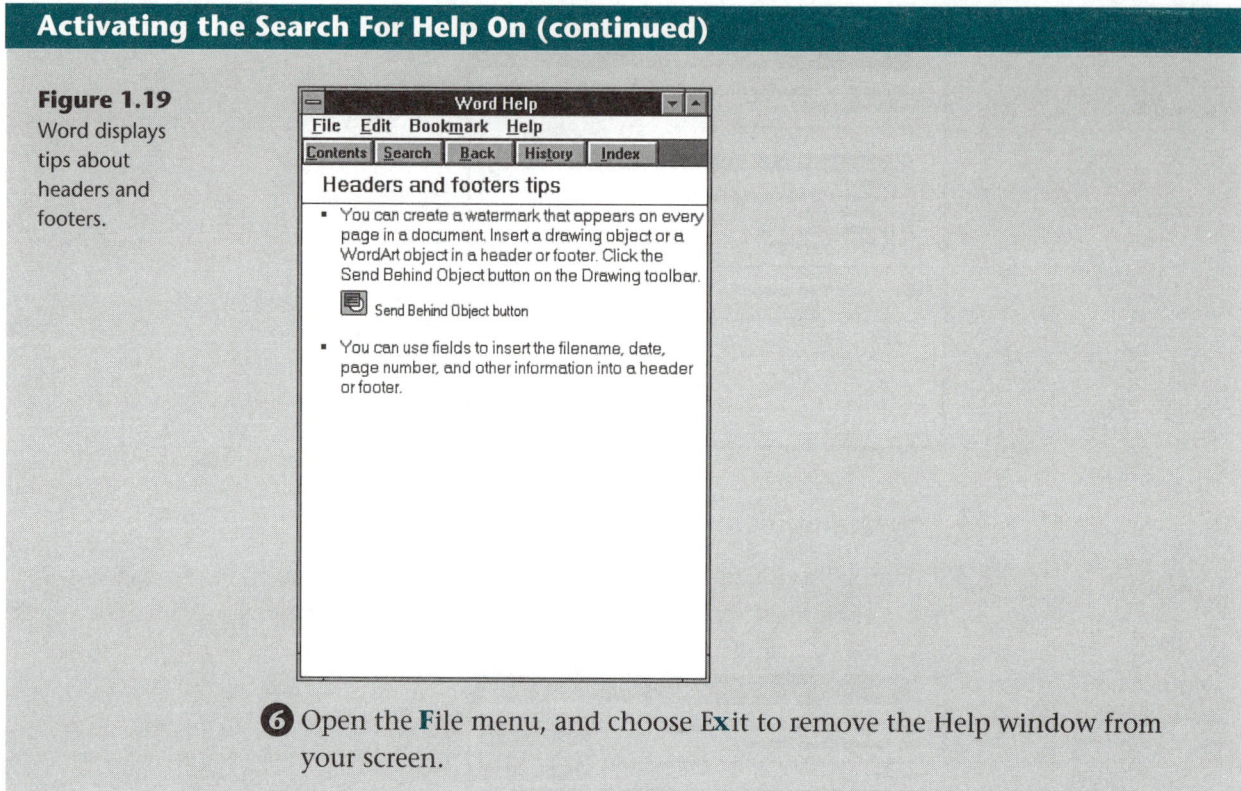

❻ Open the **F**ile menu, and choose E**x**it to remove the Help window from your screen.

Using the Index

The **I**ndex from the **H**elp menu displays a button for each letter of the alphabet and an index list. You can use the button or the list to find help on a specific topic. If you need help on page layouts, for example, you can click the letter *P* and selected topics beginning with *P* appear. You then can click the topic you want, and Word displays the Help information on that topic.

Using Context-Sensitive Help

Any time you are in the process of doing something and need help, you can press F1 to access Help. When you press F1, you get instant information about your current situation. If you press F1 after opening the **F**ile menu and highlighting **N**ew, for example, Help about the New command in the File menu appears.

Getting Help about a Command

Sometimes you want to get help before you select a command or click a toolbar button. Press Shift+F1, and the pointer changes to the arrow-and-question-mark shape shown in figure 1.20.

Use this pointer to click a menu name and then choose a command, or to click a toolbar button. Instead of executing the command or completing an action, Word displays information about the command or toolbar button.

If you activate the Help pointer and then decide you don't want to use it before you select a command or toolbar button, press Esc.

Figure 1.20
The pointer changes to the arrow-and-question-mark shape you see here.

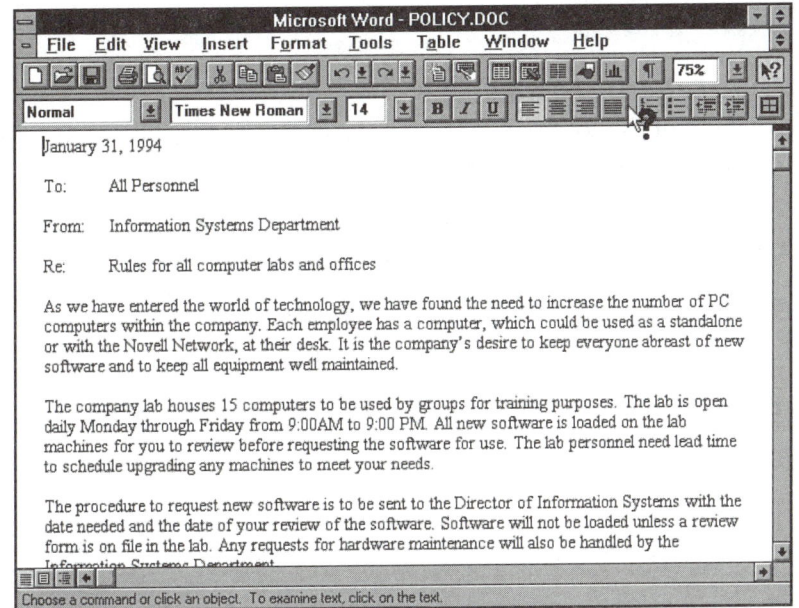

Getting Help about a Dialog Box

As is common in many other Windows applications, every dialog box in Word has a Help button. Click this button to display a window that explains how to use that dialog box.

Objective 7: Close Word

After you have finished working with Word and have saved your work, you need to exit the program.

> **Closing Word**
>
> To close the application, choose Exit from the File menu.
>
> If you choose Exit before saving your work, Word warns you and gives you the opportunity to save the file.

Chapter Summary

In this chapter, you have become familiar with Word's basic functions. You learned the basics of starting Word, creating a new document, entering text, saving the document, and printing the document. You used both with the mouse and the Word toolbars.

In the next chapter, you learn to retrieve and edit documents.

Checking Your Skills

True/False Questions
For each of the following statements, circle *T* or *F* to indicate whether the statement is true or false.

T *F* 1. Although you can use Windows and Word by using only a keyboard, both programs are easier to use with a mouse.

T *F* 2. Word windows cannot be changed to accommodate the preferences of the user or the requirements of the word processing project.

T F 3. Clicking a button in the toolbar saves keystrokes.

T *F* 4. The Formatting toolbar can be used to start the Spelling Checker.

T F 5. If you choose Exit before saving your work, Word warns you and gives you the opportunity to save the file.

T F 6. You can create newspaper-style columns at the beginning of a document.

T F 7. Large buttons are easier to see but take up a considerable amount of valuable screen space.

T F 8. You can open many Window documents at one time, each in its own window.

T F 9. You can use the Save As dialog box to assign a file name to your document and to specify the disk drive and directory to which you want to save it.

T *F* 10. The black commands on a menu are not available at the current time; the gray commands are available at the current time.

Multiple-Choice Questions
In the blank provided, write the letter of the correct answer for each of the following questions.

_____ 1. If the word you type is too long to fit on the line, Word places all the characters of that word at the left end of the next line using the __*a*__.

   a. word wrap feature

   b. margin release feature

   c. automatic formatting

   d. default settings

   e. hard return

_____ 2. Which one of the following does NOT appear on the opening screen?

   a. Document Control menu

   b. menu bar

   c. scroll bars

      d. pointer bar

      e. status bar

____ **3.** The term that means "to fill the entire screen" is ___b___.

      a. minimize

      b. maximize

      c. restore

      d. enlarge

      e. expand

____ **4.** One of the three Standard toolbar buttons you can click to open a drop-down *list* box is the ___a*b___ button.

      a. Zoom control

      b. Undo

      c. Help

      d. New

      e. Save

____ **5.** The commands to save a document can be found on the ___c___ menu.

      a. Save

      b. Edit

      c. File

      d. Utilities

      e. Format

____ **6.** You can see on-screen all text in the font and size you have chosen by using ___d___.

      (a.) Print Preview

      b. AutoFormat

      c. WYSIWYG

      d. Zoom

      e. Show/Hide

____ **7.** The flashing vertical bar in the text area of the document is known as the ___b___.

      a. cursor position

      b. insertion point

      c. keyboard position

d. button location

e. mouse icon

____ **8.** A yellow flag displaying the button's name when you point to a button in a toolbar is known as a ___d___.

a. flag

b. menu

c. tool button

d. ToolTip

e. Help

____ **9.** Three buttons at the left end of the horizontal scroll bar enable you to choose ___b___.

a. text alignment

b. different views of the document

c. fonts in the document

d. from a list document

e. which documents to print

____ **10.** When a toolbar is in the rectangular format, it is known as a ___a___ toolbar.

a. standard

b. fixed

c. horizontal

(d.) floating

e. vertical

Fill-in-the-Blank Questions

In the blank provided, write the correct answer for each of the following questions.

1. When you click the __print preview__ button in the Standard toolbar, you cannot change any settings in the Print dialog box.

2. A Word feature that automatically moves a complete word to the beginning of a new line whenever text overflows the right margin is known as __word wrap__.

3. Each menu contains commands grouped by _____.

4. Word provides you with two ways of confirming a selection—by clicking OK or pressing __enter__.

5. In the File Name text box, you can type a name containing up to ___8 (+3)___ characters for the document.

6. When you start Word, the application opens a new document called _document 1_.

7. The _split box_, a small black box just above the arrow at the top of the vertical scroll bar, splits the current window into two panes so that you can see two parts of the same document simultaneously.

8. If you point to one of the buttons in a toolbar, the _Tool tip_ [status bar] displays a message indicating what will happen when you click that button.

9. While you work in Word, you choose items from menus, toolbars, and _icons_.

10. At the bottom and right side of the screen are the horizontal and vertical _scroll_ bars.

Applying Your Skills

Review Exercises

Exercise 1: Changing Toolbars

To become as efficient as possible using Word, you may want to change the buttons on the Standard and Formatting toolbars to those functions you use frequently. For example, you probably will use Open, Close, Save, and Print frequently, but you may not need Columns.

1. Select **V**iew, **T**oolbars, **C**ustomize.
2. Change three buttons on each of the two toolbars.
3. Then return the toolbars to their original buttons.

Exercise 2: Creating MEDICAL.DOC

In this exercise, you create a new document titled MEDICAL.DOC.

1. Type the following document.

    June 24, 1995

    Mr. Tom Smith
    Seaside Lane
    Slippery, PA 16057

    Dear Patient:

    We are proud to announce the opening of our new location on Boston Post Road. We have increased our staff for the efficient operation of the new facility.

    We are extending our invitation for you to visit the facility on Sunday, July 10, from 10:00 AM to 3:00 PM. All the doctors will be available for questions.

The new facility will allow us to have new extended hours: Monday through Friday from 8:00 AM to 8:00 PM and on Saturday from 6:00 AM to 12:00 PM. We look forward to seeing you on the 10th.

Sincerely,

Samuel Baker, MD

2. Save the file to your data disk as **MEDICAL.DOC**.

Exercise 3: Creating and Saving a Document
In this exercise, you create and save a document.

1. Type the following document.

   To: Planning Committee Members

   From: Samuel Simones
            Chairperson

   RE: Change of date and time of meeting

   The date for the next meeting has been changed to March 9, 1995 in the conference room. Our speakers for the meeting cannot attend the March 2nd meeting, and their presence is required. Also, the decision date has been moved to March 31st rather than March 15th. My apologies for any inconveniences these delays may have caused.

2. Save the file to your data drive as **FIRST.DOC**.

Exercise 4: Using the Standard Toolbar to Create a Document
You can use the Standard toolbar to create a document.

1. Using the Standard toolbar, open a new document, and type the following:

   Employee Evaluation Guidelines

   1. Employer must contact you two weeks prior to an on-the-job visit.
   2. Employer must supply a list of tasks to be reviewed.
   3. Employee must have a portfolio of all tasks listed.
   4. Employee may review completed evaluation.
   5. Any responses from employee on evaluation must be received within two weeks of report.

2. Save the file to your data disk as **GUIDELINE.DOC**.

Exercise 5: Using the Formatting Toolbar
Using the Formatting toolbar, follow these instructions:

1. Click Bold, and then type

   This is bold.

2. Click Italics, and then type

    This is Italics.

3. Click Underline, and then type

    <u>This is underlined.</u>

4. Click Center, and then type

    This is centered.

5. Click Bold, Underline, and Align Right, and type

    <u>Look how this appears.</u>

6. Save the file to your data disk as **BUTTON.DOC**.

Continuing Projects

Project 1: Practice in Using Word
Practice using Word by following these steps:

1. Using the Standard toolbar, open a new document, and select the Normal template.

2. After reviewing the chapter, type the steps necessary for a fellow worker to enter Word text.

3. Print the document, using the standard toolbar.

4. Save the file to your data drive as **STEPS.DOC**

Project 2: Federal Department Store
You work at Federal Department Store and want to create a list of items with descriptions and prices to be eventually formatted in a brochure.

1. To begin this venture, type the following items, using the Formatting toolbar as needed.

    <u>Classic Soccer Shorts</u>

    Our classic soccer shorts for active sports and cool summer wear. Made from lightweight, quick-drying 2.5 oz. nylon. Elasticized waist with drawcord gives custom fit. Unlined or lined. $15.00.

    <u>Short Sleeve Striped Rugby</u>

    Rib-knit collar and 3-button placket. Placket and collar band reinforced with sturdy, colorful cotton twill. $29.99

2. Save the file to your data disk as **CATALOG.DOC**.

Project 3: Real Entertainment Corporation
You work for Real Entertainment Corporation and have been asked to create a company newsletter. The first step in planning any publication is to find out what is happening in the company. After sending notices to the various departments,

making them aware of the newsletter and requesting any articles or advertisements to be included, the initial newsletter is sent to clients.

1. Type the following paragraph:

Real Entertainment Corporation

I bet you're wondering if Real Entertainment Corporation makes movies, signs on new actors, markets musical groups, and so on. Well, now you will find out the real facts about us in our new monthly newsletter.

Real Entertainment Corporation is involved in bringing entertainment to your home, your office, or your organization. For the last 10 years of operation, we have brought joy to many people in the form of music, videos, casino games, and comedy shows. We have an entertainment center, located at our corporate headquarters, that you may visit to review material before signing a contract.

We hope we have sparked your interest in our company and that you will read our monthly newsletter that will include the latest in entertainment offerings, scheduled events opened to the public, lists of contributions made to needy organizations, and much more!!

2. Save the file to your data disk as **RECD.DOC**.

Chapter 2
Editing a Document

In the course of your daily work, you will have certain documents that you use over and over. In this chapter, you learn how to open and make changes to existing documents.

AutoCorrect
Word's built-in capability to correct certain typing mistakes while you are typing.

You learn how to move the insertion point to the locations you want to edit and how to move, copy, and delete text in the document. Because in Word you can open more than one document at a time, you also learn how to move and copy text between documents. You learn to use Word's built-in feature, *AutoCorrect*, to make corrections to the document as you type. Imagine—typing a document and your spelling mistakes are corrected immediately!

After making all changes to a file, you should always save it if you want to use it at a later date.

Objectives

By the time you finish this chapter, you will have learned to

1. Open an Existing Document
2. Move Around in a document
3. Use AutoCorrect to Prevent Mistakes
4. Use Basic Editing Features
5. Work with More Than One Document

Objective 1: Open an Existing Document

In Chapter 1, you learned that when you start Word a blank document opens on-screen and is labeled *Document1*. To create a new document, you simply start typing. To work on an existing document, however, you must open that document.

Opening a Recently Used Document

Word remembers the last four documents you opened and lists their names at the bottom of the File menu. You can open any of these documents by clicking the document name in the File menu (see figure 2.1).

Figure 2.1
The names of the last four files you opened are listed at the bottom of the File menu.

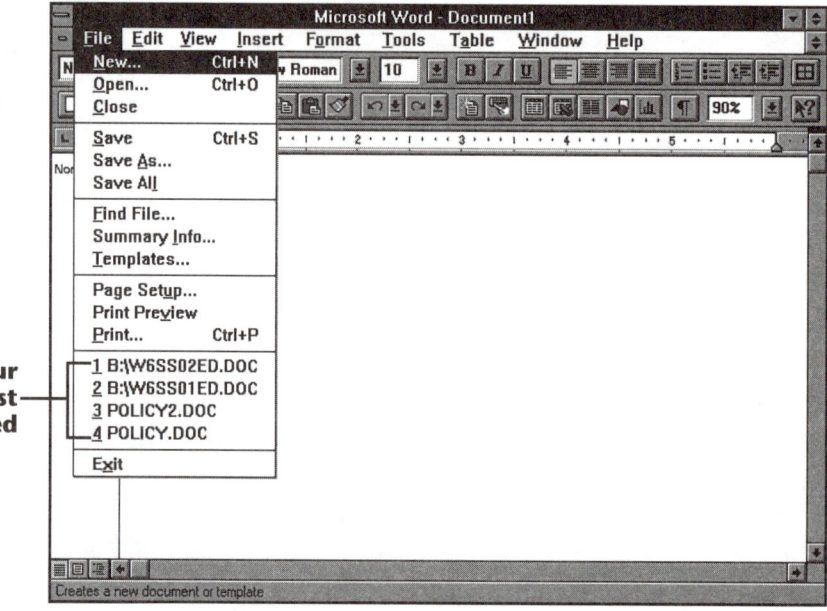

The four files last opened

If the document you need has not been used recently, you cannot use the list to open the document.

Opening a Document

You can open an existing document by choosing a menu command or a button in the Standard toolbar. To open POLICY.DOC, follow these steps:

1. From the File menu, choose the Open command.

   or

   Click the Open button on the Standard toolbar.

   Whether you use the menu command or the toolbar button, Word displays the Open dialog box (see figure 2.2).

Figure 2.2
Use the File, Open menu commands or click the Open button to display the Open dialog box.

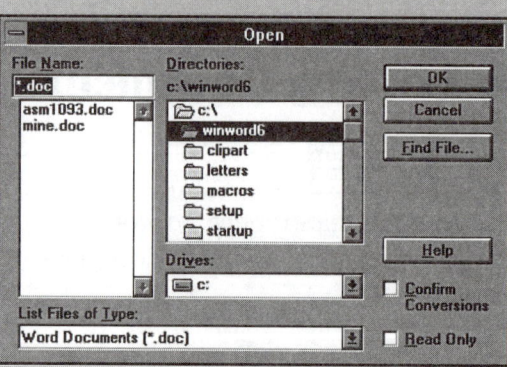

Move Around in a Document   37

> The File **N**ame list in the Open dialog box shows all files in the current directory that have names with the DOC extension.
>
> If POLICY.DOC is in the current directory, ignore step 2. If the document is not shown and is on a different disk or in a different directory, you must select that disk or directory.
>
> ❷ You can choose the drive in the Dri**v**es list box and the directory in the **D**irectories list box. Choose the drive containing your data disk. (Figure 2.2 shows drive C chosen.)
>
> ❸ Type the name of the document, **POLICY.DOC**, in the File **N**ame text box.
>
> ❹ Choose OK. The dialog box closes, and the document appears on-screen.
>
> **Note:** *Instead of selecting the name of the document and then choosing OK, you can simply double-click the name of the document in the File **N**ame list box. You can use this technique with most dialog boxes.*
>
> ❺ Keep the document open.

The opened document is used in the following sections.

Objective 2: Move Around in a Document

When you revise a document, you have to move the insertion point to the text that needs changing. Word provides many ways to use the mouse or the keyboard to move the insertion point.

Using the Mouse to Move the Insertion Point

To use the mouse to move the insertion point, position the mouse pointer where you want the insertion point to be and then press the left mouse button. If you want to move the insertion point to a part of the document that does not appear in the window, first use the scroll bars or one of the other methods described in this chapter to display that part of the document.

> **Tip**
>
> The scroll bars are very useful tools in editing; using them makes moving through a document quicker than using ⬆ and ⬇ or [PgUp] or [PgDn].

You can display or hide the scroll bars on-screen. Removing scroll bars or hiding scroll bars gives more work area on-screen.

Changing the Display of Scroll Bars

To change the display of scroll bars, follow these steps:

❶ From the **T**ools menu, choose **O**ptions. The Options dialog box appears (see figure 2.3).

Figure 2.3
The Options dialog box displays the View tab options.

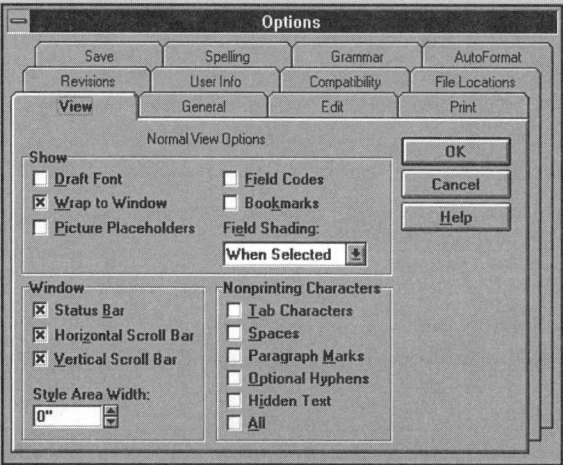

❷ Click the check box for **V**ertical Scroll Bar.

❸ Choose OK. The display of scroll bars changes (see figure 2.4).

Figure 2.4
The horizontal scroll bar is the only scroll bar displayed.

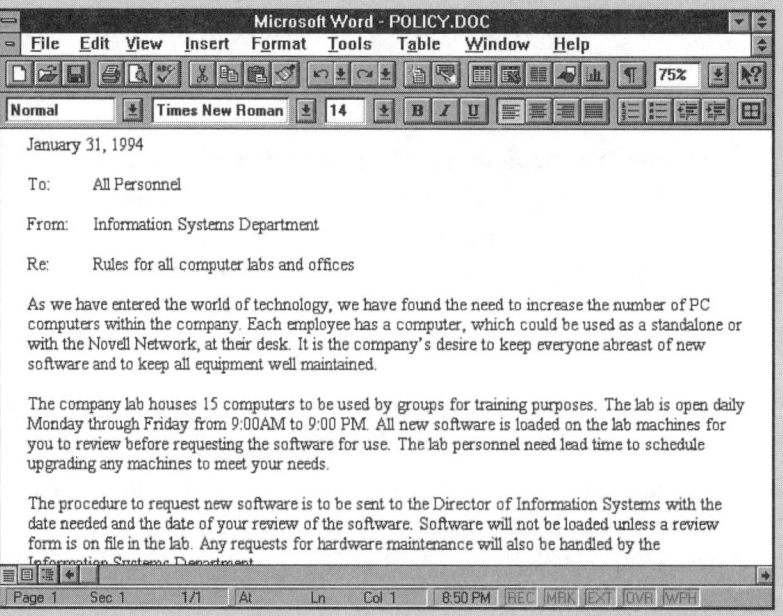

❹ Click **T**ools, **O**ptions, View tab and make sure that each scroll bar option has an × in the check box.

The position of the scroll box on the vertical scroll bar indicates the position of the text in the window relative to the beginning and the end of the document. The position of the horizontal scroll bar indicates the position of the text in the window relative to the left and right margins. When you create a new document or open an existing one, the scroll box is at the top of the scroll bar because the beginning of the document is in the visible window.

You can use the mouse to move to a document area in three ways:

- The scroll box
- The scroll bar
- The scroll arrows

Scrolling in a Document

To practice using these methods of moving within the POLICY.DOC, follow these steps:

1 Point to the box, hold down the left mouse button, and drag the box the direction in which you want to move through the document.

2 Click the area between the scroll box and the top arrow. This action moves one screen at a time through the document.

3 Point to the down scroll arrow and hold down the left mouse button. This actions moves you quickly through the document.

4 Click the up scroll arrow. This action moves you more slowly through the document.

Caution
The insertion point does not move until you click the new location.

You have not yet moved the insertion point. After you finish scrolling, you must place the mouse pointer where you want the insertion point to be and then press the left mouse button to move the insertion point to the new location.

If you have problems... If Word jumps back to the position where the insertion point was before you began to scroll and inserts the text there, you started typing before you clicked the new location.

Using the Keyboard to Move the Insertion Point

Using the keyboard to move the insertion point is often faster than using the mouse, particularly in large documents. Table 2.1 lists key combinations for moving the insertion point.

In Word, you can return to any one of the most recent three insertion point positions. To do this, press ⇧Shift+F5 one, two, or three times. If you press ⇧Shift+F5 a fourth time, the insertion point returns to its original location.

Note: *When you save a document, Word stores the last three insertion point positions. When you reopen the document, you can press ⇧Shift+F5 one, two, or three times to move directly to those positions.*

Table 2.1 Moving the Insertion Point with the Keyboard

Key Combination	Effect
←	Moves the insertion point one character to the left.
→	Moves the insertion point one character to the right.
↑	Moves the insertion point up one line.
↓	Moves the insertion point down one line.
Ctrl+←	Moves the insertion point one word to the left.
Ctrl+→	Moves the insertion point one word to the right.
Home	Moves the insertion point to the beginning of the line.
End	Moves the insertion point to the end of the line.
Ctrl+↑	Moves the insertion point to the beginning of the current paragraph. If the insertion point is already at the beginning of a paragraph, this key combination moves the insertion point to the beginning of the preceding paragraph.
Ctrl+↓	Moves the insertion point to the beginning of the next paragraph.
PgUp	Moves the insertion point up by the height of one window.
PgDn	Moves the insertion point down by the height of one window.
Ctrl+PgUp	Moves the insertion point to the top of the current window.
Ctrl+PgDn	Moves the insertion point almost to the bottom of the current window.
Alt+Ctrl+PgUp	Moves the insertion point to the top of the preceding page.
Alt+Ctrl+PgDn	Moves the insertion point to top of the next page.
Ctrl+Home	Moves the insertion point to the beginning of the document.
Ctrl+End	Moves the insertion point to the end of the document.

Moving to a Specific Location

You can go directly to a specific location in a document in three ways:

- Press F5 (the Go To key).
- From the Edit menu, choose Go To.
- Double-click the page number in the status bar.

In each case, Word displays the Go To dialog box (see figure 2.5).

Figure 2.5
Use the Go To dialog box to move to a specific page or to other specified places in a document.

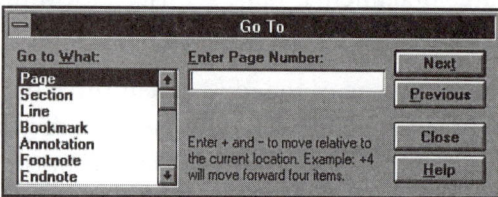

Note: *The Go To dialog box does not close automatically when you move to a new location. You must press* Esc *(or click the Close button) to close the dialog box.*

As you can see in the Go to **W**hat list box, you can go to many different types of locations: page, section, line, bookmark, annotation, footnote, endnote, field, table, graphic, equation, or object. In the list box, you select the type of location you want to go to, identify the location by typing its number or name in the Text box, and then press Enter.

Using the Go To Dialog Box

To use the Go To dialog box, follow these steps:

1. With the POLICY.DOC document open in Word, press F5 to display the Go To dialog box.

2. In the Go to **W**hat list box, click Line.

3. If the insertion point is not in the **E**nter Line Number text box, point to that box and click to place the insertion point there.

4. Type **15** for the line number and press Enter.

5. Click the Close button. Word immediately displays the specified line.

Instead of going to a line specified by its number, you can go forward or backward in the document by a specific number of pages. To do this, in step 4, you would type the plus sign (+) or minus sign (–), a number, and press Enter. For example to move forward three lines in the document, type **+3**; to move backward four lines, type **–4**.

You can use the same technique to move to a specific page number (or up or down by a specific number of pages) in the current document, but first you must select Page in the Go to **W**hat list box.

Objective 3: Use AutoCorrect to Prevent Mistakes

Before you learn to correct mistakes, take a look at one of the ways Word helps prevent mistakes in the first place. Most of us have fingers that don't always do what we want. It's quite common for people to type *adn* when they mean *and* or *teh* instead of *the*. Word can detect and correct these and similar types of errors automatically while you are typing. This feature is called AutoCorrect. When AutoCorrect is turned on, you see what it does on-screen.

In case you are wondering what to do if you really intend to type *adn* or *teh*, don't worry. You can turn off AutoCorrect.

Turning AutoCorrect On and Off

When you install Word, AutoCorrect is initially enabled so that Word corrects certain spelling mistakes while you type. However, if other people use Word on your computer, they may have turned off AutoCorrect. To turn AutoCorrect on or off, follow these steps:

❶ From the Tools menu, choose the AutoCorrect command to open the AutoCorrect dialog box (see figure 2.6).

Figure 2.6
Use the AutoCorrect dialog box to specify several automatic corrections Word can make while you type.

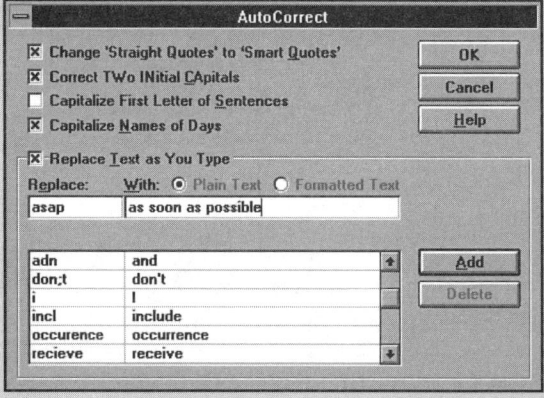

❷ Look to see whether the Replace Text as You Type check box is checked. If the box is checked, AutoCorrect is on and corrects certain spelling mistakes while you type. If the box is not checked, AutoCorrect is disabled; click the box or type Alt+T to turn on AutoCorrect.

❸ Choose OK to close the dialog box.

Now that you know how to activate AutoCorrect, you are ready to see how it works.

Experimenting with AutoCorrect

To see AutoCorrect in action, make sure that you have activated it (refer to the preceding tutorial). Then follow these steps:

❶ Move the cursor to a blank area of the document.

❷ Type **adn** and press Spacebar. Word should change *adn* to *and*. Pressing Spacebar activates Word to recognize immediately the three characters as a word and changes them to *and*.

This demonstration shows how AutoCorrect works. When you start a new word, AutoCorrect does nothing until you finish that word by typing a space or a punctuation character such as a period or comma (not an apostrophe). Then AutoCorrect checks what you have typed against its list of errors and, if it finds a match, automatically corrects the error.

Changing the AutoCorrect List of Errors

You may find times when you need to change AutoCorrect's list of errors—in the lower part of the AutoCorrect dialog box. To do so, you can scroll down the list of errors to see what is currently there. Then you can delete, change, or replace entries and add new ones. All changes you make take effect when you choose OK to close the dialog box. If you cancel the dialog box by clicking Cancel or by pressing (Esc), you lose all changes.

Adding a New Error Entry

You can add a new entry to AutoCorrect's list of errors. To have AutoCorrect spell out the abbreviation *DOS* as the phrase *Disk Operating System*, for example, follow these steps:

❶ Open the AutoCorrect dialog box if it is not already open.

❷ If the **R**eplace text box contains text, click the right end of the text and then press (Backspace) until you delete the existing text. This step is not necessary if you have just opened the dialog box.

❸ Type the error you want to replace—**DOS** in this case. You can type up to 31 characters but cannot include any spaces.

❹ Press (Tab) to move to the **W**ith text box.

❺ Type the replacement, **Disk Operating System** (see figure 2.7). Word allows up to 255 characters. You can have spaces in the replacement text.

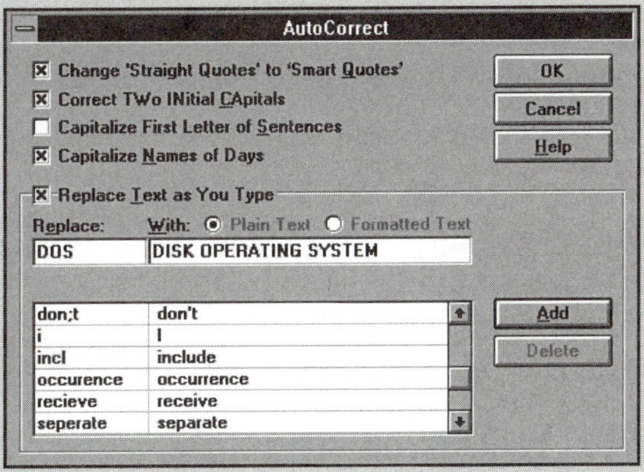

Figure 2.7
Enter the text in the Replace and With text boxes.

❻ Click the **A**dd button in the dialog box.

❼ Choose OK to close the dialog box and to put the changes into effect.

❽ To confirm that this addition works properly in a document, type **DOS** followed by a space in POLICY.DOC. You should see the words *Disk Operating System* in place of what you typed.

Objective 4: Use Basic Editing Features

Copy
To make a duplicate of selected text and then place it in the Clipboard.

In this section, you learn how to use the Insert and Overtype modes, display nonprinting characters, select text, delete text, and insert blank lines. You also learn how to *copy*, move, and delete text and how to undo editing changes you have made.

Understanding Insert and Overtype Modes

Insert mode
A mode in which inserted text moves existing text to the right and down.

When you first open a Word document and start typing, Word is in *Insert mode*. In this mode, Word inserts the characters you type to the left of the insertion point, and text on the right side of the insertion point moves to the right. If this movement causes words to move beyond the right margin, word wrap moves those words to the next line. In the status bar, when OVR (an abbreviation for overtype) is dimmed, Word is in Insert mode. *Overtype mode* replaces characters as you type over existing text, so you usually will want to work in the Insert mode.

Overtype mode
A mode in which the characters you type replace existing characters.

Inserting Blank Lines

To insert blank lines into your document, Word must be in Insert mode. If OVR is black in the status bar (indicating that it is active), Word is in Overtype mode. To switch to Insert mode, double-click OVR in the status bar so that the three letters become gray.

After making certain that Word is in Insert mode, position the insertion point where you want to insert a blank line and press [⏎Enter] twice.

To switch from Overtype to Insert mode, press [Insert] again, or again double-click OVR in the status bar.

Adding Text to the Document

Suppose that after you review POLICY.DOC, you realize another paragraph needs to be added to it. You can add text to the document by following these steps:

❶ Move the insertion point to the end of the third paragraph.

❷ Press [⏎Enter] twice.

❸ Type the following paragraph:

> It has been brought to our attention that software is being purchased through individual divisions. This software must be registered, and if equipment problems arise, the division will not have continued softwear and hardwear support. If all procedures are followed, a smooth operation will continue.

Note: *Some words have been intentionally misspelled in the preceding paragraph.*

❹ Compare your work with figure 2.8.

Figure 2.8
The new text has been added with intentional misspellings.

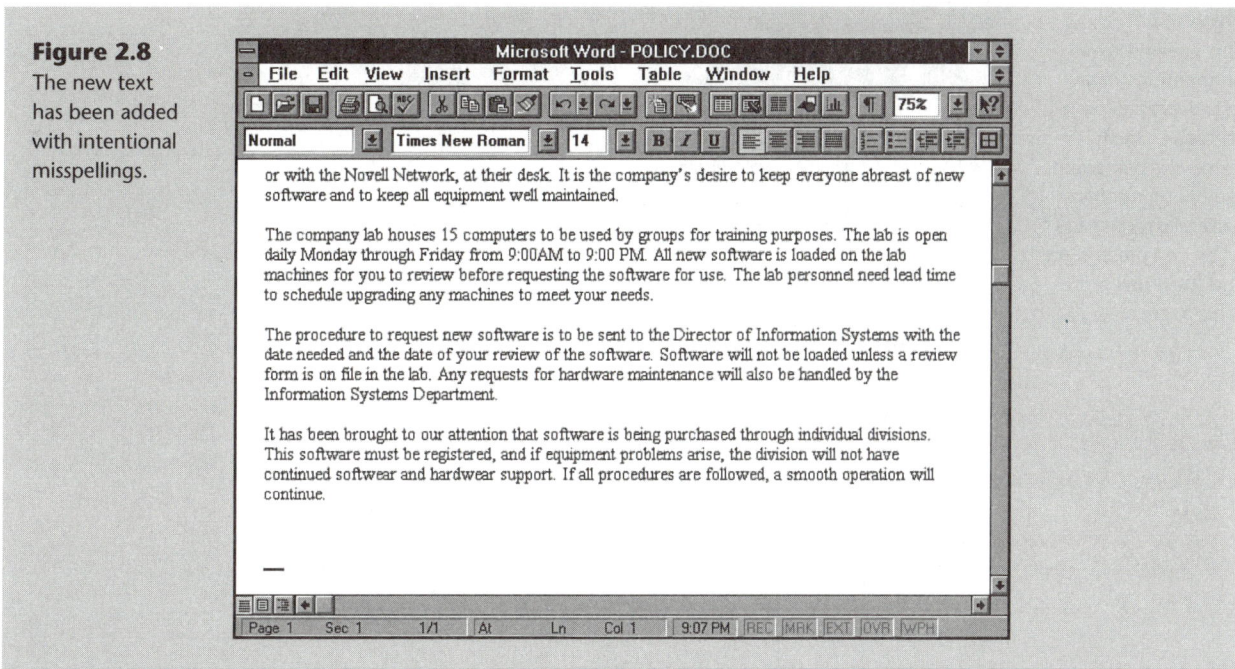

Displaying Nonprinting Characters

When you press most keyboard keys, your screen displays the corresponding character, and, when the time comes for printing, the printer prints it. This is not the case for all keys, however.

When you press ↵Enter, Tab⇆, or Spacebar, the insertion point moves on-screen without displaying a character. These keys, and some other keys that do not display or print a character, are known as nonprinting characters.

Sometimes you need to know which nonprinting characters are causing the insertion point to move. If a line has a blank space in it, for example, you may need to know whether a tab caused the space or whether someone just pressed the Spacebar several times.

 Word can display special symbols to represent nonprinting characters. Position the mouse pointer on the Show/Hide button in the Standard toolbar, and click (see figure 2.9).

> **If you have problems...** If your document is displaying nonprinting characters and you click the Show/Hide button but nothing happens, the display may be turned on in the **T**ools, **O**ptions menu. Access that menu, and change the setting by clicking the check boxes in the Nonprinting Characters box.

Figure 2.9
This screen shows nonprinting characters: the raised period represents each space; the paragraph symbol represents a hard return (inserted when you press [⏎Enter]); and the arrow represents a tab.

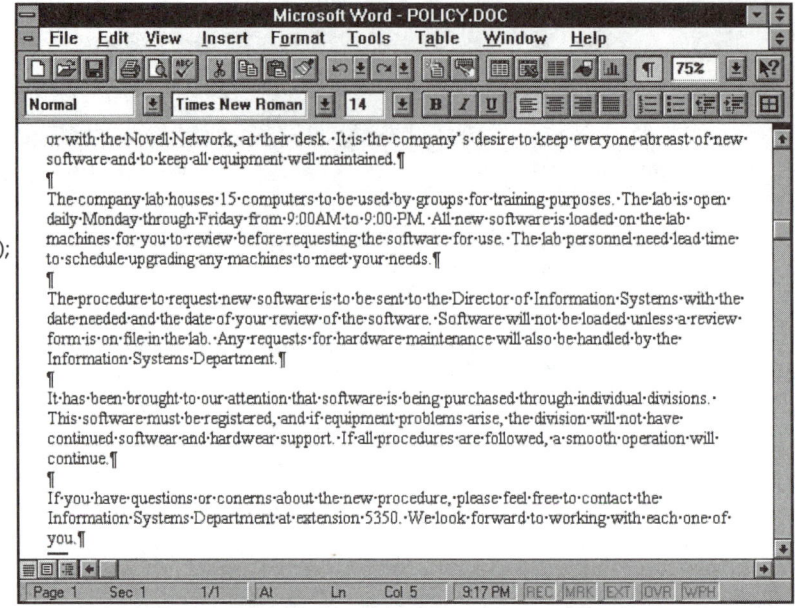

Note: *You can use the **T**ools menu to select nonprinting characters individually.*

To hide nonprinting characters, click the Show/Hide button again.

Selecting Text

Word operates on the principle that you must identify what you want to change before you can change it. To identify text, you select it by using the mouse or the keyboard (see figure 2.10).

Figure 2.10
Selected text appears on-screen as white characters on a black background, whereas unselected text appears as black on a white background.

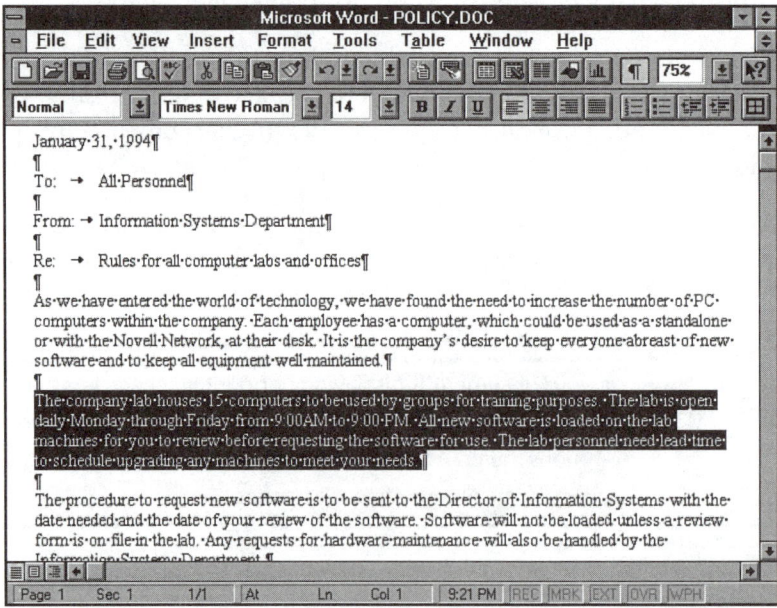

Being Careful with Paragraph Marks

Quite often you select text because you want to delete it or move it. If that text is at the end of a paragraph and you want to select just the text without changing the paragraphing, be careful not to select the paragraph mark—whether it is visible or hidden. (If paragraph marks are hidden, it's a good idea to click the Show/Hide button in the Standard toolbar so that paragraph marks are visible.)

In most cases, there are two good reasons for not deleting or moving a paragraph mark:

- The text to follow should start a new paragraph.
- The paragraph mark contains information that controls the formatting of text in the preceding paragraph.

If the paragraph is double-spaced and italicized and the following paragraph is single-spaced with normal text, deleting the paragraph mark changes the first paragraph to the second paragraph attributes.

Selecting Text with the Mouse

Selection bar
The selection bar is the region just to the right of the line that separates the style area from the text area.

When you select text with the mouse, you can use the *selection bar*, an area at the left side of the text area. The selection bar is not marked in any way, but when you position the mouse pointer in the selection bar, the pointer appears as an arrow pointing up and slightly to the right (see figure 2.11). You can use the selection bar to select text or highlight text for changes such as underlining or bold facing. Table 2.2 lists techniques for using the mouse to select text.

Figure 2.11
When you position the mouse pointer in the selection bar, the pointer appears as an arrow pointing up and slightly to the right.

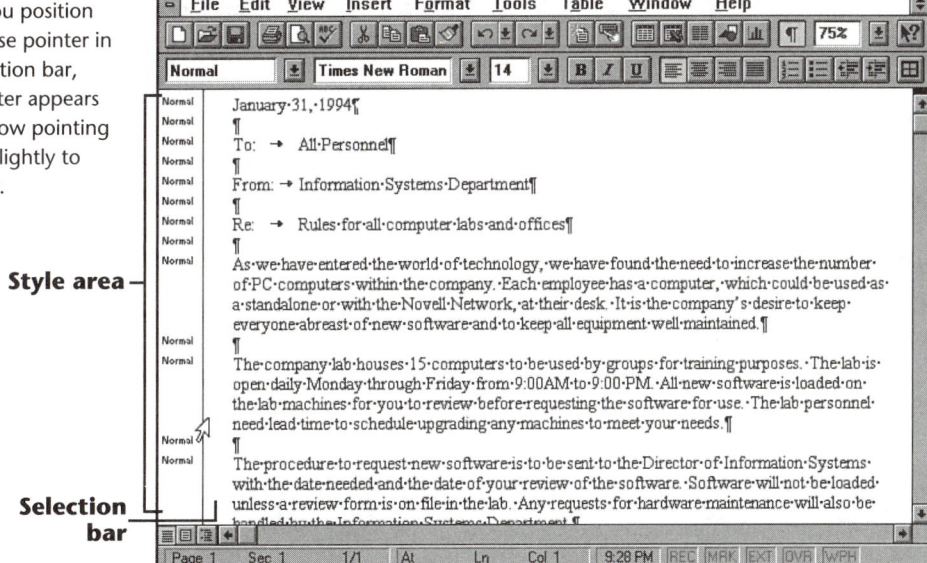

Style area

Selection bar

Caution

If you have chosen to display a style area at the left side of your screen, the selection bar is the region just to the right of the line that separates the style area from the text area. When you are using the mouse to select text, make sure that you point in the selection bar, not in the style area, when you want to use the selection bar. Clicking the mouse pointer in the style area selects the entire paragraph.

Table 2.2 Selecting Text with the Mouse

To select	Use the mouse
Any block of text	Point to the beginning or end of the text, press and hold down the mouse button, drag the pointer to the other end of the text you want to select, and then release the mouse button. Word highlights the text as you select it.
	Or click the beginning or end of the text and then press ⇧Shift while you click the other end of the text you want to select. Word highlights the text when you click the second time.
A word	Double-click the word.
A line	Click in the selection bar at the left end of the line.
Multiple lines	Point to the selection bar at the left of the first or last line. Press and hold down the mouse button while you drag the mouse pointer down or up the selection bar to the left of the line at the other end of the range of lines. Word highlights the lines as you select them.
A sentence	Press Ctrl, and click anywhere in the sentence.
A paragraph	Double-click in the selection bar to the left of the paragraph.
	Or click in the style area to the left of the paragraph.
	Or triple-click anywhere within the paragraph.
Several adjacent paragraphs	Click in the selection bar to the left of the first or last paragraph you want to select to select that paragraph. Then press and hold down the mouse button while you drag to include other paragraphs in the selection. Word highlights the paragraphs as you select them.
	Or click in the selection bar to the left of the first or last paragraph you want to select to select that paragraph. Then press ⇧Shift while you click in the selection bar to the left of the paragraph at the other end of the range. Word highlights the paragraphs when you click the second time.
A document	Triple-click in the selection bar or press Ctrl and click in the selection bar.

To deselect text, click anywhere in the document, including the selected area.

Using the Keyboard to Select Text

To select text with the keyboard, you use techniques very similar to the techniques for moving the insertion point with the keyboard, as detailed in table 2.1 earlier in this chapter. In many cases, you simply add ⇧Shift to the key combination you use to move the insertion point (see table 2.3).

Table 2.3 Selecting Text with the Keyboard

Key Combination	Effect
⇧Shift+←	Selects one character to the left.
⇧Shift+→	Selects one character to the right.
Ctrl+⇧Shift+←	Selects to the beginning of the word.
Ctrl+⇧Shift+→	Selects to the end of the word.

Key Combination	Effect
Shift+Home	Selects to the beginning of the line.
Shift+End	Selects to the end of the line.
Shift+↑	Selects to the same horizontal position in the preceding line.
Shift+↓	Selects to the same horizontal position in the next line.
Ctrl+Shift+↑	Selects to the beginning of the paragraph.
Ctrl+Shift+↓	Selects to the end of the paragraph.
Shift+PgUp	Selects to the top of the current window.
Shift+PgDn	Selects to the bottom of the current window.
Ctrl+Shift+Home	Selects to the beginning of the document.
Ctrl+Shift+End	Selects to the end of the document.
Ctrl+A	Selects the entire document. You also can press Ctrl+5 on the numeric keypad.

To deselect the selected text, press any arrow key.

Extending a Selection

With Word, you can select any amount of text by extending a selection. Most text selections are of words or paragraphs, but sometimes you want to select multiple paragraphs. Use the EXT indicator on the status bar to select more than one paragraph when you click the mouse.

Using the Mouse to Extend a Selection

To use the mouse to extend a selection in POLICY.DOC, follow these steps:

❶ Place the insertion point at the beginning of paragraph four.

❷ Double-click EXT (extend) in the status bar. The indicator turns black to show that Extend Selection is on.

❸ Click the end of text you want to select. The selected text is highlighted to show that it is selected.

❹ Turn off Extend Selection by double-clicking EXT.

Note: *Word automatically turns off Extend Selection when you perform an operation on the selected text. To turn off Extend Selection without extending the selected text, double-click the indicator. Extend Selection is off when EXT is gray.*

❺ Press an arrow key to deselect the text.

In the preceding tutorial, you used a mouse to extend a selection of text. You also can use the keyboard to select text. Whichever method you use, the Extend Selection saves time in working with a document.

50 Editing a Document

> ### Using the Keyboard to Extend a Selection
>
> To use the keyboard to extend a selection in POLICY.DOC, follow these steps:
>
> **1** Place the insertion point at the beginning of paragraph four.
>
> **2** Press `F8`. The EXT indicator in the status bar turns black to show that Extend Selection is on.
>
> **3** Press `F8` four times to extend the selection. The first press turns on Extend Selection; the second extends the selection to the end of the current word; the third, to the end of the current sentence; and the fourth, to the end of the current paragraph.
>
> **4** To return the selected text to the previous increment, press `Shift`+`F8`.
>
> **5** Press `Esc` to turn off Extend Selection.
>
> **6** Place the insertion point at the beginning of the document, and press `F8`+`9`. Word extends the selection to the first 9 in *1994*.
>
> When you press the key for a letter or other character, including punctuation marks and nonprinting characters such as `Tab` and `Enter`, you extend the selection to the next occurrence of that character.
>
> **7** Press the following keys to change the selection: `↓`, `←`, `→`, `PgUp`, `PgDn`, `↑`, `Home`, and `End`.
>
> **8** Press `Esc` to turn off Extend Selection.

Word automatically turns off Extend Selection when you perform an operation on the selected text. To turn off the Extend Selection without doing anything with the selected text, as you did in the tutorial, press `Esc`. Extend Selection is off when EXT is gray.

Deleting with Shortcut Keys

Word provides keyboard shortcuts for deleting blocks of text (see table 2.4).

Table 2.4 Deleting Text

Key Combination	Effect
`Backspace`	Deletes the selected text or deletes one character to the left of the insertion point.
`Ctrl`+`Backspace`	Deletes one word to the left of the insertion point.
`Del`	Deletes the selected text or deletes one character to the right of the insertion point.
`Ctrl`+`Del`	Deletes one word to the right of the insertion point.
`Ctrl`+`X`	Deletes the selected text and places it in the Clipboard.

Moving, Copying, and Deleting Text

One of the benefits of using Word is the ease with which you can move, copy, and delete text within your documents. You don't have to plan sentences, paragraphs, or even documents in detail before you start. Just type as thoughts come into your mind. Later you can polish your work by moving or copying words within sentences, sentences within paragraphs, and paragraphs within the document.

Moving text is removing the text from its current position and placing it in a new position. You can use one of the following methods to move text:

- The Cut and Paste buttons in the Standard toolbar
- The Cu**t** and **P**aste commands in the **E**dit menu
- The Move key (F2)
- The mouse
- The *Spike*

Spike
Word's specialized version of the Clipboard. You can store multiple entries in the Spike.

Paste
To place the contents of the Clipboard into a document.

Copying text is making a duplicate of the text and placing the duplicate in a new location. The original text remains in its current location. You use one of the following methods to copy text:

- The Copy and Paste buttons in the Standard toolbar
- The **C**opy and **P**aste commands in the **E**dit menu
- The Copy key
- The mouse

Deleting text is either completely removing a section of text or removing the section and then replacing it with other text. To delete text, you can use one of the following methods:

- The **C**lear command in the **E**dit menu
- The Overtype mode
- The Backspace key
- The Delete key

Deleting and Replacing Characters

To delete and replace characters in POLICY.DOC, follow these steps:

❶ Move the insertion point to the *e* in *softwear*.

❷ Press [Del] once.

❸ Move the cursor to the space after the *r* in *software*.

❹ Type the character **e**.

❺ Repeat the steps for the word *hardwear*.

You should become familiar with each method of moving, copying, and deleting and should use whichever one is appropriate in each specific situation. Although

52 Editing a Document

you will most frequently want to copy text within a document, you can use each method to copy text between Word documents. In addition, you can use the methods that involve the Clipboard to copy text into different Windows applications, such as into an Excel worksheet.

The Clipboard

Clipboard
A temporary storage area for text and graphics.

When you move, copy, or delete text or graphics in Windows, Word for Windows, and other Windows applications, you make extensive use of the *Clipboard*. The Clipboard is a temporary storage area you can use to move and copy text or graphics within a document or between different documents. You can select anything in a document and put it into the Clipboard. Then you can move the contents of the Clipboard to a different place in the same document or to another document.

Cut
To remove selected text from the document and store it in the Clipboard.

The Clipboard can contain only one item at a time, but the one item can be almost any size. When you move or copy text to the Clipboard, that text completely replaces whatever was previously in the Clipboard. The text that goes into the Clipboard stays there until you *cut* or copy something else to the Clipboard or until you exit Word.

Placing a section of text into the Clipboard has two steps:

1. Select the text you want to move.

2. Choose the command to cut or copy that text.

When you cut text, you remove it from your document and place it in the Clipboard. In contrast, when you copy text, that text remains in your document and a copy of it goes into the Clipboard. You cut when you want to move something; you copy when you want to place a copy somewhere else.

In the following tutorials, you use the Clipboard to store text for further use.

Using the Toolbar to Move Text

The Standard toolbar contains two buttons, Cut and Paste, for moving text. To use the toolbar buttons, follow these steps:

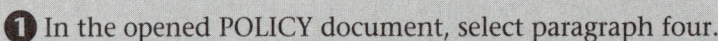 In the opened POLICY document, select paragraph four.

 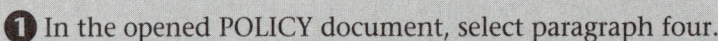 Click the Cut button in the Standard toolbar. Word removes the selected text from the document and places it in the Clipboard.

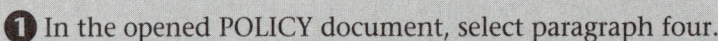 Place the insertion point on the first character in paragraph three.

 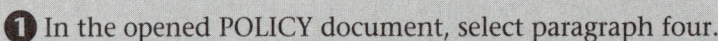 Click the Paste button in the Standard toolbar. At the insertion point, Word pastes a copy of the text that is in the Clipboard (see figure 2.12).

Figure 2.12
The text is moved to the new location.

The moved text

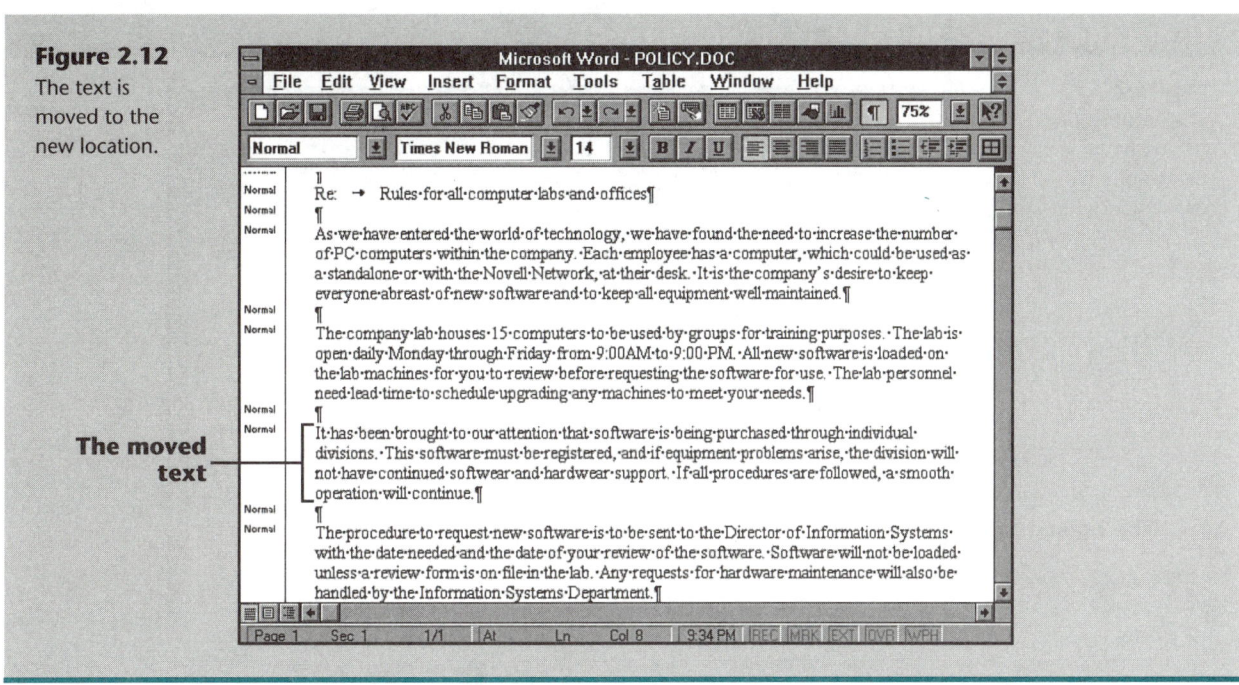

Note: *If you cut or copy something to the Clipboard and then change your mind, you can undo your action. See "Undoing Your Mistakes," later in this chapter.*

Using the Toolbar to Copy Text

The Standard toolbar also has a Copy button. To use the toolbar button to copy text, follow these steps:

1. Select paragraph four of the POLICY document.

2. Click the Copy button in the Standard toolbar. Word leaves the selected text in the document and places it in the Clipboard.

3. Place the insertion point on the first character in paragraph three.

4. Click the Paste button in the Standard toolbar. At the insertion point, Word pastes a copy of the text that is in the Clipboard (see figure 2.13).

Using the Toolbar to Copy Text (continued)

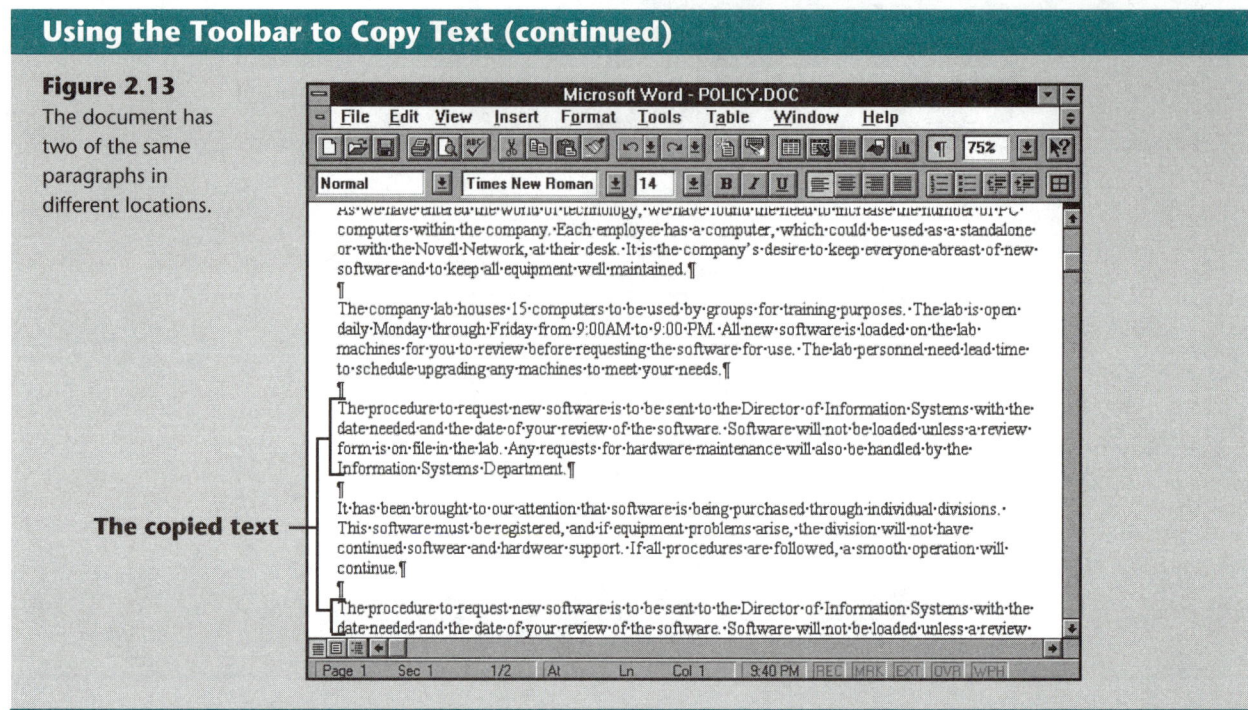

Figure 2.13
The document has two of the same paragraphs in different locations.

The copied text

You have moved and copied text to the Clipboard using the toolbar. In the next tutorials, you move and copy using the Edit menu.

Using the Edit Menu to Move Text

You can move text by choosing commands from the **E**dit menu. To use the menu, follow these steps:

1 In the opened POLICY.DOC, select paragraph three.

2 From the **E**dit menu, choose the Cu**t** command. Word removes the text from the document and places it in the Clipboard.

3 Place the insertion point after paragraph three.

4 From the **E**dit menu, choose the **P**aste command. At the insertion point, Word pastes a copy of the text that is in the Clipboard (see figure 2.14).

Figure 2.14
The paragraph is moved to a new location.

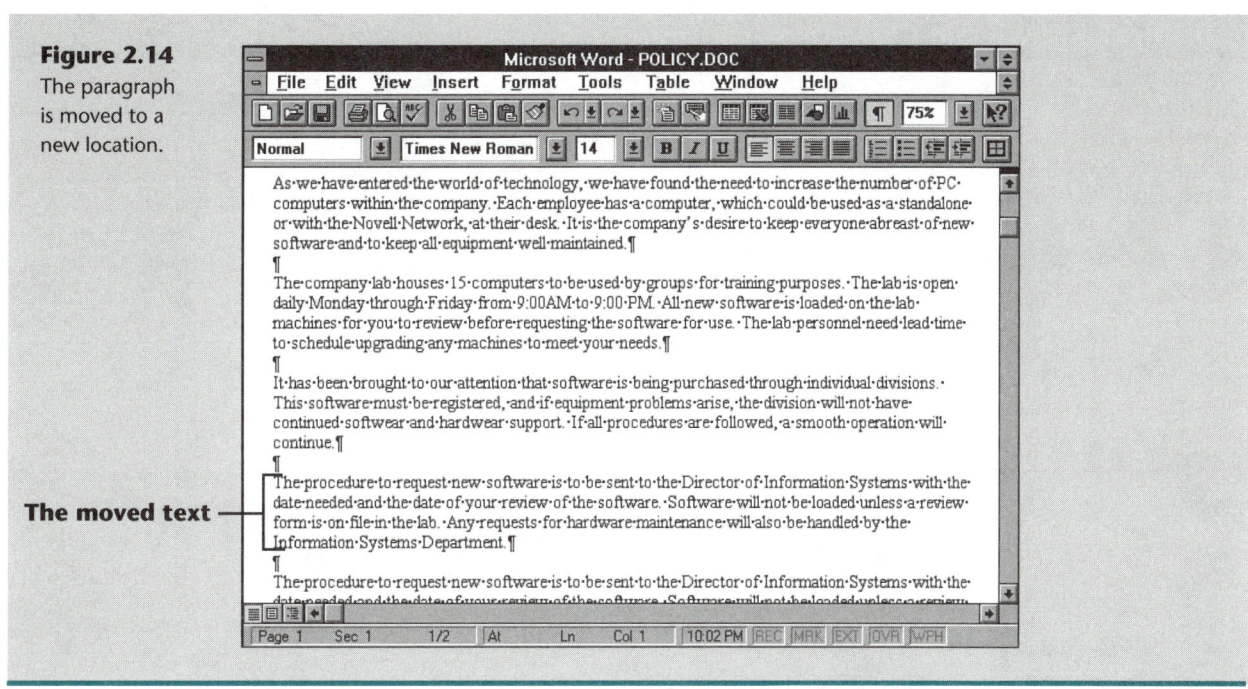

The moved text

To copy text, just choose the **E**dit, **C**opy command rather than the Cu**t** command in step 2.

Using the Move and Copy Keys

Using F2 (Move) and ⇧Shift+F2 (Copy) to move text does not involve the Clipboard.

Note: *In Word 6.0, F2 works completely differently from the way it did in previous versions.*

To use F2 to move text in POLICY.DOC, follow these steps:

1. Select paragraph four to move.

2. Press F2 (Move). The prompt Move to where? appears in the status bar (see figure 2.15).

(continues)

Using the Move and Copy Keys (continued)

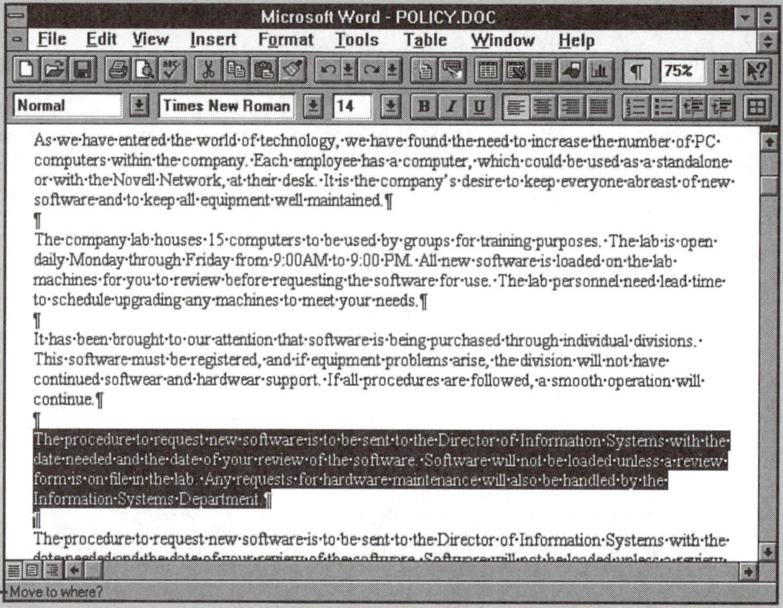

Figure 2.15
The Move To prompt appears in the status bar.

The Move To Where? prompt

❸ In the opened POLICY document, place the insertion point before paragraph three.

❹ Press ⏎Enter. The selected text moves from its original position to its new position at the insertion point (see figure 2.16).

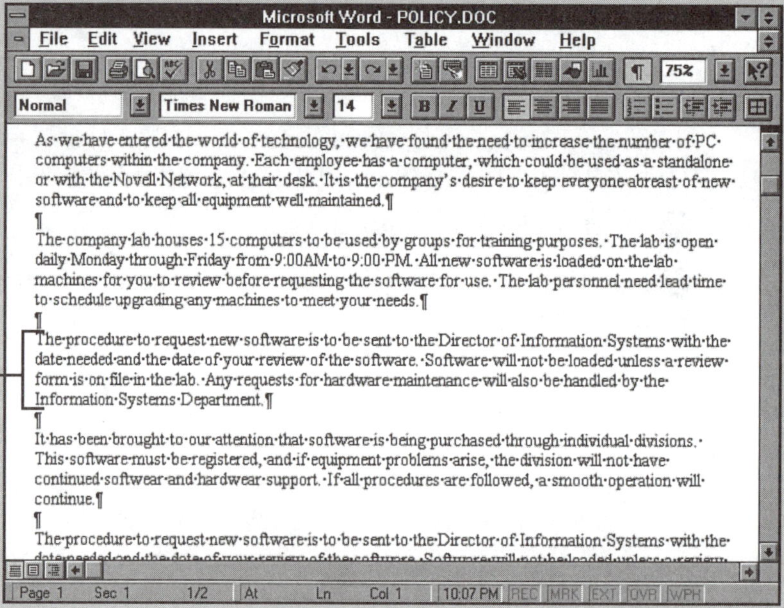

Figure 2.16
The text is moved to a new location.

The moved text

Copying text using ⇧Shift+F2 leaves the text in its original position and invokes the Copy to Where? prompt.

Dragging Text

You can use the mouse to move or copy text in two ways: by dragging the text or by pressing the right mouse button. In both cases, the text moves without involving the Clipboard. To use the mouse to drag text, follow these steps:

❶ In the opened POLICY.DOC, select paragraph three to move.

❷ Position the mouse pointer anywhere within the selected text.

When you move the mouse pointer onto the selected text, the pointer becomes an arrow.

❸ Hold down the left mouse button. The pointer changes its shape (see figure 2.17).

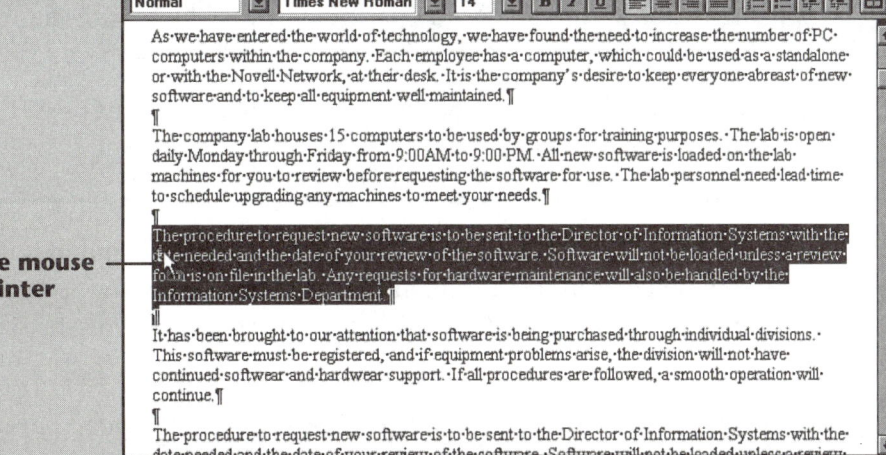

Figure 2.17
The mouse pointer changes shape, becoming a dotted insertion point with a box attached.

❹ Drag the mouse pointer to the new place for the text, after the existing paragraph four; and then release the mouse button. The text moves from its previous position to the new one.

Note: *Use the dotted insertion point, not the box, to indicate where you want to place the copied or moved text.*

To copy and drag text, press and hold down Ctrl, and then press and hold down the left mouse button. Drag the mouse pointer to the place where you want a copy of the selected text, release the mouse button, and then release Ctrl. The text is copied to the new position.

Using the Spike to Move Text

The Spike is Word's extended version of the Clipboard. The Clipboard can hold only one item at a time. The Spike, however, can hold many items. The Spike is used exclusively for moving text, not for copying. You can repeatedly select items and place them in the Spike without losing previously selected items. As can the Clipboard, the Spike can hold text and graphics.

Use the Spike when you need to move items from several different places, even from several different documents, to one new place. When you retrieve the items from the Spike, they appear in the same order that you placed them into the Spike, with individual items separated by paragraph marks. When you retrieve items from the Spike, you can leave those items in the Spike, or you can clear the Spike. To use the Spike, follow these steps:

1. In the opened POLICY.DOC, select paragraph four to move to the Spike.

2. Press Ctrl+F3. Word removes the selected text from the document and adds it to the Spike.

3. Repeat steps 1 and 2 for paragraph three to be moved to the Spike.

4. Place the insertion point after paragraph three. Make sure that the insertion point is at the beginning of a line or is preceded by a space.

5. Press Ctrl+Shift+F3. Word places the material in the Spike at the new place in the document and deletes the text from the Spike.

To insert the text without emptying the Spike, type **spike** and press F3. The text in the Spike appears in the document, but also remains in the Spike. If you move more text to the Spike, Word adds that text to the text already there.

Undoing Your Mistakes

Everyone makes mistakes. Word makes it easy for you to undo your incorrect actions and then do them correctly. This version of Word remembers not only your most recent action, but an entire sequence of actions. What's more, after you have undone one or more actions, Word can automatically redo those actions for you.

You can undo and redo actions either by clicking buttons in the Standard toolbar or by choosing commands in the **E**dit menu.

Using Undo

You can use the Undo button in the Standard toolbar to undo one or more actions. The button to the right of the Undo button is the Redo button. Each of these buttons has a down-pointing arrow that opens a drop-down list box.

To undo one action at a time, click the Undo button. The first time you click the button, Word undoes your most recent action. The next time you click it, Word undoes the action immediately before that. You can continue choosing the button to undo more previous actions.

Using Undo in a Document

If you want to undo a series of actions, Word offers a better way than undoing those actions one at a time. To see Undo in action in the opened POLICY.DOC, follow these steps:

❶ Cut the word *hardware* from one place in the document.

❷ Paste it after paragraph three and after paragraph four.

 ❸ To undo those three actions (cut, paste, and paste), click the Undo button three times or click the down arrow of the Undo button and click each action.

The word will be deleted from the new positions and appear in the original.

One mistake you might make is to undo an action and then realize that you didn't want to undo it after all. Fortunately, Word keeps track of each action you undo so that you can subsequently redo it—that is, undo the undo.

Using Redo

To see how the Redo button works, follow these steps:

❶ Highlight the word *software* in POLICY.DOC.

❷ Press Del to delete the word.

❸ Then click the Undo button in the Standard toolbar to undo the deletion.

If you open the Undo list box at this point, Word shows that your latest action was Clear, which is the name of the command in the **E**dit menu that corresponds to pressing Del.

 ❹ Click the Redo button in the Standard toolbar, the button to the right of the Undo button.

This reverses the insertion of the word you deleted earlier so that the word is immediately deleted once again.

Word also remembers a sequence of undo actions. If you again cut a word and paste it twice and then undo all three actions, for example, Word remembers these three undo actions. To experiment with this feature, click the down arrow at the right side of the Redo button in the Standard toolbar (see figure 2.18).

Figure 2.18
The Redo drop-down list box shows the most recent actions that were redone.

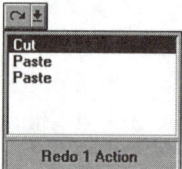

To redo all three actions, select all three items with the mouse, just as you did in the Undo list box. When you release the mouse button, Word redoes the three actions.

Note: *There is a significant difference between the Undo and Redo lists. Whereas the Undo list is always available, the Redo list is available only immediately after you have undone actions. If you take any action, such as typing text, after undoing actions, you cannot redo those actions.*

Using the Edit Menu to Undo and Redo Actions

You can undo actions one at a time, starting from the most recent, by opening the **E**dit menu and choosing the **U**ndo command (see figure 2.19).

Figure 2.19
When you open the **E**dit menu, the **U**ndo command is followed by the name of your most recent action—**U**ndo Clear in this example.

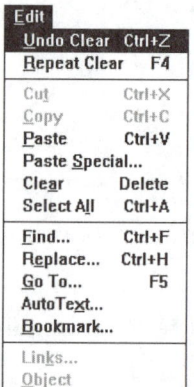

To undo the most recent action, choose the **U**ndo command. You can step back, one action at a time, by repeatedly opening the **E**dit menu and choosing the **U**ndo command.

The second command in the **E**dit menu is sometimes **R**edo and other times **R**epeat. If there are actions available to redo, the command is **R**edo; if there are no actions to redo, the command is **R**epeat.

Suppose that you have used the **U**ndo command to undo one or more actions and then, before doing anything else, you open the **E**dit menu again. In this case, the second item in the menu is **R**edo, which you can choose to redo the most recent undone action. If you did do something else, such as typing text, after an undo, however, there is nothing to redo. Therefore, the second item in the **E**dit menu is **R**epeat.

Repeating an Action

After choosing a command or clicking a toolbar button, you can repeat the same action. Just open the **E**dit menu, and choose the **R**epeat command.

If you choose a command or click a toolbar button and then undo the action, the **E**dit menu contains the **R**edo command instead of the **R**epeat command, as explained in the preceding section.

Objective 5: Work with More than One Document

In Word, you work with documents in windows. You can open several documents at the same time, each in its own window. By default, Word maximizes the document window so that only one open window is visible at a time. The active window is the window that contains the document on which you are currently working and that contains the insertion point. Any action you take affects only the active document.

Word enables you to

- Work with several documents, each in its own window.

Pane
A portion of a window.

- Split a window into two parts, called *panes*, and work with different documents in each pane.

When you have two or more documents open at the same time, you can easily copy or move text between them. You also can refer to information in one document while working with another document.

Working with Different Documents in Separate Windows and Views

To open more than one document, open each document just as you open a single document. If the documents are not maximized, their windows are stacked on top of each other so that only the most recently opened document is completely visible; you can see only the edges of the other documents. If the documents are maximized, only the most recently opened one is visible. To make an open document active, switch to its window by following these steps:

① Using the New File button, open a new document.

② Open the **W**indow menu. Your menu probably will not match the one shown in figure 2.20.

Figure 2.20
A list of open documents appears at the bottom of the Window menu.

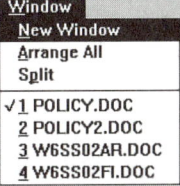

③ Select POLICY.DOC. That document becomes completely visible.

Each document is independent; you can work in any document without affecting the other open documents. You can, however, move and copy text between documents by using the Clipboard.

Moving or Copying Text between Documents

To move or copy text between documents, follow these steps:

1. With POLICY.DOC still open, open FIRST.DOC.

2. Open the **W**indow menu, and click `POLICY.DOC` on the list. That document becomes active and is displayed on-screen.

3. Select the first paragraph of text to copy from the POLICY document.

 4. Cut or copy the text by clicking the Cut or Copy button in the Standard toolbar or by choosing the **C**u**t** or **C**opy command in the **E**dit menu.

5. Use the **W**indow menu to switch to the FIRST.DOC document where you want to place the cut or copied text.

6. Place the insertion point where you want the cut or copied text to appear.

 7. Paste the text into the document by clicking the Paste button in the Standard toolbar or by choosing the **P**aste command in the **E**dit menu.

Working with Different Documents on the Same Screen

To use F2 (Move) or Shift+F2 (Copy) or the mouse to move or copy text between two documents, both documents must be open and visible on-screen.

Note: *The two documents do not have to be visible at the same time if you cut or copy to the Clipboard.*

To make two or more documents visible on-screen at the same time, open those documents. Then open the **W**indow menu and choose the **A**rrange All command (see figure 2.21).

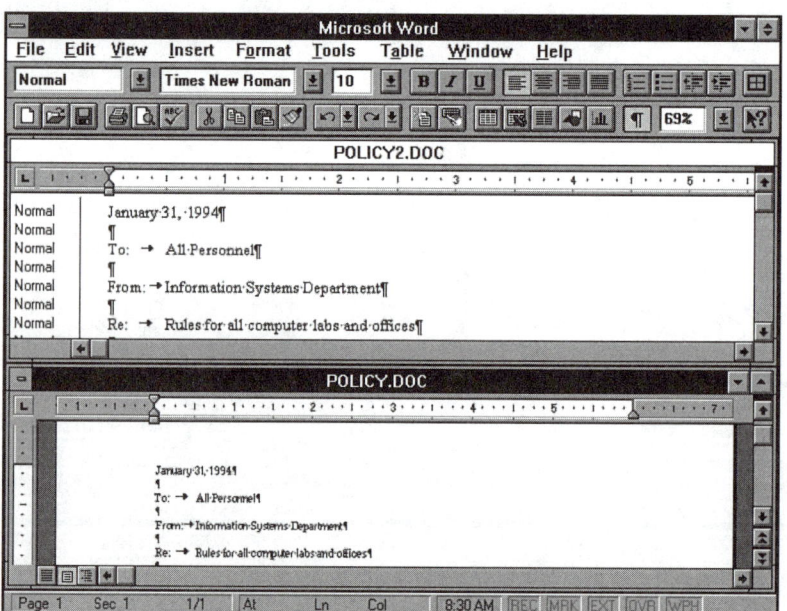

Figure 2.21
In this example, two documents are shown in separate windows within the Word window.

To make a document active, place the insertion point anywhere inside that document's window.

Note: *When you choose the **A**rrange All command, Word divides the screen into as many windows as needed to display all the open documents. If four documents are open, for example, Word divides the space within the Word window into four windows, with each open document occupying one window. Working in small windows is difficult. Do not choose the **A**rrange All command when many documents are open unless you need to see all the open documents on one screen.*

To return to working in one window, you can do either of the following:

- Close all but one open document.

- Maximize the active document. To maximize a document, choose the Maximize button at the right end of the document's title bar.

Working with One Document in Two Panes

To view and work in two parts of the active document at the same time, you can divide the document window into two panes. You can scroll and work in each pane independently. This feature is particularly useful when you want to move or copy text between distant parts of a long document. You can split the screen into two panes and then view the source text in one pane and the destination area in the other pane.

To split the screen into panes by using the mouse, follow these steps:

❶ In the opened POLICY.DOC, point to the split box at the top of the vertical scroll bar (see figure 2.22).

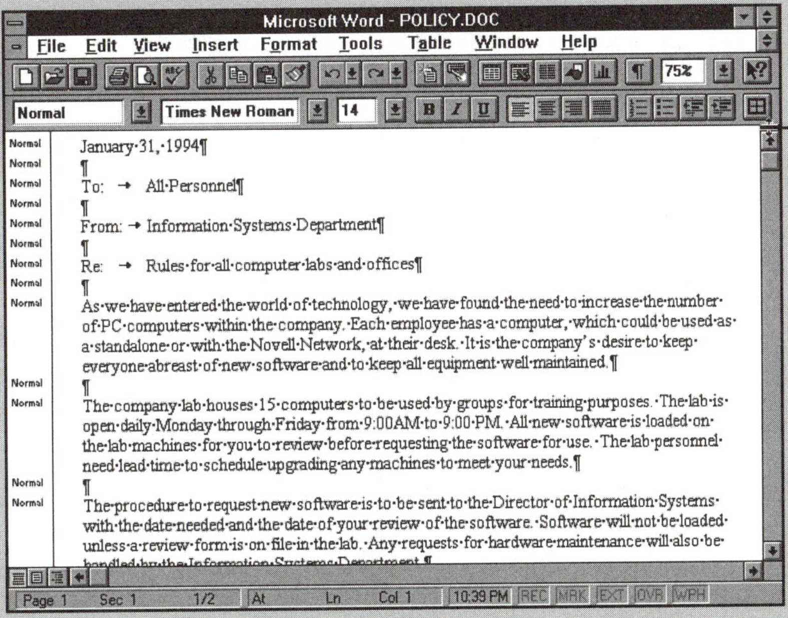

Figure 2.22
When you position the mouse pointer on the split box, the mouse pointer shape changes to a double-ended arrow.

The split box

(continues)

> **Working with One Document in Two Panes (continued)**
>
> ❷ Double-click the split box, dividing the text area into two equal panes.
>
> ❸ The pane that contains the insertion point is the active pane. To make the inactive pane active, click anywhere inside the inactive pane.
>
> ❹ Press F6 to switch back to the other pane.
>
> ❺ Double-click the split box again to return to a full-sized window. (You also can use the **W**indow Remove **Sp**lit option to return to the full-sized window.)

With two panes open and different parts of the same document shown on-screen, you can easily copy or move text from one part of a document to another by using the methods previously described.

> **Tips**
>
> To create panes of different sizes, drag the split box down the vertical scroll bar to indicate where you want the screen to split.
>
> To change the size of the panes, point to the split box, press the mouse button, and drag up or down.

Displaying Documents in Different Views

Word can display several different views of the same document. You can use these views to focus on various aspects of a document and to make editing easier. You can display a document in six views:

- Normal
- Outline
- Page Layout
- Full Screen
- Print Preview

Changing between Views

The easiest way to switch between the three most commonly used document views is to choose the buttons at the left end of the horizontal scroll bar (see figure 2.23). You learn about the other three views later.

Work with More than One Document   65

Figure 2.23
In figure 2.23, the pointer is on the Page Layout button, and that button is identified by a ToolTip.

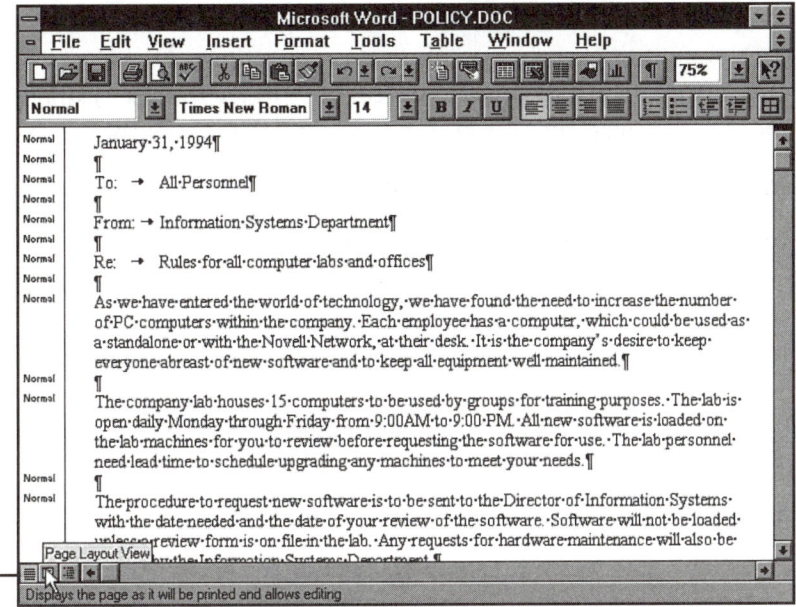

The view buttons

From left to right, the three buttons at the left end of the horizontal scroll bar select the Normal, Page Layout, and Outline views of a document.

You also can use the **V**iew menu to choose document views (see figure 2.24).

Figure 2.24
You can use the first three commands in the **V**iew menu to select **N**ormal, **O**utline, or **P**age Layout views of a document.

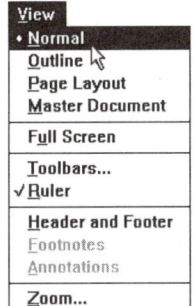

Whether you use buttons in the scroll bar or commands in the **V**iew menu, the highlighted button in the scroll bar identifies the current view. Also, when you open the **V**iew menu, Word displays a bullet on the left side of the currently selected view.

Deciding Which View to Use

Normal view is the default and, generally, the most useful view. You will probably do most of your work in this view.

In Normal view, you can see character and paragraph formatting; alignment; tab positions; and line, section, and page breaks. In this view, you do not see headers, footers, footnotes, or side-by-side columns, or how the document will actually look on a printed page.

Page Layout view shows all the formatting in the document—including headers, footers, footnotes, columns, and frames—in their correct positions. You can edit and format text in this view; you can also move frames by dragging with the mouse. However, the screen response is a little slower than in Normal view.

In Page Layout view, a vertical ruler is added at the left side of the screen.

In Page Layout view, two additional buttons, each with a double-headed arrow, appear at the bottom of the vertical scroll bar. When you click the button with the double-headed up arrow, the document scrolls up one page; when you click the button with the double-headed down arrow, the document scrolls down one page.

 Outline view enables you to work with a document in outline form, providing that you have applied suitable heading styles to titles and subtitles in the document. In Outline view, the various levels of headings are automatically indented to show the structure of a document. You can collapse a document so that only headings are displayed.

Changing the View of POLICY.DOC

Print Preview gives you a good idea of what a page will look like when you print it. Looking at pages with Print Preview before you print them is always a good idea.

To display POLICY.DOC in Print Preview, follow these steps:

 ❶ Choose the Print Preview button in the Standard toolbar.

or

From the File menu, choose Print Preview. Figure 2.25 shows POLICY.DOC in Print Preview.

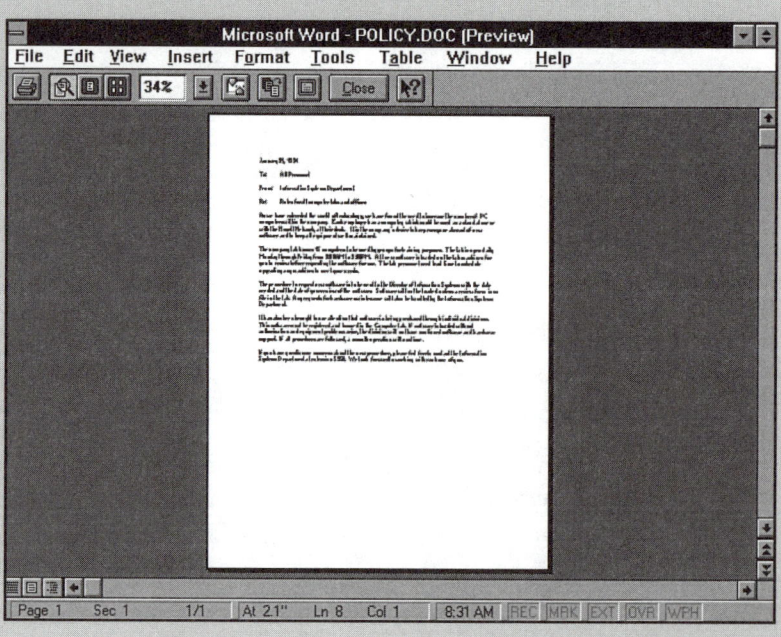

Figure 2.25 Print Preview shows you a miniature version of how your document will look when printed.

Word automatically scales the document so that a complete page is shown on-screen. When you switch to Print Preview with either of these methods, Word automatically scales the image so that you can see a complete page. Unless you have a very large monitor, you cannot see individual characters, but you can see the overall layout of the page. Unlike previous versions of Word, this version enables you to change the magnification of the image so that you can see individual characters. You can edit text in this view.

❷ Click the Zoom Control box in the toolbar. The Zoom Control drop-down list box appears (see figure 2.27). Unlike the other items in the Standard toolbar, Zoom Control consists of a text box that shows the current magnification and a down arrow that provides access to a drop-down list.

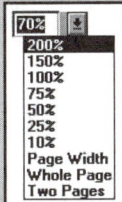

Figure 2.26
The zoom control drop-down box.

❸ Choose 75 percent from the drop-down list.

Note: *You also can type **75** in the text box that shows the current magnification, (you don't need to type the percent symbol), and press* ⏎Enter.

❹ Using the Overtype mode, change *January* to **June**.

❺ Turn off the Overtype mode.

❻ Using the Undo button on the Standard toolbar, return the month to January.

❼ Click the Normal View button on the horizontal scroll bar to return POLICY.DOC to the Normal view.

❽ Save the file to your data disk as **POLICY2.DOC**. Then print the document with all the changes, and compare the document to the printout from Chapter 1.

Print Preview does not limit you to looking at one page at a time. You can click the Multiple Pages button in the Print Preview toolbar (the fourth button from the left) to see as many as six miniature pages at a time.

Using Full Screen View

Sometimes you want to see as much of a page as possible, and you want to be able to read what is on the page. That's why Word provides a Full Screen view feature. Figure 2.27 shows a Full Screen view.

Figure 2.27
The Full Screen view eliminates everything except the text area, so that you can see as much text as possible.

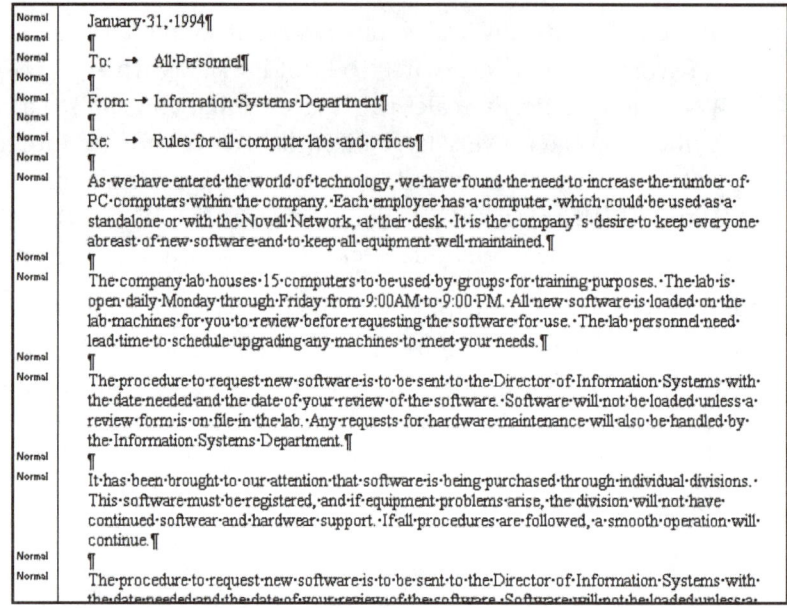

To display your document in Full Screen view, open the **V**iew menu and choose the F**u**ll Screen command. To return to the previous view, click the icon at the bottom right side of the screen. You can edit in Full Screen view, just as you can in Normal view. You can even open menus and select commands, but you have to remember which Alt+key combinations to use.

Chapter Summary

You have edited a document, added text, and used the move and copy features. Your survival skills have increased because now you can open an existing document, edit the document, and continue to use the save and print feature from Chapter 1.

You are able to open more than one document and share text between the windows. This feature saves retyping if text can be used in multiple documents. In Chapter 3, you learn how to use Word to check and improve your work.

Checking Your Skills

True/False Questions

For each of the following statements, circle *T* or *F* to indicate whether the statement is true or false.

T F **1.** Word remembers the last four documents you opened and lists their names at the bottom of the **E**dit menu.

T F **2.** If you highlight the command Cu**t** from the **E**dit menu, you can press F1 to get help on the Cu**t** command.

T F **3.** Moving the insertion point with keyboard is often slower than using the mouse.

T **F** 4. To insert a blank line in a document, you press ⬇ twice.

_T_ F 5. Moving text physically moves the text to another part of the document.

T **F** 6. You can open an existing document by choosing a menu command or a button in the Formatting toolbar.

_T_ F 7. When you click **S**how Topics, the Search dialog box shows a list of topics related to the word in the text box.

(T F 8. When you revise a document, you have to move the insertion point to the text that needs changing.

T **F** 9. The position of horizontal scroll bar indicates the position of the text in the window relative to the top and bottom margins.

_T_ F 10. You can add a new entry to the AutoCorrect list of errors.

Multiple-Choice Questions

In the blank provided, write the letter of the correct answer for each of the following questions.

____ 1. In Word, you can select any amount of text by extending a selection, clicking the __c__ indicator on the status bar.

  a. INS

  b. REC

  c. EXT

  d. OVR

  e. WPH

____ 2. Use the Go To dialog box to move to a specific __e__.

  a. page

  b. line

  c. bookmark

  d. table

  e. all the above

____ 3. To find a similar word to replace one in your document, use the __a__ feature.

  a. Spell Check

  b. Thesaurus

  c. AutoGrammar

  d. AutoFormat

  e. AutoCorrect

____ 4. To move or copy text, you can select the text using __d__.

   a. the mouse

   b. the keyboard

   c. Extend Selection

   d. a, b, c

   e. a and b only

____ 5. Documents can be displayed in different views, excluding __b__.

   a. Normal

   b. Table of Contents

   c. Outline

   d. Full Screen

   e. Print Preview

____ 6. To display the Open dialog box, click the __a__.

   a. Open button

   b. File button

   c. New button

   d. File Name

   e. status bar

____ 7. To insert blank lines into your document, Word must be in the __b__ mode.

   a. Edit

   b. Insert

   c. OVR

   d. REC

   e. MRK

____ 8. When the nonprinting characters display, the raised period represents a(n) __c__.

   a. comma

   b. semicolon

   c. space

   d. tab

   e. indent

9. You can display special symbols to represent nonprinting characters by clicking the __d__.

    a. Hide/Show button

    b. Zoom button

    c. Magnify button

    d. Show/Hide button

    e. View menu

10. If you click in the selection bar at the left end of the line, you will select __c__.

    a. a block of text

    b. a word

    c. a line

    d. multiple lines

    e. a page

Fill-in-the-Blank Questions

In the blank provided, write the correct answer for each of the following questions.

1. When you revise a document, you have to move the ___insertion___ point to the place that needs changing.

2. In the status bar, when ___OVR___ is dimmed, Word is in the Insert mode.

3. Moving text involves ___highlighting___ text and placing the ___insertion point___ in a new location.

4. To insert blank lines into your document, Word must be in the ___Insert___ mode.

5. If you need to see as much of a page as possible, and you want to read what is on the page, Word provides a ___document___ (Full screen) view feature.

6. ___Revising___ (Deleting) text is either completely removing a section of text or removing the section and replacing it with other text.

7. The position of the scroll box on the ___horizontal___ (vertical) scroll bar indicates the position of the text in the window relative to the beginning and the end of the document.

8. In the ___insert___ mode, Word inserts the characters you type to the left of the insertion point, and text on the right side of the insertion point moves to the right.

9. When you select text with the mouse, you often use the ___selection bar___, an area at the left side of the text area.

10. To deselect text, ___click___ anywhere in the document, including the selected area.

Applying Your Skills

Review Exercises

Exercise 1: Adding Text to FIRST.DOC

To add text to FIRST.DOC, follow these steps:

1. Open the FIRST.DOC from Chapter 1, Review Exercise 1, and add the following text:

    The agenda for this meeting will include the two-year plan for the merger between the design and the assembly groups. A team approach is stressed in producing the new product line, which includes integrating the marketing, sales, and designing phase.

2. Save the file to your data disk as **FIRST.DOC**.

Exercise 2: Using Help to Learn More about Magnification

To practice using Help, follow these steps:

1. Access the **H**elp screen, and select the **S**earch On Help.
2. Type the letter **M** for *magnification*.
3. Select the topic Magnification to display Help information.
4. Read the information Help displays.
5. Exit the Help menu.

Exercise 3: Changing Views

Open MEDICAL.DOC, and display the document in the following views:

a. Normal view

b. Page Layout view

c. Page Preview

Exercise 4: Editing Text

To practice editing text, follow these steps:

1. Open GUIDELINE.DOC.
2. Move item #3 to item #2.
3. Add the following text:

    If the employee cannot comply with rules stated above, then a written notification must be received within five (5) working days after receipt of guidelines.

4. Save the file to your data disk as **GUIDELINE.DOC**.

Exercise 5: Copying Text

To practice copying text within a document, follow these steps:

1. Open the BUTTON.DOC.

2. Copy each sentence to a new location, adding it to the existing text. For example, copy statement with bold to the last statement in the document.

3. Save the file to your data disk as **BUTTON.DOC**.

Continuing Projects

Project 1: Practice in Using Word

Practice using Word by following these steps:

1. Add the word *phone* to the AutoCorrect, and replace the word with *telephone*.

2. Type the following text:

    Schedule of Events

    January 31

    The anniversary committee met and discussed the necessary fund raisers to be accomplished for the next six months. People were assigned specific jobs.

    Refreshments donated by Dunkin Donuts.

    February 6

    The publication committee met and worked on signs and articles on upcoming events to be published in the local newspapers.

    A representative visited six restaurants and facilities to reserve the date. All information will be reviewed by the entire committee on March 3.

    February 8

    Sent letters to business organizations requesting donations and support. Follow-up phone calls will be done.

3. Add the sentence that begins "Refreshments....." to the end of every paragraph under each date.

4. Display the document in different views.

5. Print the document.

6. Save the file to your data disk as **SCHEDULE.DOC**.

Project 2: Federal Department Store

Continue developing the Federal Department Store brochure by following these steps:

1. Open the CATALOG.DOC.

2. Add the following text:

    <u>New Sport Sandal</u>

    Our best sandal for pavement, trail, and shore—made for walking or hiking in total comfort. Ultra-lightweight rubber and polyurethane construction. **Men's or Women's $35.00.**

    <u>Easy-Care Cardigan</u>

    Classic V-neck style cardigan, knit from 100% acrylic yarns. Easy to care for, with minimal wrinkling or pilling. Full-button front and roll-back rib-knit cuffs. **$27.00**

3. Copy the New Sport Sandal Item paragraph to the end of the document.

4. Change the first New Sport Sandal… to New Men's Sport Sandal; and the second New Sport Sandal… to New Women's Sport Sandal.

5. Delete Men's for pricing in the Women's sandal, and delete Women's in the Men's for pricing.

6. Using spike, move the Sweater description to the third item in the list.

7. Preview the document.

8. Save the file to your data disk as **CATALOG.DOC**.

Project 3: Real Entertainment Corporation

Continue working with the Real Entertainment Corporation newsletter by following these steps:

1. Open the document REC.DOC.

2. Access AutoCorrect, and add the word *group*, and replace it with *department*.

3. Add the word *US* and replace it with *United States*.

4. Type the following text:

    Marketing Group

    Our job is to contact businesses, both profit and non-profit, within the US. Form letters are sent initially, and follow-up telephone calls are made. We find five out of ten telephone calls result in at least a need for a presentation of the materials. Out of the five, we have been able to capture two contracts. This is a start, but we want the 20% to grow to 50% and so on. The newsletter can be our new marketing tool.

5. Move the paragraph "We hope we have sparked..." to the end of the document.

6. Display this document and the Schedule document in different panes.

7. Display the document in full view.

8. Print the document.

9. Save the file to your data disk as **REC.DOC**.

Chapter 3
Checking Your Work

In this chapter, you learn about the process of editing documents. Most individuals proofread their own documents and find checking their spelling, selection of words, and grammar to be time-consuming. This chapter introduces you to the Spelling Checker, Thesaurus, and Grammar Checker—features of Word designed to help you improve the quality of your documents. You also learn to search a document for selected text, special characters, or formatting and how to replace each with other text or formatting.

Objectives

By the time you finish this chapter, you will have learned to

1. Check Your Spelling
2. Use the Thesaurus
3. Check Your Grammar
4. Find and Replace Text

Objective 1: Check Your Spelling

Dictionary
An area for storing words frequently used in documents. Word contains a dictionary, but it may not contain all the words used in your document. Custom dictionaries can be created.

You should always check the spelling of each document you create. The Spelling Checker is only one of the tools you can use for this purpose. Remember that the Spelling Checker checks only individual words, without regard to their context. It cannot alert you to errors such as typing *no* rather than *know*, *too* rather than *two*, *principal* rather than *principle*, and so on.

You can use the Spelling Checker to check a single selected word, a selected block of text, or an entire document. Word always checks the spellings in your document against the spelling of words in its main *dictionary*. In addition, you can instruct Word to compare words in your document with those in one or more custom *dictionaries* you have created. When the Spelling Checker encounters a word it doesn't recognize, you can correct the word or add it to one of your custom dictionaries.

Note: *The Grammar Checker checks grammar and spelling; if you check grammar, you do not need to check spelling separately.*

Detecting and Correcting Unrecognized Words

You can start the Spelling Checker by using any of the following methods:

- Click the Spelling button on the Standard toolbar.
- Choose the **S**pelling command from the **T**ools menu.
- Press F7.

Checking the Spelling in a Document

To check the spelling in the open POLICY2.DOC document, follow these steps:

❶ Place the insertion point at the beginning of the document.

 ❷ Click the Spelling button on the Standard toolbar.

or

From the **T**ools menu, choose the **S**pelling command.

or

Press F7.

❸ Word begins checking the document and finds and highlights the word *Novell*, which it does not recognize. The Spelling dialog box appears (see figure 3.1).

Figure 3.1
The Spelling dialog box displays the unrecognized word in the Not in Dictionary text box and suggests possible replacement words in the Suggestions list box.

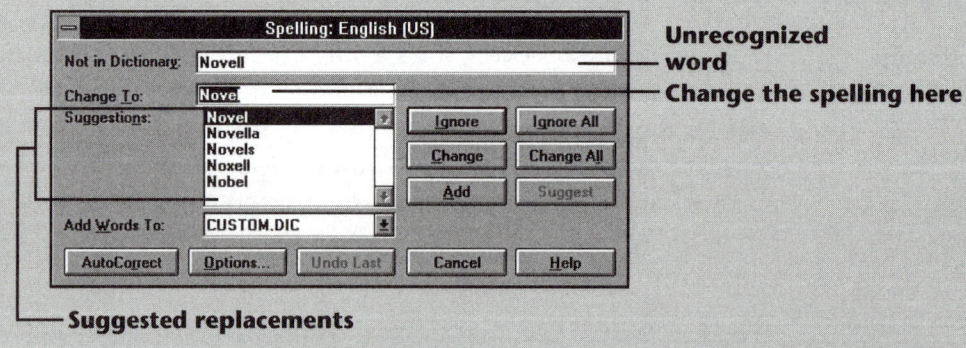

Note: *If no words appear in the Suggestions list box, click the Suggest button.*

❹ Suggested spellings appear in the Suggestions list box. Because the highlighted word is spelled correctly, click the **I**gnore All button to leave all occurrences of the same word unchanged. Word continues to check the spelling without taking any action on the highlighted word.

If Word displays a misspelled word with suggested changes, click the **C**hange button to replace the word with the correct spelling in the Change **T**o text box. Choose Change A**l**l to replace all occurrences of this word in the remainder of the document.

❺ Continue checking the spelling of the document, repeating the preceding steps.

❻ Save the file to your data disk, but do not close it.

Note: You can click the Cancel button or press Esc *at any time to stop the Spelling Checker. Word displays a message box telling you that the checking of the spelling is complete. Choose OK.*

- To change a highlighted word to a word that does not appear in the Suggestions list box when you know the correct spelling, click anywhere in the document window (or press Ctrl+Tab), and edit the word directly in the document. The **I**gnore button in the Spelling dialog box becomes the **S**tart button; click this button when you are ready to resume checking the spelling.

- To change a highlighted word to a word that does not appear in the Suggestions list box when you do not know the correct spelling, type your best guess at the spelling of the word in the Change **T**o text box, and click the **S**uggest button. Word displays similar words in the Suggestio**n**s list box. Click one of the suggested words to place it in the Change **T**o text box, and then click the **C**hange or Change A**l**l button, as appropriate.

- To undo up to five of your last spelling changes, click the **U**ndo Last button. Each time you click this button, Word returns the word you changed most recently to its original spelling. If you change the words *hte* to *the* and *thier* to *their* and click **U**ndo Last twice, for example, **U**ndo changes *their* back to *thier* first, then makes the other change.

- When the Spelling dialog box indicates a repeated word and you want to delete one of the words, simply click the **D**elete button.

Working with Custom Dictionaries

When you install Word, it has one dictionary, called the *main dictionary*. You can choose a main dictionary in one of many languages.

The main dictionary does not contain every word that you may want to use, particularly if you work with material that has specialized terminology. To solve this problem, Word enables you to create as many custom dictionaries as you want.

You can then select one or more of your custom dictionaries to use any time you use the Spelling Checker.

It is a good idea to create custom dictionaries for different subjects. If you frequently create documents about computers and also documents about finances, for example, you may want to create two different custom dictionaries to handle the terminology specific to each subject.

Creating a Custom Dictionary

To create a custom dictionary, you use the Spelling Options dialog box. You can access that dialog box from **O**ptions button in the Spelling Checker or from the **T**ools menu.

To create a custom dictionary, follow these steps:

1 From the **T**ools menu, choose **O**ptions.

2 Click the Spelling tab to display the Spelling Options dialog box. The Spelling Options dialog box appears (see figure 3.2).

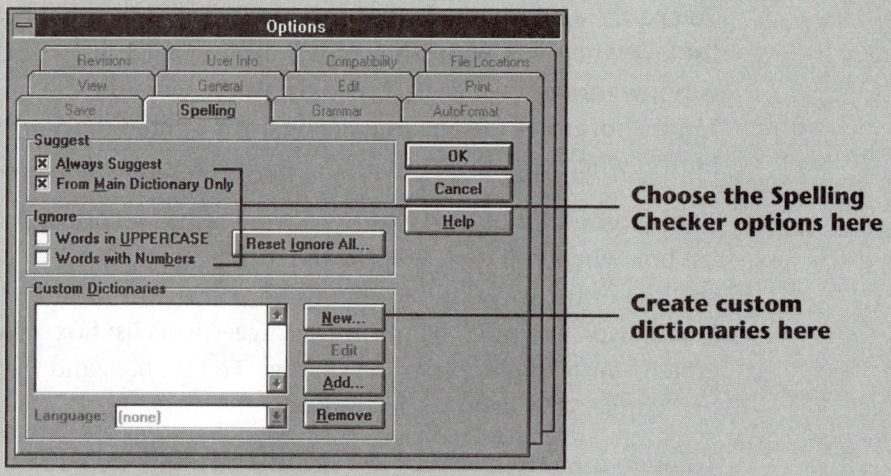

Figure 3.2
Use the Spelling Options dialog box to create custom dictionaries and to control various aspects of Word's Spelling Checker.

3 Click the **N**ew button to display the Create Custom Dictionary dialog box (see figure 3.3).

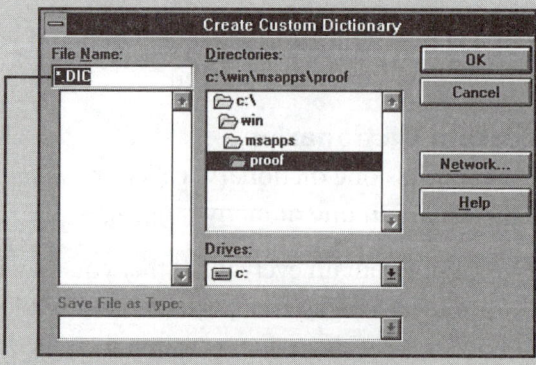

Figure 3.3
Use the Create Custom Dictionary dialog box to store words related to a specific topic that you refer to frequently.

You name your custom dictionary in the Create Custom Dictionary dialog box.

④ In the File **N**ame text box, enter **class** for your custom dictionary name. Remember to limit the name to eight characters because Word uses the name as an actual file name and automatically attaches the custom dictionary file name extension (DIC); you do not have to type it.

⑤ Choose OK to return to the Spelling Options dialog box (see figure 3.4).

Figure 3.4
The name of your first custom dictionary is now listed in the Custom **D**ictionaries list box.

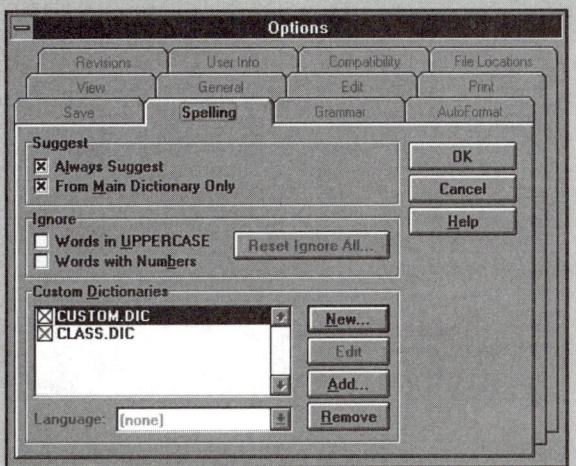

Notice that an × appears in the check box next to the custom dictionary's name; this × means that Word uses this dictionary, as well as the main dictionary, when it checks spelling. If you do not want Word to compare words with entries in this custom dictionary, click the check box to deselect it.

⑥ Choose OK to confirm settings and leave the Spelling Options dialog box.

Now you have a custom dictionary into which you can insert words that will be used frequently in appropriate contexts.

Specifying the Custom Dictionary or Dictionaries

As mentioned previously, Word always checks spelling by referring to the main dictionary. Word can also check spelling by referring to one or more custom dictionaries. You can specify which custom dictionaries Word uses.

Note: *Specify only the custom dictionaries that are appropriate for your current work. Each additional custom dictionary that you specify slows down the spell-checking process.*

To specify the custom dictionary or dictionaries to be used in the opened POLICY2.DOC, follow these steps:

(continues)

Specifying the Custom Dictionary or Dictionaries (continued)

❶ From the Tools menu, choose Options.

❷ Click the Spelling tab to open the Spelling Options dialog box (see figure 3.5).

Figure 3.5
Use the Spelling Options dialog box to select a custom dictionary to use in checking the spelling of a document.

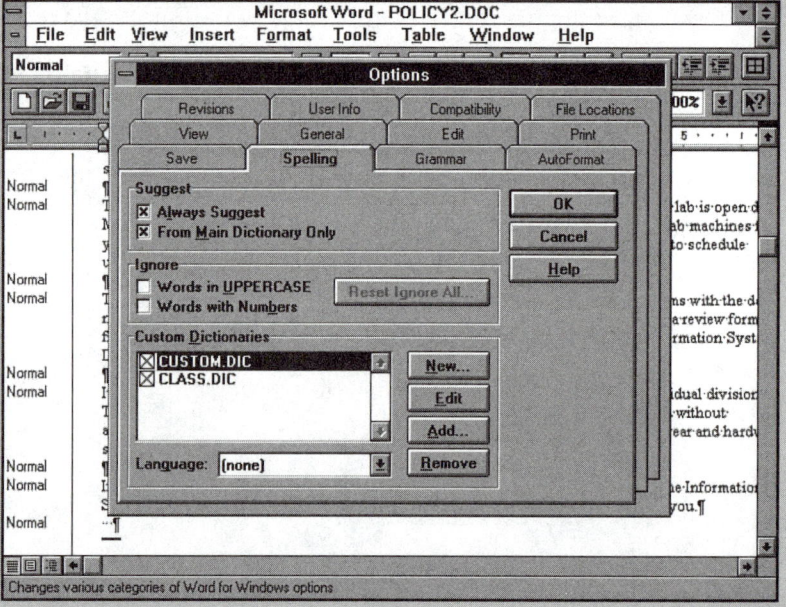

❸ In the Custom Dictionaries list box, click the check box next to CLASS.DIC to select it.

❹ Choose OK to return to the document.

With the custom dictionary available, you are ready to add words to it.

Adding a Word to Your Custom Dictionary

The easiest way to add words to a custom dictionary is to open or create a document that contains the words that you want to add, and then run the Spelling Checker.

To add a word to your CLASS.DIC custom dictionary while in POLICY2.DOC, follow these steps:

❶ In the Spelling Options dialog box, select the CLASS.DIC custom dictionary check box (see figure 3.6).

Figure 3.6
The Spelling dialog box appears, showing the first word in your document that is not in the main dictionary.

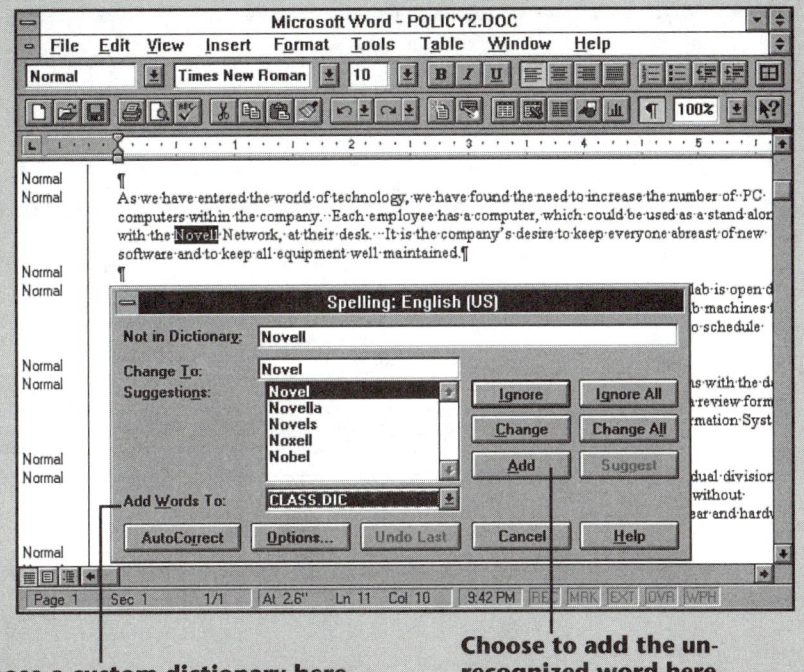

Choose a custom dictionary here

Choose to add the unrecognized word here

❷ Choose **T**ools, **S**pelling to begin checking the spelling.

❸ When the Spelling Checker highlights the unrecognized words, choose the CLASS.DIC custom dictionary in the Add **W**ords To drop-down list.

❹ Click **A**dd. Word adds *Novell* to the selected custom dictionary and searches for the next unrecognized word.

After you have added the initial collection of words in your custom dictionary, you can add more words as they occur in your work. Adding words that are specific to your business saves time in the spell-checking process.

Choosing Other Spelling Options

In the Spelling options dialog box, you can choose other options to control the way Word checks spelling. Some of the options include the following:

- Choosing whether Word always makes suggestions when it encounters an unknown word
- Choosing whether Word ignores words in uppercase letters
- Choosing whether Word ignores words that include numbers

Objective 2: Use the Thesaurus

While you are creating or editing a document, you can use the Thesaurus to find synonyms, antonyms, and related words for words you use in your document.

Activating the Thesaurus

To use the Thesaurus in POLICY2.DOC to find synonyms, antonyms, and related words, follow these steps:

1 Place the insertion before the word *arise*.

2 From the **T**ools menu, choose the **T**hesaurus command.

Word selects the word, and the Thesaurus dialog box appears (see figure 3.7).

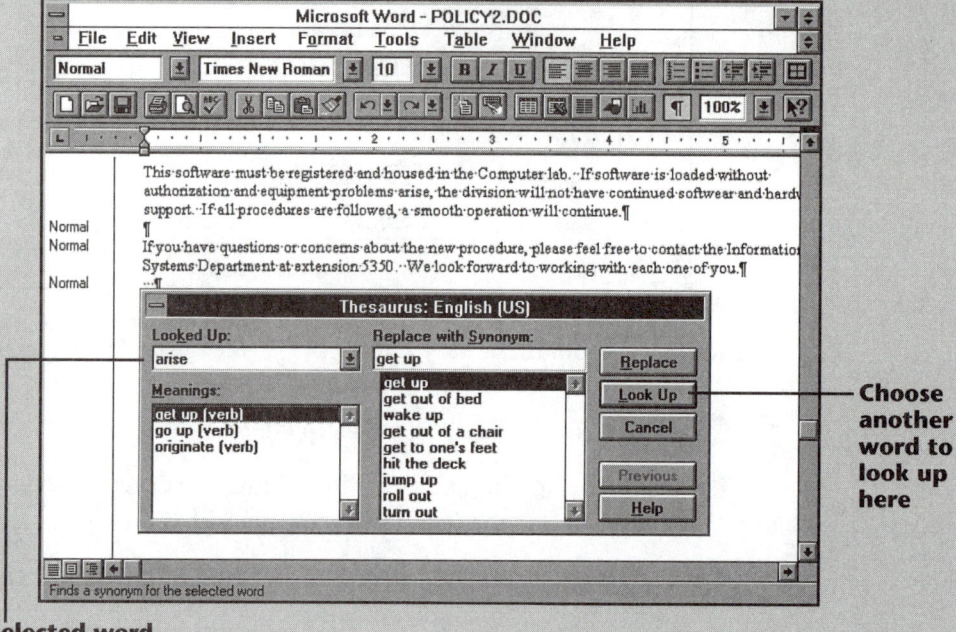

Figure 3.7
Word displays the selected word, a list of synonyms, and a list of meanings.

The word *arise* is displayed in the Looked Up text box.

Meanings of the word appear in the Meanings list box, and synonyms appear in the Replace with **S**ynonym list box.

3 Select `originate (verb)` in the Meanings list box. A new list of synonyms appear in the Replace with **S**ynonym list box.

4 Select `occur` in the Replace with **S**ynonym list box.

When you click a different word in the **M**eanings list box, synonyms for that word appear in the Replace with **S**ynonym list box.

5 Click **R**eplace. The word *arise* is replaced with *occur*.

6 Choose Cancel to return to your document.

7 Save the file to your data disk as **POLICY2.DOC**.

In the Thesaurus dialog box, you can do any of the following:

- Replace a selected word in your document by choosing a word in the Replace with **S**ynonym list box and clicking the **R**eplace button.

Synonym
A word that has the same (or nearly the same) meaning as another word. The Thesaurus suggests synonyms.

- Search for more possible *synonyms* by clicking a word in the Replace with **S**ynonym list box and then clicking the **L**ook Up button. Word moves the word you chose into the Loo**k**ed Up text box and displays the meanings and synonyms for the new word.

- Search for even more possible synonyms by clicking a word in the **M**eanings list box. Word displays a new list of synonyms in the Replace with **S**ynonym list box. If you click a word in the Replace with **S**ynonym list box and then click the **L**ook Up button, Word moves the word you chose into the Loo**k**ed Up box and displays the meanings and synonyms for the new word.

Note: *Double-clicking the word produces the same result as clicking the word and then clicking the **L**ook Up button.*

Antonym
A word that means the opposite (or nearly the opposite) of another word. The Thesaurus suggests antonyms for some words.

The topics *Antonyms* or Related Words may appear in the **M**eanings list box. If you choose either of these, the Replace with **S**ynonym list box changes to a Replace with **A**ntonym list box or a Replace with **R**elated Word list box. The Replace with **A**ntonym list box displays a list of words that mean the opposite of the original word. The Replace with **R**elated Word list box displays a list of words related to the original word. To return to the Replace with **S**ynonym list box, click any other word in the **M**eanings list box.

You can type a word in the **R**eplace With text box. When you choose the **L**ook Up button, Word looks up the word you typed. When you choose the **R**eplace button, Word replaces the selected word in the document with the word you typed.

To cancel the operation and return to the document, click the Cancel button or press `Esc`.

Note: *If Word cannot find a synonym for the word you selected, it displays words with similar spellings in the **M**eanings box.*

Objective 3: Check Your Grammar

Readability statistics
A dialog box displaying the word, character, paragraphs, and sentence counts; calculating average sentences per paragraph, average words per sentence, and average characters per word; and reporting the reading level of the document.

Word's Grammar Checker helps you identify sentences that have questionable style or grammatical structure. It also suggests corrections for many grammatical errors. By default, the Grammar Checker uses grammar and style rules for business writing, checks spelling, and displays *readability statistics* after checking the grammar. To change these and other options for the Grammar Checker, click the **O**ptions button in the Grammar Checker dialog box or the **O**ptions command on the **T**ools menu. See Chapter 9 for more information on changing options.

The Grammar Checker can check the grammar in all or part of a document. To check only part of a document, select the text you want to check before you start the Grammar Checker.

To begin checking the grammar in a document, choose **T**ools, **G**rammar. Word immediately begins checking the document. When Word finds a sentence with questionable grammar, it highlights the questionable sentence and displays the Grammar dialog box.

In the Grammar dialog box, you can do any of the following:

- To make a suggested change, choose a suggestion from the **Su**ggestions list box and then click the **C**hange button.

  Note: *You also can choose a suggestion by double-clicking it.*

- To make a correction by editing the document yourself, click somewhere in the document window (or press Ctrl+Tab) and then edit the sentence. The **I**gnore button becomes the **S**tart button. When you are ready to resume checking the grammar, click this button.

- To ignore Word's suggestion, click the **I**gnore button to skip over the questionable item. If the Grammar Checker finds other problems within the same sentence, Word highlights it in the **S**entence box.

- To ignore all Word's suggestions relating to the current sentence, click the **N**ext Sentence button.

- To ignore the current problem and all subsequent occurrences of the same problem in the document, click the Ignore **R**ule button.

- To see an explanation of the error Word has detected, click the **E**xplain button.

You can stop checking the grammar at any time by clicking the Cancel button or pressing Esc.

If Word is checking spelling and grammar and finds a misspelled word, it displays the Spelling dialog box. Make any spelling corrections as you normally would.

When you start checking grammar at a location other than the beginning of your document and you reach the end of the document, you have the option of continuing the grammar check from the beginning.

Using the Grammar Checker

To check the POLICY2.DOC grammar using the Grammar Checker, follow these steps:

1 Position the insertion point at the beginning of the document.

Note: *To check the grammar for a block of text, select the block of text first.*

2 From the **T**ools menu, choose **G**rammar.

Word begins to examine the spelling and grammar in your document and highlights the first sentence with questionable grammatical structure or style. The Grammar dialog box appears (see figure 3.8).

The Sentence text box contains the questionable sentence, in this case the questionable sentence is *Each employee has a computer, which could be used as stand alone or with the Novell Network at their desk.* The Suggestions list box displays suggestions for improving the questionable sentence, in this case Word suggests that the verb group may be in the passive voice.

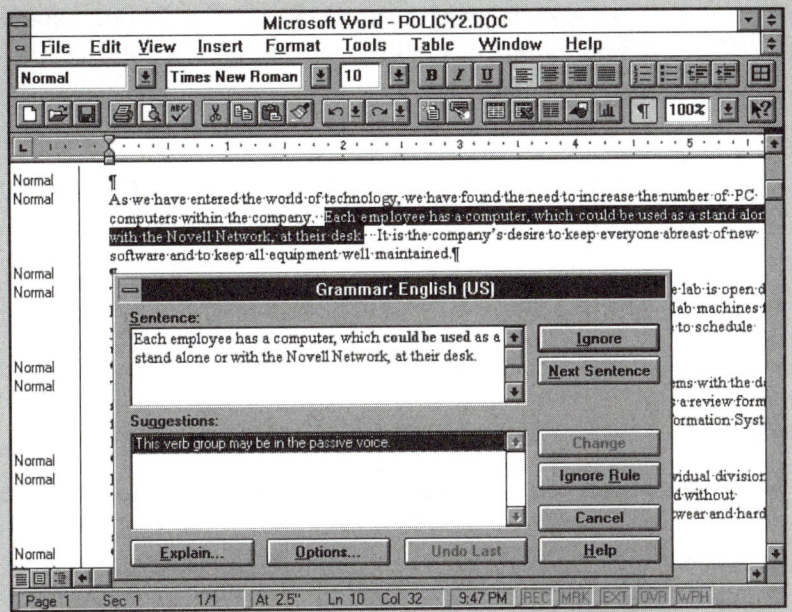

Figure 3.8
When Word finds a sentence with questionable grammatical structure or style, it highlights the sentence and displays the Grammar dialog box.

❸ Choose **I**gnore to ignore Word's suggestion and continue checking the document.

❹ When Grammar Checker is finished checking the document, it displays the Readability Statistics dialog box (see figure 3.9). Choose OK to clear the dialog box from your screen and return to your document.

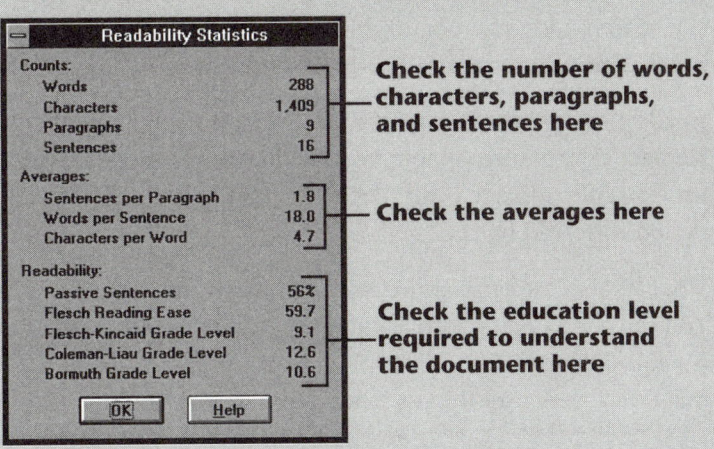

Figure 3.9
If you did not change the defaults in the Options Grammar dialog box, the Readability Statistics dialog box appears when you finish checking the grammar.

❺ Save the file to your data disk as **POLICY2.DOC**.

In the Readability Statistics dialog box, the Counts figures are the number of words, characters, paragraphs and sentences in the document. The Averages figures are the average number of sentences per paragraph, words per sentence, and characters per word. The entries under Readability can be explained as follows:

- *Flesch Reading Ease* is based on the average number of words per sentence and the average number of syllables per 100 words. The higher the number, the easier the document is to read.

- *Flesch-Kincaid Grade Level* represents the school grade level required for a as stand alone or with the Novell Network at their desk. The Suggestions list box displays suggestions for improving the questionable sentence, in this case Word suggests that the verb group may be in the passive voice.

- *Coleman-Liau Grade Level* represents another estimate of grade-level requirements.

- *Bormuth Grade Level* represents yet another estimate of grade-level requirements.

Objective 4: Find and Replace Text

Find
A Word feature that locates a specific word or phrase within a document.

Most people tend to make the same kinds of mistakes over and over when they create documents. If you know that you often spell a word incorrectly, you can use Word's Spelling Checker to find and correct that word. But what if the incorrect spelling is the correct spelling for a different word—if you have a tendency to use the word *principle* when you mean to use *principal*, for example. In this case, the Spelling Checker doesn't help you solve these problems. However, Word's **F**ind command can be very useful.

The **F**ind command can also be a great help if you are editing another person's document and that person has consistently used an incorrect spelling. If the author uses *thier* instead of *their*, you can use the **F**ind command to quickly and easily locate each occurrence of *thier*. Word provides a **R**eplace command that can search an entire document and automatically replace every occurrence of a misspelled word, such as *thier*, with the correctly spelled word, *their*.

In addition to Word's capability of searching for specific words, the **F**ind and **R**eplace commands enable you to change repeated character strings. You can, for example, replace every occurrence of a period followed by two spaces with a period followed by one space.

You can also use **F**ind and **R**eplace to locate and change nonprinting characters. You can modify character formatting, for example, by searching for and changing the formatting codes indicating italics or boldface. The **F**ind and **R**eplace commands are very useful tools when you want to check and improve a document.

Searching a Document for Text

Many times the same phrase is used throughout a document. Word can search the document for a specific word, phrase, or format. To search through POLICY2.DOC to find specific text, follow these steps:

1 From the **E**dit menu, choose the **F**ind command to display the Find dialog box (see figure 3.10).

❷ In the Find What text box, type the word **computer**. As soon as you start typing, the previously disabled Find Next button becomes enabled.

❸ From the Search drop-down list, choose All to have Word search the entire document.

❹ Choose Find Next. Word begins the search and highlights the first occurrence of computer.

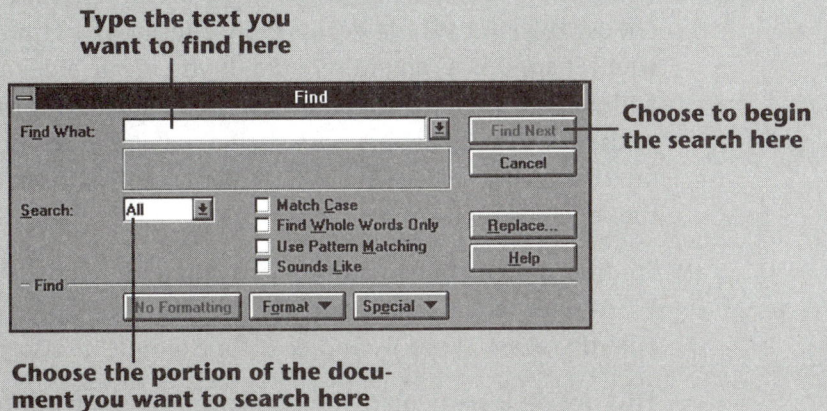

Figure 3.10
Use the Find dialog box to specify information that you want Word to find.

❺ To find the next occurrence of computer, choose the Find Next button again.

Whether the search is successful or not, the Find dialog box remains on-screen.

❻ When the search is complete, Word displays a message box (see figure 3.11) indicating that the search is finished. Choose OK to return to the Find dialog box.

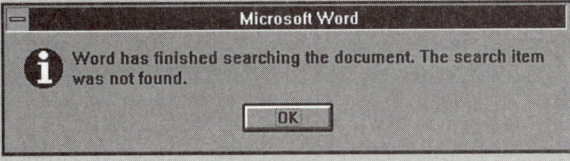

Figure 3.11
Word displays this message box after completing the search.

❼ Press ⏎Enter or choose Cancel to return to the document.

Narrowing the Search

You can take several actions to narrow Word's search of a document. Narrowing the search helps Word to quickly find exactly the information you want.

- Searching Part of a Document. By default, Word searches an entire document. If you want to search only a specific part of a document, select that part before opening the Find dialog box.

- Controlling the Search Direction. From the Search drop-down list, you can control the direction of a search. By default, Word searches from the insertion point toward the end of the document (the Down option). If you want to search from the insertion point toward the beginning of the document, choose the **U**p option.

- Matching Case. By default, Word does not distinguish between uppercase and lowercase letters when searching a document. If you want to find text that appears in the exact combination of uppercase and lowercase letters, choose the Match **C**ase check box. Word finds only those words in which the case of each character matches the case entered in the Fi**n**d What text box.

- Find Whole Words Only. To make a search even more efficient, you can choose the Find **W**hole Words Only check box to find the information only when it appears as an entire word. If you create a document about animals and you tell Word to search for *cat,* for example, Word finds every occurrence of the consecutive letters *c-a-t,* such as *catalog, category, allocate, catch,* and so on. If you choose the Find **W**hole Words Only Check box, Word finds only the specified text.

- Finding Words That Sound Alike. If you choose the Sounds **L**ike check box, Word finds words that sound like the word you entered in the Fi**n**d What text box. If you ask Word to find *here,* for example, it also finds *hear.*

    This option is particularly helpful if you have a habit of typing *no* when you mean *know,* and vice versa. After finishing your document, you can use either *no* or *know* as your search string, and then choose the Sound **L**ike option. Word finds every occurrence of both words, enabling you to double-check your usage.

Wild-card character
Characters that you can use to represent one or more other characters.

- Using Pattern Matching. You can use the Use Pattern **M**atching option to specify a word or phrase using *wild-card characters* ?, which represents any one character or no characters, and *, which represents any sequence of characters. This option is particularly useful when you don't know the exact spelling of the word you want to find.

Using Wild Card Characters in Word Searches

To use wild card-character in word searches in POLICY2.DOC, follow these steps:

1 From the **E**dit menu, choose the **F**ind command to display the Find dialog box.

2 In the **F**ind What text box, type the word **reg***. As soon as you start typing, the previously disabled **F**ind Next button becomes enabled (see figure 3.12).

Figure 3.12
Use the Find dialog box to search for specific text.

❸ Open the **S**earch drop-down list box, and choose All to search the entire document.

❹ Choose the Use Pattern **M**atching check box.

❺ Click **F**ind Next.

Word finds words that begin with the letters *reg.*

Whether the search is successful or not, the Find dialog box remains on-screen.

❻ When the search is complete, Word displays the message box indicating that the search is finished. Choose OK to return to the Find dialog box.

❼ Press Esc or choose Cancel to return to the document.

Up to this point, you have searched for characters that correspond to keyboard keys that can be seen on-screen. Word also enables you to find nonprinting characters and other special characters such as paragraph marks, tabs, and line breaks.

Note: *In Chapter 2, you displayed nonprinting characters. To locate a paragraph ending or a tab, Word can search the document for these nonprinting characters. See Chapter 5 for information on including special characters in your documents.*

Finding Special Characters

To find special characters in POLICY2.DOC, follow these steps:

❶ From the **E**dit menu, choose the **F**ind command to display the Find dialog box. Be sure to deselect Use Pattern **M**atching and choose Match **C**ase.

❷ Choose the Sp**e**cial button at the bottom of the Find dialog box. Word displays a list of special characters (see figure 3.13).

Figure 3.13
When you choose the Sp**e**cial button, Word displays a list of non-printing and other special characters.

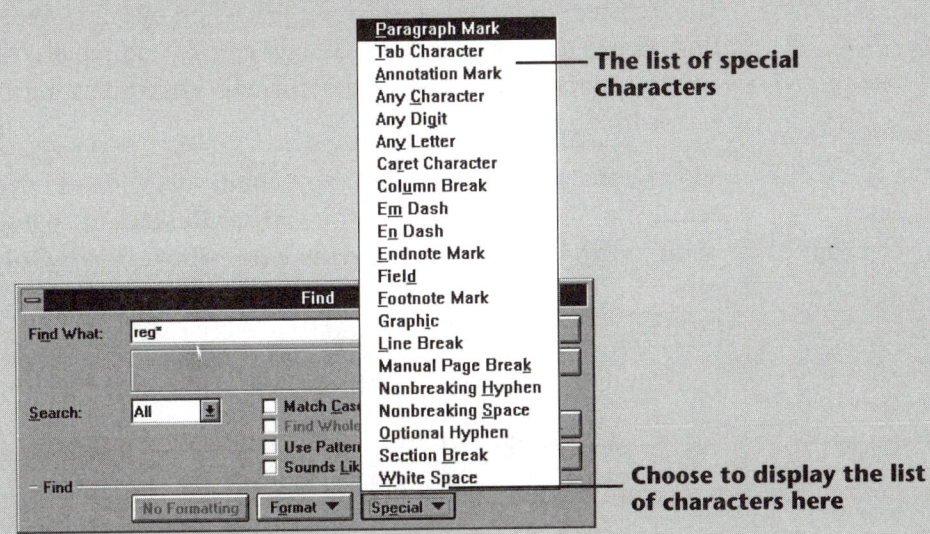

(continues)

Finding Special Characters (continued)

3 Choose **P**aragraph Mark as the special character to find (see figure 3.14).

Figure 3.14
The symbol for the paragraph mark appears after you choose Paragraph Mark as the special character to find.

4 Choose **F**ind Next. Word highlights the first occurrence of a paragraph mark in your document.

If Word cannot find such an occurrence, a message is displayed telling you that the search item was not found.

Note: *If nonprinting characters are hidden, Word highlights the blank positions where the marks occur in the document.*

> **Tip**
>
> If you know that ^p represents a paragraph mark, you can type it directly in the **Fin**d What text box rather than choosing it from the special character list.

Replacing Text, Special Characters, or Formatting

When you use the **F**ind command, Word highlights the first occurrence of the word or string of characters that you specify. You then do what needs to be done with the highlighted text.

The **R**eplace command works as an extension of **F**ind. With **R**eplace you can find occurrences of specified character groups and replace each occurrence with another character group or find occurrences of formatting characters and replace each with another character.

Suppose that you create a document about cats and later decide that the material actually applies more to dogs; you can use **R**eplace to change every occurrence of *cat* to *dog*. Unless you choose the Find **W**hole Words Only option described earlier in this chapter, however, you may not be pleased to find that every *catastrophe* becomes a *dogastrophe,* and that every *catalog* becomes a *dogalog*.

You can replace information throughout a document in two ways:

- Click the **R**eplace button in the Find dialog box.

- From the **E**dit menu, choose **R**eplace.

Either way, when you choose **R**eplace, Word displays the Replace dialog box.

Replacing Text

To find and replace text in POLICY2.DOC, follow these steps:

1 Move the insertion point to the top of the document.

2 From the Edit menu, choose Replace. The Replace dialog box appears (see figure 3.15).

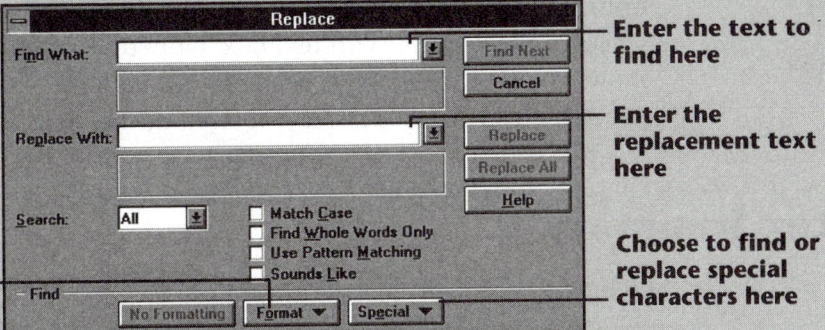

Figure 3.15
Use the Replace dialog box to find and replace specified text.

3 Type **lab**, in the Find What text box.

4 Type **room**, as the replacement text, in the Replace With text box.

5 Choose Replace All to have Word automatically replace all occurrences of *lab* with *room* (see figure 3.16).

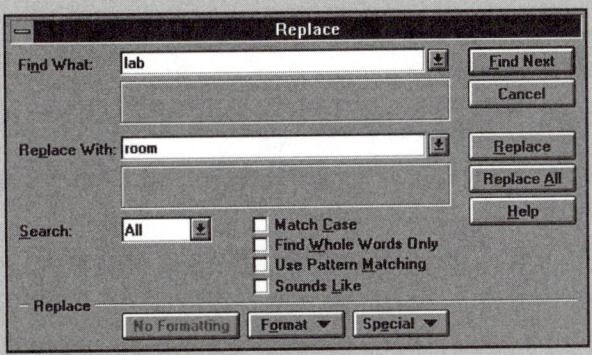

Figure 3.16
Use the Replace dialog box to specify that each occurrence of lab be replaced with room.

Note: *If you use Replace All and find that you have replaced more than you expected, you can choose Undo from the Edit menu to undo all the replacements.*

6 Save the file to your data disk, and then close it.

Two more points should be mentioned about how the Replace command works:

- *Matching the case of the replacement string.* If you do not choose the Match Case check box in the Replace dialog box, Word attempts to set the case of characters in the replacement word to match the original word. If the word to be replaced appears at the beginning of a sentence with an initial capital letter, for example, the replacement word is inserted with an initial capital as well. But if you *have* checked Match Case, Word finds and replaces only the words

Caution
Although Replace All can be very convenient, use it with care. If you forget to select the Find Whole Words Only check box, you accidentally may replace parts of words, which will result in words that do not make sense.

94   Checking Your Work

in your document that match the case of each character in the search string. In addition, the replacement word appears in your document exactly as it was entered in the Replace With text box, without regard for the case of characters in the word that was replaced.

- *Using spaces or no space as the replacement string.* If you want to replace a word with nothing (not even a space) leave the Replace With text box empty, and make sure that no replacement format is specified. If you want to replace a word with one or more space characters, simply enter the desired number of spaces in the Replace With text box. Only the position of the insertion point shows you that spaces have been entered because spaces don't appear on-screen (even if Word is displaying nonprinting characters).

Chapter Summary

In this chapter, you have learned how to use Word's Spelling Checker, the Thesaurus, and Grammar Checker to proof your documents. You have also learned how to find and replace specific text, characters, or formatting characters in a document.

In Chapter 4, you learn how to manage your files. Managing your files enables you to perform commands such as copying within Word. You are responsible for your documents, not only in creation and printing, but also in being able to open and making changes efficiently.

Checking Your Skills

True/False Questions

For each of the following statements, circle *T* or *F* to indicate whether the statement is true or false.

T F **1.** The **F**ind and **R**eplace commands enable you to locate and change nonprinting characters.

T F **2.** By default, Word distinguishes between uppercase and lowercase letters when searching a document.

T F **3.** The Spelling Checker checks individual words without regard to context.

T F **4.** The main dictionary contains all the words that are in Webster's Dictionary.

T F **5.** The Grammar Checker identifies sentences that have questionable style or grammatical structure.

T F **6.** Word always checks the spelling in your document against the main dictionary.

T F **7.** If Word displays a misspelled word with suggested changes, click the **I**gnore All button.

T F **8.** You can click the Cancel button or press Esc at any time to stop the Spelling Checker.

T F **9.** To undo up to ten of your last spelling changes, click the **U**ndo Last button.

T F **10.** You name your custom dictionary in the Create Custom Dictionary dialog box.

Multiple-Choice Questions

In the blank provided, write the letter of the correct answer for each of the following questions.

____ **1.** A specific format that Word can search for is ____.

    a. character

    b. pitch

    c. font

    d. code

    e. template

____ **2.** The wild-card characters used to search for a pattern match are ____.

    a. + and -

    b. * and ,

    c. * and ?

    d. / and *

    e. ? and .

____ **3.** If you select the Sounds **L**ike option, Word finds ____.

    a. *new* and *knew*

    b. *made* and *maid*

    c. *can* and *could*

    d. *sew* and *so*

    e. a, b, and d

____ **4.** When using the Spelling Checker, to replace the highlighted word with the word that appears in the Change **T**o text box, ____.

    a. choose the **C**hange button

    b. choose the Suggest button

    c. click anywhere in the document window

    d. choose **C**hange All

    e. choose the **U**ndo button

5. To replace a word with a word similar in meaning, click a word in the Replace With _____ list box.

    a. Meanings

    b. Synonyms

    c. Related Words

    d. Antonyms

    e. Cancel

6. A Word feature that locates a specific word or phrase within a document is _____.

    a. Search

    b. Locate

    c. Find

    d. Replace

    e. Look

7. If Word highlights a word that is spelled correctly, you click _____.

    a. Change To

    b. Change All

    c. Ignore

    d. Skip

    e. Continue

8. When the word *cta* is changed to *cat* and then *teh* is changed to *the*, the Undo last change displays _____.

    a. cta

    b. cat

    c. teh

    d. the

    e. no word

9. To create a custom dictionary, you use the _____.

    a. Options on the Tools menu

    b. the Spelling Options dialog box

    c. the Grammar Options dialog box

    d. the Tools menu

    e. the Customize feature

___ **10.** While creating or editing a document, you can use the Thesaurus to find ____.

   a. synonyms

   b. antonymns

   c. related words

   d. homonyms

   e. a, b, and c

Fill-in-the-Blank Questions

In the blank provided, write the correct answer for each of the following questions.

1. By default, Word searches an entire document or the part of the document _____ or _____ the insertion point.

2. The wild-card character _____ represents any one character or no characters, and _____ represents any sequence of characters and searches for _____ strings.

3. If you ask Word to find *there*, it also finds *their* using the _____ option.

4. Word always checks the spellings in your document against the spelling of words in its _____ dictionary.

5. You can use the Thesaurus to find _____, _____, and _____ words while you are creating or editing a document.

6. You can use the _____ to check a single selected word, a selected block of text, or an entire document.

7. You can click _____ or press [Esc] at any time to stop the Spelling Checker.

8. Adding words that are specific to your business to the dictionary _____ time in the spell-checking process.

9. The Replace With _____ list box displays a list of words that mean the opposite of the original word.

10. When you choose the **L**ook Up button, Word looks up the word you typed in the _____ text box.

Applying Your Skills

Review Exercises

Exercise 1: Using Find and Spelling Checker

To practice using Find and Spelling Checker, follow these steps:

1. Open FIRST.DOC.

2. Find all occurrences of *meeting*.

3. Check the spelling of the document.

Exercise 2: Using Find, Replace, and Spelling Checker
To use Find, Replace, and Spelling Checker, follow these steps:

1. Open MEDICAL.DOC.

2. Replace all occurrences of *We* with *They*.

3. Check the spelling of the document.

4. Save the file to your data disk as **MEDII.DOC**.

Exercise 3: Using the Grammar Checker and the Thesaurus
To practice using the Grammar Checker and the Thesaurus, follow these steps:

1. Open MEDICAL.DOC.

2. Run the Grammar Checker, and make any necessary corrections.

3. Use the Thesaurus to find synonyms for *facility* and *extended*.

4. Save the file to your data disk as **MEDICAL.DOC**.

Exercise 4: Using the Spelling Checker and Grammar Checker
To use the Spelling Checker and the Grammar Checker, follow these steps:

1. Open STEPS.DOC.

2. Add the steps to using the Spelling Checker and Grammar Checker to the document.

3. Check the spelling of the document.

4. Save the file to your data disk as **BUTTON.DOC**.

Exercise 5: Using Find, Replace, and Spelling Checker
To use Find, Replace, and Spelling Checker, follow these steps:

1. Open GUIDELINE.DOC.

2. Replace every occurrence of *evaluation* with *rating*.

3. Check the spelling of the document.

4. Save the file to your data disk as **GUIDELINE.DOC**.

Continuing Projects

Project 1: Practice in Using Word
Practice using Word by following these steps:

1. Open SCHEDULE.DOC.

2. Use the Grammar Checker to check the document.

3. Use the Thesaurus to find synonyms for *committee*.

4. Use **Fi**n**d** and **R**eplace to find the word *met* and to replace it with *convene*.

5. Save the file to your data disk as **SCHEDULE.DOC**.

Project 2: Federal Department Store

Continue developing the Federal Department Store brochure by following these steps:

1. Open CATALOG.DOC.

2. Use the Thesaurus to find synonyms for *active*, *comfort*, and *easy*.

3. Create a custom dictionary called *STOCK*, and add the following words:

    lightwear

    drawcord

4. Check the spelling of the document.

5. Save the file to your data disk as **CATALOG.DOC**.

Project 3: Real Entertainment Corporation

Continue working with the Real Entertainment Corporation newsletter by following these steps:

1. Open REC.DOC.

2. Use the Grammar Checker to check the document.

3. Create a custom dictionary called REC.

4. Use the Thesaurus to find synonyms for *involved*.

5. Use **F**ind and **R**eplace to find the word *contract* and replace with *agreement*.

6. Save the file to your data disk as **REC.DOC**.

CHAPTER 4
Managing and Printing Files

As you work in Word, you will create numerous documents—many with information you will want to reuse. As the number of documents grows, you will find it more difficult to identify specific documents or to remember their contents. You may have difficulty finding the document that contains the information you need.

Word provides some features that will help you manage documents. In this chapter, you learn how to use the features to open, delete, copy, and print one or more documents. You learn how to specify various printing options to print a selection, the current page, specific pages, or an entire document.

You also learn how to incorporate information from other documents and other applications into a Word document. All the features help you to perform your job more efficiently.

Objectives

By the time you finish this chapter, you will have learned to

1. Use Summary Information
2. Find Files
3. Compare Versions of the Same Document
4. Insert Files from Word and Other Programs
5. Print a Document

Objective 1: Use Summary Information

Summary information
Information you supply about a document. Word can use this information in its searches for documents.

In Word, you can save *summary information* with a file. The information you can provide consists of the following:

- A document title
- A subject description
- The author's name

Keywords
Important words that occur in a document. Word can search for all documents that have the keywords you specify.

- A list of *keywords*
- Comments

Each of these categories of summary information can contain up to 255 characters. Word does not insist that you provide this information. If you do, however, you will be able to find specific documents much more easily than if you just rely on file names.

In addition to the summary information you supply, Word maintains certain statistics about each document. You can use some of these statistics to help find documents.

Creating Summary Information

You create summary information by filling in blanks in the Summary Info dialog box. There are two ways to display this dialog box:

- From the **F**ile menu, choose Summary **I**nfo.
- Check the Prompt for Summary Info box in **T**ools, **O**ption, Save to cause Word to open the Summary Info dialog box the first time you save a file.

When you first display the Summary Info dialog box, all the text boxes (except the **A**uthor text box) are blank. The **A**uthor text box contains the name entered during installation of the program. It can be changed to the current user's name by typing the new name in the **A**uthor text box (see figure 4.1).

Figure 4.1
Word automatically places the user's name in the **A**uthor text box.

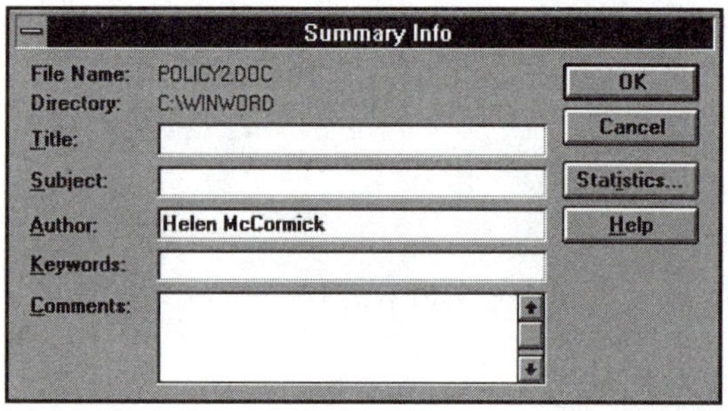

If you have saved the file previously, the file name and the directory in which it is saved are shown at the top of the dialog box.

Initially, the **T**itle text box contains a flashing insertion point. To place information into the text boxes, type the appropriate data in each text box, pressing Tab to move from box to box. Take care to be consistent. Remember that you will subsequently use the information in these boxes to help find files.

The title you use depends, of course, on the type of documents you write. If you primarily write letters to customers or clients, you can use the **T**itle text box of the Summary Info dialog box for customer and client names. Then you can use the **S**ubject text box for words that represent categories of letters, including phrases that start with such words as Proposal, Invoice, Response, Question, and so on. In the **K**eywords text box, you can list project names, people's names, or sites—whatever terms help you identify a document. You can use the **C**omments text box to summarize the entire document.

If you are using Word to prepare technical documents, on the other hand, you can use the **T**itle text box for the main title of a document and the **S**ubject text box for chapter or section numbers and titles. In the **K**eywords text box, you can list words that identify important topics covered in the document, and you can use the **C**omments text box to summarize each document.

If you use Word for several purposes, it's a good idea to have a separate subdirectory for each type of document—one subdirectory for correspondence, another for reports, and so on.

After you complete the text boxes, choose OK to close the dialog box. Word saves the summary information you provide when you save the document.

Entering Summary Information

To enter summary information for POLICY2.DOC, follow these steps:

1 Open the POLICY2.DOC.

2 From the **F**ile menu, choose Summary **I**nfo.

3 Type **Policy Information Sheet**, in the Title Box.

Press Tab to move to the next box.

4 Type **computers, software, departments** in the Subject text box. You could enter any other topics included in the document.

5 Type **Helen Ryan, Joe Camera** in the Keywords text box.

You could also enter any keywords that relate to this document.

6 Type your own name in the **A**uthor text box.

7 Choose OK to close the dialog box.

Viewing Document Statistics

To view document statistics, open the Summary Info dialog box and click the Stat**i**stics button (see figure 4.2).

Figure 4.2
Use the Document Statistics dialog box to learn more about your document.

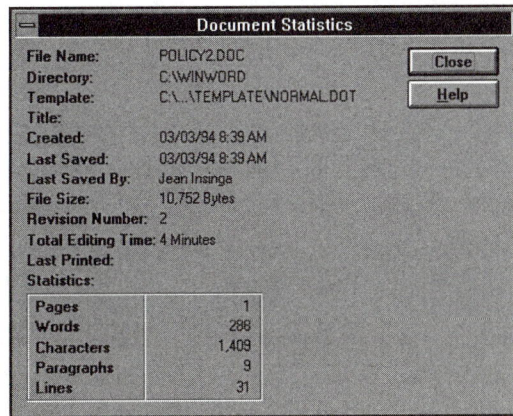

104 Managing and Printing Files

The Document Statistics dialog box contains useful information about a document. You cannot edit these statistics. As you will see later in this chapter, however, these statistics can be printed. Click Close to return to the Summary Info dialog box.

Objective 2: Find Files

Word provides two methods you can use to find a file, both of which you access by way of the Find File command in the File menu. One method is based on file names; the other uses summary information.

Finding Files with Find File

Path
The DOS term that represents the location of a file. The path generally consists of a drive name (such as A, B, or C) and directory name(s) separated by backslashes (\).

From the Find File dialog box, you can view information about documents without opening them. You can search for documents, and view and edit summary information. You also can open, print, delete, copy, and preview documents.

Note: *Using the Find File dialog box requires some knowledge of DOS file names, DOS wild-card characters, DOS directories and subdirectories, and an understanding of paths. If you are not familiar with these subjects, you should review an introductory DOS book such as Que's* MS-DOS 6 QuickStart.

Searching for a File

To search for the file POLICY2.DOC, follow these steps:

❶ From the File menu, choose Find File. Word displays the Search dialog box (see figure 4.3).

Figure 4.3
Use the Search dialog box to find a file.

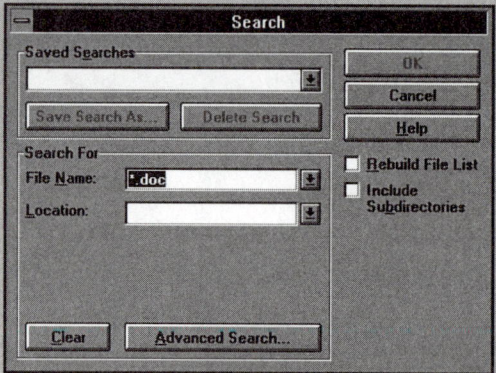

❷ Type **POLICY2.DOC**, replacing the text in the Search For File Name text box.

Note: *Rather than type out the entire file name, you can use the * wild-card character to represent omitted characters, as in POL*.DOC.*

❸ In the Location text box, type the path name of the directory you want to search. Use the location of your data disk.

If the path includes subdirectories, click the Include Subdirectories check box to place a × there. Word then searches the directory you have specified in the Location text box and its subdirectories.

④ Choose OK to start the search (see figure 4.4).

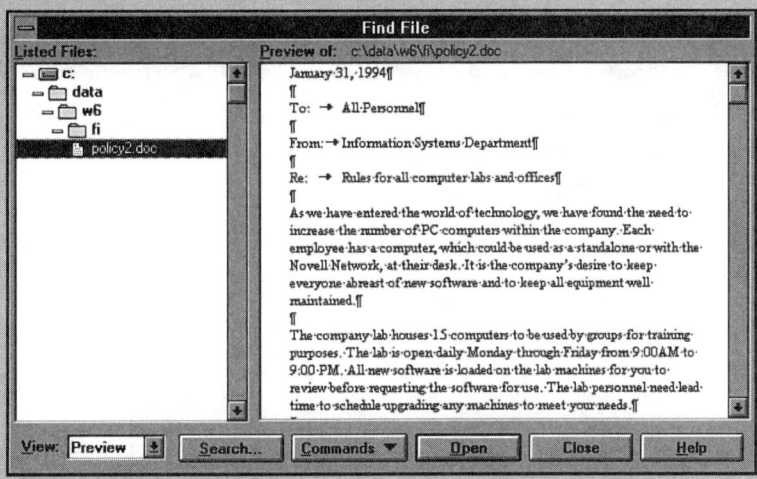

Figure 4.4
After completing a search, the Find File dialog box contains a list of files at the left side in alphabetical order by file name, and a preview of the beginning of the selected file at the right.

Note: *If you want to search for any file other than a Word file (or any other file having a DOC extension), open the File Name drop-down list box and select a file name extension. Alternatively, replace *.DOC in the File Name text box with another file name, using DOS wild-card characters if you want.*

To see a preview that shows the beginning of any file in the list, click the file name and the screen splits, displaying the file to right and the name of the file to the left.

When you use Find File, you can open the file for editing by clicking the **O**pen button at the bottom of the Find File dialog box. You also can access several additional functions by clicking the **C**ommands button at the bottom of the dialog box. When you click the **C**ommands button, you see a menu from which you can choose the following options:

- Open **R**ead Only. The document opens so that you can read the whole file, but you cannot edit it or add to it.

- **P**rint. The Print dialog box opens so that you can print the document. See information about printing later in this chapter.

- **S**ummary. The Summary Info dialog box opens for you to read or change.

- **D**elete. The document is deleted.

- **C**opy. You can make a copy of the document, giving it a different file name.

- Sor**t**ing. You can change the order in which Find File lists files. Instead of sorting in alphabetical order by file name, you can sort documents by author name, creation date, name of user who last saved each document, date each document was last saved, or document size. You also can list documents by file name or by the names you placed in the Title text box for each document's summary information.

After you finish working in the Find File dialog box, click the Close button to close it. Alternatively, you can click the **S**earch button to return to the Search dialog box.

Using Summary Info to Search for Files

Earlier in this chapter, you learned that Word can help you locate files by using the information you place in the various Summary Info text boxes. To do so, follow these steps:

1. From the **F**ile menu, choose **F**ind File to display the Search dialog box.

2. Choose **S**earch, and then click the **A**dvanced Search button dialog box (see figure 4.5).

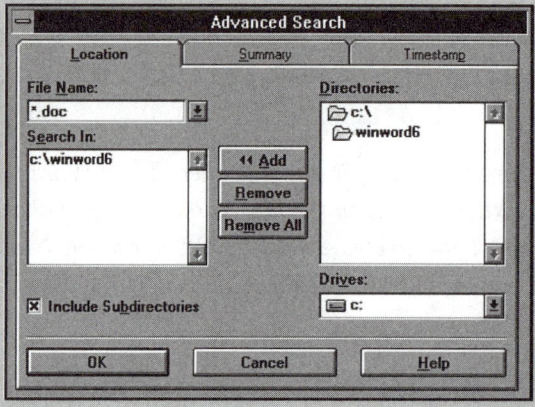

Figure 4.5
The Advanced Search dialog box has **L**ocation, **S**ummary, and Timestam**p** sections.

3. Choose **L**ocation.

4. From the Dri**v**e list box, select the drive containing your data disk.

5. Type ***.DOC**.

6. Choose OK.

The search dialog appears with the designated drive and directory listed. You can search for another file at this time or exit the Search dialog box.

It is important to understand that all the search criteria you specify are additive: Word finds only those documents that satisfy every item of the criteria you specify in the three sections of the Advanced Search dialog box. Word ignores any criteria that are empty. If you want to search for a document that you remember creating during the last three months of 1993, for example, you enter 10/1/93 into the Created **F**rom text box, 12/31/93 into Created **T**o text box, and your own name (exactly as it appears in the **A**uthor text box within the Summary Info dialog box). Subsequently, when you ask Word to search, it finds the documents you created within that range of dates.

Objective 3: Compare Versions of the Same Document

Sometimes in working with several versions of a document, you may find that you have two versions of a file, and you're not sure which one to keep. Word's capability to compare documents can be very useful at times like this.

Comparing Documents

To compare two versions of a document, follow these steps:

1. Open POLICY2.DOC.

2. From the **T**ools menu, choose Re**v**isions to show the Revisions dialog box (see figure 4.6).

Figure 4.6
Use the Revisions dialog box to compare document versions.

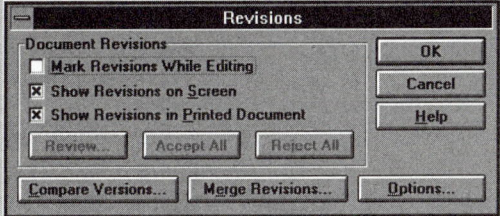

3. Click the **C**ompare Versions button to display the Compare Versions dialog box.

4. In this dialog box, either type or select the name of the document, POLICY.DOC, you want compared to the open POLICY2.DOC, and then choose OK.

5. Close, but do not save the compared POLICY2.DOC.

The open (original) document appears with all differences between it and the comparison document marked in two ways. Vertical lines in the left margin draw attention to lines that are different in the comparison document. Also, the original document shows any changed or replacement characters in blue with deleted characters in strikethrough formatting, and replacement characters underlined (see figure 4.7).

Figure 4.7
A comparison between an original and a revised document shows deleted text struck through and new text underlined. Vertical bars at the left of the text draw attention to all lines that contain changes.

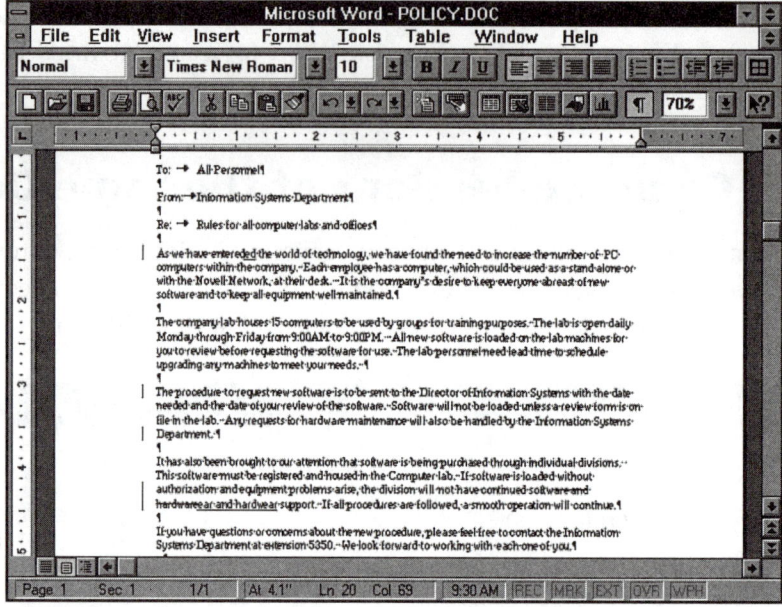

Objective 4: Insert Files from Word and Other Programs

Word offers three ways to insert information into a document. In earlier chapters, you learned to insert information by typing characters from the keyboard, including characters accessed by shortcut keys and characters available in the Symbol dialog box. In Chapter 2, you learned to paste information into Word from the Clipboard. Whatever you copy or cut from Word or another application into the Clipboard, you can paste into a document.

In this section, you learn to bring information into Word by inserting a file. Files created by Word and many other applications can be inserted into a document.

Inserting a File into a Document

To insert a file into POLICY2.DOC, follow these steps:

1. Open POLICY2.DOC.

2. Place the insertion point at the end of the document.

3. Open the **I**nsert menu (see figure 4.8).

Figure 4.8
The bottom part of the **Insert** menu lists the types of files you can insert.

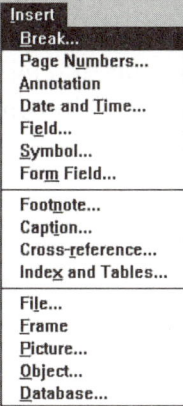

④ Click Fi**l**e to insert text in a format compatible with Word. Word displays a dialog box in which you can choose a file.

Note: *You can also click Frame, Picture, Object, or Database to insert other types of information. In all cases except Frame, Word responds with a dialog box that asks for details about what you want to insert.*

⑤ Select the file FIRST.DOC to insert.

⑥ Choose OK. The file you select is inserted into your document.

If you click **P**icture in step 3, you can insert graphics created in many types of graphics applications.

Objective 5: Print a Document

Word offers many printing options, including the following:

- The printer to use
- The document to print
- The number of pages of the document to print

If you have problems... If you have trouble printing, open and read the PRINTERS.DOC document that Microsoft ships with Word for Windows. This document contains information about printers, including common problems and their solutions.

Managing and Printing Files

Selecting a Printer

Chapters 5 and 6 of this book stress the importance of ensuring that a printer has been selected before you do any character or paragraph formatting. Word knows the capabilities of the selected printer and will offer you only formatting options that are compatible with that printer.

If you need to select or change the selection of your printer, the process is straightforward. Selecting a printer is really a matter of selecting a printer driver, a file on your hard disk. Word can use any printer driver that's installed in Windows. If you need to install a printer driver, however, you must exit Word and use the Windows Control Panel to install the driver.

Displaying the Selected Printer

To display the printer that Word is prepared to use, follow these steps:

1. From the File menu, choose Print to display the Print dialog box.

2. Locate the name of the printer that Word is currently prepared to use.

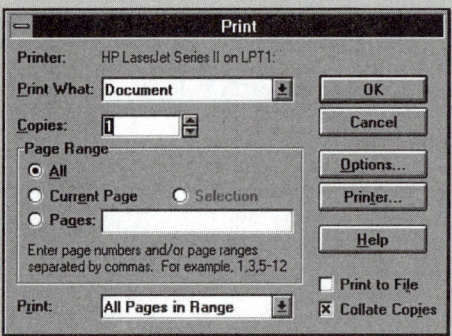

Figure 4.9
The top line of the Print dialog box shows which printer Word is prepared to use.

3. Choose OK.

The printer is usually selected before you use Word. You may have times when you need to change the selected printer—if a new printer is purchased or if your computer is connected to more than one printer, for example.

Changing a Printer Selection

To change a printer selection, follow these steps:

1. From the File menu, choose Print.

    or

    Press Ctrl + P.

② Click the Printer button in the Print dialog box to display the Print Setup dialog box (see figure 4.10).

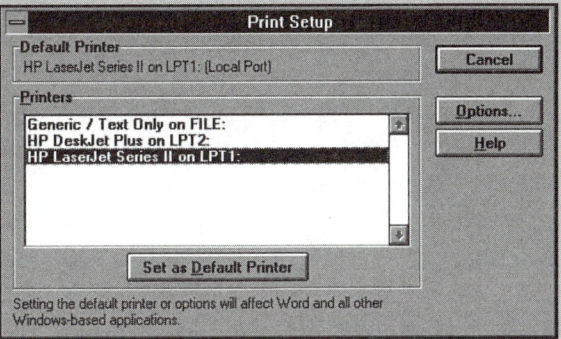

Figure 4.10
The Printers list box shows all printer drivers installed for use with Windows applications. The list you see on-screen will be different from the list shown here.

③ Click the name of any printer.

④ Click the Set as Default Printer button at the bottom of the dialog box. The Default Printer section at the top of the dialog box changes.

⑤ Click Cancel to return to the original setting.

⑥ Press Esc to leave the Print dialog box.

Printing an Entire Active Document

To print one copy of the entire active document, click the Print button (the fourth button from the left) in the Standard toolbar. If you need more control over printing, choose Print from the File menu, and then use the Print dialog box to change the settings.

Printing Selected Pages of the Active Document

From the active document, you can print one or more individual pages, as well as one or more groups of consecutive pages.

Choosing Options in the Print Dialog Box

You can choose from several options in the Print dialog box. To do so, follow these steps:

① Open POLICY2.DOC.

② From the File menu, choose Print to display the Print dialog box.

③ Make sure that the number in the Copies text box is 1.

The Page Range section of the dialog box has four option buttons:

- All. Print all pages of the document
- Current Page. Print only the page that contains the insertion point.

(continues)

Choosing Options in the Print Dialog Box (continued)

- **Pa**g**es.** Print specific pages, defined by page numbers—for example: 1-5.
- **Selectio**n**.** Print only what is selected in the document (available only if something is selected in the document).

④ Type **1** in the Page Range section.

⑤ Choose OK to start printing.

Note: *When you specify more than one copy to be printed, leave Collate Copies checked if you want Word to print one complete copy of the specified pages in page-number order, then the next complete copy, and so on. If this option is unchecked, Word prints the specified number of copies of the first page, then the copies of the second page, and so on. Having Word collate copies is convenient but slow; having Word print without collating is usually much faster but less convenient.*

Selecting Printing Options

Word offers many options that are not used often but are useful. To access these options, click the **O**ptions button in the Print dialog box to display the Print section of the Options dialog box (see figure 4.11).

Figure 4.11
Use the Print section of the Options dialog box to choose many printing options.

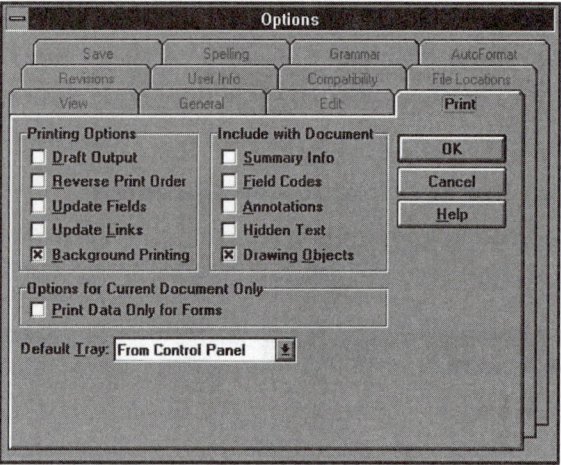

The following list describes the printing options.

- **D**raft Output. Word prints a draft-quality version of the document.
- **R**everse Print Order. Word prints pages starting from the last page of the document.
- **U**pdate Fields. Any fields—such as date and time fields—are updated to current values.

- **U**pdate **L**inks. Word updates any information in the document that is linked to another file.
- **B**ackground Printing. You can work in Word while a document is being printed.

In addition to choosing these printing options, you can choose whether to print the following:

- **S**ummary Info. Word prints summary information on a separate page at the beginning of each document.
- **F**ield Codes. Word prints field codes instead of field values. The field codes are used in merged letters discussed in Chapter 9.
- **A**nnotations. Word prints annotations with each document. Any annotations inserted for notes within a document can be printed as well.
- **Hi**dden Text. Word prints hidden text.
- Drawing **O**bjects. Word prints any objects drawn within Word.

You can click these options to place or remove the × in the corresponding check boxes; then choose OK to return to the Print dialog box.

Printing Special Information

In addition to printing document pages, Word can print certain special information. To access these options, open the **P**rint What drop-down list box in the Print dialog box (see figure 4.12).

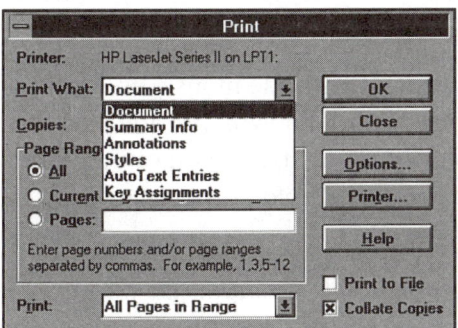

Figure 4.12
Use the Print What list box to print special information.

In this list box, you can choose to print your document, the document's summary information, annotations that have been made to the document, descriptions of styles used in the document, AutoText entries for the current template (as well as those assigned to all templates), or key assignments that apply to the current template. You click the appropriate item in the list and then choose OK to start printing.

Printing to a File

When you want to print a Word document on a printer connected to a computer other than the one you are using, you can print your document to a file on a disk. Then you can take or send that file to the other computer and print it there by using the DOS Print command, even if the other computer does not have Word installed.

To print to a file, click the Print to File button in the Print dialog box. Subsequently, when you choose OK, Word asks you to provide a name for the file.

Using the Find File Command to Print

You can print documents that are not open by using the Find File command in the File menu. You can print more than one document at a time or print the summary information for one or more documents that are not open. To do so, follow these steps:

1. From the File menu, choose Find File.

2. Select the document titled MEDICAL.DOC to print.

3. Click the Commands button, and choose Print.

   The Print dialog box appears.

4. If the settings are what you want, choose OK to print the document.

To print more than one document, you must select all the documents you want to print in the Find File dialog box before you choose the Print button.

To select more than one document with the mouse, hold down Ctrl and click the file names. If you make a mistake, hold down Ctrl and click the incorrect file name again. To select documents listed sequentially, you can click the first file name and then either drag the mouse pointer or hold down Shift and click the last file name to highlight the other file names.

Note: *The processes for selecting multiple documents are the same for copying, deleting, and opening documents as for printing them.*

Chapter Summary

In the work environment, one very important part of your job is to document your work. Using the Word summary information feature, you can specify aspects of the file, such as the author or what the document covers. This information is helpful to another person who has been asked to add information to the file. Being able to locate files quickly will make your job easier. The ability to find files, insert files, print files, print special information, and print an envelop are made easy using Word.

In the next chapter, you will learn how to enhance a document by changing fonts and working with character formats.

Checking Your Skills

True/False Questions

For each of the following statements, circle *T* or *F* to indicate whether the statement is true or false.

T F **1.** The summary information is saved as a separate file.

T F **2.** Word finds files based on file names and on summary information.

T F **3.** A comparison between an original and a revised document shows deleted text with underlines and new text with strikethrough.

T F **4.** Files created by Word and many other applications can be inserted into a document.

T F **5.** Selecting Pa**g**es from the Print dialog box prints all pages of the document.

T F **6.** When you first display the Summary Info dialog box, all the text boxes are blank.

T F **7.** From the Find File dialog box, you can view information about documents without opening them.

T F **8.** Rather than type out the entire file name, you can use the ? wild-card character to represent more than one omitted character, as in HEL?.DOC.

T F **9.** The Print dialog box opens so that you can print the document.

T F **10.** By selecting Copy from the Commands pop-up menu in the Find File dialog box, you can make a copy of the document, giving it a different name.

Multiple-Choice Questions

In the blank provided, write the letter of the correct answer for each of the following questions.

___ **1.** The summary information does not include ____.

    a. a document title

    b. a subject description

    c. date and time of document creation

    d. a list of keywords

    e. comments

___ 2. When you click the **C**ommands button on the Find File dialog box, you see a menu that enables you to _____.

   a. Open **W**rite only

   b. **P**rint

   c. **M**ove

   d. **D**elete

   e. b and d

___ 3. The document that shows any changed or replacement characters in blue with strikethrough on deleted characters and underlining on replacement characters is the _____ document.

   a. revised

   b. original

   c. backup

   d. new

   e. old

___ 4. To insert files from Word and other programs, _____.

   a. open the **I**nsert Menu and click **F**ile

   b. press [Insert] and type the name of the file

   c. open the **F**ile Menu and select the file

   d. Open the **W**indow Menu and select the file

   e. you need a utility program

___ 5. To print only what is selected in the document, click _____.

   a. All

   b. Cur**r**ent Page

   c. Pa**g**es

   d. Selectio**n**

   e. **F**ull Page

___ 6. The **S**ummary Info box containing the name entered during installation of the program is _____.

   a. the document title

   b. a subject description

   c. the **A**uthor

   d. keywords

   e. comments

____ **7.** The document statistics dialog box contains all but _____ count.

    a. word

    b. page

    c. line

    d. character

    e. spelling

____ **8.** Word provides two methods you can use to find a file, which are based on _____.

    a. file names and keywords

    b. keywords and file statistics

    c. file names and file statistics

    d. keywords and summary information

    e. file names and summary information

____ **9.** To set a document so that it opens and you can read but not edit or add to the whole file, choose the _____ option.

    a. **P**rint

    b. **S**ave **A**s

    c. **S**ummary

    d. **O**pen **R**ead Only

    e. **S**orting

____ **10.** The three sections in the Advanced Search dialog box are _____.

    a. **L**ocation, **S**ummary, **D**ate

    b. **L**ocation, **S**tatistics, **D**ate

    c. **D**irectory, **S**ummary, **T**imestamp

    d. **L**ocation, **S**ummary, **T**imestamp

    e. **D**rive, **D**irectory, **S**ummary

Fill-in-the-Blank Questions

In the blank provided, write the correct answer for each of the following questions.

1. In the _____ text box, you can list words that identify important topics covered in the document.

2. To view document statistics, open the _____ dialog box and click the Statistics button.

3. You can use the _____ dialog box to compare document versions.

4. From the _____ menu, click _____ to insert text in a format compatible to Word.

5. When you want to print a Word document on a printer connected to a computer other than the one you are using, you can print your document to a _____ on a disk.

6. Each of these categories of summary information can contain up to _____ characters.

7. Word automatically places the user's name in the _____ text box.

8. All the search criteria you specify are _____: Word finds only those documents that satisfy every item of the criteria you specify in the three sections of the Advanced Search dialog box.

9. When you use Find File, you can open the file for editing by clicking the _____ button at the bottom of the Find File dialog box.

10. From the _____ menu, you can choose Re**v**isions.

Applying Your Skills

Review Exercises

Exercise 1: Using Summary Information

To practice using the Summary Info feature, follow these steps:

1. Open the document titled FIRST.DOC.

2. Type the subject of the document, your name, and one keyword in the summary dialog box.

3. Print the document and summary information.

4. Save the file to your data disk as **FIRST.DOC**.

Exercise 2: Using Find Files

To practice using Find Files, follow these steps:

1. Access the **F**ind Files option.

2. Find all the DOC files on your disk.

3. Find all files that begin with the letter *P*.

4. Copy FIRST.DOC to **SECOND.DOC** on your disk.

5. Open the file titled STEPS.DOC.

6. Add text listing the steps to find files with the same extension.

7. Save the file to your data disk as **STEP2.DOC.**

8. Compare STEPS.DOC with STEP2.DOC.

Exercise 3: Printing Files

To review printing files, follow these steps:

1. Open GUIDELINE.DOC.
2. Add the summary information to the file.
3. Print MEDII.DOC, using the Find File menu.
4. Print GUIDELINE.DOC to a file.
5. Save the file to your data disk as **GUIDELINE.DOC**.

Exercise 4: Adding Text to BUTTON.DOC

To review material covered in this chapter, follow these steps:

1. Open BUTTON.DOC.
2. Add the new toolbar buttons used in this chapter with descriptions, as in the following example:

    Find File: Locate a file or files in a specified directory.

3. Add summary information for the BUTTON.DOC, including keywords like toolbar, button bar, and so on.
4. Print the document and the summary information.
5. Save the file to your data disk as **BUTTON.DOC**.

Continuing Projects

Project 1: Practice in Using Word

In the following steps, use Insert File to accomplish the project.

1. Open the file titled MEDICAL.DOC.
2. Insert the file SCHEDULE.DOC.
3. Add some summary information.
4. Save the file to your data disk as **NEWMED.DOC**.
5. Print NEWMED.DOC to a file titled **PRMED.PRN**.

Project 2: Federal Department Store

Continue your work on the catalog for the Federal Department Store by following these steps:

1. Open a new document.

2. Type the following:

    New World Trade Outfitters

    Looking for easy to care and lasting clothing for the casual look!! Well, here we are with a new line for both men and women. We have a 24-hour catalog service and will overnight the item if in stock. Call us at 800-377-5577 for a brochure.

3. Insert the CATALOG.DOC file.

4. Add summary information to the file.

5. Save the file to your data disk as **OUTFIT.DOC**.

6. Print the document.

Project 3: Real Entertainment Corporation

Continue your work on the newsletter for Real Entertainment Corporation by following these steps:

1. Open a new document.

2. Enter the following paragraphs:

    Deadline dates for publications:

    March 25, 1994

    April 27, 1994

    May 15, 1994

    June 20, 1994

3. Save the file to your data disk as **DATES.DOC**.

4. Open the file titled REC.DOC.

5. Insert the file DATES.DOC into REC.DOC.

6. Add the summary information.

7. Save the file to your data disk as **RECDATES.DOC**.

8. Print RECDATES.DOC with its summary information.

CHAPTER 5
Enhancing the Text in a Document

Character formatting
The process of specifying the font, font size, style, color, and placement of characters.

After the document has been proofed, documented, and stored in a known location, you are ready to "dress it up." With Word, you can control the appearance of text in a document in many ways. You can enhance the appearance of a word or phrase by using boldface type or italics, for example, or by using type of a particular size or with specific characteristics. In Word, these aspects of text appearance (as well as others) are known as *character formatting*. Word also enables you to use characters besides the ones that appear on your keyboard.

Objectives

By the time you finish this chapter, you will have learned to

1. Change Fonts and Font Sizes
2. Improve the Appearance of Text
3. Change Character Spacing
4. Set and Restore the Default Character Format
5. Remove and Copy Character Formatting

Overview of Formatting

Word divides formatting into three categories: *character formatting*, *paragraph formatting*, and *page formatting*. Each category enables you to format a document in many ways. This chapter covers character formatting and tells how to use it.

Some aspects of formatting are affected by the printer that you select to print your document. Before you begin formatting a document, make sure that the correct printer is selected. To do so, choose **P**rint from the **F**ile menu to open the

Font
A complete set of characters, all similar in appearance.

Formatting toolbar
An on-screen bar that provides shortcuts for character and paragraph formatting.

Print dialog box. The top line of this dialog box states the name of the currently selected printer. If the correct name is shown, click the Cancel button to close the dialog box. If the correct name is not shown, refer to Chapter 4 for information about selecting a printer.

Characters are letters, numbers, punctuation marks, and symbols. In Word, you can change the *font*, font size, style, color, and placement of characters. You can also format text so that it remains hidden (to include nonprinting notes to yourself, for example).

Note: *You can select specific character formatting before you type the characters, or you can type the characters, select them, and then apply the desired formatting.*

Each time you open a new document, Word initially uses defaults for all aspects of character formatting. You can change default character formatting, however, by using the *Formatting toolbar*, the keyboard, or the Font dialog box. Table 5.1 lists the character attributes you can change using each of these methods.

Table 5.1   Character Formatting Methods

Method	Character Attributes
Formatting toolbar	Changes font, font size, and font style.
Keyboard	Changes font, font size, and font style, as well as specifying various types of underlining. With the keyboard, you also can capitalize characters or show them as small capital letters, move characters to the subscript or superscript positions, and hide characters so they don't print.
Font dialog box	Specifies font, font size, font style, and various types of underlining. You can capitalize characters or show them as small capital letters, move characters to the subscript or superscript positions, or hide characters. You also can select from 16 colors and adjust the spacing between characters.

Although the Font dialog box provides the most options, applying character formatting with the Formatting toolbar or the keyboard is usually faster than applying formatting by using the dialog box.

Objective 1: Change Fonts and Font Sizes

Point
A unit used to measure the size of typographic characters. One point is approximately 1/72 inch.

Traditionally, the word *font* refers to a set of characters of the same typeface, all of which have the same size and style. But Word, like other word processing and desktop publishing programs, uses the word *font* more broadly. In Word, a font is a set of characters of the same typeface, including all sizes and styles available with that typeface. Each font has a name, such as Century Schoolbook, Helvetica, or Symbol. To a traditional printer, *Helvetica 12-point italic* is a font. To Word, Helvetica is a font that contains characters in many different sizes and in four font styles.

Windows (and therefore Word) supports fonts that are designed for various purposes. The TrueType fonts supplied with Windows and Word provide characters that appear on-screen almost exactly as they will look when printed by laser printers, as well as by certain other types of printers. Other fonts, such as the Roman and Script fonts supplied with Windows, are designed for use with a pen plotter. This section shows you how to use the Font dialog box to determine the type of printer for which each font is intended.

Note: *For best results, make sure that you select fonts intended for the type of printer you are using.*

Each font has a distinctive look. Because Word supports WYSIWYG (what-you-see-is-what-you-get), the characters that you see on-screen very closely resemble the characters that are eventually printed on paper. As you learn later in this chapter, you can see what a font looks like before you use it by displaying it in the Font dialog box.

TrueType fonts are scalable, which means that you can display and print each font in a wide range of sizes. In Word, you can specify font sizes ranging from 1 to 1,638 points in half-point increments (one point is equal to approximately 1/72 inch). This wide range of sizes is available if you are using most laser printers; it is more limited for some other printers.

Note: *Newspapers, magazines, and similar publications use 9-point to 12-point characters for most text. Headlines use 14-point or larger character sizes. You also can specify the space between lines in points.*

You might want to create a document on one computer and then print it from another computer. A possible problem arises if the two computers have different fonts available. When you create the document, however, you can specify fonts that are available on the computer to be used for printing but not on your computer. Just be aware that characters will neither appear correctly on-screen nor print correctly until you move the document to the computer that has the specified fonts available.

You can choose a font and a font size before you type the characters, or you can type the characters, select them, and then choose a font and font size. You can choose the font and font size by using the Formatting toolbar, the Font dialog box, or the keyboard.

Displaying the Formatting Toolbar

You can use the Formatting toolbar to change the font, font size, and font style. To use the Formatting toolbar, however, you must display it on-screen. If the Formatting toolbar is not already displayed on your screen, follow these steps:

❶ From the **V**iew menu, choose **T**oolbars. The Toolbars dialog box appears (see figure 5.1).

(continues)

Displaying the Formatting Toolbar (continued)

Figure 5.1
When the Toolbars dialog box appears, it shows a list of available toolbars with an × by the side of each one that is already displayed.

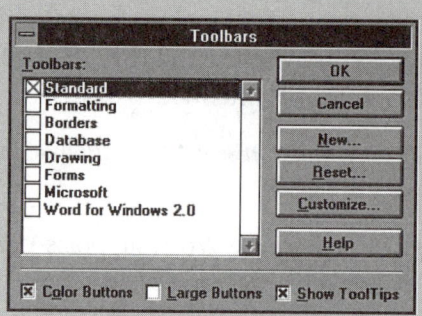

② Click in the check box to the left of Formatting in the list; an × appears in the box.

③ Choose OK to close the dialog box and redisplay the Word window (see figure 5.2).

Figure 5.2
The Formatting toolbar appears at the top of the text area.

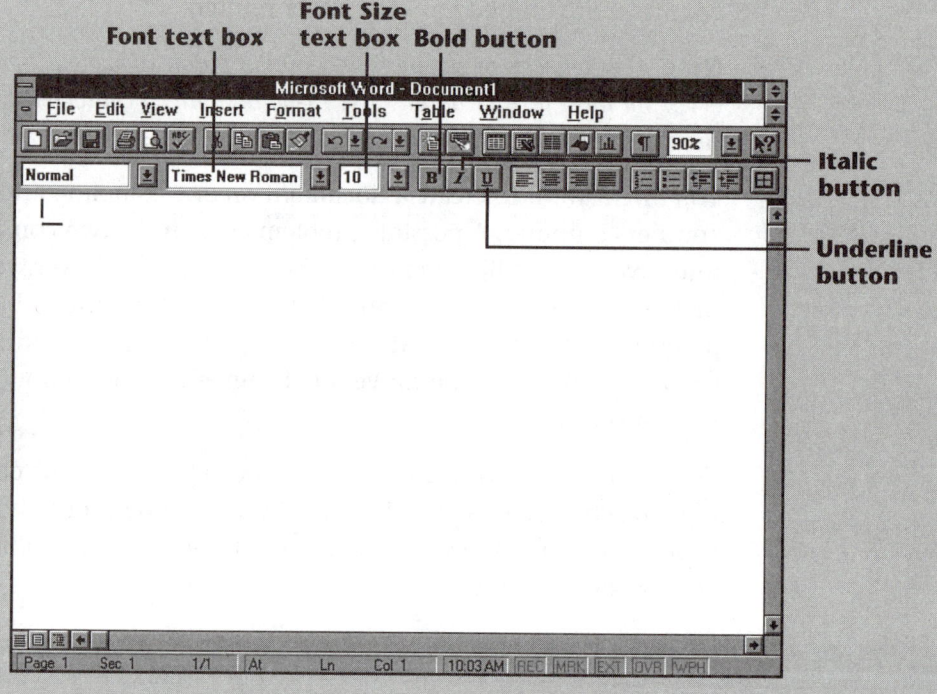

The text in the document is the default font setting when the program was installed.

You can use the Formatting toolbar to change font style and size, change the typeface to bold, italic, or underline and to align text.

Using the Formatting Toolbar to Change the Font

You can use the Formatting toolbar to change the font of a selected word, paragraph, or document. To use the toolbar, follow these steps:

1 In the open POLICY2.DOC, select *PC computer*. The Font text box on the Formatting toolbar shows the current font name.

2 Click the down arrow to the right of the Font text box to open the Font drop-down list box (see figure 5.3).

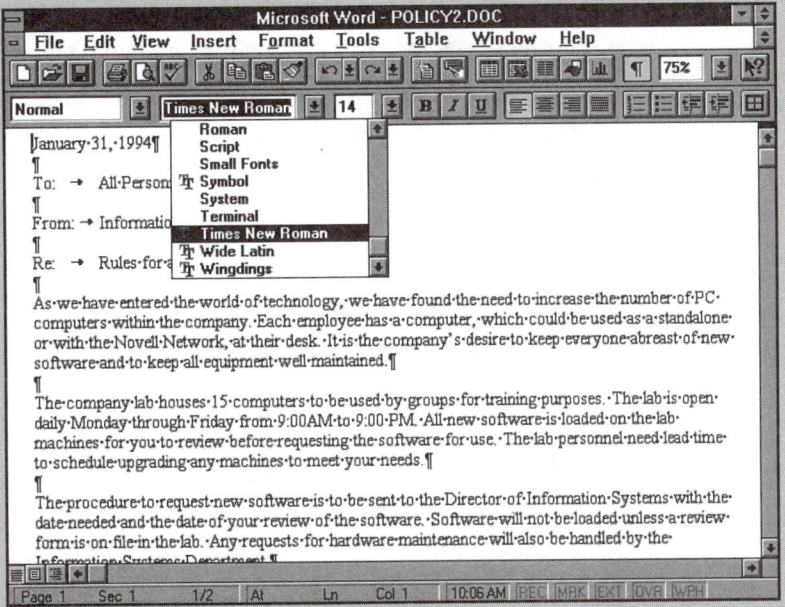

Figure 5.3
Use the Font drop-down list box to select a font.

The Font drop-down list box has two sections. At the top are the names of the fonts you have used recently. Below that is an alphabetical list of all the fonts available on your computer. The double-T symbol to the left of the names indicates TrueType fonts.

3 Click the name of the font, Times New Roman.

Note: *If you want to select a font which has a name starting with a letter toward the end of the alphabet, type the first letter of the font's name. The Font list immediately scrolls to the first font name that starts with that letter. This technique can be much faster than scrolling through the entire list of names.*

 **4** Click the Bold and Italic buttons on the toolbar.

5 Keep the document open.

That font is immediately applied to all selected characters in your document. If no characters are selected, that font is applied at the insertion point; characters you enter there appear in the selected font.

Using the Formatting Toolbar to Change the Font Size

To use the formatting toolbar to change the font size, follow these steps:

❶ In the open POLICY2.DOC, place the insertion point in front of the *J* in *January* and select the heading text, the date, *To, From,* and *Re,* for which you want to change the size. The Font Size text box in the Formatting toolbar shows the current size.

❷ Click the down arrow to the right of the Font Size text box to open the Font Size drop-down list box (see figure 5.4).

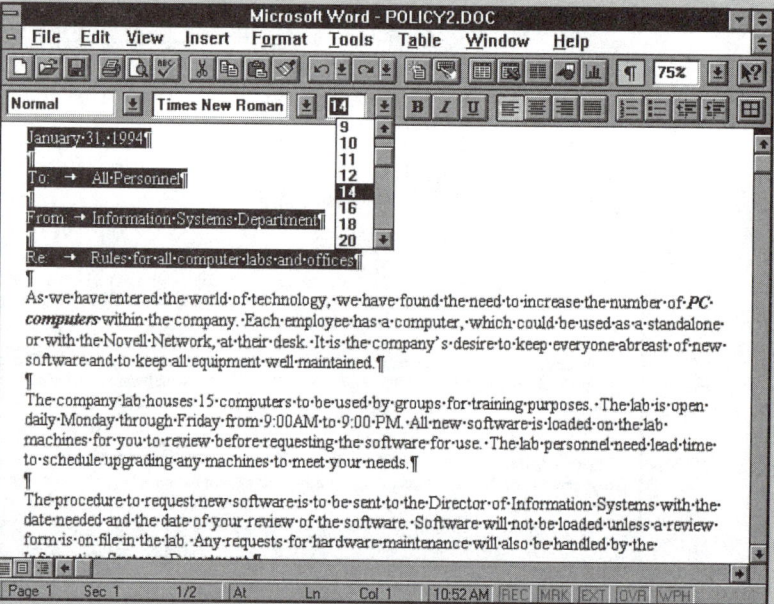

Figure 5.4
The Font Size list box shows some suggested font sizes.

❸ Click the font size, 16, in the list of suggested sizes, and observe the change in the document.

Note: *You are not limited to the font sizes in the list box. To use a size that does not appear in the list, simply type the size you want to use in the Font Size text box and then press* ⏎Enter. *If you want to change the font size to 9.5 points, for example, type* **9.5** *and press* ⏎Enter.

❹ Return the document to font size 14 by repeating the preceding steps.

❺ Keep the document open.

You also can use the Font dialog box to change the font and font size easily.

Using the Font Dialog Box to Change the Font and Font Size

To change the font and font size from the Font dialog box, follow these steps:

1 In the open POLICY2.DOC, select the paragraph beginning with "The Company lab houses...".

2 From the Format menu, choose Font to open the Font dialog box (see figure 5.5).

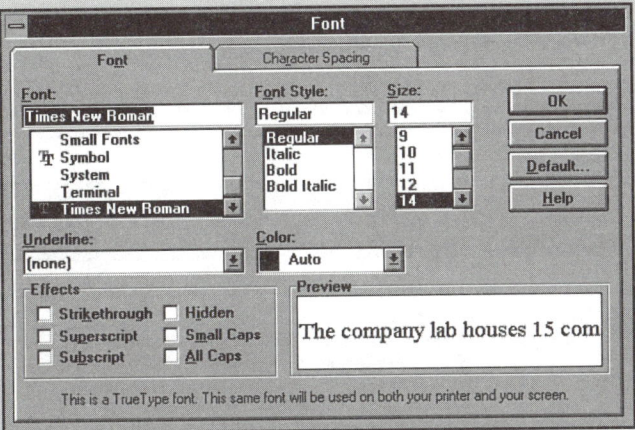

Figure 5.5
Use the Font dialog box to change character formatting.

The Font dialog box contains two sections; the first changes many character properties. The second section modifies character spacing and is covered later in this chapter.

3 Choose Arial, one of the available fonts from the Font list box. The Preview box in the lower right corner of the dialog box shows a sample of the font you have chosen. A brief message providing information about the chosen font appears across the bottom of the dialog box.

4 Choose 14 from the Size list box. The Preview box shows the new character size.

5 Choose OK to accept the font and size changes and return to the document. Figure 5.6 shows the change in the paragraph.

(continues)

Using the Font Dialog Box to Change the Font and Font Size (continued)

Figure 5.6
The highlighted paragraph is now in Arial font.

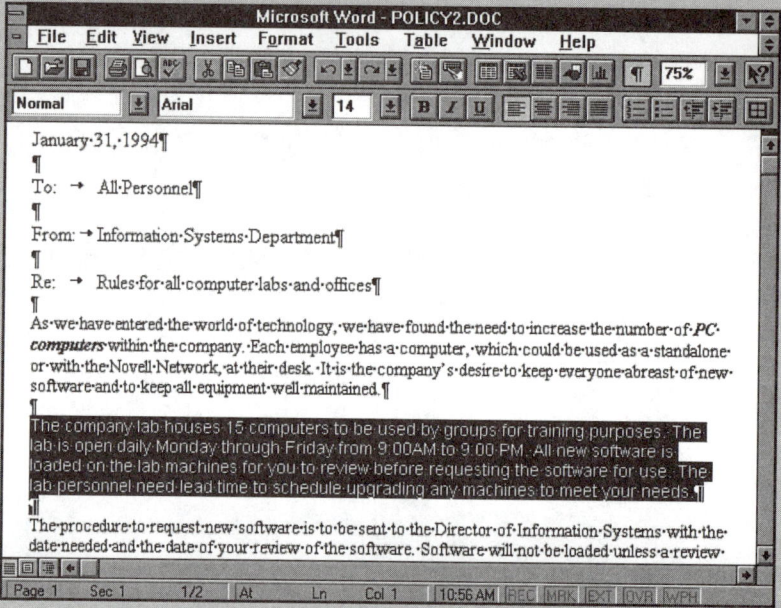

Note: *You also can open the Font dialog box by clicking the right mouse button when the pointer is located anywhere in the text area of the screen. A shortcut menu appears. Choose Font to open the dialog box.*

6 Keep the document open.

If you are more comfortable with the shortcut keys, you can change the font and font size using the keyboard.

Using Shortcut Keys to Change the Font and Font Size

To change the font and font size using the keyboard, follow these steps:

1 In the open POLICY2.DOC, select the last paragraph.

2 Press the shortcut key combination, Ctrl+] to increase the font size by one point, as listed in table 5.2.

The font size used in the paragraph changes.

If you press Ctrl+Shift+F, the current font name is highlighted in the Formatting toolbar. You can change the font by typing a new font name and then pressing Enter.

Table 5.2 Shortcut Keys for Changing the Font and Size

Shortcut Key	Effect
Ctrl+Shift+F	Activates the Font list text box in the Formatting toolbar.
Ctrl+Shift+Q	Selects the Symbol font.
Ctrl+]	Increases font size by one point.
Ctrl+[	Decreases font size by one point.
Ctrl+Spacebar	Restores default character format.

Objective 2: Improve the Appearance of Text

You can use *character style*s and effects to enhance the appearance of text in many ways. Table 5.3 lists the available styles and effects.

Character style
A particular variation of the appearance of characters in a font. Many, but not all, fonts can appear in roman (what Word calls *regular*), italic, bold, or bold-italic styles.

Table 5.3 Character Styles and Effects

Name	Style or Effect
regular	Characters appear in normal type (what printers call roman type).
bold	Characters appear in boldface type.
italic	Characters appear in italic type.
~~strikethrough~~	Characters appear as though they should be removed from the text.
hidden	Characters do not appear on-screen unless you choose to display them; they do not print unless you choose to print them. See Chapter 8 for more information about using hidden text.
SMALL CAPS	Characters are all uppercase, but the first character of each word is the assigned point size and the rest of the characters have a slightly smaller point size.
ALL CAPS	Characters are all uppercase.
single underline	Words and the spaces between them are underlined.
words only underline	Words are underlined, but spaces between them are not.
double underline	Words and spaces have a double underline.
dotted underline	Word and spaces have a dotted underline.
superscript	Characters are raised by three points and shown in a smaller size.
subscript	Characters are lowered by three points and shown in a smaller size.
color	Characters can be shown on-screen and, if you have a color printer, printed in a color other than black.

You can choose character styles and effects before typing characters, or you can enter the characters, select them, and then choose styles or effects. You can choose styles using the Formatting toolbar; you can choose styles and effects using the Font dialog box or the keyboard.

Using the Formatting Toolbar to Change the Font Styles

To use the Formatting toolbar to apply or remove the regular, bold, italic, and single underline styles, follow these steps:

1. In the open POLICY2.DOC, select "Information Systems Department" in the last paragraph.

2. Click the Formatting toolbar button labeled *I* (Italic). The text changes (see figure 5.7).

Figure 5.7
The text appears in italics.

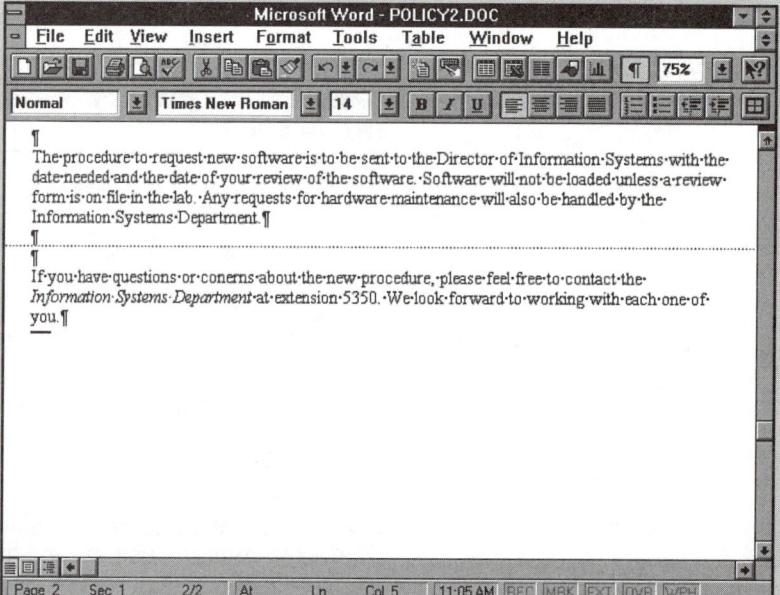

3. Keep the document open.

Each formatting button can appear in two positions on-screen: *raised* or *pressed*. If a button is in the raised position, the corresponding character style is Off; if a button is in the pressed position, the corresponding character style is On. The default state, in which all three buttons are raised, indicates the regular (roman) style (characters are not bolded, italicized, or underlined).

To change the position of a button from raised to pressed or from pressed to raised, point to it and click the left mouse button. You can click the three buttons to change styles individually or to apply combinations of styles. If the Bold and Underline buttons are both pressed, for example, the resulting character style is bold and underlined.

Improve the Appearance of Text   **131**

Using the Font Dialog Box to Change Font Styles

You can change more aspects of character style and effect by using the Font dialog box than you can by using the Formatting toolbar. In the dialog box, you can specify the bold, italic, strikethrough, hidden, small caps, all caps, and underline styles. You also can choose a color.

1 In the open POLICY2.DOC, select *registered*, in the fourth paragraph to change the font styles.

2 From the Format menu, choose Font to open the Font dialog box.

3 Click Bold Italic in the Font Style list box.

4 In the Effects area at the bottom of the screen, click the check boxes representing Strikethrough, and All Caps. An × appears in the check boxes next to the format aspects you want to use.

5 Under Font style, choose Italic. The word *registered* is now in bold, italic, and all caps (see figure 5.8).

Figure 5.8
Use the Font dialog box to change the way text appears in your document.

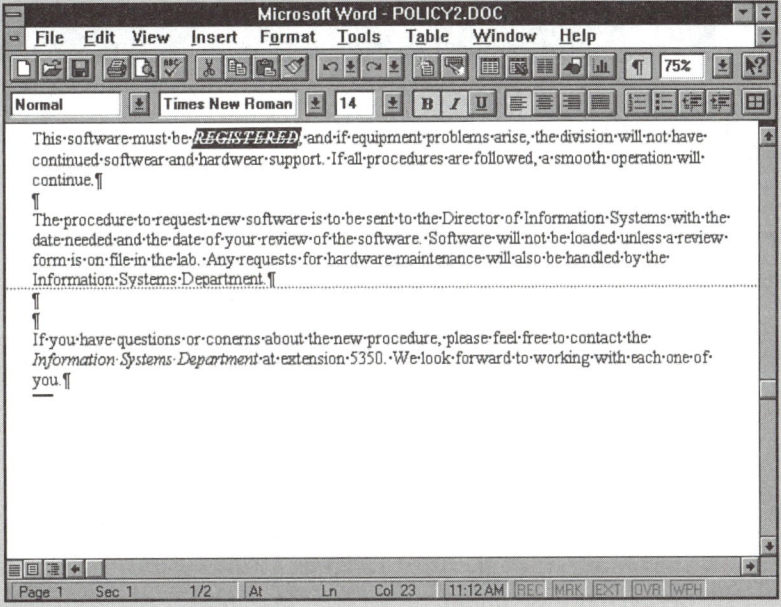

6 Choose OK to accept your formatting changes and return to the document.

Note: *As in most dialog boxes, you can click the Cancel button to close the dialog box without any of your choices affecting the selected text or the Help button to display information about the dialog box. See "Setting and Restoring the Default Character Format," later in this chapter, for information about the Default button.*

7 Keep the document open.

The text in the document has been formatted using the Formatting toolbar and the Format menu. You also can use the keyboard to change fonts.

Using the Keyboard to Change Font Styles

To apply styles and effects to text characters by using the shortcut keys, follow these steps:

1 In the open POLICY2.DOC, select "Information Systems" in the third paragraph to change the style.

2 Press Ctrl+U to apply the underline font style.

The text is now underlined.

Note: *If you have selected the option to display hidden text, you select text, and then you use the shortcut key to hide it, the text is marked with a dotted underline. You can select the text again and use the same shortcut key to remove the dotted underline and return it to normal text. If you have selected the option to hide hidden text, you select text, and then you use the shortcut key to hide it, the text completely disappears from the screen. You cannot redisplay the text by pressing the shortcut key.*

Table 5.4 Font Style Keyboard Shortcuts

Shortcut Key	Style
Ctrl+U	Single underline (words and spaces between them)
Ctrl+Shift+W	Word underline (words but not spaces between them)
Ctrl+Shift+D	Double underline (words and spaces between them)
Ctrl+Shift+B	Bold
Ctrl+Shift+I	Italic
Ctrl+Shift+A	All Caps
Ctrl+Shift+K	Small Caps
Ctrl+Shift+H	Hidden

Note: *You can press a sequence of shortcut keys to add two or more styles and effects. If you press Ctrl+Shift+B and then Ctrl+Shift+I, for example, the entered or selected characters appear in boldface and italic.*

You can also press the shortcut key Shift+F3 to change the case of characters. The first time you press the shortcut key, the selected words appear with only the first letters of each word capitalized. The second time you press the shortcut key, the selected words appears with all characters capitalized. If you press the shortcut key a third time, all the characters revert to their original lowercase state.

If you start with words that were initially entered in all uppercase letters, pressing the shortcut key once switches all uppercase to all lowercase. Pressing the shortcut key again sets only the first character of the selected text to uppercase. Pressing it a third time makes all characters uppercase.

Objective 3: Change Character Spacing

When Word displays characters on-screen (and when it prints them), it puts a certain amount of space between the characters. You can reduce or increase this standard spacing. Three reasons for changing character spacing are the following:

- To improve a document's appearance. Sometimes you may want to have a short memo fill an entire page rather than have the memo print at the very top of the page. Spacing can expand the characters, thus increasing the number of lines of the document.

- To make text fit into a limited space. You may have a document that needs to be presented as one page, and one paragraph overflows to a second page. If you select the paragraph and condense the text, the document will return to one page.

- To expand text to fill an area. As well as improving a document's appearance, you may be given a specific area in a document in which to type text and expanding the characters can fill the area.

Using the Font Dialog Box to Change Character Spacing

To change the character spacing, follow these steps:

1. In the open POLICY.DOC, select the characters *January*, for which you want to change the spacing.

2. From the F**o**rmat menu, choose **F**ont to open the Font dialog box, which displays the Font section.

3. Click the Cha**r**acter Spacing tab to display the Character Spacing section shown in figure 5.9.

(continues)

Using the Font Dialog Box to Change Character Spacing (continued)

Figure 5.9
Use the Font dialog box's Character Spacing section to change character spacing, alter character position, or select kerning conditions.

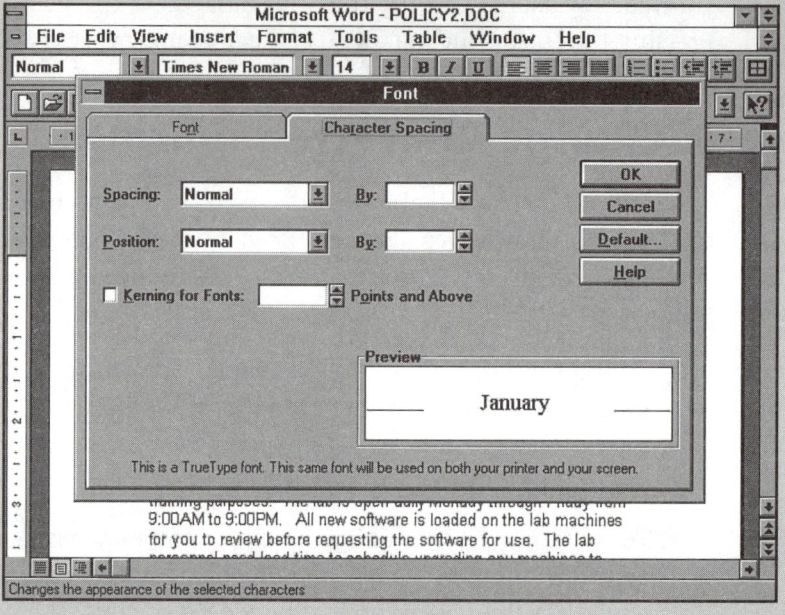

In this dialog box, you can do any of the following things:

- Open the **S**pacing drop-down list box, and choose Expanded or Condensed. Then expand or condense the spacing between characters in one-tenth-point increments.

- Open the **P**osition drop-down list box, and specify whether you want the selected text to be raised or lowered. Using this method (as opposed to the Superscript or Subscript style options in the Font dialog box), you can choose the distance you want to raise or lower the characters. This feature is helpful if the document includes mathematical fractions; you can raise or lower the numbers for a more vertical appearance.

Kern
To adjust the spacing between characters.

- Click the **K**erning for Fonts check box, and choose the character size at which you want automatic *kerning* to take effect.

④ Open the **S**pacing drop-down list box.

⑤ Choose Condensed.

⑥ Condense the spacing to 1.

⑦ Choose OK. The text is condensed (see figure 5.10).

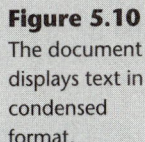

Figure 5.10
The document displays text in condensed format.

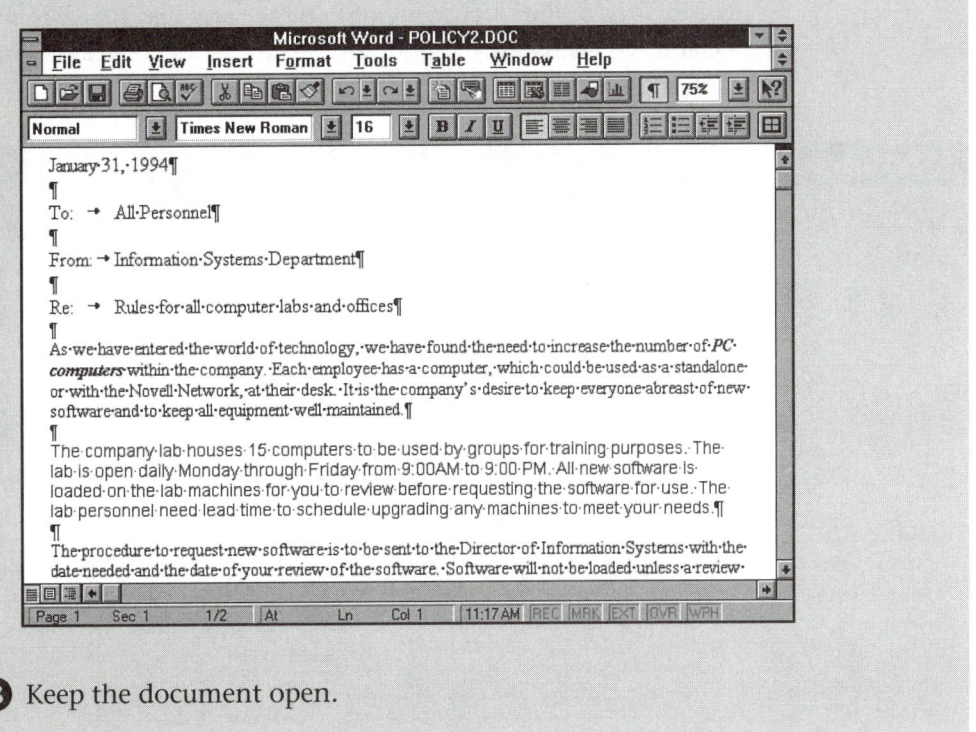

⑧ Keep the document open.

Note: Characters occupy a specific amount of space, which in many cases varies from character to character. To give the document a professional appearance, certain letters such as i will occupy noticeably less space than others. TrueType font files (and some other types of font files) include information about character spacing. Word can use this information to optimize character spacing. The apparent excessive space between certain pairs of characters is more obvious for larger font sizes. By default, Word applies automatic kerning for characters that are 10 points or larger in size. You can change the minimum font size at which Word applies kerning.

Objective 4: Set and Restore the Default Character Format

Each time you open a new document and start typing, Word uses a preselected font, font size, and type style. This font, size, and type style is known as the *default font*.

When you installed Word on your computer, the default font was probably *Times New Roman*, the default font size was probably *10 point*, and the default style was probably *Regular*. If you are satisfied with the font, size, and style you normally use, you will want to keep those settings. But if you normally use the *Arial* font and prefer a 12-point font size, you can easily change the default values to meet your needs. Then you don't have to change the font every time you start a new document.

If you open a new document and change any text to a format other than the default, you can easily restore the text to the default, as explained in the next section.

Setting a Default Character Format

To set the default character format in the opened POLICY2.DOC, follow these steps:

1. From the **Fo**rmat menu, choose **F**ont to open the Font dialog box.

2. Select Courier New Font, 12.

3. Click the **D**efault button. The confirmation dialog box appears (see figure 5.11).

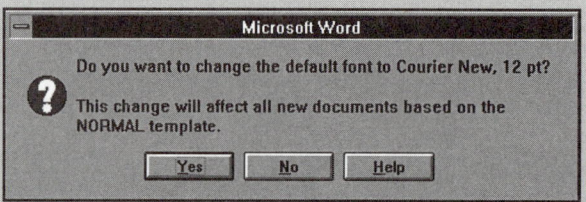

Figure 5.11
Word displays a dialog box that asks you to confirm your choice of a default font.

4. Click **Y**es to confirm your choice. Word closes both dialog boxes and returns to the document screen.

If you want to, you can open a new document and start typing. The characters you type appear on-screen in the new default format.

The new default font is stored permanently; the next time you start Word, it uses the new default font. After changing the default settings, however, you can revert to the original settings at any time.

Restoring the Default Font

When you work with a document, you may reach a point at which you have changed the fonts, font sizes, and font styles and then decide that you prefer the default font after all. Fortunately, you can easily change the text back to the default font. Simply follow these steps in the opened POLICY2.DOC:

1. Select the text *Information Systems* in the last paragraph to restore to the default font. Figure 5.12 shows how the text appears.

Figure 5.12
The document displays selected text in italic.

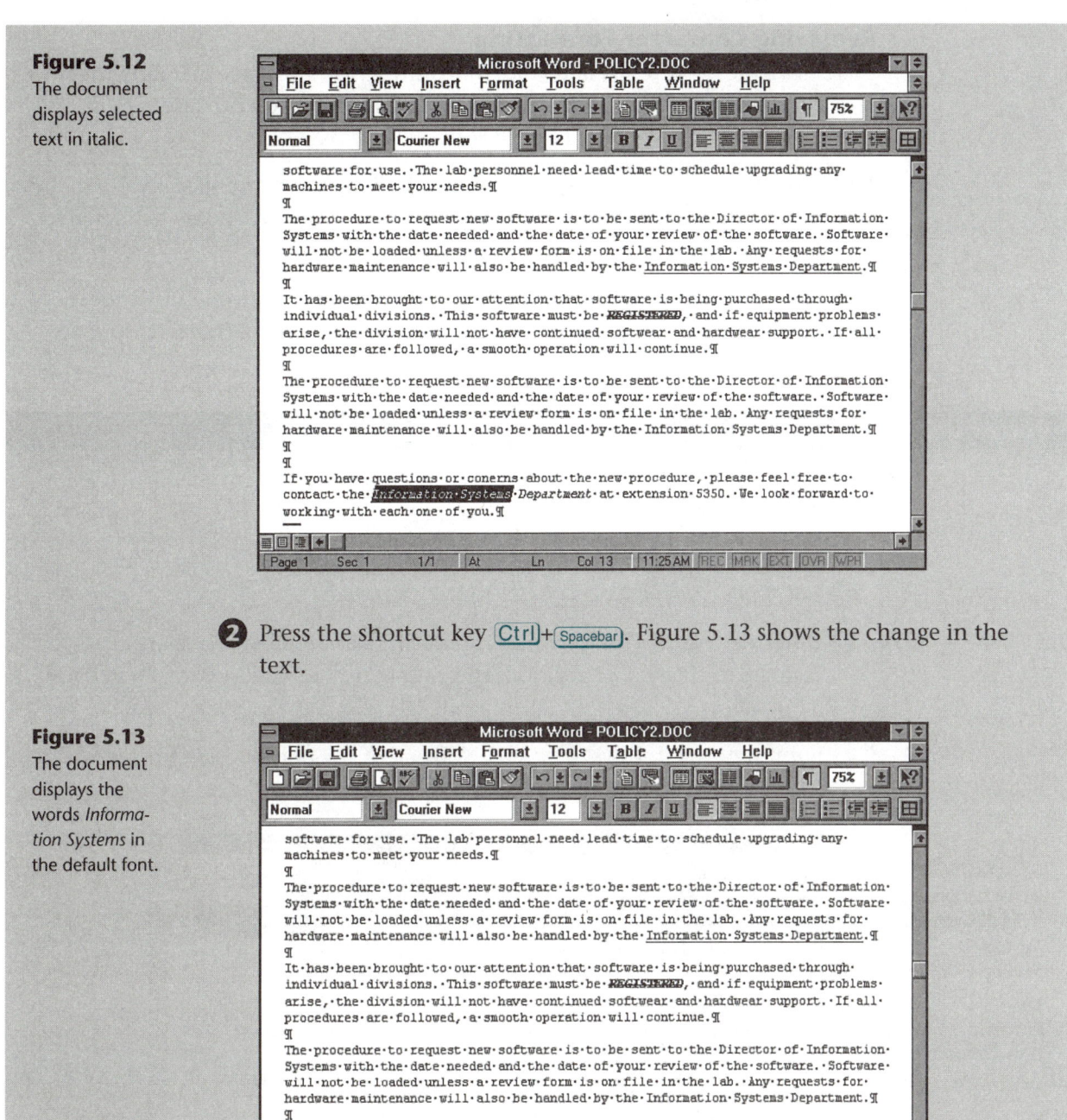

Figure 5.13
The document displays the words *Information Systems* in the default font.

❷ Press the shortcut key Ctrl+Spacebar. Figure 5.13 shows the change in the text.

This section provides only a brief introduction to the concept of Word's defaults.

Objective 5: Remove and Copy Character Formatting

If you change your mind about the character formatting you applied, you can revert to the default format, as described, or you can remove any combination of character formatting options. You can also copy the character formatting used in one block of text to other blocks.

Removing Character Formatting

To remove the Bold, Italic, and Underline font styles, select the text, and then click the appropriate button on the Formatting toolbar. You can also remove font styles using the keyboard or the Font dialog box.

If you use the Font dialog box, you can see all the currently applied styles. To remove a font style, simply click its check box. You also can choose a different font style from a list box.

To remove any other format options in the Font dialog box, you must choose another format from the same list. After you finish removing character formats, choose OK to return to the document.

Copying Character Formatting

You can copy the formatting of characters without copying the characters themselves. To copy the character formatting used in one block of text to another block of text in the opened POLICY2.DOC, follow these steps:

1 Select *Information Systems* in the third paragraph.

2 Click the Format Painter button in the Standard toolbar. The button changes to the *pressed* position, showing that it is active and ready to paint a format.

3 Point to the *N* in *Novell Network*. Notice that the pointer is an I-beam with a paintbrush at its left side (see figure 5.14).

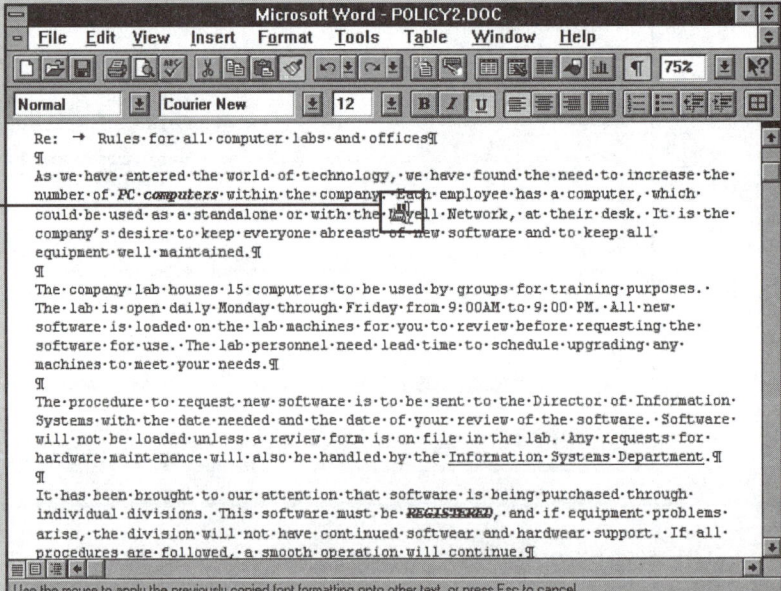

Figure 5.14
Drag the Format Painter button to highlight the text to be formatted.

The Format paintbrush

4 Press the mouse button and drag to highlight *Novell Network*.

When you release the mouse button, the text changes to the new format, the Format Painter button returns to the raised position, and the pointer becomes a normal I-beam (see figure 5.15).

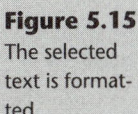

Figure 5.15
The selected text is formatted.

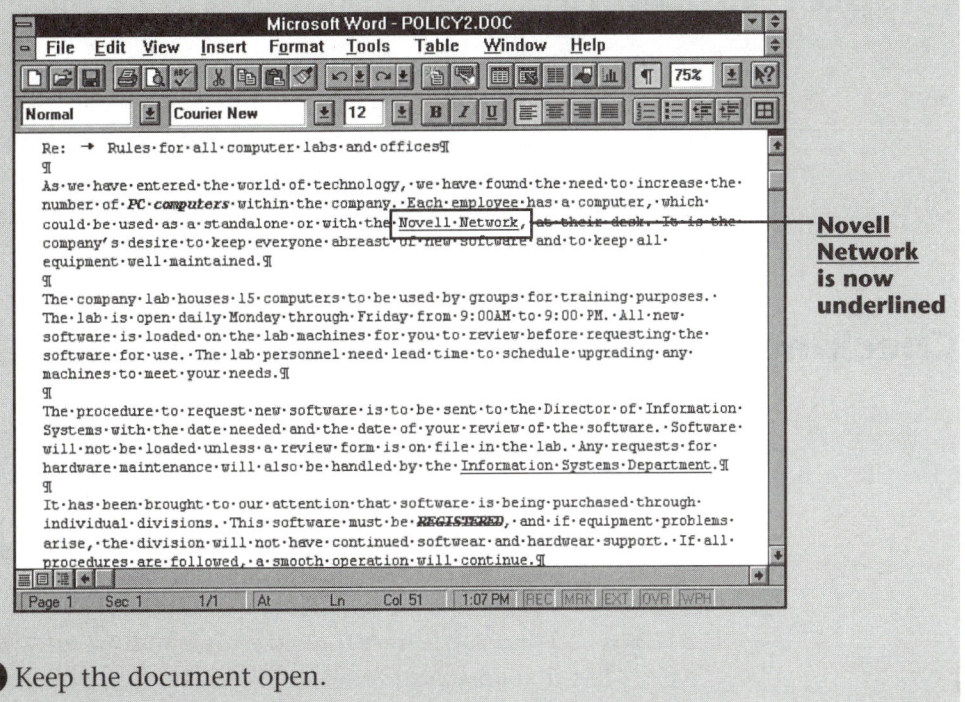

Novell Network is now underlined

⑤ Keep the document open.

Note: If you click the Format Painter button to make it active and then decide you don't want to copy a format, simply click the button again (or press Esc *) to deactivate the button.*

You can use the Format Painter in a slightly different way if you want to copy a format to several blocks of text. Instead of clicking the Format Painter button a single time to activate it, double-click it. This technique keeps the Format Painter active so that you can copy a format to several blocks of text—one after the other. After you have finished copying the format, click the Format Painter button again (or press Esc) to deactivate it.

Using the Keyboard to Copy Character Formatting

You also can use shortcut keys instead of the Format Painter button to copy a character format. Follow these steps:

① From the open POLICY2.DOC, place the insertion point, after the *P* in *PC computer*, within the text that has the format you want to copy.

② Press Ctrl+⇧Shift+C.

③ Select the text *extension 5350* to change.

④ Press Ctrl+⇧Shift+V.

⑤ Close the document without saving the changes.

Chapter Summary

Your document at this point may look very busy because of the variety of formats applied to the text. Now you can now see the power of Word for Windows, however. You can take a simple document and change the font of the character or groups of characters to give it the professional appearance. In Chapter 6, you will work with indenting, tabs, line control, and many other features of paragraph formatting.

Checking Your Skills

True/False Questions

For each of the following statements, circle *T* or *F* to indicate whether the statement is true or false.

T F **1.** A font is a set of characters of the same typeface, including all sizes and styles available with that typeface.

T F **2.** The TrueType fonts supplied with Windows and Word provide characters that appear on-screen differently from how the fonts will print.

T F **3.** TrueType fonts are scalable, which means that you can display and print each font in a wide range of sizes.

T F **4.** You can press a sequence of shortcut keys to add four or more styles and effects.

T F **5.** The default font is the preselected font each time you open a new document and start typing.

T F **6.** You can copy the formatting of characters without copying the characters themselves.

T F **7.** You can use the Font dialog box to change the font and font size easily.

T F **8.** Pressing Ctrl+Spacebar increases the font by one point.

T F **9.** If you select Hidden character effect, characters do not appear on-screen, but they do print.

T F **10.** When you select two consecutive words and click the Underline button, just words are underlined and not the space between the words.

Multiple-Choice Questions

In the blank provided, write the letter of the correct answer for each of the following questions.

_____ **1.** A font in Word which contains characters in many different sizes and in four font styles is _____.

   a. Roman

   b. Script

c. Courier

d. Helvetica

e. Times symbol

____ 2. To change the font for a word in the document, you must _____.

a. place the insertion point on the first letter of the word and select the font

b. place the insertion point at the first letter of the word and select the entire word and then select the font

c. select the font desired first and then select the text

d. select the font desired first and then type the word

e. place the insertion point at the end of the word and select the font

____ 3. In the Font dialog box, you can specify all the styles except _____.

a. bold

b. italic

c. hidden

d. lowercase letters

e. strikethrough

____ 4. Reasons for changing character spacing are all the following but _____.

a. improve a document's readability

b. keep the letters from being spaced properly

c. make text fit into a limited space

d. expand text to fill into an area

e. all the above

____ 5. To copy the formatting of characters without copying the characters themselves, use the _____ button.

a. Format Selection

b. Format Painter

c. Format Toolbar

d. Copy

e. Drawing

____ 6. Word divides formatting into which three categories?

a. character, paragraph, and sentence formatting

      b. character, sentence, and page formatting

      c. sentence, page formatting, and paragraph

      d. character, paragraph, and page formatting

      e. word, paragraph, and page formatting

____ **7.** Which of following changes only font, font size, and font style?

      a. Standard toolbar

      b. Formatting toolbar

      c. keyboard

      d. Font dialog box

      e. Formatting menu

____ **8.** If selected text is not to show on-screen or to print, it is _____.

      a. removed

      b. deleted

      c. hidden

      d. covered

      e. strikethrough

____ **9.** To boldface a word, you can _____.

      a. select the text and click the Bold button

      b. select the text and press Ctrl+B

      c. press Ctrl+B

      d. click the Bold button and type the word

      e. both a and d

____ **10.** If you want to increase the font size of selected text, you can _____.

      a. select a font size less than the default

      b. click the Increase Indent button

      c. click the Zoom button

      d. select a font size other than the default

      e. increase the font size by increments of .5

Fill-in-the-Blank Questions

In the blank provided, write the correct answer for each of the following questions.

1. Traditionally, the word _____ refers to a set of characters of the same typeface, all of which have the same size and style.

2. The Font Dialog Box enables you to change the _____ and _____ easily.

3. _____ means changing the space between selected pairs of characters to improve the appearance of a document.

4. Characters raised by three points and shown in a smaller size are _____characters.

5. To remove font styles, simply select the appropriate text and then click the font styles to be removed in the _____ toolbar.

6. _____ formatting is the process of specifying the appearance of text.

7. Although the Font dialog box provides the most options, using the Formatting toolbar or the _____ is usually faster than the dialog box.

8. You can use the Formatting toolbar to change the font and font size and to apply _____.

9. If no characters are selected, the font is applied at the _____ point.

10. If you press Ctrl+Shift+F, the current _____ name is highlighted in the Formatting toolbar.

Applying Your Skills

Review Exercises

Exercise 1: Applying Font Styles

To review applying formats before you type the text, open a new document and follow these steps:

1. Type the following passage, activating the format for fonts and font sizes before you type the text. For example, to italicize the word *font*, press Ctrl+Shift+I, and then type *font*.

   In WORD, you are able to change *font* and *font sizes* before typing the text. Display the Formatting Toolbar, and **click** to the right of the Font text box to open the Font drop-down list box. To type this text, select *Times New Roman* and click on font size, **14**.

2. Save the file to your data disk as **FONTS.DOC**.

Exercise 2: Changing Fonts in FIRST.DOC

Practice changing character formatting by following these steps:

1. Open FIRST.DOC, and select all the dates in the document.

2. Change the font to Helvetica, font size 16, and click Bold Italic.

3. Save the file to your data disk as **FIRST.DOC**.

Exercise 3: Changing Fonts in SCHEDULE.DOC

To practice changing fonts, follow these steps:

1. Open SCHEDULE.DOC, and select all the dates in the document.
2. Change the font for each date of each meeting to Times Roman 14, Bold, and Underline.
3. Save the file to your data disk as **SCHEDULE.DOC**.

Exercise 4: Changing Font Sizes and Copying Formatting

To check your skills in changing font sizes and copying formatting, follow these steps:

1. Open GUIDELINE.DOC, and change the font size for the heading to 16 and the font size for item number one to 14.
2. Copy the font size 14 format to item number 5.
3. Save the file to your data disk as **GUIDELINE.DOC**.

Exercise 5: Applying Font Styles and Sizes

To retain what you have learned about changing fonts and font sizes, follow these steps:

1. Open STEPS.DOC.
2. Add the steps to change fonts and font sizes, using the font style Helvetica and font size 12.
3. Boldface and underline each command used. For example:

    Boldface: To apply bold formatting you would....

4. Save the file to your data disk as **STEP2.DOC**.

Continuing Projects

Project 1: Practice in Using Word

To practice using character formatting, follow these steps:

1. Open the MEDICAL.DOC.
2. Change the font size for the Date to 14.
3. Italicize the inside address of the letter.
4. Boldface the salutation of the letter.
5. Underline *6:00AM - 12:00PM*.
6. Copy the format used in the Salutation to the word *Sincerely*.
7. Copy the format of the date to *Samuel Baker, MD*.
8. Save the file to your data disk as **MEDICAL.DOC**.

Project 2: Federal Department Store

Continue your work on the catalog for the Federal Department Store by following these steps:

1. Open CATALOG.DOC.
2. Change the font style of the first item name to italics, font size 14.
3. Change the character spacing for the item description to .3.
4. Copy the format of the first item name to all the item names.
5. Copy the format of the character spacing to the other descriptions.
6. Select the price for item one, and change to hidden display.
7. Save the file to your data disk as **CATALOG.DOC**.

Project 3: Real Entertainment Corporation

Continue your work on the newsletter for Real Entertainment Corporation by following these steps:

1. Open REC.DOC.
2. Change the font to Helvetica and the font size to 16 for the Headings (Real Entertainment Corporation and Marketing Department).
3. Italicize *Real Entertainment Corporation* in the first paragraph.
4. Boldface the *20%* and *50%* in the Marketing paragraph.
5. Underline *home*, *office*, and *organization* in the second paragraph.
6. Change the character spacing for *home*, *office*, and *organization* in the first paragraph to expanded by .3.
7. Copy the italicize format from *Real Entertainment Corporation* to the words *much more* in the last paragraph; and to the words *new marketing tool* in the second paragraph.
8. Save the file to your data disk as **REC.DOC**.

CHAPTER 6

Formatting a Paragraph

Paragraph formatting
The process of specifying the appearance of paragraphs—setting the tabs, the indentation and alignment of paragraphs, and line spacing.

In Chapter 5, you learned how to enhance the appearance of text by using character formatting. On the job or at work, however, you may be required to indent text, double-space text, set up tables using tabs within a document, align text, or use other *paragraph-formatting* options. In this chapter, you learn how to create emphasis by applying borders and shading to paragraphs, how to create bulleted and numbered lists, and how to use the outlining feature.

Objectives

By the time you finish this chapter, you will have learned to

1. Set the Unit of Measurement
2. Set Tab Positions and Tab Alignment
3. Indent Paragraphs
4. Align Paragraphs
5. Use Automatic Hyphenation
6. Control Line Spacing
7. Remove and Repeat Paragraph Formatting
8. Apply Borders and Shading to Paragraphs
9. Create Bulleted and Numbered Lists
10. Create an Outline

An Overview of Paragraph Formatting

In Word, the word *paragraph* has a more specific meaning than it does in grammar: a paragraph is not necessarily a series of related sentences but rather any amount of text or graphics followed by a *paragraph mark* that appears on-screen as ¶ if you have chosen to show nonprinting characters.

Note: *If nonprinting characters are not showing on-screen, click the Show/Hide button in the Standard toolbar. Click the button again when you want to hide nonprinting characters.*

Paragraph formatting controls these attributes of paragraphs:

- Tab positions and alignment
- Indentation
- Paragraph alignment
- Line spacing
- Paragraph spacing
- Numbering or *bulleting* paragraphs
- Borders and shading

Bulleting
To place a marker at the beginning of each item in a list.

Word stores all paragraph formatting in the paragraph mark at the end of each paragraph. If you delete a paragraph mark, you delete all the paragraph formatting information it contains. The paragraph formatting of the text preceding the deleted paragraph mark then changes to the formatting of the next paragraph mark.

Note: *Be careful with paragraph marks, particularly when nonprinting characters are hidden so that you cannot see paragraph marks. Do not delete or move a paragraph mark without considering the effect on the paragraph formatting of the preceding text.*

In Word, you can apply various aspects of paragraph formatting by using several methods:

- The horizontal ruler and the mouse
- The Tabs dialog box
- The Paragraph dialog box
- The keyboard
- The Formatting toolbar

Table 6.1 lists the paragraph attributes you can apply by using each of these methods.

Table 6.1 Paragraph Formatting Methods	
Method	**Paragraph Attributes**
Ruler and mouse	Tab positions and alignment, and indentation.
Tabs dialog box	Default tab spacing, custom tab positions and alignment, and leader characters.

Method	Paragraph Attributes
Paragraph dialog box	All the Tabs dialog box options (default tab spacing, custom tabs, alignment, and leaders) plus indentation, paragraph alignment, line spacing (before, after, and within paragraphs), page breaks within paragraphs, and line number suppression.
Keyboard	Hanging indents and paragraph alignment.
Formatting toolbar	Paragraph alignment, also bulleted or numbered paragraphs.

Note: *You can apply paragraph formatting before or after you type the text. To apply paragraph formatting after you type the text, select the paragraphs you want to format and then apply the format.*

The Paragraph dialog box provides the most complete way to format paragraphs because it includes most of the paragraph formatting options. Although using the Formatting toolbar or the ruler is faster than using the Paragraph dialog box, fewer formatting options are available.

As mentioned at the beginning of Chapter 5, some aspects of formatting are affected by the printer Word expects to use to print your document. Before working with formatting, open the Print dialog box to confirm that the correct printer is selected.

Objective 1: Set the Unit of Measurement

By default, Word displays rulers calibrated in inches and displays measurements in inches; however, you can choose centimeters, points, or picas rather than inches.

Switching from One Measurement Unit to Another

To switch from one measurement unit to another, open the POLICY2.DOC and follow these steps:

❶ From the **T**ools menu, choose **O**ptions to display the Options dialog box. The dialog box appears.

❷ Display the General section of the dialog box.

❸ Open the **M**easurement Units drop-down list box at the bottom of the dialog box (see figure 6.1).

(continues)

Switching from One Measurement Unit to Another (continued)

Figure 6.1
Use the Measurement Units drop-down list box to choose inches, centimeters, points, or picas.

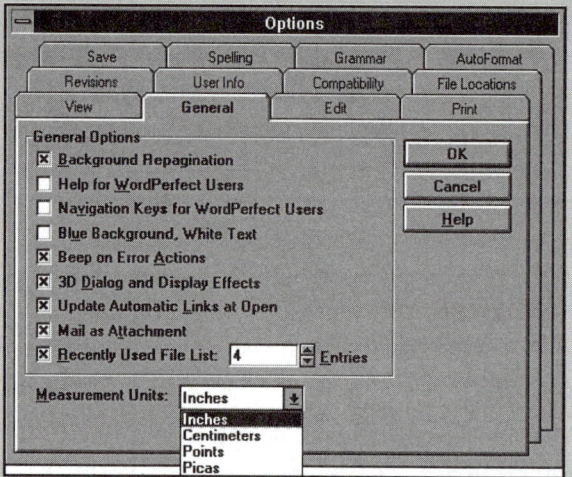

❹ Click Centimeters, and then choose OK to close the dialog box. The ruler is calibrated in the chosen units.

❺ Following the preceding steps, set the Measurement Unit to Inches.

❻ Keep the document open.

Most dialog boxes display measurements in terms of the units you selected. The screens shown in this book all use inches.

Note: *Points and picas are measurement units used in the printing industry. A point is approximately 1/72 inch, and 12 points is equal to a pica.*

The measurement unit you choose tells Word how to interpret measurements you type. As you will see later in this chapter, for example, you can set a tab position by typing its position measured from the left margin. With inches selected as the measurement unit, you can set a tab at the one-inch position by typing 1. Word interprets that number as one inch.

Even when you select inches for the measurement unit, however, you can define measurements in another unit by typing a two-letter abbreviation after the number:

- To set a measurement of one centimeter, use 1 CM.

- To set a measurement of one point, use 1 PT.

- To set a measurement of one pica, use 1 PI.

If you choose a measurement unit other than inches and want to specify one inch for a special section, type 1 IN or 1 ". The space between the number and the abbreviation is optional.

Objective 2: Set Tab Positions and Tab Alignment

You don't always want the text in a document to begin at the left margin. You may want to indent the first line of each paragraph, for example. Don't press the space bar several times to do this, as you might be accustomed to doing on a typewriter. Use the Word tab feature.

Word has two types of tabs: default tabs and custom tabs. Although Word does not show default tab positions in the horizontal ruler, default tabs are set at 1/2-inch intervals whenever you start a new document and apply to every paragraph in a document. Default tabs are always left-aligned. When you press → and then type, the text you type starts at the tab position and flows toward the right margin.

Custom tabs are those you place in the document. A custom tab applies only to those paragraphs that are selected when you create the tab. You can place custom tabs wherever you want, but Word deletes all default tabs to the left of them. Custom tabs may be left-aligned, center-aligned, right-aligned, or decimal-aligned, defined as follows:

Alignment	Description
Left	Text starts at the tab position.
Center	Text is centered on the tab position.
Right	Text ends at the tab position.
Decimal	Decimal points (periods) align at the tab position.

Custom tab positions are shown in the horizontal ruler, with different symbols indicating each type of alignment (see figure 6.2).

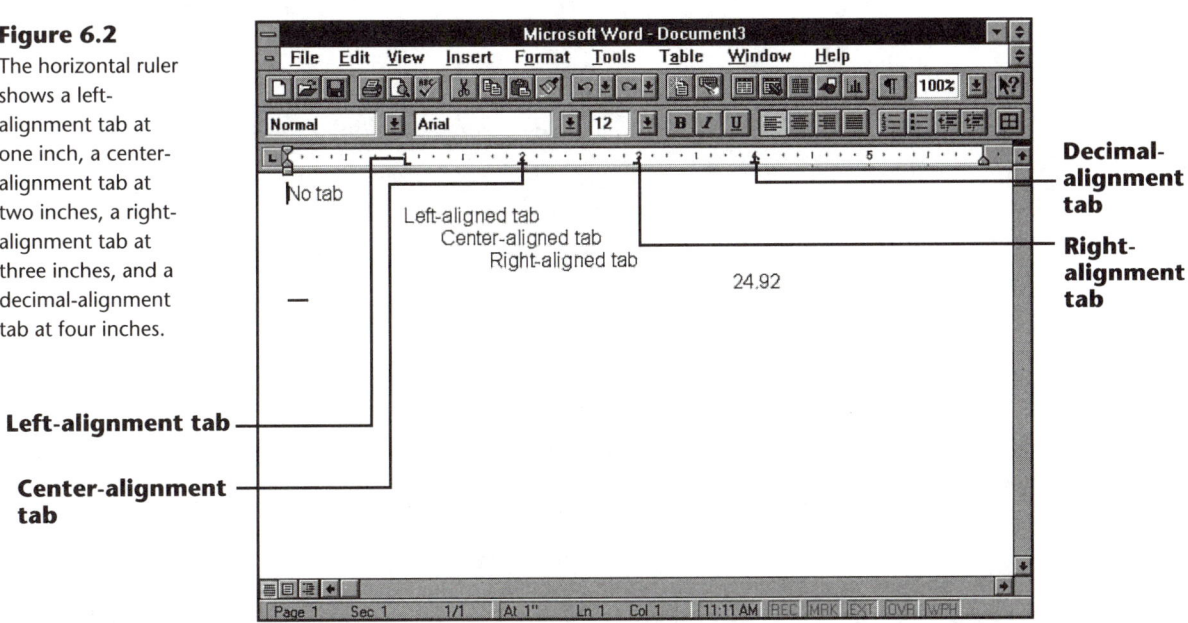

Figure 6.2
The horizontal ruler shows a left-alignment tab at one inch, a center-alignment tab at two inches, a right-alignment tab at three inches, and a decimal-alignment tab at four inches.

Notice that the ruler starts at the left edge of the document. The highlighted region in the ruler is the space between the left and right margins. You learn to set the position of these margins in Chapter 7.

The preceding illustration shows the effect of the four types of tab alignment. The first line contains text for which no tab is set, so the text starts at the left margin. The second line of text starts at a left-alignment tab. The third line is centered on a center-alignment tab. The fourth line ends at a right-alignment tab. The decimal point (period) in the number on the fifth line is aligned on a decimal-alignment tab.

You can fill the space at the left of a custom tab stop with dots, dashes, or underscore characters (known as leader characters). This is often done in tables, such as the table of contents at the front of this book.

Throughout this section, the term *tab* refers to custom tabs unless otherwise stated. You can set and delete custom tabs and change tab alignment by using one of these methods:

- The horizontal ruler and the mouse
- The Tabs dialog box

Using the Ruler and the Mouse to Set and Move Tabs

You can use the ruler and the mouse to set and delete custom tabs. Open POLICY2.DOC, and follow these steps.

1 If the Ruler is not displayed, open the **V**iew menu, and choose **R**uler.

2 Place the insertion point at the end of the document to begin using new tab positions.

3 Set the type of tab to add by clicking the symbol **L** at the extreme left end of the horizontal ruler.

Note: *Each time you click, the symbol changes—rotating through left, center, right, and decimal alignment. The three triangles on the ruler (one at the right end and two at the left end) control indentation, described later in this chapter.*

4 Place the insertion point at 2 inches inside the ruler to add a tab, and click the mouse button.

Word creates a custom tab at that location and deletes all the default tab stops to the left of it.

5 Repeat these steps to set a tab at 4.5 inches.

6 Type the following text, using the tabs, and press ⏎Enter twice:

    Serial Number   Name of Software   Price

7 Keep the document open.

To move a custom tab, drag it to the right or left in the ruler. To remove a custom tab stop, drag it down off the ruler (see figure 6.3).

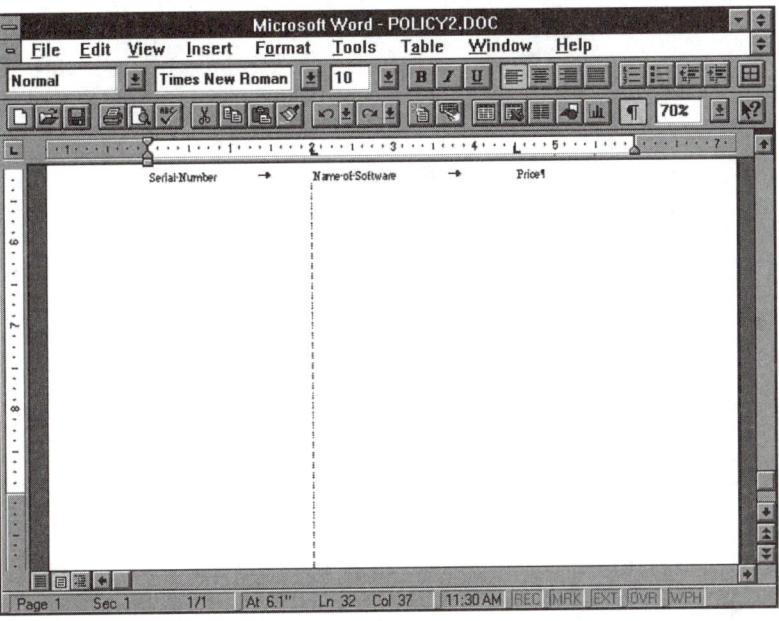

Figure 6.3
When you point to a tab position in the ruler and press the mouse button, a dashed line extends into the text area. As you drag, the dashed line moves, making it easy to align a tab with text already in the document.

Using the Tabs Dialog Box to Set, Change, and Delete Tabs

Using the Tabs dialog box, you can set tabs at precise points that are not obtainable by clicking or dragging in the ruler.

1. In the opened POLICY2.DOC, place the insertion point at the beginning of the line under the headings to begin using new tab positions, or select the paragraphs to which you want to add tabs.

2. From the Format menu, choose Tabs (see figure 6.4).

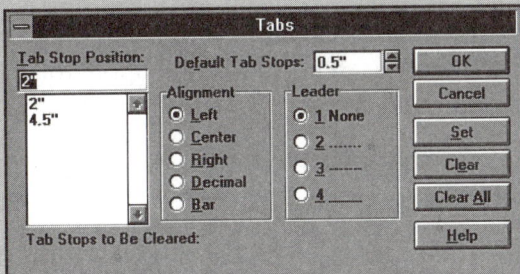

Figure 6.4
Use the Tabs dialog box to set or clear tab stops, set the spacing of custom tabs, and choose leader characters. If some custom tabs are already set, the dialog box lists them.

(continues)

Using the Tabs Dialog Box to Set, Change, and Delete Tabs (continued)

3 To set a custom tab, type **2"**, the position relative to the left margin in the **T**ab Stop Position text box. As soon as you type a number, the **S**et and Cl**e**ar buttons at the right side of the dialog box become active.

4 Choose **L**eft from the Alignment box.

5 Choose **1** for None to fill the space preceding the custom tab with dots, dashes, or a line, choose a character in the Leader box.

6 Click the **S**et button to store the custom tab setting. The position of the tab is shown in the Tab Stop Position list box.

When you set a custom tab, Word deletes all default tabs to the left of it.

7 Clear the 4.5-inch tab.

8 Repeat steps 3 through 6 to set additional custom tabs. Each tab position is added to the list box.

Set Tab 2 at 4.75 inches, select **D**ecimal for alignment and **1** for None.

9 Choose OK to accept all the tab settings and close the dialog box. The position of the tabs is indicated in the horizontal ruler.

10 Add the following text to the new tab line, and press ⏎Enter after all lines.

A1234	Word 6.0 For Windows	395.99
C4576	Excel 4.0 For Windows	449.99
P8909	Power Point 2.0	199.99

11 Save the document.

When you have two or more paragraphs selected and you open the Tabs dialog box, the box lists only those tab positions that apply to all the selected paragraphs. Each paragraph may have other tabs set.

The **B**ar alignment option causes Word to draw a vertical line through the paragraph at the specified tab position.

To remove a custom tab, click it in the **T**ab Stop Position list box, and then click the Cl**e**ar button. To clear all custom tabs, click the Clear **A**ll button. When you remove a custom tab, Word automatically re-creates default tabs in their normal positions to the right of the remaining custom tabs.

Note: *You can open the Tabs dialog box from the Paragraph dialog box or by double-clicking within the horizontal ruler. If you double-click where no tab currently exists, Word creates a tab at that position and opens the Tabs dialog box.*

Objective 3: Indent Paragraphs

Hanging indent
The first line of a paragraph starts further left than the remaining lines.

You can indent paragraphs by moving their left and right margins toward the center of the page. You can even extend paragraphs into the margins. Using Word, you can create a variety of indents, including *hanging indents*.

You can change paragraph indentation by using one of several methods:

- The horizontal ruler and the mouse
- The Formatting toolbar
- The keyboard shortcuts
- The Paragraph dialog box

Using the Formatting Toolbar to Change Indentation

By using the Indentation buttons in the Formatting toolbar, you can indent the left edge of paragraphs to default or custom tab positions, or change the indentation of paragraphs that are already indented.

The second button from the right in the Formatting toolbar—the *Increase Indent button*—increases paragraph indentation by moving the left edge of paragraphs to the right. The button at the left of this one—the *Decrease Indent button*—decreases indentation by moving the right edge of paragraphs to the left.

Indenting Paragraphs

1 In the opened POLICY2.DOC, place the insertion point at the beginning of paragraph two to begin indenting or select the paragraphs you want to indent.

If necessary, create a tab at the position in the horizontal ruler at which you want to indent paragraphs.

2 Click the Increase Indent button to indent the text to the next default or custom tab position.

If the selected paragraphs are already indented, click the Increase Indent button to increase the indentation.

or

Click the Decrease Indent button to decrease the indentation (see figure 6.5).

3 Keep the document open.

(continues)

Indenting Paragraphs (continued)

Figure 6.5
The text here is indented to the first tab position. Notice the triangular indentation marks near the left end of the ruler have moved to the indentation position.

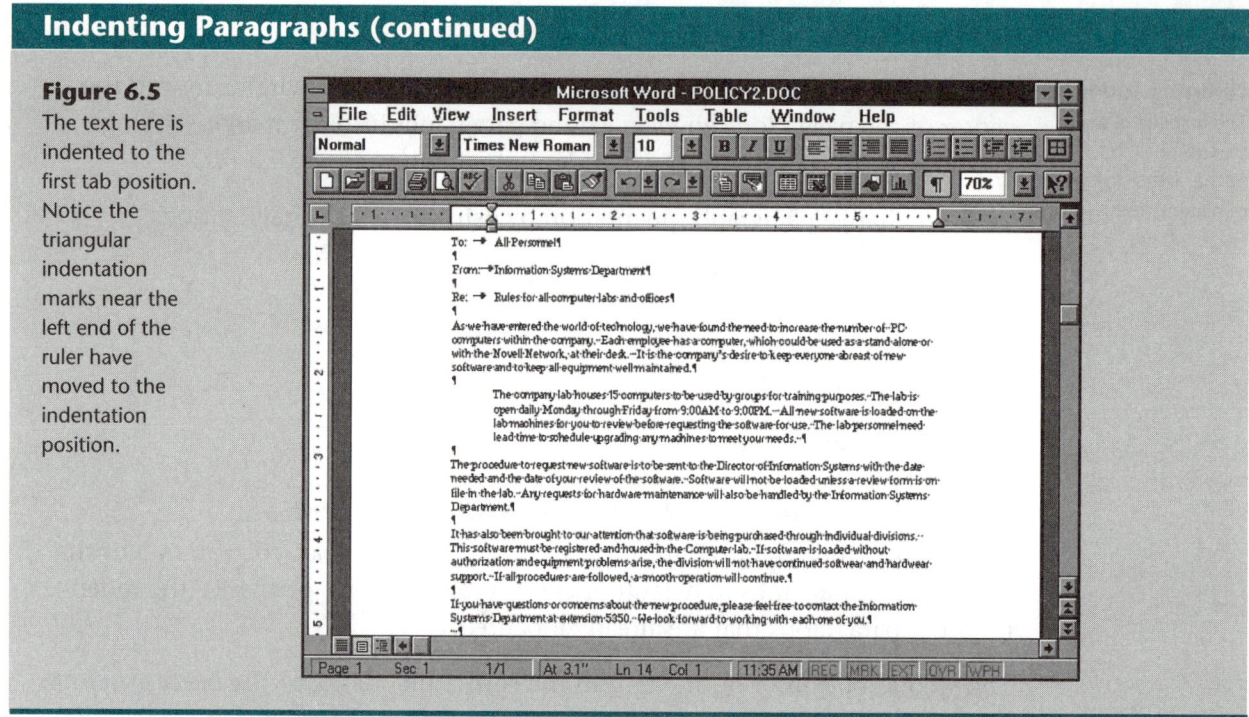

Using the Keyboard to Indent Paragraphs

You can use the keyboard to set normal and hanging indents based on default or custom tab positions.

Setting a Normal Indent

To set a normal indent in POLICY2.DOC, follow these steps:

1. Place the insertion point at the beginning of paragraph.

2. Press Ctrl + M to indent paragraph four to the first tab position (see figure 6.6).

Figure 6.6
The text in paragraph four is indented.

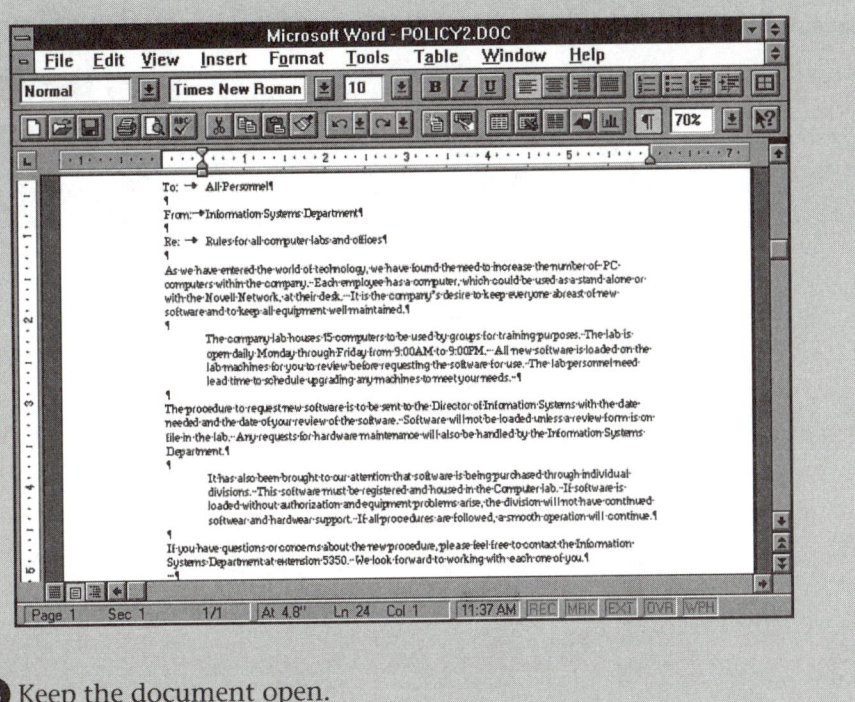

③ Keep the document open.

You can press the same shortcut key to indent the paragraph to subsequent tab positions.

To decrease paragraph indentation, press the key combination Ctrl+Shift+M.

Creating a Hanging Indent at the First Tab

To create a hanging indent at the first tab, follow these steps:

① In the opened POLICY2.DOC, place the insertion point at the beginning of paragraph one to begin a paragraph with a hanging indent.

② Press Ctrl+T to indent all lines except the first line to the first tab position (see figure 6.7).

(continues)

Creating a Hanging Indent at the First Tab (continued)

Figure 6.7
All lines are indented except the first line.

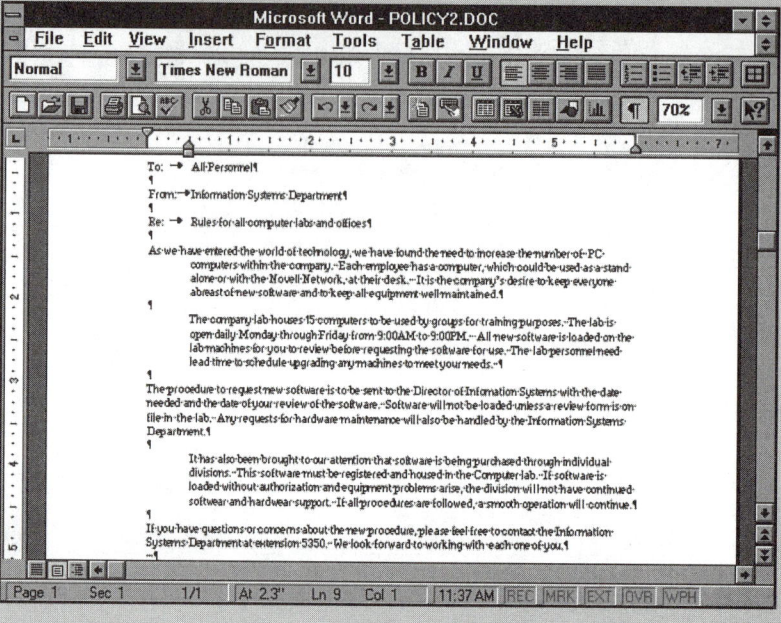

❸ Keep the document open.

You can press the same shortcut key to increase the hanging indent to subsequent tab positions.

To decrease paragraph indentation, press the key combination Ctrl+⇧Shift+T.

Using the Ruler and the Mouse to Indent Paragraphs

You can indent a paragraph by dragging indentation markers in the ruler. With this method, you can indent the following:

- The left side of a paragraph
- The right side of a paragraph
- The first line of a paragraph differently than other lines in the same paragraph

When you look at the preceding illustrations that show the ruler or or when you look at your screen, you see that the left end of the ruler contains a triangular marker at the top and another at the bottom, and the right end of the ruler contains one triangular marker at the bottom. You can control indentation by dragging these markers.

To indent a paragraph in POLICY2.DOC by dragging indentation markers in the ruler follow these steps:

❶ Place the insertion point inside paragraph three.

② Point to the indent marker at the right end of the horizontal ruler, and drag the marker about an inch to the left. As you drag, a dotted, vertical line moves in the document. When you release the mouse button, the right edge of the paragraph moves to the indented position.

③ Point to the lower indent marker at the left end of the horizontal ruler, and drag the marker about an inch to the right. When you release the mouse button, the left edge of all lines except the first line of the paragraph move to the indented position.

④ Point to the upper indent marker at the left end of the horizontal ruler, and drag the marker about an inch to the right. When you release the mouse button, the left edge the first line of the paragraph moves to the indented position (see figure 6.8).

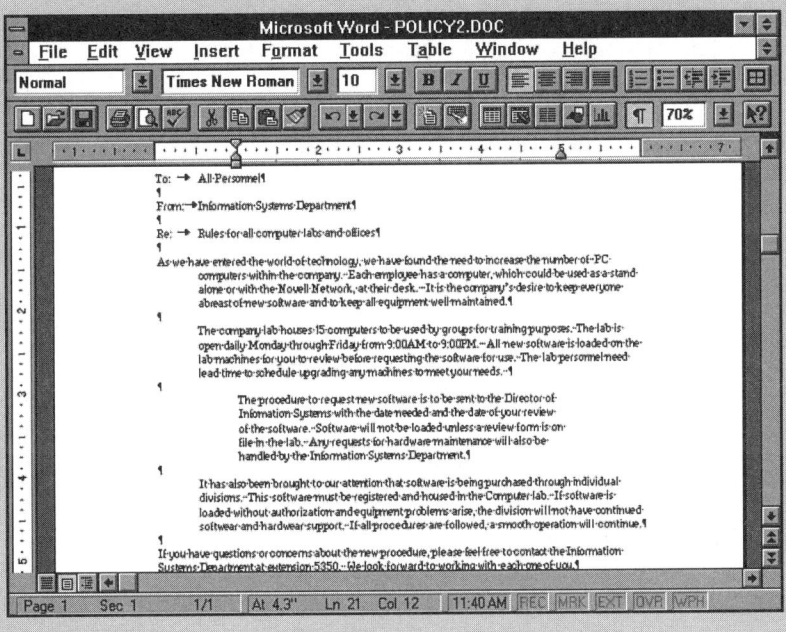

Figure 6.8
Paragraph three is indented by the steps just described. Note the positions of the indent markers in the ruler.

To extend the right edge of a paragraph into the right margin, drag the right indentation marker in the ruler into the margin.

Extending the left edge of a paragraph into the left margin is a little more complicated because you don't see the left margin in Normal view. There are two ways to solve this problem:

- Change to Page Layout view by opening the **V**iew menu and choosing **P**age Layout.

- Hold down ⇧Shift and click the left scroll arrow in the horizontal scroll bar.

The second method enables you to see the left margin while the document is in Normal view.

After you have made the left margin visible, you can drag the upper or lower left indent marker (or both) into the left margin. Word does not allow you to drag an indentation marker beyond the paper size set in the Page Setup dialog box.

Using the Paragraph Dialog Box to Indent Paragraphs

Using the Paragraph dialog box, you can set indentations to precise measurements that you cannot obtain by dragging in the ruler. You must select the paragraphs you want to indent before you open the Paragraph dialog box.

To open the Paragraph dialog box, open the **Fo**rmat menu and choose **P**aragraph. If necessary, click the **I**ndents and Spacing tab to show that section of the dialog box (see figure 6.9).

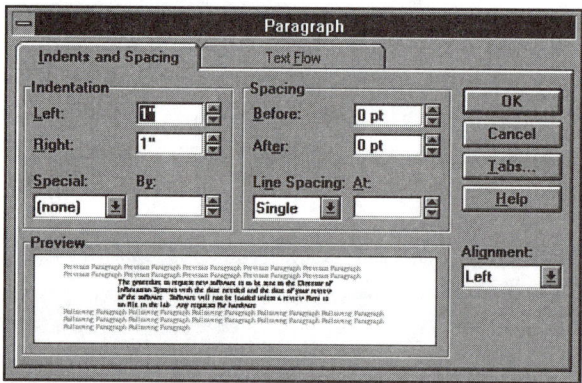

Figure 6.9
In the Indentation area, you can indent from the left or right margins or create special indentations.

While you work with the Paragraph dialog box, the Preview box indicates the effect of the choices you make.

You can set indentation measurements by clicking the arrows at the right of the **L**eft or **R**ight text boxes or by typing measurements in those boxes. Positive numbers move the indentation toward the center of the document; negative numbers move the indentation away from the center and even into the margins. Although Word shows abbreviations for measurement units in the text boxes, you don't have to type these abbreviations unless you want to use a measurement unit other than the default.

The measurement in the **L**eft text box defines the left indentation for all lines in the selected paragraph. To set the indentation of the first line of a paragraph at a different position than the indentation of the remaining lines, open the **S**pecial drop-down list box (see figure 6.10).

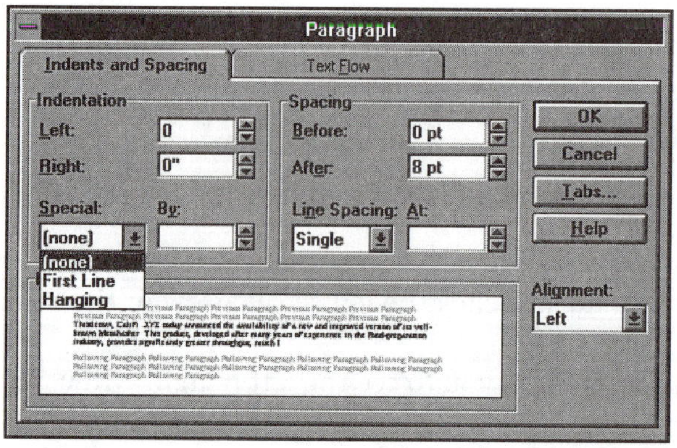

Figure 6.10
Use the Special drop-down list box to define an indentation for the first line of a paragraph.

Indenting the First Lines of Paragraphs to the Right

To move the indentation of the first lines of paragraphs to the right in POLICY2.DOC, follow these steps:

1. Place the cursor on the first letter of the first paragraph.

2. From the Format Paragraph menu dialog box, open the Special drop-down list box, and click First Line.

3. Use the arrows in the First Line text box to increase the indentation of the first line to 1.5, or type the number **1.5**. Word allows only positive numbers in the Special drop-down list box.

4. Choose OK.

5. Keep the document open.

You have indented paragraphs in various ways. After you have tried each exercise, you will find one method you use frequently.

Creating a Hanging Indent

To create a hanging indent in POLICY2.DOC, complete the following steps:

1. Place the cursor on the first letter of the second paragraph.

2. From the Format Paragraph menu dialog box, open the Special drop-down list box, and click Hanging.

3. Use the arrows in the Hanging text box to increase or decrease the distance the first line hangs over the remainder of the paragraph to 1, or type the number **1**. Word allows only positive numbers.

4. After you have set indentation measurements, choose OK to apply those values to the selected paragraphs in your document.

5. Choose OK.

6. Keep the document open.

Objective 4: Align Paragraphs

In Word, you can align text to the left or right margin, center text, or justify text. Figure 6.11 shows examples of the different alignments.

Figure 6.11
Here are examples of left-aligned, center-aligned, right-aligned, and justified text.

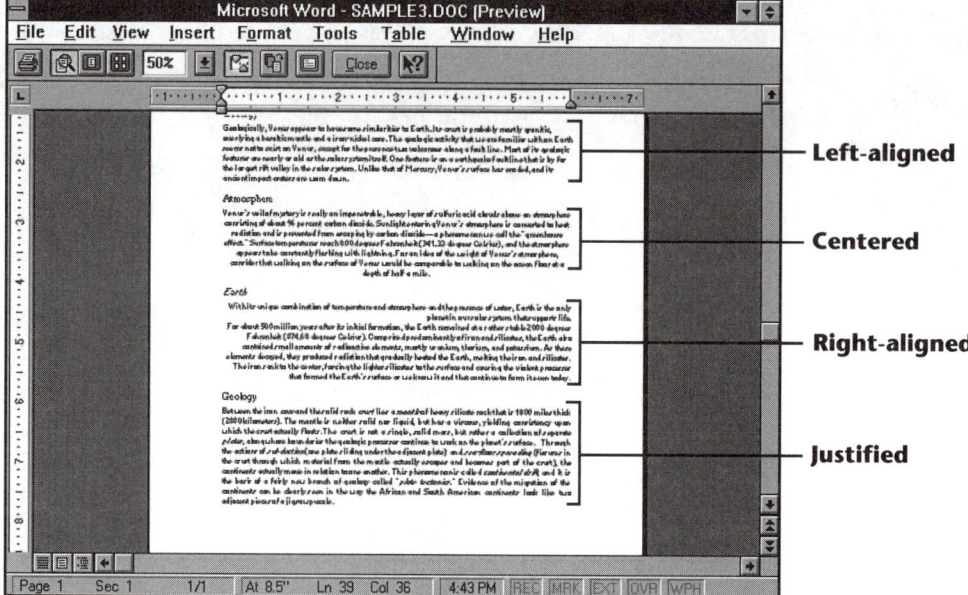

The paragraph at the top of the preceding illustration is left-aligned; all lines start at the left margin, and the right margin is ragged. The second paragraph is center-aligned; each line is centered on the page so that both margins are ragged. The third paragraph is right-aligned; all lines end exactly at the right margin, and the left margin is ragged. The bottom paragraph is justified; Word automatically adjusts the space between words so that all the lines except the last line in a paragraph start and end exactly at the margins.

You can change paragraph alignment, using one of three methods:

- The Formatting toolbar
- The keyboard
- The Paragraph dialog box

Using the Formatting Toolbar to Set Paragraph Alignment

To change paragraph alignment, place the insertion point in the paragraph, and click an alignment button. To set the alignment for a new paragraph, click an alignment button, and then type the text.

The Formatting toolbar contains four alignment buttons:

Button	Alignment
	Align Left
	Center
	Align Right
	Justify

When the insertion point is within a single paragraph or when a single paragraph is selected, one of the four alignment buttons is down to indicate the current alignment. If two or more paragraphs with different alignments are selected, all four alignment buttons are up.

Using the Keyboard to Set Paragraph Alignment

You can change paragraph alignment from the keyboard. Select one or more paragraphs, and then press one of the following key combinations:

Key Combination	Alignment
Ctrl+L	Align left
Ctrl+E	Center
Ctrl+R	Align right
Ctrl+J	Justify

To align a new paragraph, press one of these shortcut keys, and then type the paragraph.

Using the Paragraph Dialog Box to Set Paragraph Alignment

To use the Paragraph dialog box to set paragraph alignment in POLICY2.DOC, follow these steps:

1. Place the insertion point in paragraph five to align.

2. From the Format menu, choose Paragraph to display the Paragraph dialog box (see figure 6.12).

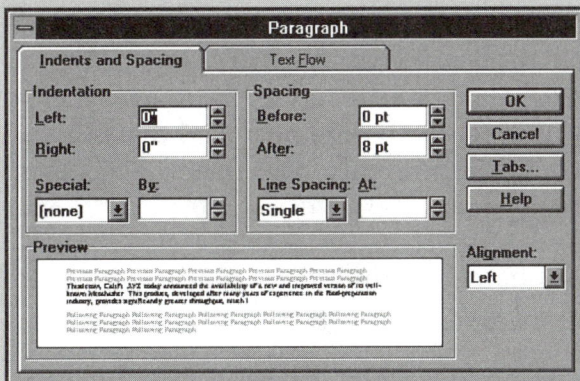

Figure 6.12
The text box at the lower right of the dialog box shows the current alignment.

3. Open the Alignment drop-down list box, and click Right.

   The alignment of paragraph five changes to right-aligned.

4. Keep the document open.

Objective 5: Use Automatic Hyphenation

Hyphens serve two purposes in the written English language:

- Hyphens join words together, as in *on-the-fly*.

- Hyphens divide words, enabling you to start a long word at the right end of one line and continue that word at the left end of the next line.

Note: *Don't confuse a hyphen with a dash. Unfortunately, on a typewriter, one key serves both purposes, but this isn't the case in Word. Use the hyphen key on the keyboard for the two purposes defined above. With NumLock turned off, you can use an en dash (Ctrl+- on the numeric keyboard) to represent a range, such as pages 1–15, or you can use the em dash (Ctrl+Alt+-) to represent a pause or break.*

Using Hyphens in a Document

When you are typing a document, you should type only the hyphens that join words together, such as *forget-me-not*. You should not normally break words at the end of a line and type a hyphen to continue the word at the beginning of the next line. Leave that for Word to do automatically.

Word offers three types of hyphens:

- Normal Hyphen. A normal hyphen acts almost like any other keyboard character. The only difference is that a word wrap occurs immediately after a normal hyphen that is close to the right margin. Press - to add a normal hyphen to your text.

- Nonbreaking Hyphen. Use this hyphen to join words that should *not* be split between lines. Press Ctrl+Shift+- to include a nonbreaking hyphen in your text.

- Optional Hyphen. Use this hyphen to join words that may be split between lines. If the entire word that contains an optional hyphen fits in a line, the hyphen is not displayed or printed. If the word occurs at the right end of the line, Word splits the word at the optional hyphen, which in this case is displayed and printed. Press Ctrl+- to include an optional hyphen in your text.

Figure 6.13 illustrates both the interaction between the three different types of hyphens and also how word wrap occurs.

Figure 6.13
The three different types of hyphenation are shown in this figure. Nonprinting characters are not displayed here.

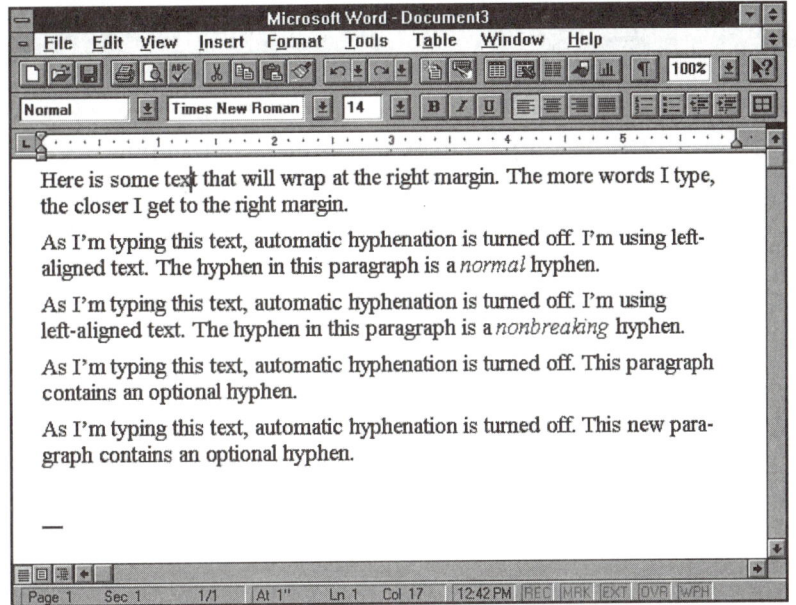

Hyphenating a Document Automatically

When you open a new document and start typing, Word does not use automatic hyphenation. Words are not broken at the right ends of lines except where you have included optional hyphens.

You can turn on automatic hyphenation before you start typing, or you can apply automatic hyphenation to existing text. To enable automatic hyphenation in the opened POLICY2.DOC, follow these steps:

1. From the **T**ools menu, choose **H**yphenation to display the Hyphenation dialog box (see figure 6.14).

Figure 6.14
Use the Hyphenation dialog box to select automatic hyphenation and to specify hyphenation parameters.

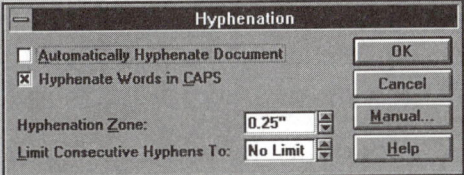

2. Click the **A**utomatically Hyphenate Document check box to turn on automatic hyphenation.

3. To disable automatic hyphenation of capitalized words, click the Hyphenate Words in the **C**APS check box to remove the ×.

4. Change the size of the hyphenation zone, and specify **3** as the maximum number of consecutive hyphens.

5. Choose OK to return to your document. Text in the document is shown hyphenated on-screen (see figure 6.15).

(continues)

Hyphenating a Document Automatically (continued)

Figure 6.15
The document displays hyphenation marks.

> As we have entered the world of technology, we have found the need to in-crease the number of computers within the company. All employees have computers, which can be used as stand-alones or with the Novell Network. It is the company's desire to keep everyone abreast of new software and to keep all equipment well-maintained.
>
> The company lab houses 15 computers to be used by groups for training pur-poses. The lab is open daily Monday through Friday from 9:00AM to 9:00PM. All new software is loaded on the lab machines for you to review before requesting the soft-ware for use. The lab personnel need lead time to sche-dule upgrading any machines to meet your needs.

❻ Keep the document open.

The *hyphenation zone* is the distance between the word at the end of a line and the right margin, within which Word tries to hyphenate words. A narrow hyphenation zone tends to reduce the raggedness of the document's right margin, whereas a wide zone reduces the number of hyphenated words.

After you have enabled automatic hyphenation, Word adjusts hyphenation as you type and edit text.

Hyphenating a Document Manually

Instead of setting Word to automatically hyphenate a document, you can use the setting for Word to suggest each place where hyphenation is possible; then you accept or reject the suggestion. To hyphenate POLICY2.DOC manually, follow these steps:

❶ Place the insertion point at the beginning of the document to start manual hyphenation.

❷ Choose **T**ools, **H**yphenation, and click the **M**anual button.

Word analyzes the document and, when it reaches a place where hyphenation is possible, displays the Manual Hyphenation dialog box (see figure 6.16).

Figure 6.16
Word offers a hyphenation suggestion.

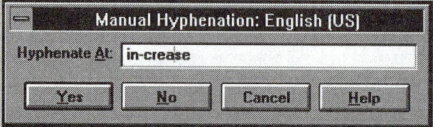

3 To accept hyphenation, click where you want to hyphenate the displayed word, and click the **Y**es button. To reject hyphenation, click the **N**o button.

To stop the hyphenation process, click Cancel.

4 Close the document.

Automatic hyphenation normally applies to an entire document; however, you can exclude specific paragraphs from hyphenation.

Excluding a Paragraph from Automatic Hyphenation

To exclude a paragraph in POLICY2.DOC from automatic hyphenation, follow these steps:

1 Open POLICY2.DOC, and select paragraph one to exclude from automatic hyphenation.

2 From the F**o**rmat menu, choose **P**aragraph to open the Paragraph dialog box.

3 If necessary, click the Text **F**low tab to display that section of the dialog box.

4 Click the **D**on't Hyphenate check box to place an × in it. The selected paragraph is no longer hyphenated (see figure 6.17).

Figure 6.17
The paragraph displays without hyphenation mark.

> As we have entered the world of technology, we have found the need to increase the number of computers within the company. All employees have computers, which can be used as stand-alones or with the Novell Network. It is the company's desire to keep everyone abreast of new software and to keep all equipment well-maintained.
>
> The company lab houses 15 computers to be used by groups for training pur-poses. The lab is open daily Monday through Friday from 9:00AM to 9:00PM. All new software is loaded on the lab machines for you to review before requesting the soft-ware for use. The lab personnel need lead time to sche-dule upgrading any machines to meet your needs.

5 Choose OK to return to your document.

6 Close the document.

If Word had previously hyphenated the selected paragraphs, hyphenation is removed. If the document is subsequently hyphenated, the selected paragraphs are excluded.

Objective 6: Control Line Spacing

Paragraph formatting enables you to control line spacing within paragraphs and line spacing between paragraphs. In each case, you can specify spacing in terms of lines or in terms of specific measurements.

By default, Word uses single-line spacing, in which the spacing between lines is determined by the size of the characters in the line. If a line contains characters of different sizes, the largest character in the line determines the line spacing. The default line spacing is a little larger than the size of the font to allow enough space between lines.

Using the Keyboard to Set Line Spacing within Paragraphs

To set line spacing, select one or more paragraphs; then press one of the following shortcut keys:

Key Combination	Line Spacing
Ctrl+1	Single
Ctrl+5	One and one-half
Ctrl+2	Double

Using the Paragraph Dialog Box to Set Line Spacing within Paragraphs

To set line spacing in POLICY2.DOC, follow these steps:

1. Select the first two paragraphs.

2. From the Format menu, choose Paragraph to open the Paragraph dialog box.

3. Choose Line Spacing. The drop-down list box appears (see figure 6.18).

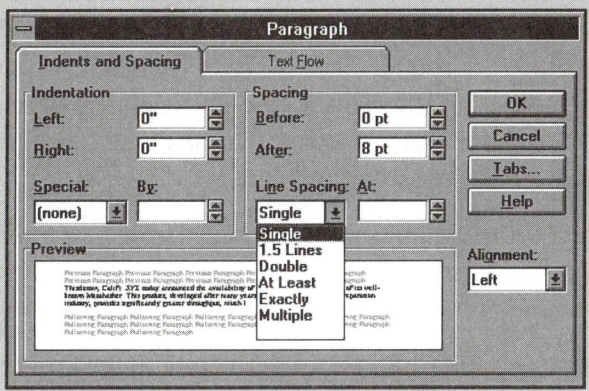

Figure 6.18
The Line Spacing drop-down list box offers a choice of six line spacings.

The available line spacings are the following:

- Single. Lines are spaced according to the height of the largest character in each line.

- 1.5 Lines. Lines are spaced at one and one-half times the height of the largest character in each line.

- Double. Lines are spaced at double the height of the largest character in each line.

- At Least. Lines are spaced at the distance set in the **A**t text box, or more if required to accommodate larger characters.

- Exactly. Lines are spaced at exactly the distance set in the **A**t text box, even if this space is not large enough to show complete characters.

- Multiple. Lines are spaced at a multiple of the size of the largest character on each line.

4 Click Double in the Line Spacing drop-down list box to set the line spacing for the selected paragraphs.

5 Choose OK to apply that spacing to the selected paragraphs.

6 Repeat the process for each of the options. When you choose At Least, Exactly, or Multiple, you must specify a value in the **A**t text box. Experiment by using different values. Remember to choose OK to leave the dialog box and see the changes to the selected paragraphs.

7 Close the document without saving it.

Setting the Space Between Paragraphs

This book has extra space between paragraphs, and you may want to format your documents similarly. If you use a typewriter, you are probably accustomed to pressing the carriage-return key to create a space between paragraphs.

In Word, you can use the same method to create extra space between paragraphs if you are working with a single-page document. If you do this for multipage documents, however, you are likely to have problems. When you edit paragraphs, the chances are that somewhere in the document the last line of a paragraph is right at the bottom of a page. Consequently, the next page will start with a blank line that doesn't look right.

To avoid this problem, you can format each paragraph to have space after it. Word automatically ignores this extra space if it comes at the top of a page. By doing this, you eliminate the possibility of pages starting with a blank line.

Formatting paragraphs with extra space before them works similarly. In this case, Word ignores the blank space before a paragraph if that paragraph is at the top of a page.

One way to set a space between paragraphs is to select a paragraph and then press Ctrl+0 (zero). This shortcut key adds a 12-point space (1/6 of an inch) before the paragraph.

Another way to set spaces is to open the **F**ormat menu and choose **P**aragraph to open the Paragraph dialog box (see figure 6.19).

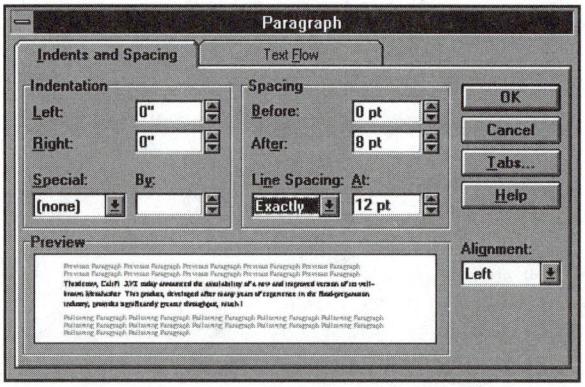

Figure 6.19
Under Spacing in the Paragraph dialog box are the **B**efore and Aft**er** text boxes.

Use the **B**efore or Aft**er** text boxes (or both) to define the space before or after the selected paragraphs. Word displays the space in points. If you type or select a number, Word interprets that number as points. You can specify the spacing in another unit of measurement by adding the abbreviation for the measurement unit after the number (see "Set the Unit of Measurement," at the beginning of this chapter, for information about this procedure).

After you have set the spacing between paragraphs, choose OK to apply the spacing you have set to the selected paragraphs.

Using the Paragraph Dialog Box Text Flow Options

So far, this chapter has presented only the **I**ndents and Spacing section of the Paragraph dialog box. The Text **F**low section provides other ways to control paragraph formatting.

Four of the option buttons in this section control the way Word separates documents into pages. With none of these options selected, Word simply creates a new page whenever the current page is full. The options in the Text Flow section modify Word's treatment of a new page.

Click the Text **F**low tab in the Paragraph dialog box to display these options (see figure 6.20).

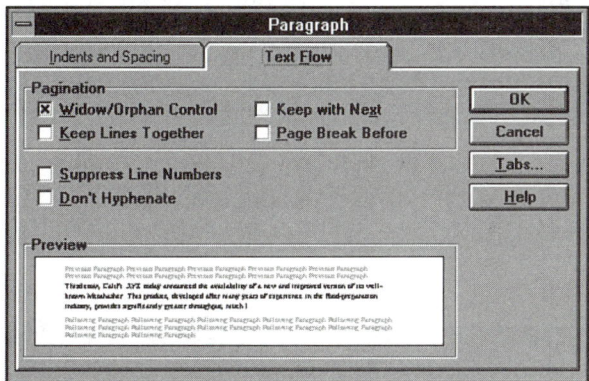

Figure 6.20
The Text Flow section of the Paragraph dialog box contains six options you can enable or disable in any combination.

The following six options are in the Text **F**low section of the Paragraph dialog box.

Option	Function
Widow/Orphan Control	Prevents the first line of a paragraph from appearing at the bottom of a page, and prevents the last line of a paragraph from appearing at the top of a page. To prevent either of these circumstances, Word moves the last line of a page to the next page whenever necessary.
Keep Lines Together	Prevents a page break within a paragraph.
Keep With Ne**x**t	Prevents a page break between the selected paragraph and the next paragraph.
Page Break Before	Always places the paragraph at the top of a new page.
Suppress Line Numbers	With line numbering selected, omits selected paragraphs from the line numbering sequence (see Chapter 7 for information about line numbering).
Don't Hyphenate	Excludes the paragraph from automatic hyphenation.

Note: *The Keep With Next option is particularly useful for headings. Apply this option to each heading paragraph to prevent the possibility of a heading occurring at the bottom of a page and the text under that heading starting on the next page.*

Click the options to enable or disable them according to your requirements.

Objective 7: Remove and Repeat Paragraph Formatting

To simplify your work, Word enables you to remove, repeat, and copy formatting quickly. To remove all paragraph formatting applied to selected paragraphs, select those paragraphs and press Ctrl+Q.

> ### Repeating Paragraph Formatting from One Paragraph to Another
>
> In the opened POLICY2.DOC, repeat paragraph formatting by following these steps:
>
> **1** Apply double-spacing to paragraph five.
>
> **2** Immediately after applying the formatting, select paragraph two to which you want to apply the same formatting.
>
> **3** From the **E**dit menu, choose the **R**epeat Paragraph command (or press F4).

If you applied several formats by using the Formatting toolbar, the ruler, or the keyboard, Word repeats each formatting operation one at a time, starting with the most recent.

Objective 8: Apply Borders and Shading to Paragraphs

Shading
A dotted pattern that creates the effect of a highlight.

Shadow
A box that creates the effect of a shadow.

With Word, you can emphasize paragraphs by *shading* or by placing borders around, above, below, or beside them.

Adding Borders to Paragraphs

Borders are lines placed above, below, or at either side of a paragraph, or any combination of these. Borders can be drawn in various line styles, thicknesses, and colors, and can include a *shadow*. A shadow adds a three-dimensional look to the border.

You can add borders by using the Paragraph Shading and Borders dialog box, or you can use the Shading toolbar.

> ### Applying a Border Completely around One or More Paragraphs
>
> To apply a border to the opened POLICY2.DOC, follow these steps:
>
> **1** Select paragraph three to which you want to apply a border. If you don't select a paragraph, Word applies the border to the paragraph that contains the insertion point.
>
> **2** From the F**o**rmat menu, choose **B**orders and Shading to display the Paragraph Borders and Shading dialog box (see figure 6.21).

Figure 6.21
You can specify the type of border you want in the Borders section of the Paragraph Borders and Shading dialog box.

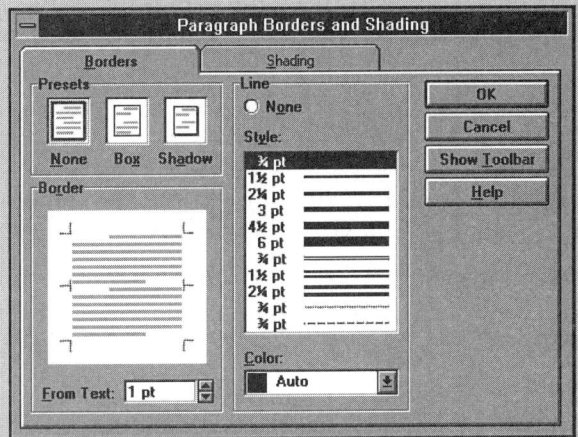

③ To select the type of border you want, click the **B**orders tab at the top of the dialog box to display that section of the dialog box. Notice that the dialog box contains a Bo**r**der sample that shows bordered text. While you make changes in this dialog box, you can see the effect of those changes in the sample.

④ Under Presets, click Sh**a**dow.

⑤ In the St**y**le list, select 3/4 (thickness).

⑥ Open the **C**olor list box, and click Blue for the color.

⑦ In the **F**rom Text text box, accept the default value for the space between the text in the paragraph and the border.

⑧ Choose OK to create the border around the selected paragraphs (see figure 6.22)

Figure 6.22
A shadow border is drawn around paragraph three.

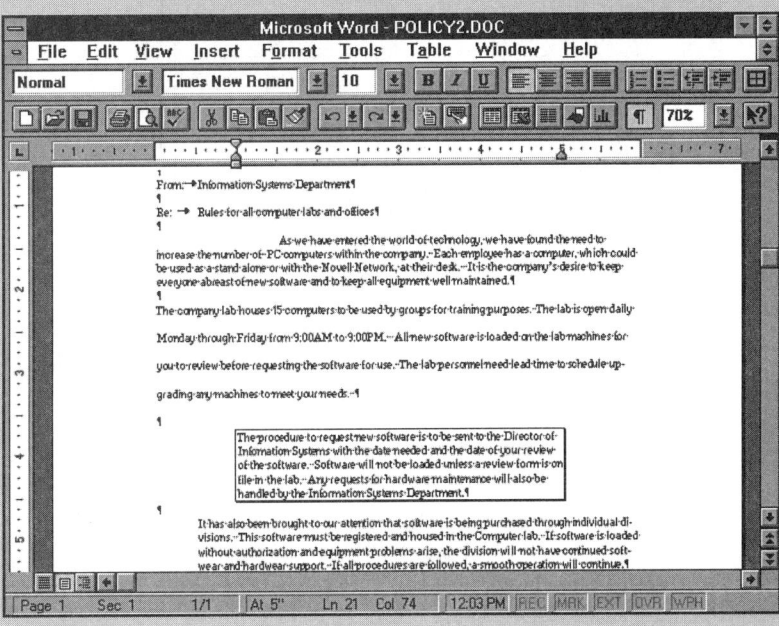

Note: *Notice that the border shown in the preceding figure extends to the margins. This occurs because these lines of text are within the margins shown in the ruler. If you want the right side of the border to be close to the text, indent the right side of the paragraphs. Then the side of the border will be at the indentation position.*

You can use the **B**order sample box to identify which sides of a border are to be drawn. You can create a border consisting of just the left and right sides, for example. When you click Bo**x** or Sh**a**dow in the dialog box, border markers appear on all four sides of the sample. You can remove the border from any side by clicking on that border in the sample. You can replace a border by clicking where that border should be in the sample. To remove the top and bottom edges of the border, just click those edges in the sample.

Using the Paragraph Borders and Shading Dialog Box

You can shade paragraphs in a similar manner to the way you add borders.

Note: *Before you spend time shading paragraphs throughout a document, shade a typical paragraph, print it, and examine the results. If you use any more than very light shading, you will probably find that it is difficult to read text within the shaded paragraph. The effect is even more pronounced when you make photocopies of shaded paragraphs.*

To shade paragraphs, select one or more paragraphs to be shaded, open the Paragraphs Borders and Shading dialog box, and select the **S**hading tab (see figure 6.23).

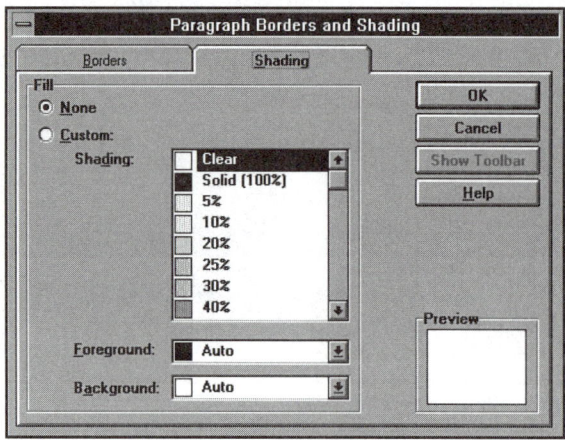

Figure 6.23
Use the Shading section to choose which shading patterns to apply to selected paragraphs.

In the Sha**d**ing list box, you can choose the percentage of gray in the shading. If you scroll further down the list box, you can choose from a variety of shading patterns. When you click a percentage of gray or a shading pattern, the Preview box at the bottom right of the dialog box shows your selection.

By default, Word creates shading with black dots on a white background and patterns with black lines on a white background. In both cases, black is the foreground color, and white is the background color. If you are going to print your work on a color printer, you can choose different foreground and background colors. Just open the **F**oreground and B**a**ckground drop-down list boxes, and choose colors.

After you have selected appropriate shading in the dialog box, choose OK to apply the shading to the selected paragraphs.

To remove shading from selected paragraphs, choose **S**hading **N**one from the Paragraph Borders and Shading dialog box, and then choose OK.

Creating Borders and Shading with the Shading Toolbar

You can display the Shading toolbar in two ways:

- Click the Show **T**oolbar button in the **S**hading section of the Paragraph Borders and Shading dialog box.

- From the **V**iew menu, choose **T**oolbars, check Borders in the Toolbars dialog box, and choose OK (see figure 6.24).

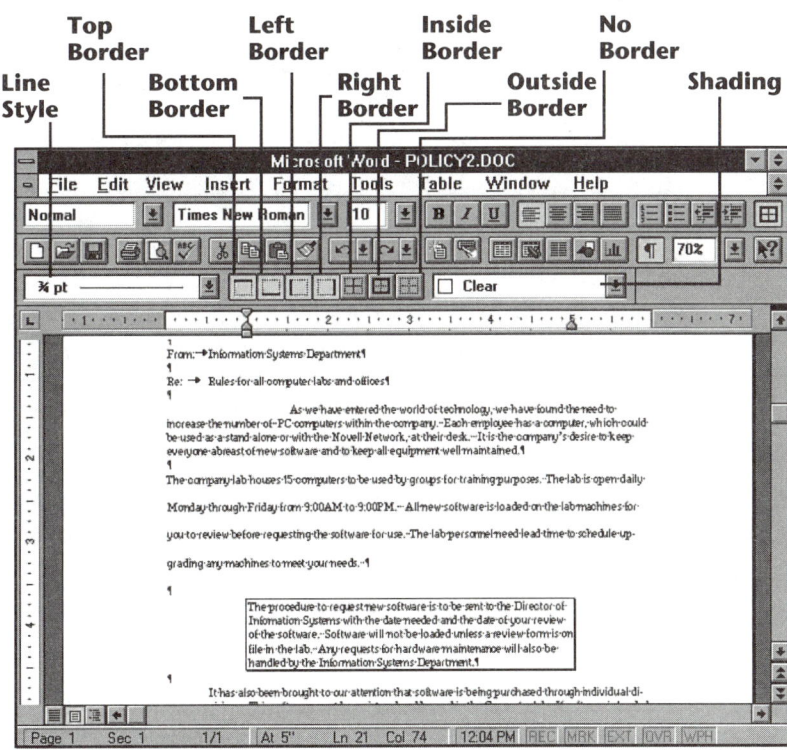

Figure 6.24
Use the Shading toolbar, shown just above the ruler, to apply borders as well as shading and patterns to selected paragraphs.

Applying Shading

To use the Shading toolbar, follow these steps:

1 Open POLICY2.DOC, and select paragraph three.

2 Click the Shading button to display the drop-down list.

3 Select 10%. The paragraph is shaded (see figure 6.25).

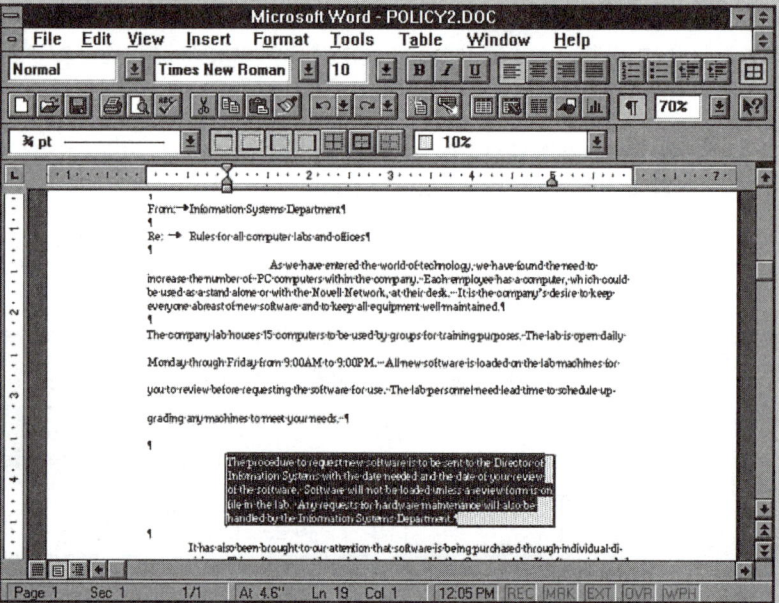

Figure 6.25
Paragraph three of the document is shaded.

4 Close the document.

5 After you have finished using the Shading toolbar, remove it by opening the **V**iew menu, choosing **T**oolbars, unchecking Borders, and choosing OK.

Objective 9: Create Bulleted and Numbered Lists

Many types of documents contain lists. To make it easy for readers to see the individual items on the list, you can put each item on a separate line rather than in a continuous paragraph.

To add more emphasis to separate items and to indicate clearly where each item begins when some items occupy more than one line, you should place a marker, known as a bullet, at the beginning of each item.

Using a bullet to mark the beginning of each item implies that the order of the items has no particular significance. In cases in which the order is important, you can number the items rather than use bullets. You can do this when you are listing the steps in a procedure or when you are listing priorities.

Word can automatically add bullets or numbers to a list.

Creating a Bulleted List

To create a bulleted list, follow these steps:

1 In the opened POLICY2.DOC, create the following list of software needed at the end of the document:

Software List

Microsoft Excel

Microsoft Word 6.0 For Windows

Microsoft Power Point 2.0

2 Select the three items to be included in the bulleted list (see figure 6.26).

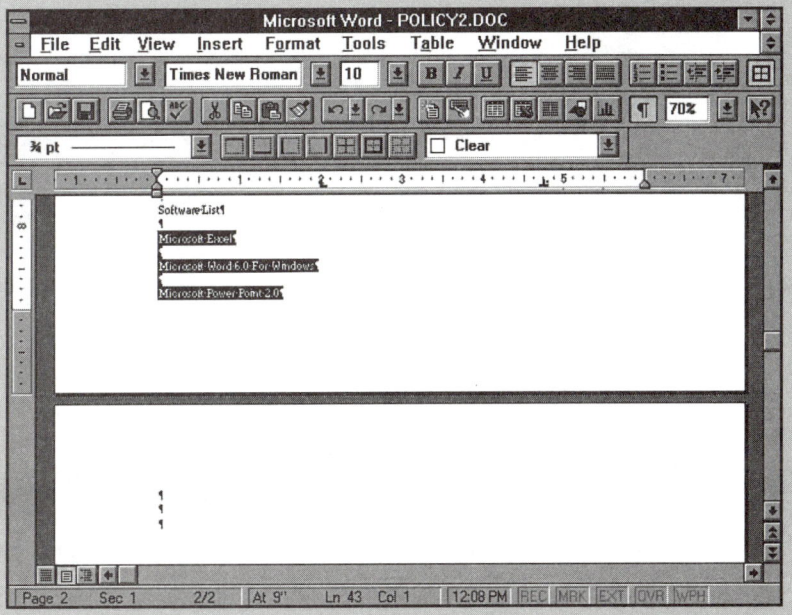

Figure 6.26
The items in the list are selected.

 3 Click the Bullets button on the Formatting toolbar (see figure 6.27).

(continues)

Creating a Bulleted List (continued)

Figure 6.27
Word automatically adds bullets to the list, as shown here.

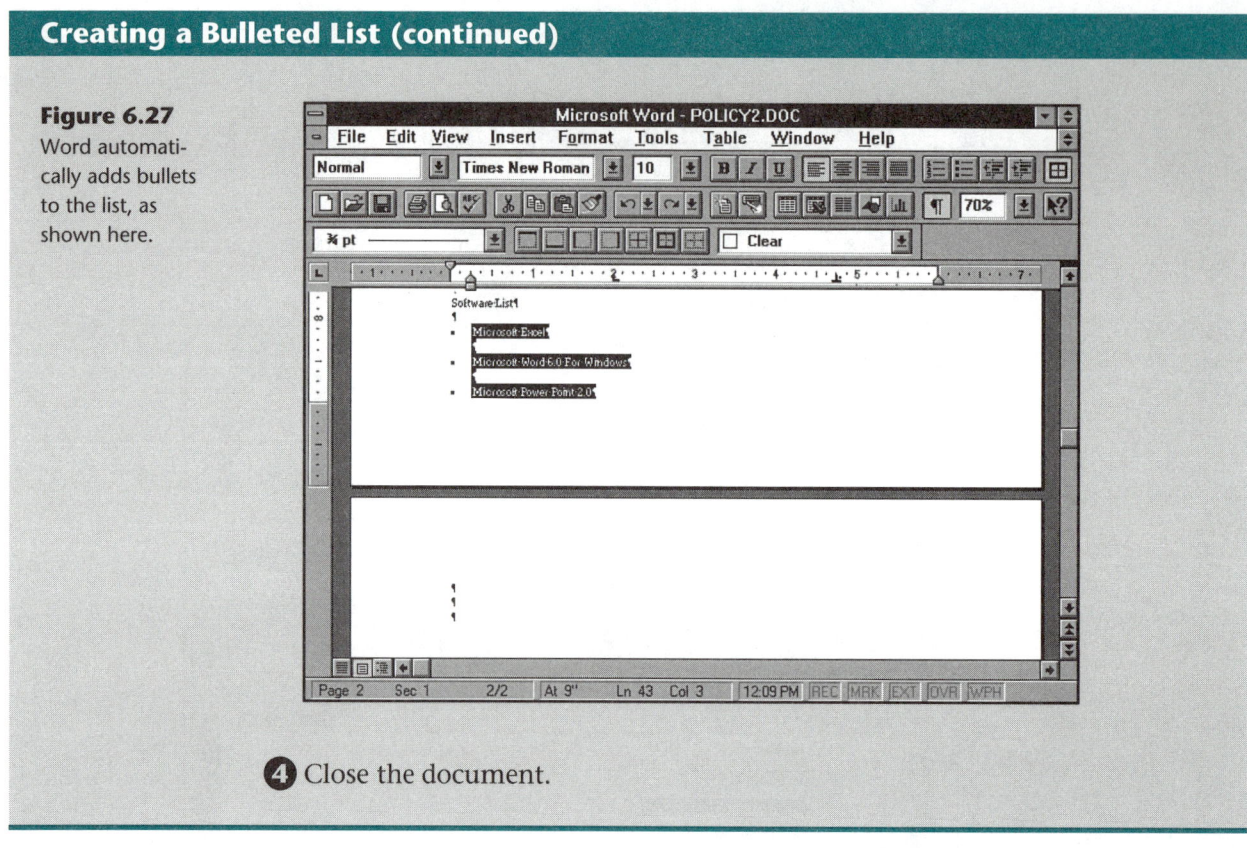

④ Close the document.

If you want a numbered list rather than a bulleted list, use the same procedure except, in step 3, click the Numbering button in the Formatting toolbar—the button immediately to the left of the Bullets button.

Tip

As always, you can undo bulleting or numbering by opening the **E**dit menu and choosing **U**ndo.

Objective 10: Create an Outline

Before you begin writing a document, particularly a long one, you should organize your thoughts by preparing an outline. You can use Word to create your outline and then, instead of referring to the outline as you write, you can prepare your document by filling in the details within the outline. As you work, you can switch back and forth between the Outline view, which focuses on the headings and structure of the document, and the Normal view of the document.

Beyond these basic capabilities, Word outlining simplifies adjusting the outline and the document. Word automatically applies to the document any structural changes you make to the outline.

Outlining is based on the standard nine heading styles of Heading 1, Heading 2, and so on. Heading 1 is used for main headings; Heading 2, for first-level subheadings; Heading 3, for second-level subheadings, and so on.

Creating an Outline

To create an outline, follow these steps:

1 Open a new document.

2 Switch to Outline view by clicking the Outline button on the horizontal scroll bar or by opening the **V**iew menu and choosing **O**utline (see figure 6.28).

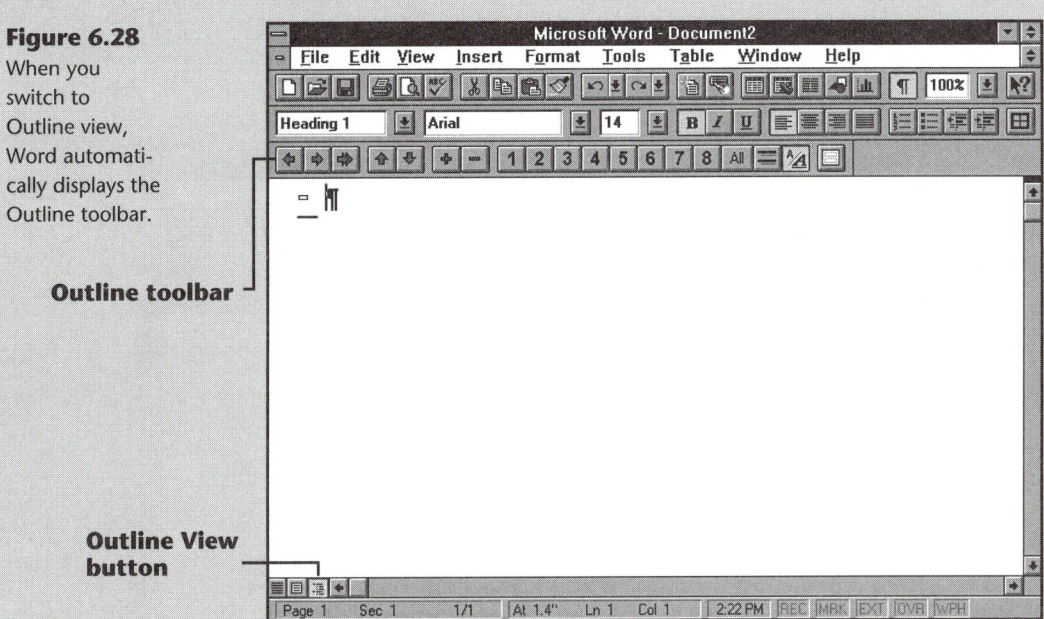

Figure 6.28
When you switch to Outline view, Word automatically displays the Outline toolbar.

Outline toolbar

Outline View button

Note: *Unlike other toolbars, you cannot display the Outline toolbar from the Toolbar dialog box. However, the Outline toolbar functions the same way that other toolbars function. When you point to a button, a ToolTip shows the button's name, and the status bar displays a brief explanation of its purpose. The Outline toolbar disappears when you switch to another view.*

The symbols on the left side of the screen indicate headings and subheadings. Initially, in an empty document, a single horizontal bar at the left indicates the location where Word expects to place the first heading.

3 Type the following heading, and press ⏎Enter:

Needs Assessment

A similar bar appears on the next line, showing that Word is ready for the next heading.

(continues)

Creating an Outline (continued)

④ Continue typing the following headings one after another, ending each by pressing `Enter`:

User Group

Software

Hardware

Maintenance

Your document should look like the one in figure 6.29.

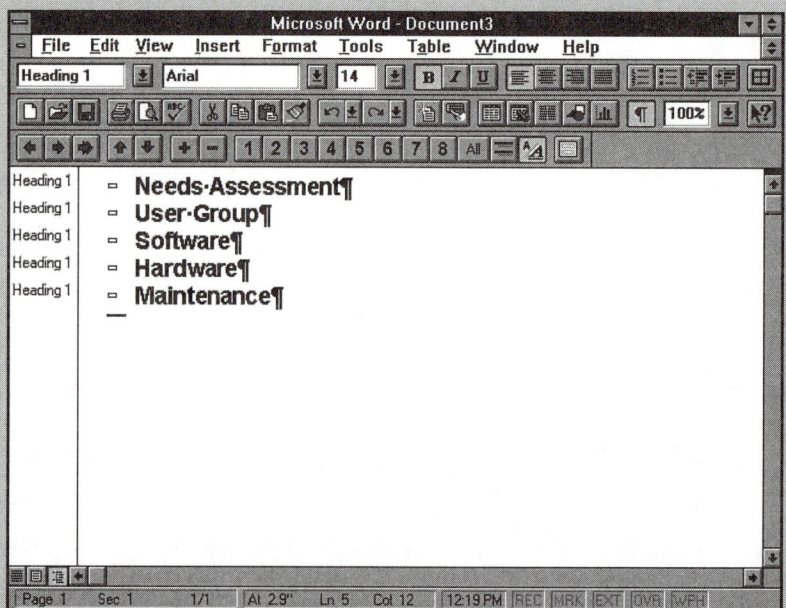

Figure 6.29
The set of main headings in an outline.

⑤ Save the file to your data disk as **SOFTWARE.DOC**, but keep the document open.

This illustration shows the headings with the style area displayed. The style area here illustrates that Word automatically assigns the Heading 1 style to your main headings, causing the heading text to appear in a certain font, font size, and font style.

After you have completed your first version of main headings, you are ready to add subheadings.

Creating Subheadings

To create subheadings in the file titled SOFTWARE.DOC, follow these steps:

① Place the insertion point at the right end of the first heading, and press `Enter` to create a new line.

Word shows a blank line with the same bar at the left as the other lines.

② To make this line a subheading, click the Demote button (the right arrow) on the Outline toolbar (see figure 6.30).

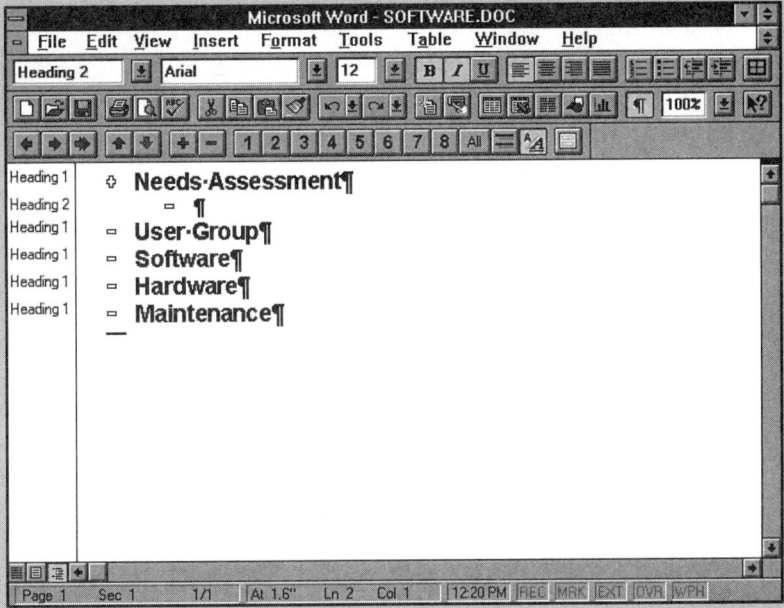

Figure 6.30
This example shows the outline after a new blank line has been created and the Demote button has been pressed.

Note: *Instead of clicking the Demote button, you can press* Tab *to enter a subheading.*

Notice that the blank line has been demoted to a subheading, with the bar moved to the right, and that the style for that line is Heading 2. Notice also that the bar at the left of the main heading above it has changed to a plus sign. The plus sign in a heading indicates that subheadings are located under it.

③ Type the following text under *Needs Assessment*, pressing Enter at the end of each line:

Present System

Volume of Data Processed

Word Force

④ Type the following text under *User Group*, pressing Enter at the end of each line:

Management

Clerical

(continues)

Creating Subheadings (continued)

5 Type the following text under *Software*, pressing ↵Enter at the end of each line:

    Accounting

    Word Processing

    Database

6 Type the following text under *Hardware*, pressing ↵Enter at the end of each line:

    IBM Compatible

7 Type the following text under *Maintenance*, pressing ↵Enter at the end of each line:

    3-Year Plan

Figure 6.31 shows the outline with the new subheadings.

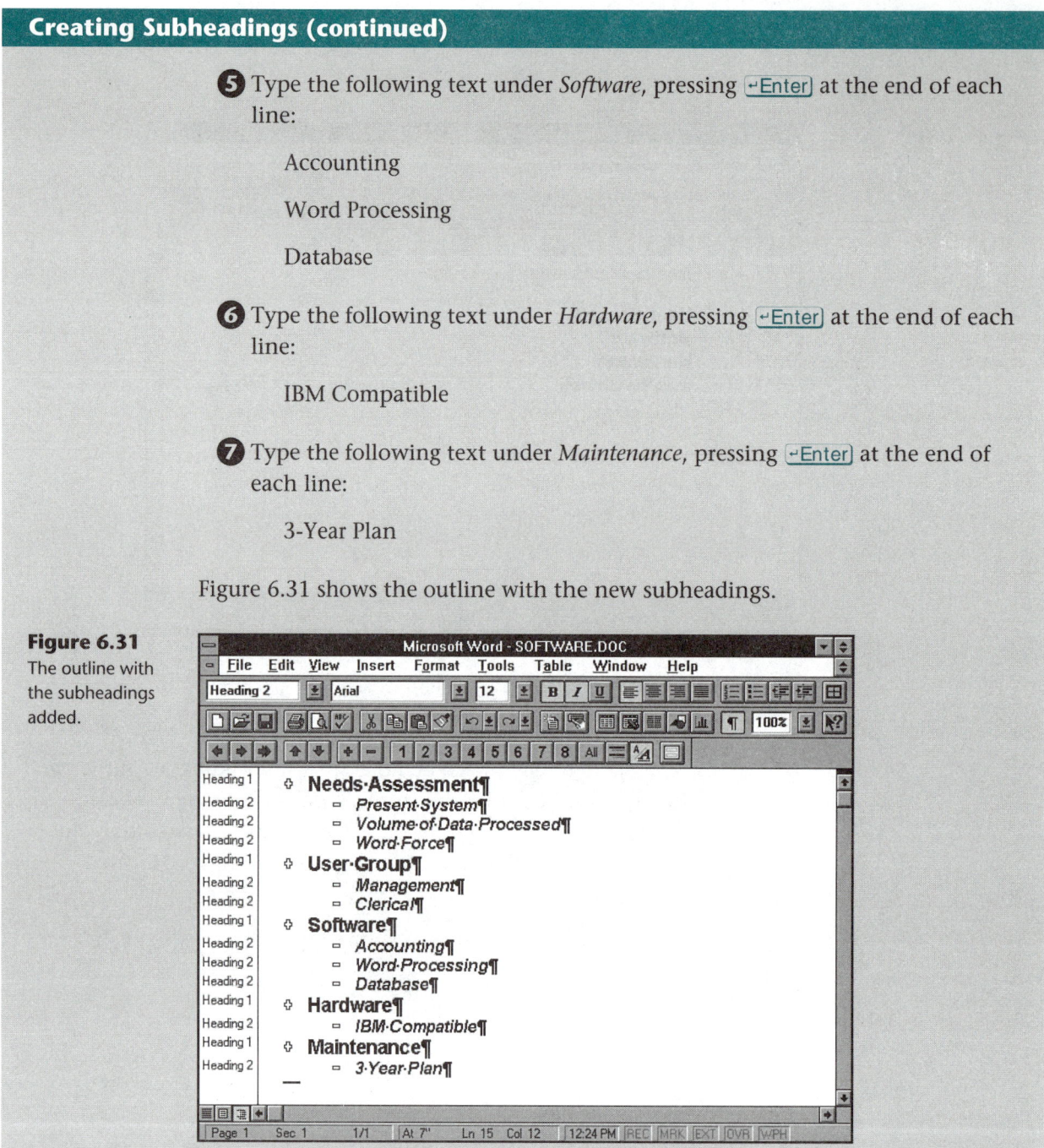

Figure 6.31
The outline with the subheadings added.

After you fill in your subheadings, you can add another level of subheadings. Although you may not use a second level of subheadings in the final document, these subheadings can serve to remind you of what you want to include in separate paragraphs.

Adding Second-Level Subheadings

You add second-level subheadings under first-level subheadings in the same way that you added subheadings under main headings. To add second-level subheadings to SOFTWARE.DOC, follow these steps:

1 Create a blank line under the subheading *IBM Compatible*.

2 Demote that line to the next level.

3 Type the text, **Digital**, and press ↵Enter (see figure 6.32).

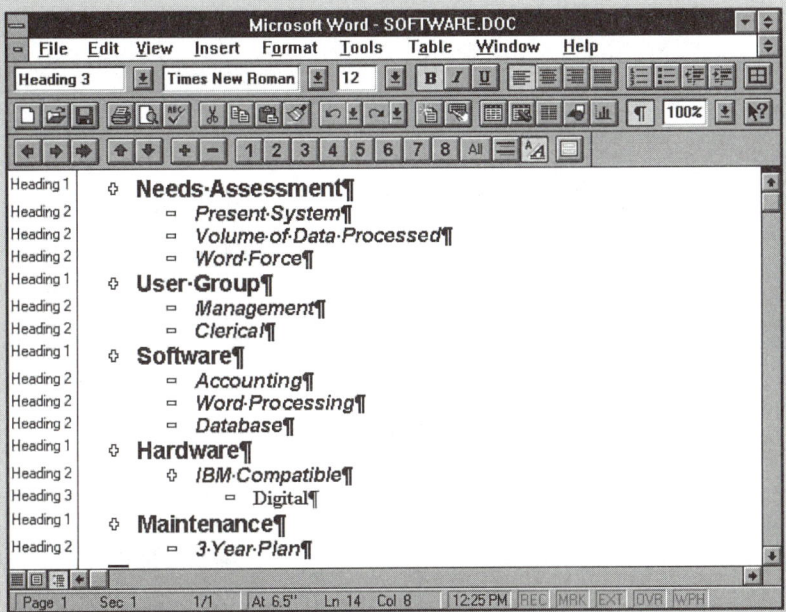

Figure 6.32
The outline displays a main heading and two sublevels.

Add as many second-level subheadings as you want. Continue in this way, adding subheadings and creating some third-level subheadings if you want. Notice that each level of subheadings is automatically given a different heading style.

4 Save and close the document.

Changing the Level of Headings

Promoting
To raise a subheading to a higher heading level.

Demoting
To move a heading to a lower heading level.

You can promote and demote items in your outline at any time. *Promoting* raises a subheading to a higher heading level—a second-level subheading to a first-level subheading, and so on. *Demoting* moves a heading or subheading to a lower level.

To promote a heading, place the insertion point within that heading and click the Promote button (at the left end of the Outline toolbar). If you want to promote or demote a heading together with the subheadings under it, select the heading and the subheadings under it by pointing to the left of the heading, pressing the mouse button, and dragging down. Release the mouse button when the heading and subheadings are all selected. Then click the Promote or Demote button in the toolbar to promote or demote the heading and subheadings as a group.

Changing the Order of Headings

At some point, you may want to change the order of the headings in your outline. To move a heading or subheading that has lower-level subheadings one position up or down in the outline, follow these steps:

1. In the opened SOFTWARE.DOC, point to the marker at the left of the Clerical heading, and click the mouse button to select the heading.

2. Click the Move Up button (the up-arrow button on the Outline toolbar). The selected heading and its subheadings immediately move up or down one position in the structure.

3. Return the selected Clerical subheading to its original position by clicking the Move Down button (the down-arrow button on the Outline toolbar).

You can move headings more than one position by repeatedly clicking the Move Up or Move Down buttons, or you can drag headings up or down by one or more positions.

Collapsing and Expanding Headings

At times, you may want to view all headings and subheadings. At other times, you may want to see only main headings, or perhaps just main headings and first-level subheadings, so that you can see the big picture without being distracted by details. This process of hiding lower-level subheadings is known as collapsing an outline. Similarly, the process of showing hidden subheadings is known as expanding an outline. You can collapse and expand the outline for the entire document or just for parts of it.

To change the levels of headings displayed, follow these steps:

1. Click the button labeled 1 on the Outline toolbar.

   Just the main headings appear; you have collapsed the outline (see figure 6.33).

Figure 6.33
Click the numbered buttons on the Outline toolbar to select the level of headings displayed.

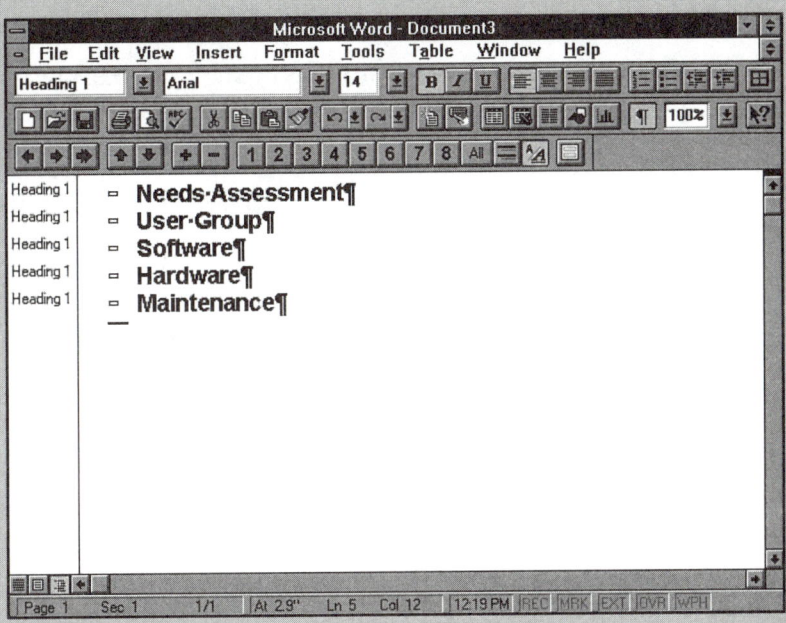

You can click the other numbered buttons on the Outline toolbar to show increasing levels of subheadings or the All button to show all levels of headings.

2 To expand the outline, place the insertion point within the first heading.

3 Click the + button on the Outline toolbar.

4 To collapse just the Needs Assessment group, place the insertion point in that group, and click the - button on the Outline toolbar.

Only the first level of heading appears.

5 Click the + button on the Outline toolbar to redisplay the Needs Assessment group.

Note: *You always know when a displayed heading has lower-level subheadings by the plus sign displayed at the left.*

When you are working with an outline, you may have ideas for paragraphs in addition to headings. You can use fourth-level headings as reminders for paragraphs then and convert these headings into text later.

Working with Text in an Outline

To convert the Software subheading in SOFTWARE.DOC into text, follow these steps:

1. Place the insertion point on the Software heading, and click the Demote to Body Text button (the double right arrow on the Outline toolbar).

   Body text is always the lowest level in the outline structure; you cannot add lower-level subheadings to body text. Word assigns the Normal style to body text.

2. Type whatever body text you want.

3. Delete the text that you just typed, leaving the word *Software*.

4. With the insertion point in the word *Software*, click the Promote button on the Outline toolbar. Software is again a heading.

If you have problems... As you type, you may find that your text does not appear on-screen. If you type the first few words and see only an ellipsis (...), the Show First Line Only button on the Outline toolbar is pressed. To deactivate that button, click the Show First Line Only button.

Remember that the collapsing and expanding of outlines is completed in the Outline view.

Returning to Normal View

After you have finished your first version of an outline, you may want to continue working on the document in Normal view. To do so in the opened SOFTWARE.DOC, follow these steps:

1. Click the Normal View button in the horizontal scroll bar.

   The Normal view of the document contains the headings, subheadings, and body text you created in Outline view (see figure 6.34). The small black squares at the left of each heading and subheading indicate that these items were created in Outline view. They do not appear in Print Preview or in the printed document.

Figure 6.34
The Normal view displays small black squares at the left of each heading and subheading, indicating that these items were created in Outline view.

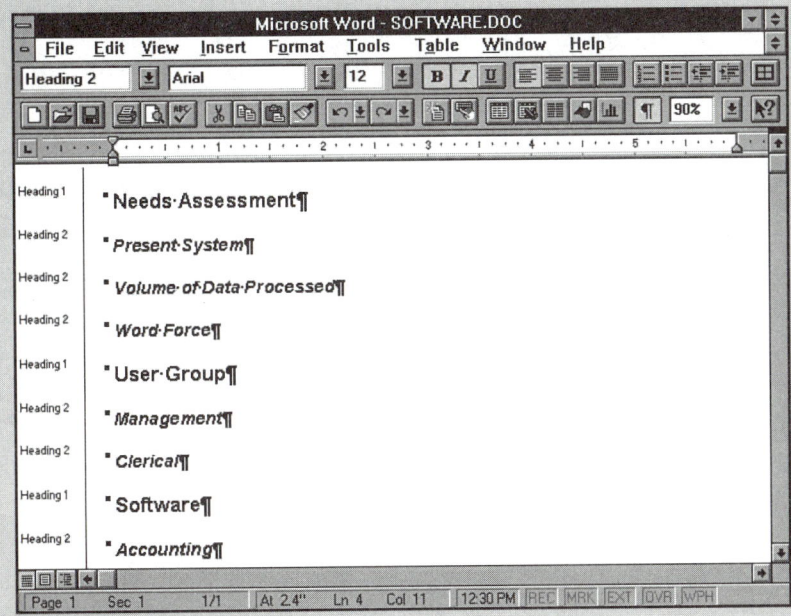

➋ Place the insertion point at the end of the Needs Assessment heading, and press ⏎Enter.

➌ Type the following paragraph:

> Computer marketers have done their job well. Most people believe that they should have a computer and feel that they are sadly behind the times if they don't have a computer. Despite the pressures by marketers, however, the first step in our study begins with two questions:
>
> Do we need to become computerized? How will we use a computer system?

Note: *To retain the structure of the document, always return to Outline view to insert or delete headings and subheadings.*

Although you can move headings and the text under them from place to place in a document using the editing techniques you learned in Chapter 3, outlining provides an easier way.

Moving Sections of the Document

To move the entire Needs Assessment group to the end of SOFTWARE.DOC, follow these steps:

➊ Switch to Outline view.

➋ Collapse the document so that only the main headings show.

(continues)

Moving Sections of the Document (continued)

3 Place the insertion point within the Software heading.

4 Click the Move Down button on the Outline toolbar.

5 Switch to Normal view. The entire Needs Assessment group has moved down (see figure 6.35).

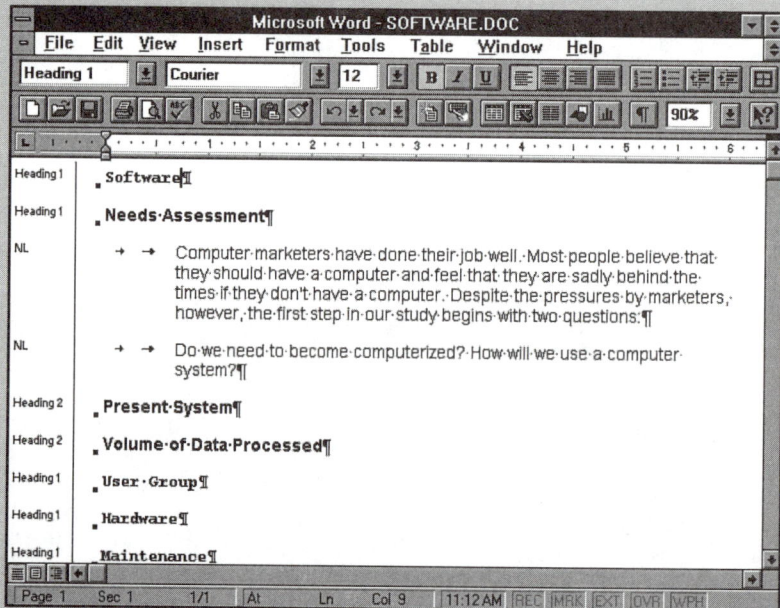

Figure 6.35
Use the Outline view to move entire sections of a document.

6 Press `Alt`+`Backspace` to return the Needs Assessment group to the beginning of the document.

When you switch back to Normal view, all text under the selected heading precedes the other heading. This process is much easier than cutting to the Clipboard and then pasting, especially if many pages of text are involved.

Numbering Headings

You can automatically number headings in Outline view. To number headings in SOFTWARE.DOC, follow these steps:

1 Change to Outline view.

2 From the Format menu, choose Heading Numbering to display the Heading Numbering dialog box (see figure 6.36).

Figure 6.36
You can choose among six numbering schemes.

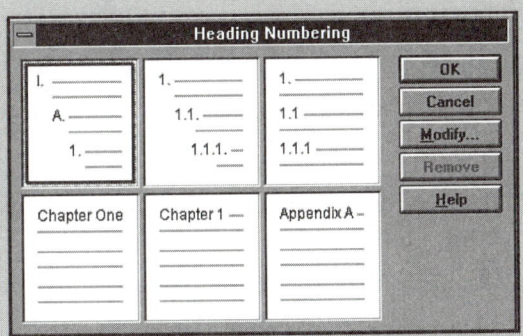

❸ Click the numbering scheme I., A., 1., and then choose OK. Word applies the numbering scheme to the outline (see figure 6.37).

Figure 6.37
Word automatically numbers your headings according to the scheme you choose.

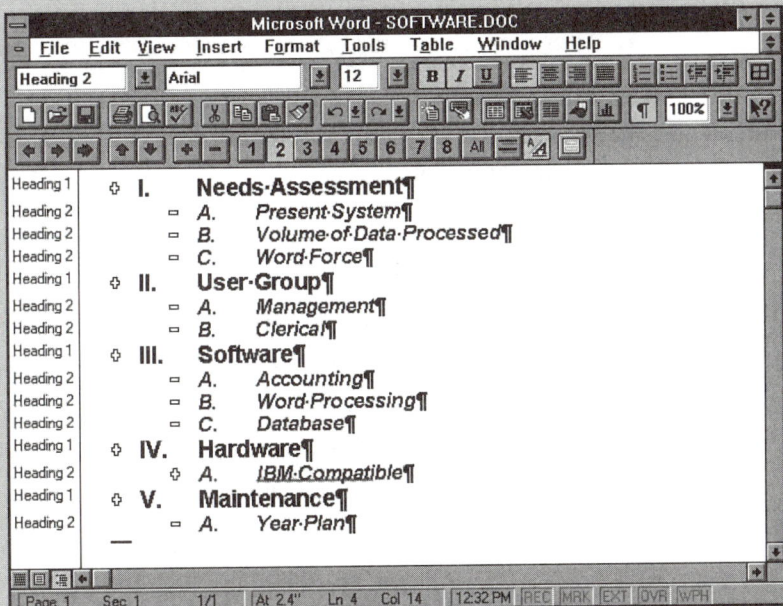

❹ Save the file to your data disk as **OUTLINE.DOC**.

Chapter Summary

This chapter contains valuable information about the Word formatting tools. You have used many formatting features and may find only selective ones to be useful. However, remember the resources available to you; you may need them in the future.

In the next chapter, you will learn to use page formatting features including changing margins, adjusting page size, adding headers and footers, and using other page layout techniques.

Checking Your Skills

True/False Questions

For each of the following statements, circle *T* or *F* to indicate whether the statement is true or false.

T F **1.** You can use the Measurement Units drop-down list box to choose inches, centimeters, points, or picas.

T F **2.** Default tabs apply only to the first and last paragraphs of a document.

T F **3.** You can indent paragraphs by moving their left and right margins toward the center of the page.

T F **4.** Word can align text to the left or right margin, center text, or justify text.

T F **5.** After you select the Outline view, you cannot return to the Normal view.

T F **6.** Word stores all paragraph formatting in the paragraph mark at the end of the paragraph.

T F **7.** You can change the distance between default tabs, but you cannot change custom tabs.

T F **8.** The measurement of the left text box defines the right indentation for all lines in the selected paragraph.

T F **9.** The Widow/Orphan Control prevents the first line of a paragraph from appearing at the top of a page and prevents the last line of a paragraph from appearing at the bottom of a page.

T F **10.** With Word, you can emphasize paragraphs by *shading* or by placing borders around, above, below, or beside them.

Multiple-Choice Questions

In the blank provided, write the letter of the correct answer for each of the following questions.

_____ **1.** With Word, you can apply various aspects of paragraph formatting by using the _____.

    a. Tabs dialog box

    b. horizontal ruler dialog box

    c. Paragraph dialog box

    d. Copy toolbar

    e. Font toolbar

Checking Your Skills

___ **2.** You can set and delete custom tabs and change tab alignment by using ___.

    a. the horizontal ruler and the mouse

    b. the Tabs dialog box

    c. the Paragraph dialog box

    d. the Format toolbar

    e. both a and b

___ **3.** You can use the keyboard to indent text to the left by pressing ___.

    a. Ctrl+I

    b. Ctrl+N

    c. Ctrl+M

    d. Ctrl+T

    e. Ctrl+L

___ **4.** The option that is **NOT** available in the Text Flow section of the Paragraph dialog box is ___.

    a. **W**idow/Orphan Control

    b. **K**eep paragraphs together

    c. **P**age Break Before

    d. **K**eep With Ne**x**t

    e. **D**on't Hyphenate

___ **5.** To add more emphasis to separate items and to indicate clearly where each item begins when some items occupy more than one line, you should place a marker, known as a(n) ___.

    a. asterisk

    b. dash

    c. equal sign

    d. bullet

    e. double asterisk

___ **6.** A tab that applies only to those paragraphs that are selected when you create a tab is a ___ tab.

    a. left

    b. decimal

    c. custom

d. default

   e. right

___ 7. Which of the following is not an alignment button on the Formatting toolbar?

   a. Align left

   b. Left Justify

   c. Center

   d. Align right

   e. Justify

___ 8. Lines spaced at double the height of the largest character in each line are said to use ____ spacing.

   a. double

   b. single

   c. 1.5

   d. At least

   e. Multiple

___ 9. To apply a border to the left of selected paragraphs, click the ____ button.

   a. Top Border

   b. Left Border

   c. Inside Border

   d. Outside Border

   e. No Border

___ 10. Unlike other toolbars, the Toolbar dialog box cannot display the ____ toolbar.

   a. Standard

   b. Border

   c. Formatting

   d. Outline

   e. Drawing

Fill-In-the-Blank Questions

In the blank provided, write the correct answer for each of the following questions.

1. The _____ dialog box provides the most complete way to format paragraphs because it includes most of the paragraph formatting options.

2. You can use the _____ and the _____ to set and delete custom tabs.

3. The _____ _____ button increases paragraph indentation by moving the left edge of paragraphs to the right.

4. If two or more paragraphs with different alignments are selected, all four _____ buttons are up.

5. The _____ zone is the distance between a word at the end of a line and the right margin, within which Word tries to hyphenate words.

6. To move a _____ tab, drag it to the right or left in the ruler.

7. You can _____ paragraphs by moving their left and right margins toward the center of the page.

8. To simplify your work, Word enables you to remove, repeat, and copy _____ quickly.

9. You can add borders by using the _____ Shading Borders dialog box.

10. Using a _____ to mark the beginning of each item implies that the order of the items has no particular significance.

Applying Your Skills

Review Exercises

Exercise 1: Indenting Paragraphs

Practice indenting paragraphs by following these steps:

1. Open the FIRST.DOC, and indent the first paragraph from both the left and right margin.

2. Create a hanging indent for the second paragraph.

3. Save the file to your data disk as **FIRST.DOC**.

Exercise 2: Using Custom Tabs

In the following exercise, you use custom tabs.

1. Open the SCHEDULE.DOC, and add the following data to the end of the document using custom tabs. The tabs could be 1.5 Left, 2.5 Left, 4.0 Center, and 6.0 Decimal for the headings.

Date	Fund Raiser	Time	Fee
04/02/94	Bake Sale	9:00AM-4:00PM	0.00
05/01/94	Fashion Show	6:00PM-11:00PM	20.00
06/01/94	Craft Fair	9:00AM-6:00PM	15.00

  2. Save the file to your data disk as **SCHEDULE.DOC**.

Exercise 3: Centering a Paragraph

Practice centering a paragraph by following these steps:

  1. Open the MEDII.DOC, and center the paragraph.

  2. Set the line spacing to double-space the paragraph.

  3. Save the file to your data disk as **MEDII.DOC**.

Exercise 4: Creating a Bulleted List

To practice creating a bulleted list, follow these steps:

  1. Open a new document, and type the following lines, creating a bulleted list.

     Word For Windows Content:

     Chapter 1 covered working with Word screens.

     Chapter 2 covered editing existing documents.

     Chapter 3 covered checking your work.

     Chapter 4 covered managing and printing files.

     Chapter 5 covered enhancing a document.

     Chapter 6 covered formatting a paragraph.

  2. Save the file to your data disk as **CONTENT.DOC**.

Exercise 5: Applying Borders and Shading

To practice applying borders and shading to a document, follow these steps:

  1. Open GUIDELINE.DOC, and add a border to item 4.

  2. Shade item 2.

  3. Save the file to your data disk as **GUIDELINE.DOC**.

Continuing Projects

Project 1: Practice in Using Word

Suppose that you are asked to write an article about how colleges and high schools communicate for the student's college search process. Create the following outline with three sublevels:

I. Orientation at the High School

      A. Fall Orientation

      B. Spring Orientation

   II. College Fairs

      A. Fall College Fairs

         1. October at Hale School

         2. November at Civic Center

      B. Spring College Fairs

         1. March at University

         2. May at Civic Center

   III. Testing

      A. Dates

         1. December

         2. May

      B. Courses

         1. Private

         2. Public

Save the file to your data disk as **COLLEGE.DOC**.

Project 2: Federal Department Store
Continue your work on the catalog for the Federal Department Store by following these steps:

1. Open OUTFIT.DOC, and center the company name.

2. Add item numbers to each item—for example, S225 for the cardigan.

3. After the opening paragraph, create the following numbered list for ordering merchandise:

   1. Select the items of your choice in the catalog.

   2. Have the item number available.

   3. Have a credit card or method of payment available.

   4. Call 1-800-233-WEAR

4. Create paragraphs with hanging indents for each item description.

5. Create borders, and shade each item name.

6. Save the file to your data disk as **OUTFIT.DOC**.

Project 3: Real Entertainment Corporation

Continue your work on the newsletter for Real Entertainment Corporation by following these steps:

1. Open the REC.DOC, and center the headings *Real Entertainment Corporation* and *Marketing Department*.

2. Double-space the second paragraph.

3. Create a hanging indent for paragraph two.

4. Copy the format of the second paragraph to the last paragraph.

5. Add shadow borders to the headings.

6. Create a bulleted list at the end of the document. Use the list as follows:

    Department Articles:

    *Sales

    *Marketing

    *Tours

    *Travel

    *Accounting

7. Save the file to your data disk as **REC.DOC**.

CHAPTER 7

Formatting a Page

Header
Text that appears at the top of each page.

Footer
Text that appears at the bottom of each page.

In Chapters 5 and 6, you worked with formatting features for characters and paragraphs. In this chapter, you learn how to use formatting features to enhance the look of your document page. In previous chapters, you changed spacing, used tabs, and bold- faced characters, but your document may still need margin adjustments or you may want it to be a three-column document. The features covered in this chapter bridge word processing and desktop publishing, showing you how to produce a professional-looking document. Specifically, you learn how to format pages; set margins, paper size, and orientation; use page numbering; insert page breaks; create headers and footers; format sections; work with columns; import pictures; and use special text effects.

Objectives

By the time you finish this chapter, you will have learned to

1. Set Margins
2. Choose Paper Size and Orientation
3. Choose a Paper Source
4. Control Pagination
5. Create Headers and Footers
6. Divide a Document into Sections
7. Divide Pages into Columns
8. Import Pictures
9. Achieve Special Text Effects

198 Formatting a Page

Objective 1: Set Margins

When you first open a document, Word has default page formats that include

- Left and right margins of 1.25 inches
- Top and bottom margins of 1 inch
- Headers placed .5 inch from the top of the page
- Footers placed .5 inch from the bottom of the page
- No *gutter* (indicated by a setting of 0 inches)

Gutter
An extra margin at the inside edge of facing pages to allow space for binding.

The defaults that you see may be different from these if the values were changed during installation, if another user changed them, or if your version of Word is set up to use a certain type of printer.

By changing margin settings, you can affect the document's length, improve the clarity of the document, or leave room for binding the document. You also can divide a document into different sections, and each section can have its own set of margins. You can change a document's left and right margins in three ways:

- Use the ruler
- Use Print Pre**v**iew
- Use the Page Set**u**p command

Using the Ruler in Print Preview Mode to Set Margins

You can set margins for both new and existing documents. Within Print Preview mode, you can change margins without returning to the document window by dragging the mouse to the new locations on the ruler.

To use the ruler to change the margins, follow these steps:

 1 Open POLICY2.DOC, and click the Page Layout View button (on the left side of the horizontal scroll bar),

or

Choose **F**ile, Print Pre**v**iew.

In both Print Preview mode and Page Layout view, you can see the left, right, top, and bottom margins.

2 Move the mouse pointer to the right margin marker on the horizontal ruler. You know you are pointing at the margin marker when the pointer changes to a double-headed arrow (see figure 7.1).

Figure 7.1
In this example, the display is the Print Preview mode, with the pointer at the right margin position within the horizontal ruler.

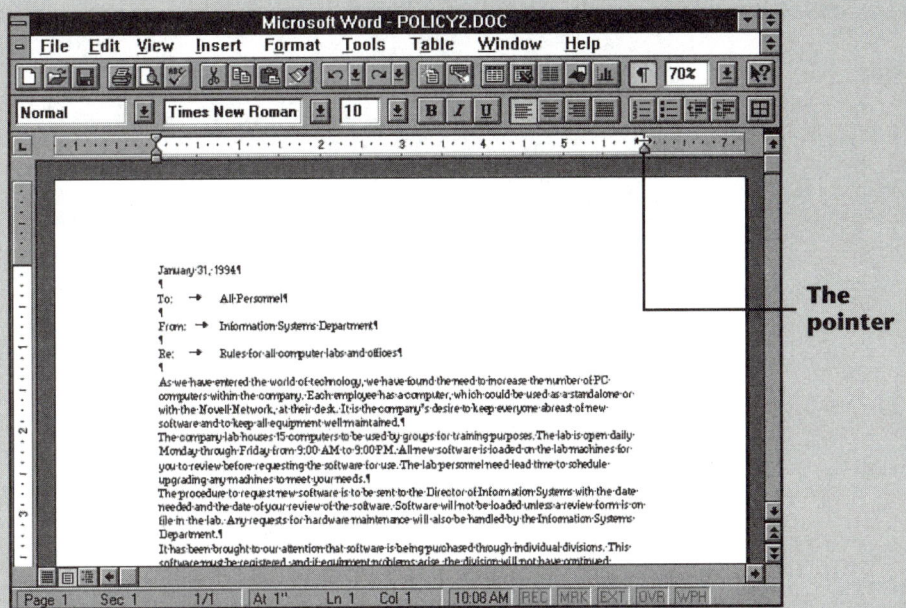

The pointer

③ Drag the left margin marker one inch to the right to adjust the width of the left margin. Drag the right margin marker one inch to the left to adjust the width of the right margin. Word updates the page display as soon as you release the mouse.

④ Move the mouse pointer to the top margin marker on the vertical ruler. You know that you are pointing at the margin marker when the pointer changes to a double-headed arrow.

⑤ Drag the top margin marker down two inches. Drag the bottom margin marker up two inches. When you release the mouse, the text in the document adjusts to the new top margin position.

In addition to using the ruler to set margins, you also can use the Page Setup command to enter values in the Page Setup dialog box.

Using the Page Setup Dialog Box to Set Margins

To use the Page Setup dialog box to set margins, follow these steps:

① From the File menu, choose Page Setup to open the Page Setup dialog box. If necessary, click the Margins tab to display the Margins section of the dialog box (see figure 7.2).

(continues)

Using the Page Setup Dialog Box to Set Margins (continued)

Figure 7.2
The Page Setup dialog box opens with the current margin values shown in text boxes.

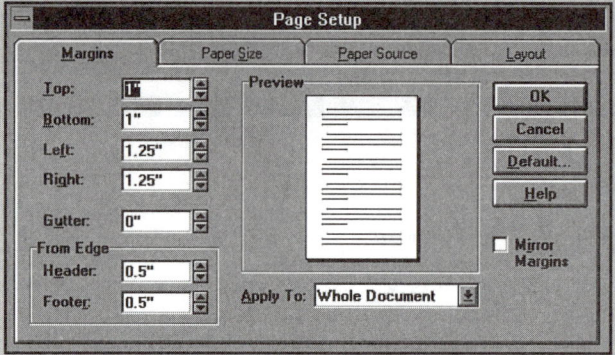

❷ Change the values in the **T**op, **B**ottom, Le**f**t, and Ri**g**ht text boxes to 2, 2, 1.5, and 1.5, respectively.

❸ If you need extra space in the gutter, set a value in the **Gu**tter text box.

Note: *The gutter is where two facing pages are joined in a bound document. Word adds the gutter value to the right margin of left pages and to the left margin of right pages. It is a good idea to have a gutter value of half an inch if you intend to print your document double-sided and bind it.*

❹ If necessary, set positions for headers and footers in the H**e**ader text box and Foote**r** text box. At this time, do not change the H**e**ader and Foote**r** default values.

❺ Choose OK to apply the margins to your document.

In the Page Setup dialog box **M**argins section, you also find the following options:

- **A**pply To. By default, Word applies your margin changes to the whole document. Later in this chapter, you see how you can divide your document into sections and have different margins in each section.

- M**i**rror Margins. When you check this option, the Le**f**t text box in the Margins section of the dialog box changes to I**n**side, and the Ri**g**ht text box changes to **O**utside. This option enables you to specify separate inside and outside margins when you intend to print your document on both sides of the paper and bind it. You can achieve the same result by specifying left and right margins, together with a gutter margin.

- **D**efault. Click this button if you want to apply the page setup settings to the current document and to save them as default values to apply to new documents.

Note: *The Page Setup dialog box is divided into four sections—**M**argins, Paper **S**ize, **P**aper Source, and **L**ayout—that you can display individually by clicking the appropriate tab. When you click the default button, changes in all four sections of the dialog box (not just the section currently displayed) are saved as the defaults.*

Objective 2: Choose Paper Size and Orientation

Orientation
A term that refers to vertical and horizontal page orientation.

Word enables you to select the paper size and orientation of a document. The default paper size is a standard business letter—8 1/2 by 11 inches. You can easily change the paper size if your document is larger or smaller. The default orientation is portrait orientation, but you can print in landscape orientation if you want your document to print across the page.

Changing the Paper Size and Orientation

To change the paper size and orientation of the opened POLICY2.DOC, follow these steps:

1 From the **F**ile menu, choose Page Set**u**p to display the Page Setup dialog box.

2 Click the Paper **S**ize tab to display the Paper **S**ize section of the dialog box (see figure 7.3).

Figure 7.3
Use the Paper Size section of the Page Setup dialog box to choose among standard paper sizes or define custom paper sizes. You can also choose Portrait or Landscape orientation.

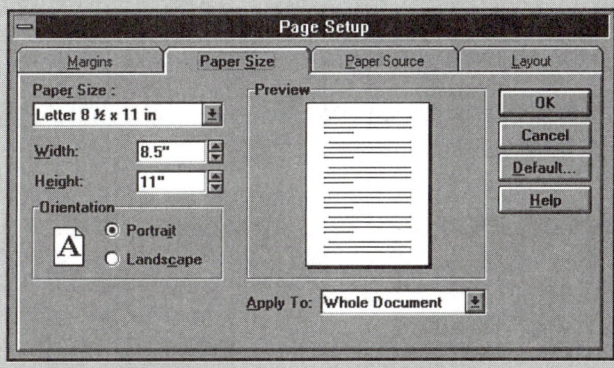

3 From the Pape**r** Size drop-down list, choose Custom Size.

4 Enter **10.5** in the **W**idth text box and **8.0** in the H**e**ight text box.

Note: *When you select a standard paper size, the numbers in the* **W***idth text box and* H**e***ight text box change to reflect the size you selected.*

The Preview section of the dialog box changes to show a miniature view of the paper size you select, whenever you make a change.

5 In the orientation area, choose Lands**c**ape.

6 Choose OK to apply the paper size and orientation to the active document.

Note: *The changes you make in the Page Setup dialog box apply to the entire document. To save these settings as defaults to use for all new documents, choose* **D***efault.*

To see the overall effect of your changes, choose the Print Pre**v**iew command from the **F**ile menu.

Objective 3: Choose a Paper Source

In Word, you can choose a source of paper on which to print your document, but only within the capabilities of your printer. Some printers can accommodate only one paper source, and some can accommodate several. With Word, you can choose which paper source to use; for example, a typical laser printer has two paper sources—manual feed and paper tray—and the potential for an optional envelope feeder.

Furthermore, you can choose one paper source for the first page of a document and another paper source for remaining pages. This capability is useful if you want to print the first page on special paper, such as letterhead, and the remaining pages on blank paper. The following tutorial can be done if your printer has different paper sources.

Choosing the Paper Source

To choose the paper source for POLICY2.DOC, follow these steps:

1. From the File menu, choose Page Setup to display the Page Setup dialog box.

2. In the Page Setup dialog box, click the Paper Source tab to display the paper source options (see figure 7.4).

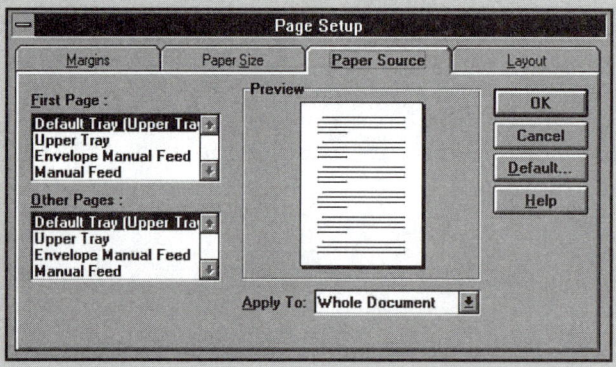

Figure 7.4
In this figure, the Paper Source section of the Page Setup dialog box displays typical laser printer settings.

3. To change the paper source for the first page of a document, choose Default Tray (Upper Tray) in the First Page list box.

4. To change the paper source for all pages except the first page of a document, choose Default Tray (Upper Tray) in the Other Pages list box.

5. Choose OK to apply these choices to your document.

Note: *The changes you make in the Page Setup dialog box apply to the entire document. Choose Default to save the new settings as defaults to use for all new documents.*

6. Close the document without saving any changes.

Objective 4: Control Pagination

When formatting documents, you often need to control pagination—the way Word separates your document into pages. In this section you learn about controlling page breaks, repaginating, and page numbering.

Setting Page Breaks

Soft page break
A page break that Word inserts after calculating that the text has filled a page.

Word automatically starts a new page whenever the current page is full based on the settings for page size, margins, font sizes, the document text, line spacing, and other relevant factors. When a page is full, Word inserts a *soft page break* in the document. As you edit or move text, Word continually recalculates the amount of text on each page and moves soft page breaks accordingly.

Hard page break
A break you insert in a document to force Word to begin a new page.

In some documents, you may want to begin a new page in a specific location. To do this, you insert a *hard page break*. Hard and soft page breaks differ in two ways:

- Word inserts soft page breaks automatically, but you must insert hard page breaks manually.
- You cannot delete a soft page break, but you can delete a hard page break.

You can insert and delete hard page breaks with a menu command or from the keyboard.

Using Menu Commands to Insert a Hard Page Break

To use a menu command to insert a hard page break in POLICY2.DOC, follow these steps:

1 Set the orientation to portrait.

2 Place the insertion point at the beginning of the second paragraph.

3 Choose **I**nsert, **B**reak. The Break dialog box appears (see figure 7.5).

Figure 7.5
The Break dialog box.

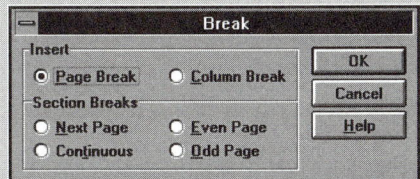

4 Choose OK to insert a hard page break at the insertion point location.

5 Close the document without saving your changes.

As you have seen, it is necessary to create page breaks within a document in specific locations. Using the menu is one method to create breaks. You also can use the keyboard to create page breaks.

Using the Keyboard to Insert a Hard Page Break

To use the keyboard to insert a hard page break in POLICY2.DOC, follow these steps:

1. Open POLICY2.DOC, and place the insertion point at the beginning of the fourth paragraph.

2. Press Ctrl+Enter to insert a hard page break into the document.

3. Save your change, but keep the document open.

Whichever method you use, the hard page break is shown in your document as a single dotted line across the page with the words *Page Break* at its center. This line does not, of course, appear in printed documents.

Deleting a Hard Page Break

To delete a hard page break in the opened POLICY2.DOC, follow these steps:

1. Click the dotted line that represents the hard page break. A small black rectangle appears on the page break line and adjacent to the left margin.

2. Press Del to remove the hard page break.

   Note: *You can cut the hard page break to the Clipboard, as described in Chapter 3, or you can place the insertion point immediately after the hard page break and press Backspace. You also can start a new page by formatting a paragraph with the **P**age Break Before option, as described in Chapter 6.*

3. Save your changes, but keep the document open.

Repaginating a Document

By default, Word calculates pagination in the *background mode*—that is, whenever you pause while typing or editing. Background repagination uses some memory; if you experience memory problems, you may want to turn off this option.

Turning off Background Repagination

To turn off background repagination in the opened POLICY2.DOC, follow these steps:

1. Choose **T**ools, **O**ptions.

2. Click the General tab to display the General section of the dialog box (see figure 7.6).

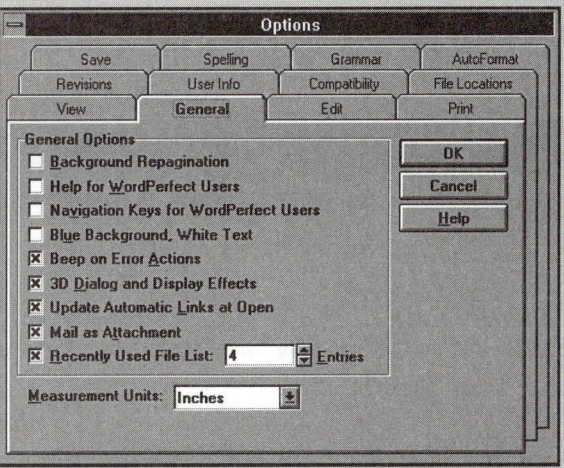

Figure 7.6
Use the General section of the Option dialog box to have repagination in the background.

❸ Click the **B**ackground Repagination check box to deselect it.

❹ Choose OK to return to the document.

❺ Close POLICY2.DOC, and save your changes.

When background repagination is off, Word still repaginates the document when you take any of the following actions:

- Print the document
- Choose Page Layout view or the Print Preview command
- Compile a table of contents or an index

Numbering Pages

Word automatically keeps track of the number of pages in a document. As you work in a document, you can see the current page number on the status bar. To print page numbers, however, you must first insert them into the document.

You can choose to print page numbers within the header at the top of each page or within the footer at the bottom of each page.

Note: *You can place the page number within the text on a page by pressing* Alt+⇧Shift+P, *as described in Chapter 5.*

Word has two methods for placing page numbers at the top or bottom of pages:

- With the Page N**u**mbers command in the **I**nsert menu
- With the **H**eader and Footer command in the **V**iew menu

In this section, you learn how to place page numbers in a document using the Page N**u**mbers command. In the next section, you learn how to add page numbers to a document using the **H**eader and Footer command.

206 Formatting a Page

When you use the Page Numbers command, you can choose where the page numbers appear, as well as their alignment and format. By default, Word places an Arabic number (1, 2, 3, and so on) in a footer on the right side of the page.

Inserting Page Numbers

To insert page numbers in the opened POLICY2.DOC, follow these steps:

❶ Position the insertion point on the first page of the document where you want numbering to begin.

❷ From the **I**nsert menu, choose Page N**u**mbers. The Page Numbers dialog box appears (see figure 7.7).

Figure 7.7
Use the Page Numbers dialog box to choose the position, alignment, and format of page numbers.

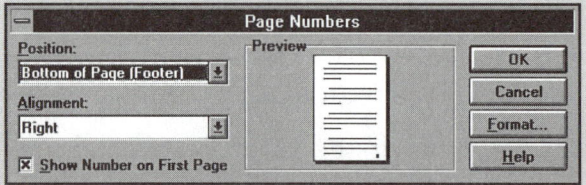

❸ From the **P**osition drop-down list, choose **T**op of Page (Header) to place the page numbers at the top of the page.

❹ From the **A**lignment drop-down list, choose **C**enter to place the page numbers centered.

Note: *The Left, Center, and Right options place page numbers within the margins; the Inside and Outside options place page numbers outside the margins.*

❺ Choose the **S**how Number on First Page check box to deselect it so that no page number will appear on the first page.

❻ Choose **F**ormat. The Page Number Format dialog box appears (see figure 7.8).

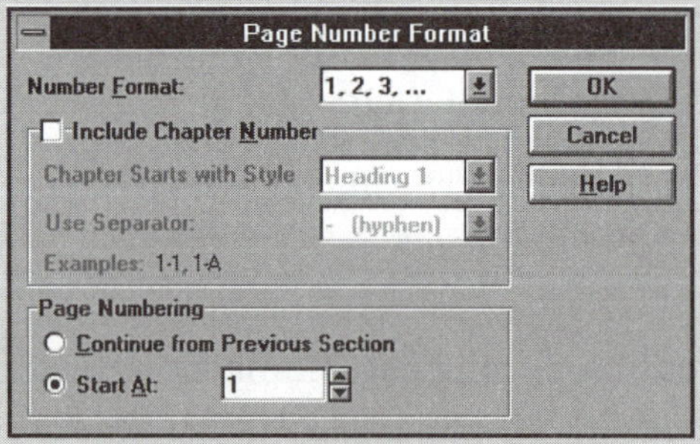

Figure 7.8
Use the Page Number Format dialog box to change the number format and the starting page number; you can also choose whether to include chapter numbers.

❼ From the Number Format drop-down list, choose i,ii,iii....

❽ Choose OK to return to the Page Numbers dialog box.

> **9** Choose OK to apply the page numbers to the document.
>
> **10** Choose OK to return to the document.
>
> **11** Close the document, and save your changes.

Note: *You can see page numbers in Page Layout view and in Print Preview mode.*

Objective 5: Create Headers and Footers

A header is the region between the top of a page and the top margin. A footer is the region between the bottom margin and the bottom of the page. With Word, you can place a header and footer on every page of a document and within the header or footer, you can enter and format text and graphics. As described earlier in this chapter, you can use the Page Setup command to define the distance from the top of the page where header text appears, and the distance from the bottom of the page where footer text appears.

When you add page numbers to a document, you add a header or footer. This type of header or footer has very limited flexibility; it can contain only a page number. In this section, you learn how to create headers and footers containing such items as page numbers, dates, the name of your document, and graphics.

You can create headers or footers that appear the same on each page of a document, or you can alternate pages—one header or footer on odd-numbered pages and a different header or footer on even-numbered pages. Different odd-page and even-page headers and footers are useful when you print on two sides of the paper and bind your documents—you can print page numbers on the outside edge of every page. You can also choose to omit the header and footer from the first page or section of a document.

You can add headers and footers to an existing document, or you can create headers and footers in a new document before that document contains any text.

When you display headers and footers, the horizontal ruler appears with two tab stop settings: a center-aligned tab at the center of the page and a right-aligned tab at the right edge of the page. These settings make it easy for you to place three elements into a header or footer: one at the left, one at the center, and one at the right.

Also, notice that there is a flashing insertion point at the top-left of the header region.

Creating a Header or Footer

To create a header or footer, follow these steps:

1 Open POLICY2.DOC, and press Ctrl+⤶Enter twice to place two hard page breaks in the document, if you have not created the page breaks. This step creates a three-page document so that you can see how headers and footers work in a multipage document.

2 From the **V**iew menu, choose **H**eader and Footer. Word displays the Header area on-screen (surrounded by a dashed line) and the Header and Footer toolbar (see figure 7.9).

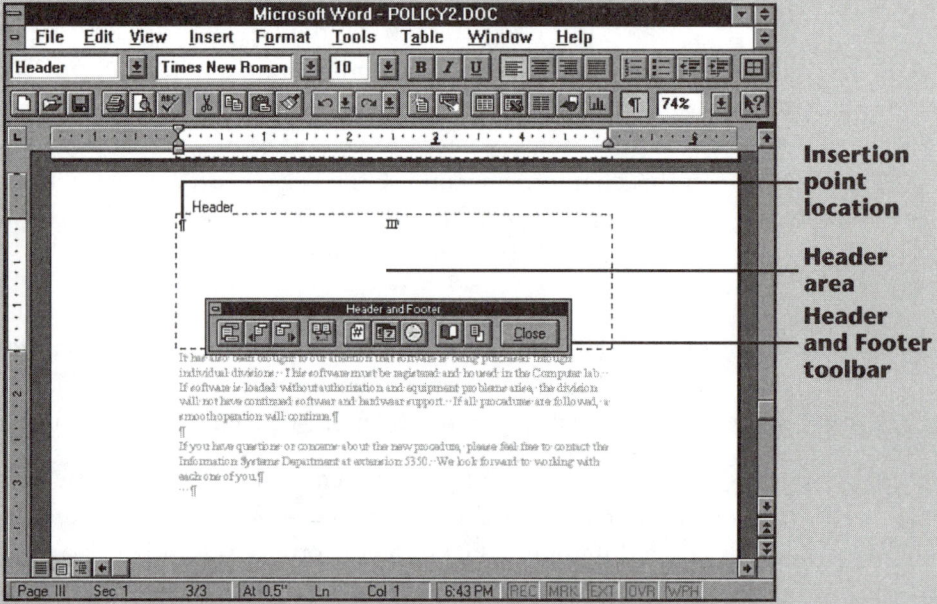

Figure 7.9
The new document appears in Page Layout view with the Header and Footer toolbar displayed and with the header region outlined at the top of the page.

3 In the Header area, type **Software Product Highlights**. The text you type appears at the top-left of the header region.

4 Press Tab twice to move the insertion point to the tab position at the right edge of the header, and click the Date button in the Header and Footer toolbar (see table 7.1) to place the current date into the header.

Note: *To place the current time in the header, click the Time button on the Header and Footer toolbar.*

5 Click the Switch from Header to Footer button on the Header and Footer toolbar, to move to the footer area (see figure 7.10).

Figure 7.10
The footer region is similar to the header region.

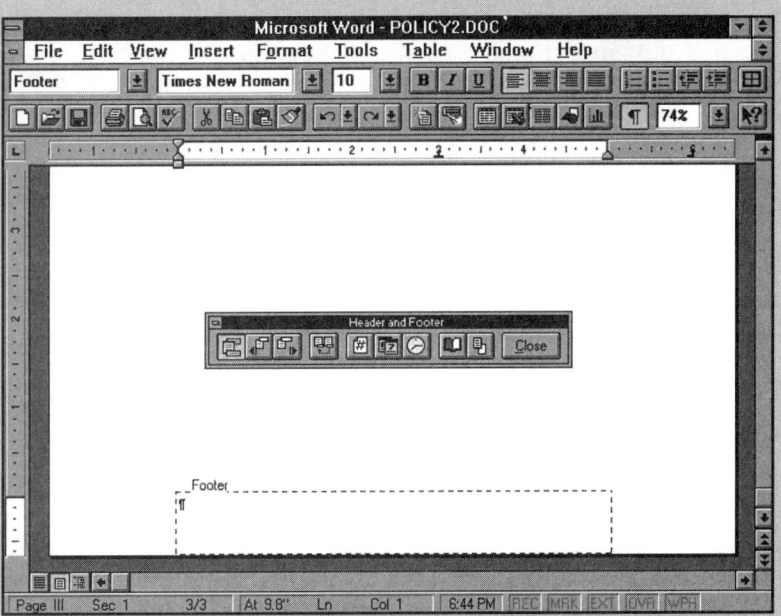

6 Type your name as you want it to appear in the footer. The characters you type appear at the left side of the footer area.

7 Press Tab twice to move the insertion point to the right margin.

8 Click the Page Number button in the Headers and Footers toolbar to insert the page number field.

9 Click the Close button in the Header and Footer toolbar to return to Normal view. To see the header and footer in place, change to Page Layout view or Print Preview mode.

10 Close the document, and save your changes.

The Header and Footer toolbar has 10 buttons (see table 7.1). As with other toolbar buttons, you can point to any button to see its name in a ToolTip and a brief description of its purpose in the status bar. From left to right, these buttons are as listed in the following table:

Table 7.1 Header and Footer Toolbar Buttons

Button	Name	Function
	Switch Between	Switches from header to footer area.
	Show Previous	Moves back to a previous section of the document that has different headers or footer.
	Show Next	Moves forward to the next section of the document that has different headers or footers.
	Same as Previous	Copies the headers or footers from the previous section of the document to the current section.
	Page Numbers	Inserts page numbers into the header or footer.
	Date	Inserts the date into the header or footer.
	Time	Inserts the time into the header or footer.
	Page Setup	Opens the Page Setup dialog box so that you can modify the header or footer settings.
	Show/Hide Document Text	Shows or hides the current document text.
	Close	Closes header or footer display and returns to the document view.

You can use all but three of these buttons in a single-section document. The second, third, and fourth buttons, are useful only when you are working with a multisection document.

Creating Different Headers and Footers for Specific Pages

So far, you have created headers and footers that appear on every page of a document. You also can change the way headers and footers appear by placing different headers and footer on different pages. To create different headers and footers on odd and even pages in the opened POLICY2.DOC, follow these steps:

1 From the **V**iew menu, choose **H**eader and Footer to display the header you created in the preceding exercise.

2 Click the Page Setup button in the Header and Footer toolbar to display the **L**ayout section of the Page Setup dialog box (see figure 7.11).

Figure 7.11
In the Headers and Footers area of the Layout section, you can set Word to display different headers and footers on different pages.

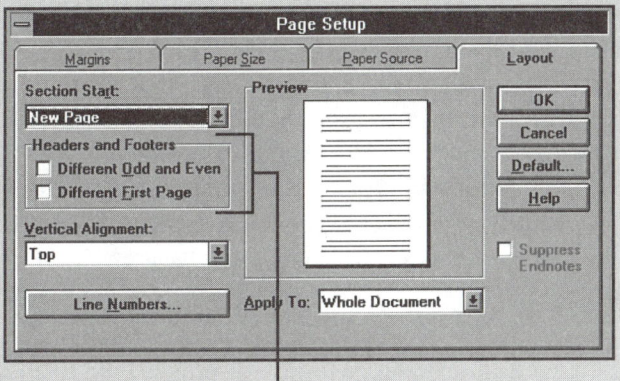

Choose Header and Footer page options here

③ Choose the check box next to Different **O**dd and Even. The Preview area changes from showing a single page to showing facing pages.

④ Choose OK to accept your changes.

⑤ Choose Close.

⑥ Choose **V**iew, **H**eader and Footer to display the header area.

The title of the header area has changed to indicate that different headers and footer will appear on different pages. The header area is now labeled *Odd Page Header*.

⑦ Save your changes, but keep the document open.

After you choose Different **O**dd and Even, the text in the odd header and footer regions appears only on odd-numbered pages. You can make changes to this text without affecting what appears in the headers and footers on even-numbered pages.

To work with even-numbered pages, click the double-down arrow at the bottom of the vertical scroll bar. You can determine if the page is even-numbered by looking at the page number in the status bar. A header region labeled *Even Page Header* and a footer region labeled *Even Page Footer* appears, in which you can work with the header and footer that will appear on even pages without affecting the odd pages.

You also can have a different header and footer (or no header and footer) on the first page of a document.

Creating a Different First-Page Header or Footer

To create a different first-page header or footer in POLICY2.DOC, follow these steps:

 ① Click the Page Setup button in the Headers and Footers toolbar to display the **L**ayout section of the Page Setup dialog box.

(continues)

> **Creating a Different First-Page Header or Footer (continued)**
>
> **❷** Deselect the Different **O**dd and Even check box, and choose the check box next to the Different **F**irst Page.
>
> **Note:** *If you do not deselect the Different **O**dd and Even check box, a unique header and footer will appear on the first page, the same header and footer will appear on all odd-numbered pages except the first, and the same header and footer will appear on all even-numbered pages.*
>
> **❸** Choose OK to return to the Header and Footer view.
>
> When even-numbered pages are displayed, the header and footer regions are labeled *Even Page Header* and *Even Page Footer*. When all odd-numbered pages are displayed, the header and footer regions are labeled *Odd Page Header* and *Odd Page Footer*. When the first page is displayed, the header and footer regions are labeled *First Page Header* and *First Page Footer*.
>
> At this stage, the odd-numbered page headers and footers, except those on the first page, contain the information you previously placed there. However, the headers and footers for the even-numbered pages and the headers and footers for the first page are empty. You can place information into these headers and footers by following the steps you used to create odd-numbered page headers and footers.
>
> **❹** Save the file to your data disk as **FORM.DOC**, but keep the document open.

Editing Headers and Footers

You can edit text in headers and footers just as you edit any other text. However, you cannot edit fields such as the Page Number, Date, and Time. Each of these, although appearing on-screen as separate characters, is one entity. You can delete the entire field, but you cannot modify individual characters in it. To delete a field, place the insertion point just to the left of the field, drag over the field to highlight it, and then press [Del].

Objective 6: Divide a Document into Sections

In Word, you can divide a document into sections, each of which can be formatted differently. If you want the formatting to be the same throughout the document, you do not need to create any sections. You *must* create a new section, however, if you want to change any of the following formatting in any part of a document:

- Margins, paper size, or page orientation
- Format, position, or sequence of page numbers
- Contents or position of headers and footers
- Location of footnotes or endnotes

- Number of columns
- Line numbering

Inserting a Section Break

To break a document into sections, insert a section break wherever you want a new section to start. You can have as many sections as you want within a document. To insert a section break in the opened POLICY2.DOC, follow these steps:

1. Place the insertion point at the beginning of the third paragraph on page 2 to start a new section.

2. From the **I**nsert menu, choose **B**reak to display the Break dialog box (see figure 7.12).

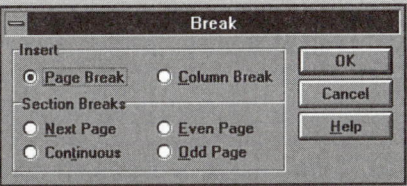

Figure 7.12
Use the Break dialog box to choose the type of break you want to insert.

The Section Breaks section of the dialog box displays four types of section breaks:

- **N**ext Page. The text after the break starts at the beginning of a new page.
- Con**t**inuous. The text after the break continues on the same page as the text before the break.
- **E**ven Page. The text after the break starts at the beginning of the next even-numbered page.
- **O**dd Page. The text after the break starts at the beginning of the next odd-numbered page.

3. Choose Con**t**inuous as the section break option, and then choose OK.

   Word starts a new section at the insertion point location.

4. Close the document, and save your changes.

   A nonprinting double line appears across the screen with the words End of Section in it, indicating where one section ends and the next begins (see figure 7.13).

(continues)

Inserting a Section Break (continued)

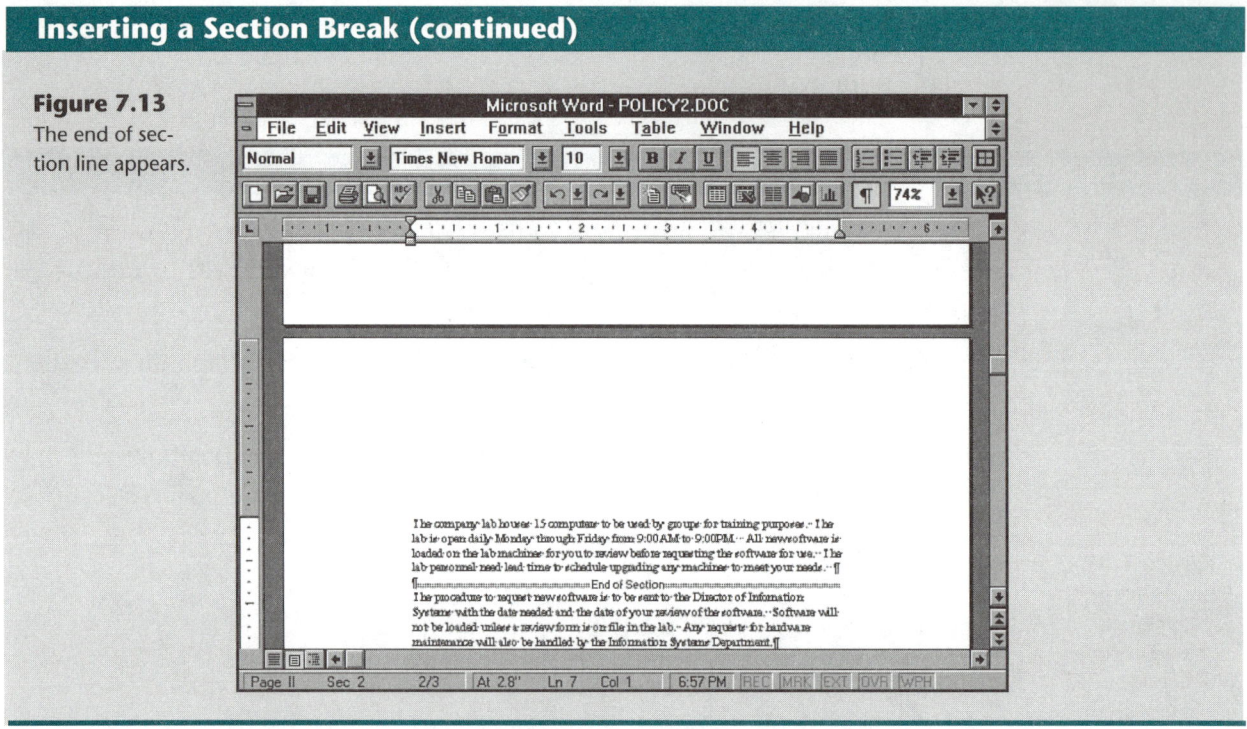

Figure 7.13
The end of section line appears.

Deleting a Section Break

Word stores all section formatting in the section break. If you delete a section break, the preceding text assumes the section formatting of the next section.

To delete a section break, position the insertion point on the double line and press Del. Alternatively, you can position the insertion point immediately after the section break, and press Backspace.

Assigning Formats to Sections

When you divide a document into sections, all sections initially have the same section formatting. You can change the section formatting of an individual section by placing the insertion point anywhere in that section and creating the formatting you want for that section. The commands you can use to assign formatting to individual sections include the following:

- **C**olumns in the F**o**rmat menu to have different numbers of columns in individual sections

- Foot**n**ote in the **I**nsert menu to change the numbering of footnotes and endnotes for individual sections

- **H**eader and Footer in the **V**iew menu to change the contents of the header and footer (including page numbering) for individual sections

- Page N**u**mbers in the **I**nsert menu to change the page numbering for separate sections

- Page Set**u**p in the F**o**rmat menu to change margins and orientation for individual sections

Word can vertically align the text within a section at the top of a page, in the center of a page, or it can vertically justify the text by adjusting the space between lines so that the text exactly fits between the top and bottom margins.

Setting the Vertical Alignment of a Section

To set the vertical alignment of a section, follow these steps:

1. Divide the document POLICY2.DOC into sections so that the text you want to align vertically is in a separate section and is the only text on a page. Create a section for the bulleted list included in the document.

2. With the insertion point within the section to be aligned, open the File menu and choose Page Set up to display the Page Setup dialog box.

3. If necessary, click the Layout tab to display the Layout section of the dialog box (see figure 7.14).

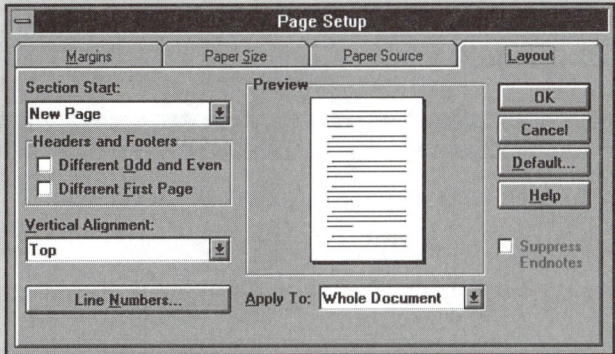

Figure 7.14
Use the Layout section of the Page Setup dialog box to specify vertical alignment.

4. From the Vertical Alignment drop-down list, choose Center.

5. Choose OK, and switch to Print Preview mode to confirm the vertical alignment.

6. Close the document, and save your changes.

Objective 7: Divide Pages into Columns

Newspaper columns
Text in columns, that flows from the bottom of one column to the top of the next.

Some documents look their best and are easiest to read when they are divided into columns. Sometimes you can fit a document on fewer pages by dividing the document into columns. In Word, you can divide pages of your documents into columns, either as *newspaper columns* or *side-by-side columns*. When you use newspaper columns, your text fills one column then starts at the top of the next column, just as it does in newspapers and magazines. Side-by-side columns display paragraphs next to each other as they do, for example, in the tables in this book.

Word offers great flexibility in the way columns look. You can control the number of columns, the width of each column, the space between columns, and where the text breaks between one column and the next.

Dividing a one-page document into columns is defining a new page format. The one-page document resembles a newspaper article. As with other page formats, column formatting applies to a complete section of a document. Therefore, if you want to have different column formats within a document, you must divide your document into sections, as described earlier in this chapter.

If you insert one or more *continuous* section breaks into a page, that page can contain several different column formats. *Continuous* section breaks appear one after the other in the document. Suppose that you want to create a page in which the text is in two columns with a heading in a single column stretching across both columns of text. To do this, you break the page into two sections, with the top section as a single column for the heading, and the lower section in two columns for the text.

Setting the Column Format

When you create a new document, by default Word creates a single-column format. If you want to create the document in two or more columns, you can specify the column format before you start typing the text, or you can complete the text and then divide the document into columns.

Formatting an Existing Document into Equal Width Columns

To format an existing document into two or more equal width columns in the opened POLICY2.DOC, follow these steps:

❶ Delete the page break after paragraph one in the document.

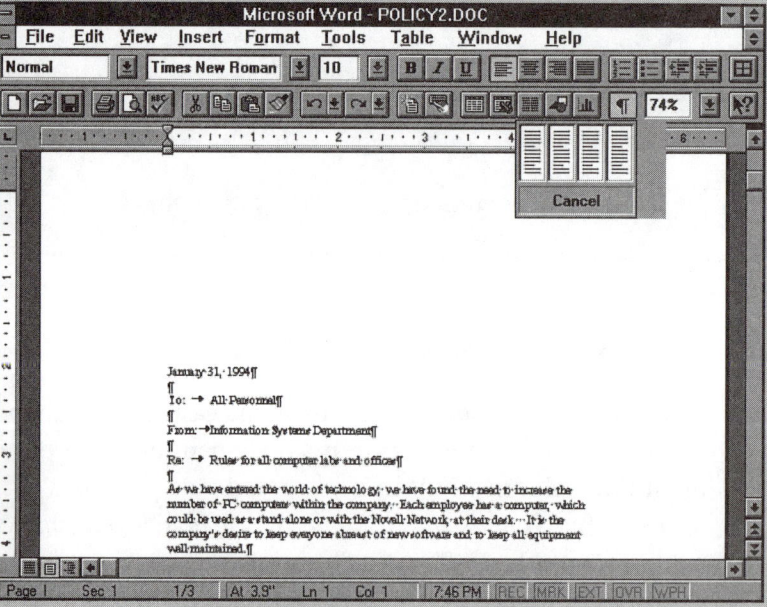

Figure 7.15
Four text columns appear when you click the Columns button.

❷ Click the Columns button on the Standard toolbar. A box with four text columns appears below the toolbar (see figure 7.15).

③ While pointing to the Columns button on the Standard toolbar, press and hold down the mouse, and drag the mouse pointer across the text columns to highlight two columns.

④ Release the mouse button.

Word divides the document into two columns (see figure 7.16)

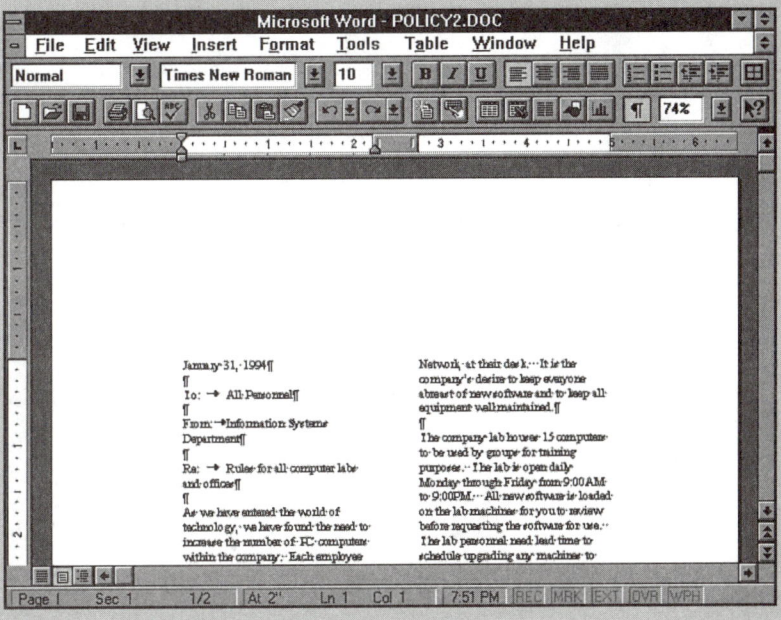

Figure 7.16
The document is divided into two columns. The horizontal ruler shows the positions of the columns and the space between the columns.

⑤ Close the document, and save your changes.

Note: *If you display the document in Normal view, you see only one column at a time. To see what the document looks like in columns, choose Page Layout view or Print Preview.*

Dividing a Page into Columns of Unequal Width

In Word, you can create a document with columns of unequal width. To create a section of a document with columns of unequal width in the opened POLICY2.DOC, follow these steps:

① Add the title *Information Systems Procedures* to the top of the document.

② Place the insertion point on the first character of paragraph one.

③ Choose **I**nsert, **B**reak to display the Break dialog box.

④ Click the Con**t**inuous option to have the section break within the page.

⑤ Choose OK to display the document in two sections on the same page (see figure 7.17).

(continues)

Dividing a Page into Columns of Unequal Width (continued)

Figure 7.17
At this stage, the page is divided into two sections, each section displayed separately in two columns.

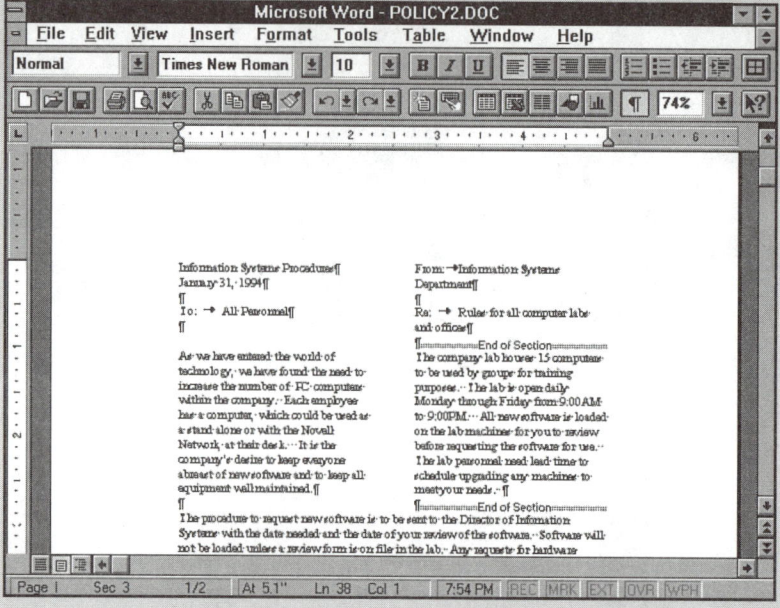

6 Change the font of the heading line to 16 and center the title.

7 Place the insertion point in the first section containing the title.

8 Click the Columns button on the Standard toolbar.

9 Drag the mouse pointer across the text columns to highlight only one column. Release the mouse button to show the first section as a single column (see figure 7.18).

Figure 7.18
The page appears with the first section as a single column.

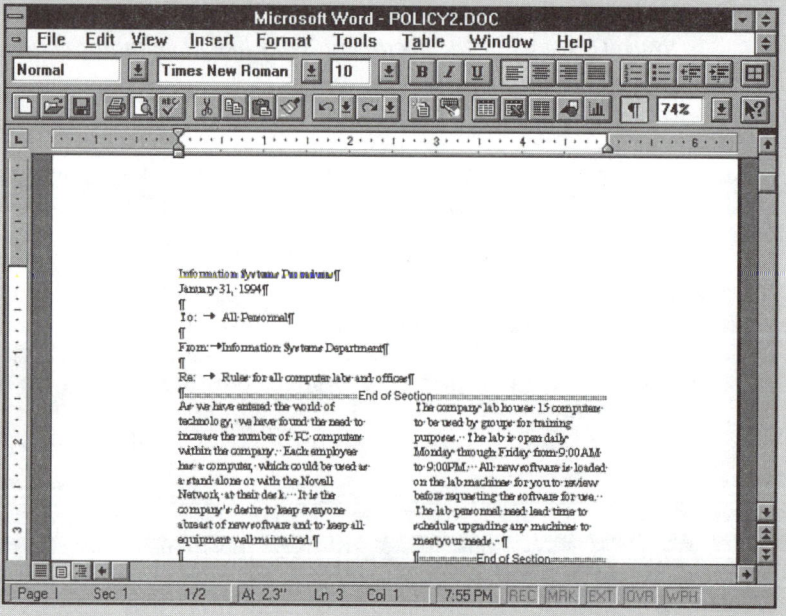

10 Close the document, and save your changes.

Changing Column Widths and Spacing

You can change the width of columns and the spacing between columns in Normal or Page Layout views or in Print Preview mode. In each case, point to the horizontal ruler and drag the margin boundaries to new positions, as described earlier in this section.

Setting Up Columns with Exact Measurements

Alternatively, you can change column widths and spacing in the Columns dialog box. You can use this method to choose up to 11 columns, to define separately the width of each, and to define the spacing between columns.

Creating Unequal Column Widths in the Columns Dialog Box

To divide a section of POLICY2.DOC into columns of unequal widths in the Columns dialog box, follow these steps:

1. Position the insertion point within the paragraph beginning with "The procedures..." to divide into columns.

2. From the Format menu, choose Columns to display the Columns dialog box (see figure 7.19).

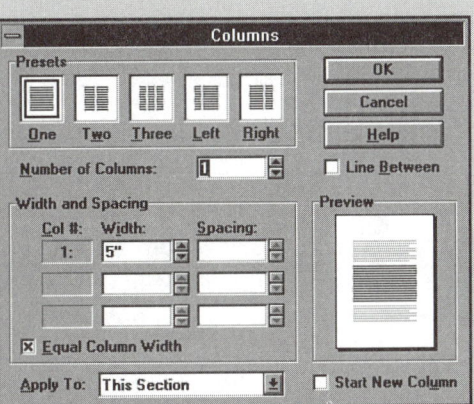

Figure 7.19
Use the Columns dialog box to choose the number of columns and their size.

3. In the Presets area, choose Three,

   or

   In the Number of Columns text box, type 3.

   In the Preview box, you can preview the page layout. The Width text box and Spacing text box show the column dimensions.

4. Click Equal Column Width.

5. Choose OK to apply the selected column format to the document.

6. Close the document, and save your changes.

Note: *If you open the Columns dialog box after you have divided a document into sections, the box shows the width and spacing between columns. You can change column width and spacing at this time.*

Placing Lines between Columns

To place separation lines between columns, open the Columns dialog box, and choose the check box next to the Line **B**etween option. Lines between columns are useful if multiple items are within the two columns. Adding separation lines also gives the columns a frame appearance.

Balancing Column Lengths

When Word divides text into columns, it fills the first column with text and then continues the text into the next column. With more than two columns, this pattern continues with subsequent columns. If there is not enough text to fill a page, this process results in columns of unequal length.

To avoid this problem, you can insert a *column break* anywhere you like in a column. Word ends the column at the break instead of at the bottom margin. You may have to experiment with the positions of column breaks to achieve the desired effect.

Inserting a Column Break

To insert a column break in the opened POLICY2.DOC, follow these steps:

1. Make sure that the document is in Page Layout view.

2. To insert a column break, position the insertion point on page two, the paragraph beginning with "If you have. . ."

3. From the **I**nsert menu, choose **B**reak to display the Break dialog box.

4. Choose **C**olumn Break, and then choose OK.

   The document reappears with the new column starting where you placed the column break marker. The marker itself is shown by a dotted line marked `Column Break`.

5. Close the document, and save your changes.

To delete the column break, click the column break marker and press ¶ .

Objective 8: Import Pictures

You can incorporate pictures directly into a Word document to enhance and clarify visually what you write in words. One source of pictures is the collection of clip art images that is included with Word. If you followed the standard installation procedures, these clip art images are available in the CLIPART directory. This directory is in the Word for Windows directory (C:\WINWORD), unless you specified another directory during installation.

Importing a Picture File

You can import graphics files from applications such as clip art files, charts that you create in a spreadsheet program, and other images created in other graphics applications. To import a picture from a graphics file into POLICY2.DOC, follow these steps:

❶ Position the insertion point in the second paragraph of the document.

❷ From the Insert menu, choose Picture. The Insert Picture dialog box appears. By default, the contents of the CLIPART directory are displayed (see figure 7.20).

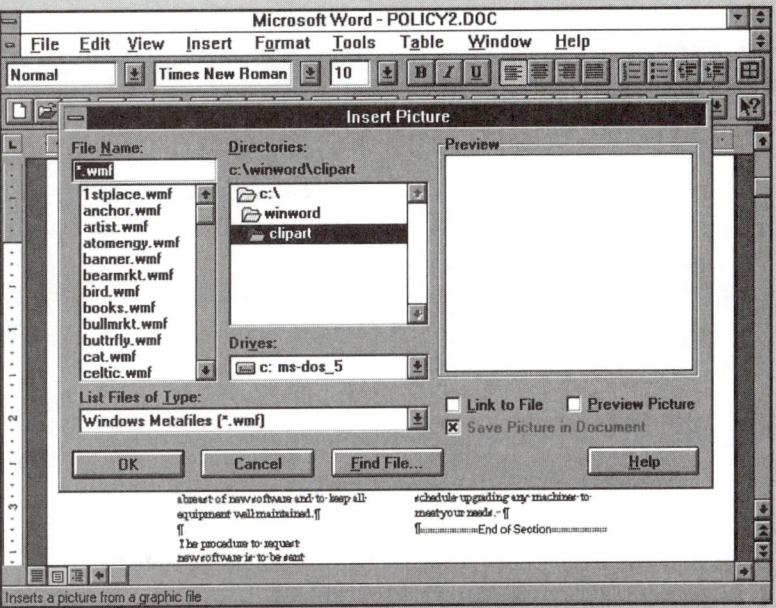

Figure 7.20
The CLIPART directory contains images included with Word.

❸ From the List Files of Type list box, choose the type of file you want to import—*.WMF.

You can choose All Graphics Files to display all files with formats that Word can convert.

❹ Select drive C; the directory, WINWORD\CLIPART; and the name of the file, COMPUTER.WMF, you want to import.

To see the contents of the selected file, choose the Preview Picture check box.

❺ Choose OK.

❻ Close the document, and save your changes.

Linking a Picture File

Normally, when you insert a picture into a Word document, the contents of the picture are saved along with the rest of your document. This is convenient because it doesn't matter if you move or delete the original picture file—the contents are stored in your document. However, a document with a number of pictures can take up a great deal of disk space and, if you modify the original picture, your Word document will not be up-to-date.

You can use the linking feature to store in your document an internal reference to the original picture. If the picture file changes, Word updates the document. Linking is also useful for saving disk space because, although the picture is in more than one application, it is stored only once.

Linking a Picture to Its Original File

To link a picture in POLICY2.DOC to its original file, follow these steps:

1. From the **I**nsert menu, choose the **P**icture command. The Insert Picture dialog box appears.

2. From the List Files of **T**ype list box, choose *.WMF.

3. Select drive C; directory, \WINWORD\CLIPART; and the name of the file, COMPUTER.WMF, to import.

4. Select the **L**ink to File check box.

    To save disk space when importing a picture, make sure that the **S**ave Picture in Document check box is *not* selected. (This check box is available only when the **L**ink to File check box is selected.)

5. Choose OK.

6. Close the document, and save your changes.

Normally, the linked picture is updated automatically when you open the Word for Windows document, or if the picture file is changed while the Word for Windows document is open. If you don't want the picture to reflect any changes to the original file, see the section on "Importing a Picture File," earlier in this chapter.

Objective 9: Achieve Special Text Effects

Watermark
An image that you can print on the background of one page or all pages in a document.

You can create a number of special text effects to enhance your Word documents. For example, you can use a text box to create a *watermark*. You can also use WordArt, a small text-manipulation program included with Word. WordArt enables you to turn text and characters into works of art. For example, if you are promoting a turkey dinner and would like the text to be printed within the turkey, you can use WordArt.

Creating a Watermark

To create a watermark in POLICY2.DOC, follow these steps:

1. Click the Drawing button on the Standard toolbar. The Drawing toolbar appears (see figure 7.21).

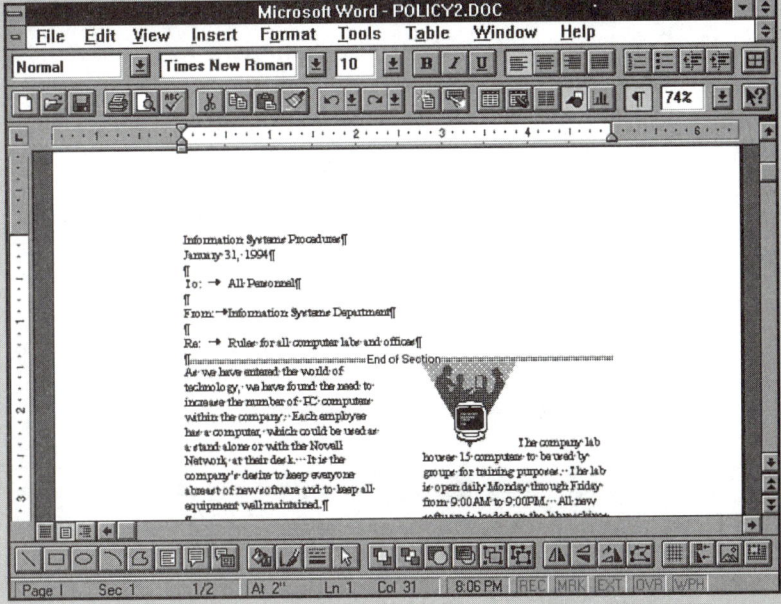

Figure 7.21
The Drawing toolbar appears across the bottom of the screen and above the status bar.

2. To use the watermark on every page of a document, choose **H**eader and Footer from the **V**iew menu.

    If you position the watermark on a particular page, it will print only on that page. If you position it in a header or footer, it will print on every page.

3. Click the Text Box button on the Drawing toolbar.

4. Drag in the header box to create a text box the size of the text or picture you want to use for your watermark.

5. Choose **P**icture, BOOKS.WMF, from the **I**nsert menu to import a picture.

    If you are using text, it is a good idea to use the Font dialog box to make the text light gray so that the watermark doesn't overwhelm the contents of the text layer that prints in front of the text box.

6. Click the Send Behind Text button on the Drawing toolbar (see figure 7.22).

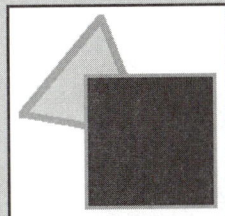

Figure 7.22
You can send a text box to the back drawing layer to get this effect.

(continues)

Creating a Watermark (continued)

You can also use any combination of drawing objects in place of a text box. To use an imported picture, however, you must use a text box.

7 Close the document, and save your changes.

Features have been added to the document to improve its appearance. Using WordArt allows text to display in a unique style and position.

Creating a Text Effect with WordArt

To create a text effect in the opened POLICY2.DOC with WordArt, follow these steps:

1 Move the insertion point to the end of the document.

2 From the Insert menu, choose the Object command. The Object dialog box appears (see figure 7.23).

Figure 7.23
Use the Object dialog box to insert objects into a file.

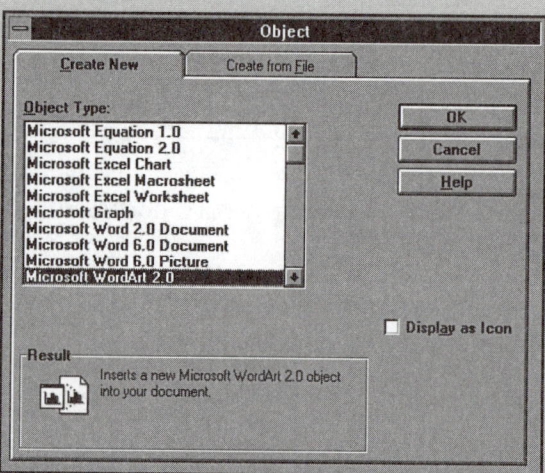

3 Click the Create New tab.

4 From the Object Type list box, select Microsoft WordArt 2.0.

5 Choose OK.

WordArt temporarily replaces Word menus with its own menus and toolbar and displays the WordArt text entry box (see figure 7.24).

Figure 7.24
WordArt temporarily replaces the Word menu and toolbar with its own menu and toolbar.

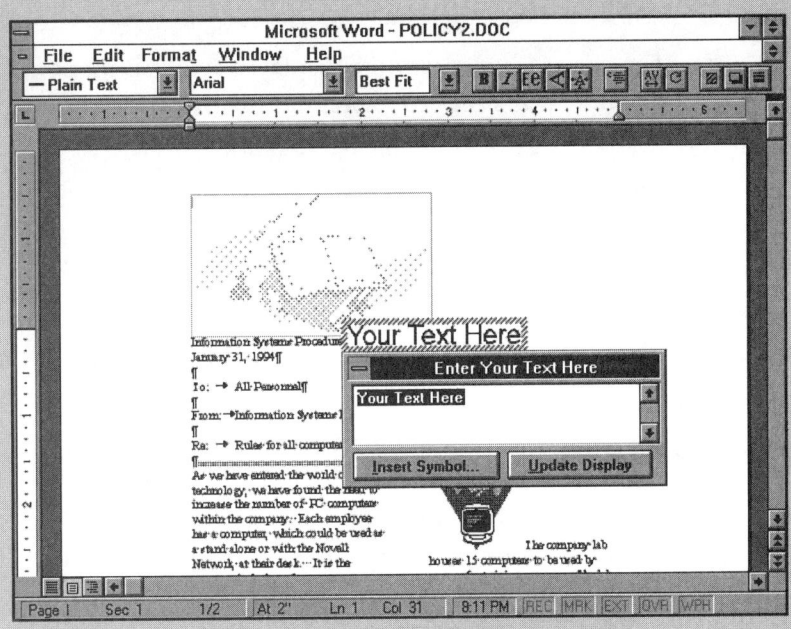

6 In the Enter Your Text Here dialog box, type the following text:

> **We need your support in this software project or people will be without both hardware and software when needed.**

7 Choose the Update Display button to apply the selected effects to your text. You can choose the Insert symbol button to choose unusual characters from the selected font.

8 Use the list boxes and buttons on the toolbar to select Circle shape, Times New Roman font, 20 Font Size, and click the Ee button upright display in the circle (see figure 7.25).

Figure 7.25
WordArt can create text effects such as this.

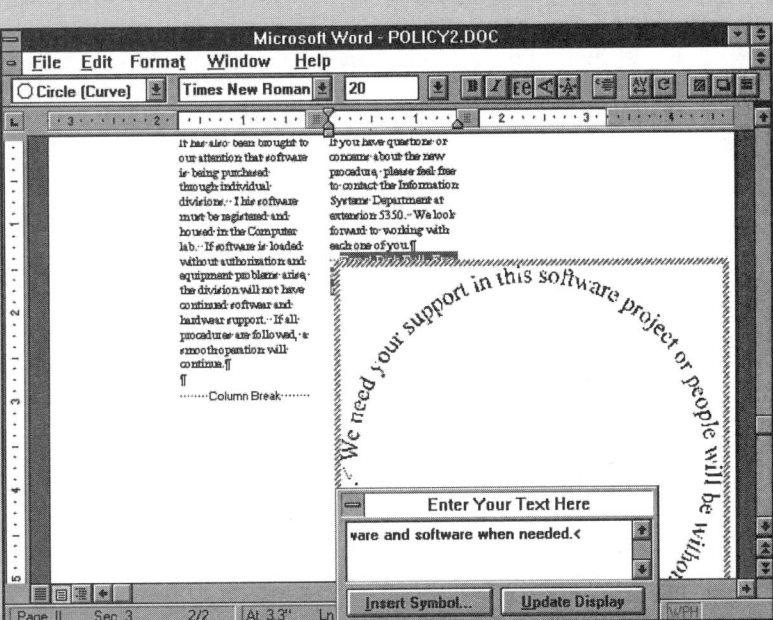

(continues)

> **Creating a Text Effect with WordArt (continued)**
>
> The changes you make are displayed in the underlying Word for Windows document. It's easy to experiment with a wide variety of effects. Try a few of the toolbar buttons to see what they do.
>
> **❾** When you are finished, click elsewhere in the document.
>
> The normal Word for Windows menus and toolbars return.
>
> **❿** Close the document, and save your changes.

Chapter Summary

After you complete this chapter, your document should contain the features of a publication. In this chapter, you have learned how to format pages and sections. You learned how to set margins, paper size and orientation, paper source, and pagination. You also learned how to use formats, outline techniques, change column structure, and add graphics. Finally, you learned how to create special text effects to further enhance your document. In Chapter 8, you learn how to create and edit tables in Word.

Checking Your Skills

True/False Questions

For each of the following statements, circle *T* or *F* to indicate whether the statement is true or false.

T F **1.** When you first open a document, your first step is to change the margin settings.

T F **2.** By default, Word starts a new page whenever the current page is full.

T F **3.** A *header* is the region between the bottom margin and the bottom of the page.

T F **4.** Word enables you to store all section formatting in the section break.

T F **5.** WordArt enables you to fit words into shapes, rotate text to any angle, and use other eye-catching features.

T F **6.** Within Print Preview mode, you can change margins without returning to the document window.

T F **7.** When formatting documents, you often need to control pagination, which is how Word separates your document into pages.

T F **8.** You can print only page numbers within the header at the top of each page.

T F **9.** Dividing a one-page document into columns is defining a new page format.

T F **10.** WordArt enables you to turn text and characters into works of art.

Multiple-Choice Questions

In the blank provided, write the letter of the correct answer for each of the following questions.

____ **1.** The left and right margin default settings in Word are _____.

    a. 1 inch for both

    b. 1.5 inches for both

    c. 1 inch and 2 inches

    d. 1.25 for both

    e. none of these answers

____ **2.** If you select landscape orientation, your document will print _____.

    a. vertically

    b. horizontally

    c. with a border

    d. in 3-D

    e. only on-screen

____ **3.** When a page is full and you continue typing, Word inserts _____.

    a. a hard page break

    b. a hard section break

    c. a soft page break

    d. a soft section break

    e. printer control characters

____ **4.** Click the _____ Header and Footer toolbar button to move to the next section of a document that has different headers or footers.

    a. Switch to Header and Footer

    b. Show Next

    c. Show Previous

    d. Same as Previous

    e. Show/Hide Document Text

_____ 5. A special text effect in Word that enables you to print an image on the background of every page or just one page in the document is called _____.

   a. graphics

   b. text art

   c. WordArt

   d. a watermark

   e. click art

_____ 6. The Page Setup dialog box is divided into four sections, and includes _____.

   a. Page **L**ayout

   b. **P**aper Location

   c. P**r**inter Location

   d. **M**argins

   e. Paper **O**rientation

_____ 7. When you display headers and footers, the horizontal ruler appears with two tab stop settings: _____.

   a. a left-aligned tab at the left edge of the page

   b. a right-aligned tab at the right edge of the page

   c. a center-aligned tab at the center of the page

   d. both a and b

   e. both b and c

_____ 8. To delete a section break, position the insertion point on the double line and press _____.

   a. [Esc]

   b. [Tab]

   c. [Enter]

   d. [Del]

   e. [Backspace]

_____ 9. You can import graphics files from applications such as _____.

   a. Clipart

   b. WordArt

   c. Watermarks

d. Art

e. Drawing

___ 10. If you display the two-column document in Normal view, you see _____.

a. both columns

b. section breaks

c. only one column

d. a blank screen in Normal view

e. a Print Preview

Fill-in-the-Blank Questions

In the blank provided, write the correct answer for each of the following questions.

1. The _____ is when two facing pages are joined in a bound document.

2. When formatting documents, you often need to control _____, which is how Word separates your document into pages.

3. A _____ is the region between the top of a page and the top margin.

4. To break a document into sections, insert a _____ break wherever you want a new section to start.

5. _____ enables you to fit words into shapes, rotate text to any angle, and use other eye-catching features.

6. Word enables you to select the _____ size and orientation of a document.

7. When a page is full, Word inserts a _____ break in the document.

8. You add a _____ or _____ when you add page numbers to a document.

9. You can place separation lines between columns by selecting an option in the _____ dialog box.

10. The _____ feature enables you to store in your document an internal reference to the original picture.

Applying Your Skills

Review Exercises

Exercise 1: Formatting FIRST.DOC

To practice formatting margins and page orientation, follow these steps:

1. Open the FIRST.DOC.

2. Set the left and right margins at 2 inches.

3. Set the top and bottom margins at 2 inches.

4. Set the page orientation to landscape.

5. Save the file to your data disk as **FIRST.DOC**.

Exercise 2: Formatting SCHEDULE.DOC
To practice formatting margins and page breaks, follow these steps:

1. Open SCHEDULE.DOC.

2. Set the top and bottom margins at 2.5 inches.

3. Create page breaks for each date.

4. Save the file to your data disk as **SCHEDULE.DOC**.

Exercise 3: Formatting MEDICAL.DOC
To practice formatting another document, follow these steps:

1. Open MEDICAL.DOC.

2. Set the top and bottom margins at 1.5 inches.

3. Change the orientation to landscape.

4. Create a new section at the top of the page, using continuous type for the break.

5. Import the clip art MEDSTAFF.WMF into the new section.

6. Save the file to your data disk as **MEDICAL.DOC**.

Exercise 4: Formatting GUIDELINE.DOC
To practice formatting columns, follow these steps:

1. Open GUIDELINE.DOC.

2. Change the one-page layout to two columns.

3. Insert column breaks for every item in the GUIDELINE.DOC. For example, 1.... should be in its own column.

4. Save the file to your data disk as **GUIDELINE.DOC**.

Exercise 5: Formatting STEP2.DOC
To practice using WordArt, follow these steps:

1. Open STEP2.DOC, and create WordArt with the following text:

    This is my security blanket when using WORD.

2. Select Circle shape and Arial size 16.

3. Save the file to your data disk as **STEP2.DOC**.

Continuing Projects

Project 1: Practice Using Word

You own a real estate company, and you want to create a flyer announcing a property new to the market. To create a flyer, follow these steps:

1. Type **WILDWOOD REALTY COMPANY** at the top of the page.
2. Move the insertion point to the top of the document, and create a section.
3. Import the clip art REALEST.WMF.
4. Move the insertion point to the end of the document, and type the following as the body of the newsletter:

    Wildwood Realty announces a new residential listing:

    A glamorous four bedroom home, nestled in the hillside of the Connecticut River. Ten acres of wooded land surround the beautiful custom landscape of this dream home. Many amenities. Open house Sunday June 5, 1995 from 9:00AM-4:00PM. Once you visit, you will never want to leave!!

5. Enhance the text with italics and boldface, and change the font size to 14.
6. Change the orientation to portrait, and change the top margin to 2 inches.
7. Save the file to your data disk as **REALEST.DOC**.

Project 2: Federal Department Store

Continue your work on the catalog for the Federal Department Store by following these steps:

1. Open OUTFIT.DOC.
2. Create a section break for the name of the company.
3. Create a section for the opening paragraph and following list.
4. Create a two-column layout for the remaining text in the document.
5. Insert a graphic CONTINEN.WMF within the company section.
6. Create column breaks after every two items.
7. Save the file to your data disk as **OUTFIT.DOC**.

Project 3: Real Entertainment Corporation

Continue your work on the newsletter for Real Entertainment Corporation. The corporation wants this newsletter to contain brief articles about each department in a bulleted list.

1. Open REC.DOC.

2. Type the following paragraphs about each department in the business:

Sales

The sales department has developed a team approach to marketing the entertainment products. Each sales representative visits or contacts organizations in his or her various locations. If the organization is interested in a site demonstration of the product, a marketing and sales person plans a presentation package. For more information, call 401-REC-CALL.

Tours

Every Monday through Friday, REC offer tours through the corporation facilities. The hours of operation are from 9:00 AM to 9:00 PM. We ask that the organization sends groups of no more than three representatives to view the facilities. We feel a small group provides a more personal tour.

Travel

REC offers special travel packages to all employees. We have a four-person department that plans trips from one day to ten days of travel. So if you are feeling down and need a lift, come and see us. Our office is open from 10:00 AM to 6:00 PM, or you can reach us at ext. 5589.

Accounting

A reminder to all employees: all forms sent in the yearly payroll package must be completed and returned by February 15 of each year. If this is not possible, please contact us immediately. Information is available on new health packages. Our office is open from 8:30 AM to 4:30 PM Monday through Friday.

3. Create a section for each heading and center it.

4. Place the insertion point on the first character of paragraph one and divide the page into a three-column structure.

5. Create a header and footer for the newsletter:

    Header: **Real Entertainment Corporation News** should be left-justified, and the date should be right-justified.

    Footer: **Give us a call at 1-800-CALL-REC** should be centered.

6. Add the clip art PARTY.WMF to the first section of the document.

7. Create a watermark, DANCERS.WMF. for the background of the newsletter.

8. Save the file to your data disk as **REC.DOC**.

CHAPTER 8
Designing Tables in a Document

In Chapter 7, you learned to format text in newspaper-style columns, where text flows from the bottom of one column to the top of the next column. Sometimes you may want to format text in columns in a different way, with related paragraphs or columns of data side by side. If you are defining terms, for example, you may want to type each term in the first column and the corresponding definition beside it in the second column. If you have a list of numerical data, as another example, you may want the data to align within columns.

Table
A set of cells that contain information.

You can create columns using tabs, but Word's *table* capabilities offer a much easier method. You can use these capabilities to present information in tables with or without lines between columns and rows. When you format data in a table, it is easy to sort it into alphabetical order and, in the case of numerical data, to perform calculations. In this chapter, you learn how to create tables, or *side-by-side paragraphs,* within your documents. You also learn how to edit and format tables in Word.

Objectives

By the time you finish this chapter, you will have learned to

1. Recognize When to Use Tables
2. Create Side-by-Side Columns and Tables
3. Enter Data in a Table
4. Select Cells, Columns, and Rows
5. Move between Cells
6. Change Column Widths and Row Heights
7. Insert and Delete Columns, Rows, and Cells

8. Move Columns, Rows, and Cells
9. Edit Text in a Table
10. Add Borders and Shading
11. Calculate Values

Objective 1: Recognize When to Use Tables

Some documents are created primarily in side-by-side format; other documents may include side-by-side paragraphs or tables. The following are some examples of documents that are primarily in side-by-side format:

- Catalogs and price lists
- Telephone directories
- Specifications
- Theatrical scripts
- Inventories and Invoices to show calculations

Side-by-side columns
Vertical lines of cells arranged beside one another on a page. Word names columns alphabetically from left to right.

Within this chapter, the lists of shortcut key functions and their definitions are examples of *side-by-side columns*.

When you create documents containing side-by-side paragraphs or tables of numerical data, you should use the Word facilities described in this chapter. In the tutorials in this chapter, you create a table in POLICY2.DOC, displaying a room schedule list. Each exercise continues from the preceding exercise. Periodically, you are reminded to save your data.

Objective 2: Create Side-by-Side Columns and Tables

Row
A horizontal line of cells. Word numbers rows consecutively from top to bottom.

To create side-by-side columns and tables with Word, you start by temporarily defining the number of columns and *rows* you want. In most cases, you know the number of columns, but you probably don't know how many rows you will need. It doesn't matter. Just make your best guess because you can change the number of rows and columns as you work.

Creating a Table

To create a table, follow these steps:

1 Open POLICY2.DOC, and position the insertion point at the end of the document.

2 Click the Insert Table button on the Standard toolbar to display a replica of a table (see figure 8.1).

Figure 8.1
A replica of a table appears when you click the Insert Table button.

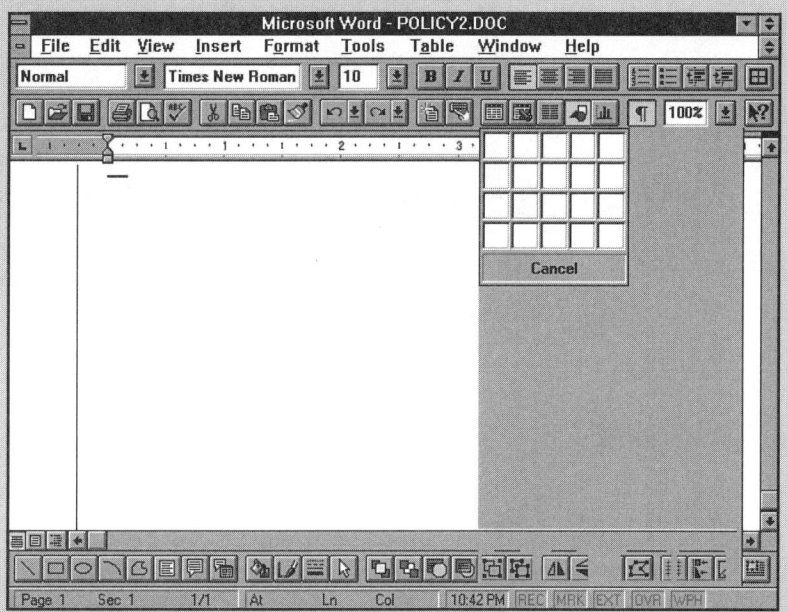

Note: *Make sure that no text is selected before you press the Insert Table button to create a table. If any text is selected, Word attempts to convert that text into a table.*

❸ Place the mouse pointer on the upper left cell in the table box.

❹ Click and drag to the right to highlight four rows and five columns.

Figure 8.2
In the table box, four rows and five columns are highlighted.

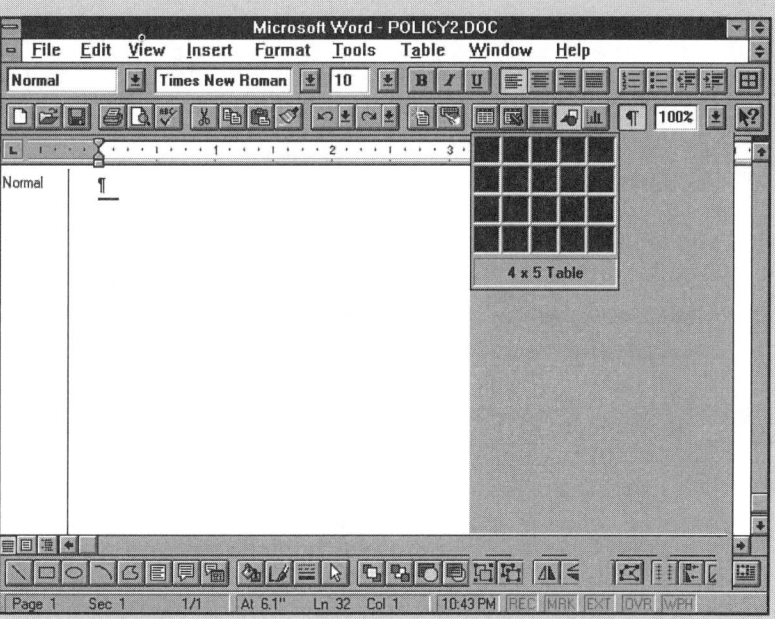

(continues)

Creating a Table (continued)

5 Release the mouse button to display a table outlined with *gridlines*.

If the gridlines do not display, choose Gridlines from the Table menu.

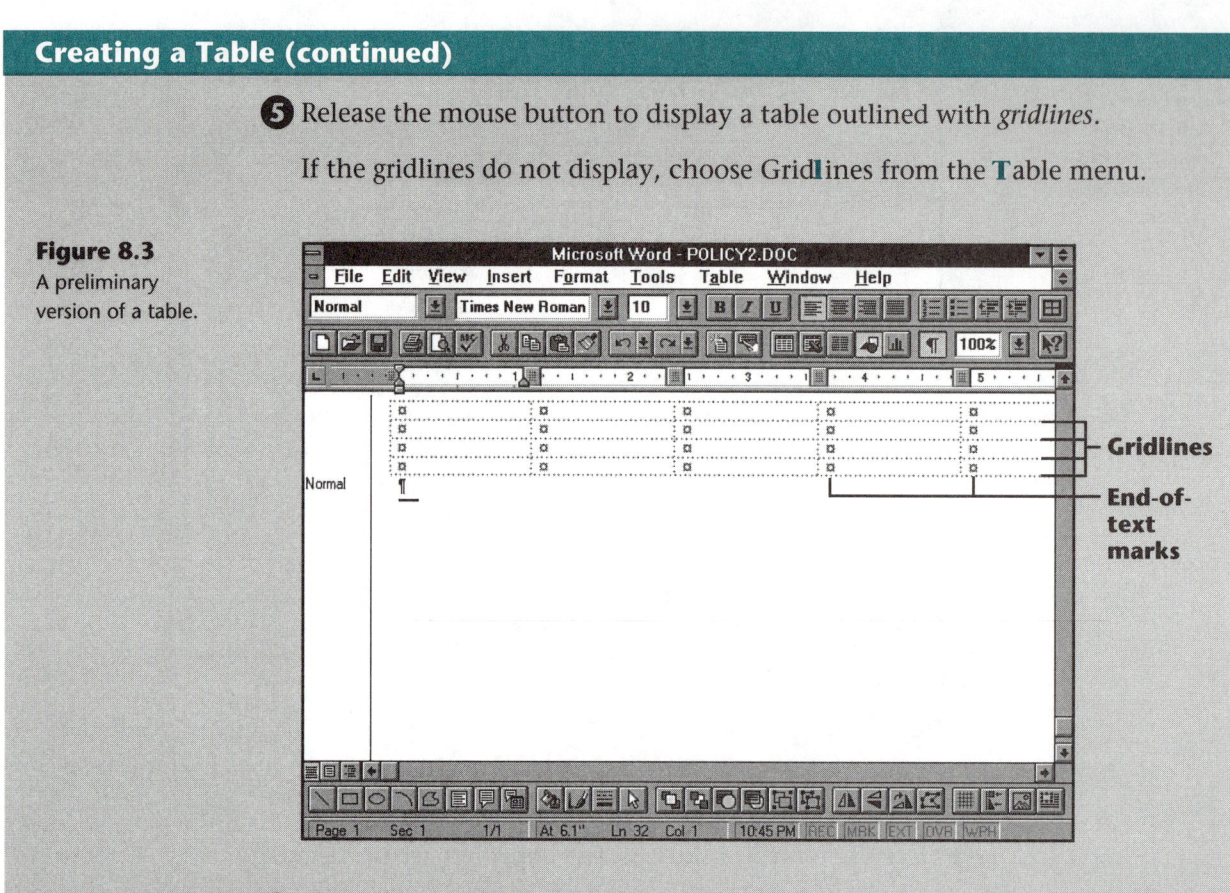

Figure 8.3
A preliminary version of a table.

6 Close the document and save your changes.

When you insert a table into a document, the horizontal ruler shows the width of each column in a table, but the usable width of each column is slightly less than the space between the vertical gridlines—to provide some blank space between columns.

By default, when you create a table, Word displays nonprinting characters such as gridlines, end-of-text marks, and end-of-row marks. Click the Show/Hide Marks button on the Standard toolbar to switch between displaying and hiding nonprinting characters.

Using the Insert Table Command to Create Tables

You can also create a table with columns of a precise width, using the Insert Table command from the Table menu. To create a table with precise column widths, follow these steps:

1 Open POLICY2.DOC, and position the insertion point at the end of the document.

2 Choose Table, Insert Table. The Insert Table dialog box appears (see figure 8.4).

Figure 8.4
You can specify the number of columns and rows for a table in the Insert Table dialog box.

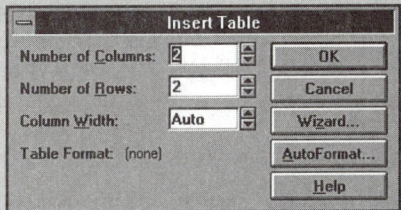

③ In the Number of **C**olumns text box, enter **2** for the number of columns in the table.

④ In the Number of **R**ows text box, enter **2** for the number of rows in the table.

⑤ In the Column **W**idth text box, choose Auto (the default) to automatically columns of equal width across the page.

⑥ Choose OK to create the table.

⑦ Close the document without saving your changes.

Objective 3: Enter Data in a Table

In a table, you enter data into *cells*. You can enter and edit data separately in each cell. Cells can contain text, numbers, or graphics. You can enter data by typing, importing from another application, or creating a drawing or chart within the cell. This chapter covers only how to enter text and numbers in cells.

Cell
The intersection of a row and a column in a table. You can store information in cells.

Note: *When you are placing or editing data in a cell, pressing a keyboard key (except for* Tab *and* Shift+Tab*) has the same effect as when you are working with normal text. When you press* Tab*, you move to the next cell; when you press* Shift+Tab*, you move to the previous cell. To place a tab within a cell, press* Ctrl+Tab*.*

Entering Column Titles

Tables should have column titles so that readers can easily understand the information. To enter column titles in a table, follow these steps:

① Open the document POLICY2.DOC. Place the insertion point in the upper left cell. The insertion point appears to the left of the end-of-text mark in that cell.

② Type **Room** in the upper left cell.

(continues)

238 Designing Tables in a Document

Entering Column Titles (continued)

3 Press Tab or click anywhere within the second cell in the first row. Type **Description** in this cell.

4 In the third column of the first row, type **Hours**.

5 In the fourth column of the first row, type **# of PCs**. Your table should look like figure 8.5.

Figure 8.5
The first row of this table contains titles for each column.

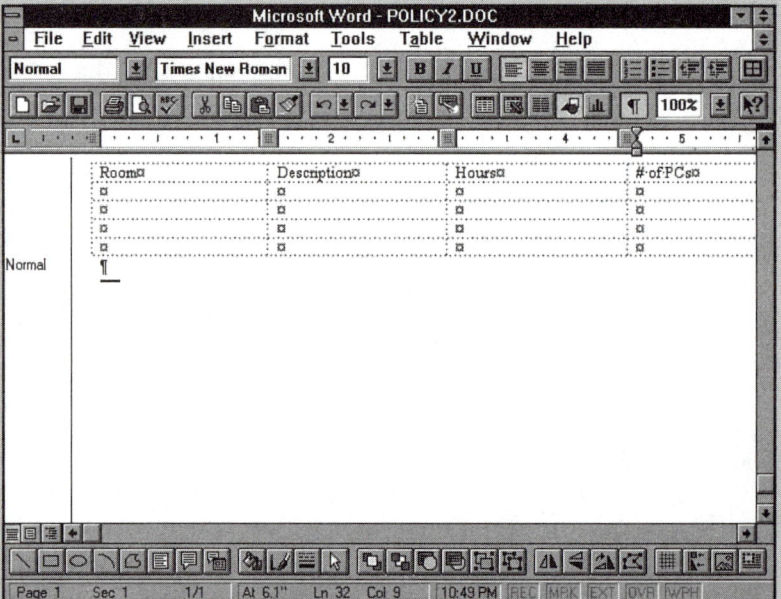

6 Save the document, but keep it open.

Entering Records in a Table

You can enter additional data in the table in the same manner that you entered the column titles. Each record constitutes a row within the table.

Entering Data in a Table

To enter the remaining data in the table, follow these steps:

1 Position the insertion point in the first cell of the second row. Type **305A**.

2 Press Tab or click within the second cell of the second row, and type the following data:

286 Nec PC computers; 1Mg of RAM; 40 Mg Hard Drive; 1 5.25 disk drive and 1 3.5 disk drive; Dot Matrix Printers (9pin)

3 Position the insertion point in the third cell of the second row, and type **2:00 PM - 5:00 PM**.

④ In the fourth cell of the second row, type **16**.

⑤ In the third and fourth rows, type the following data:

308	286 Nec PC computers; 640K; 40 Mg Hard Drive; 1 5.25 disk drive; Dot Matrix Printers (9pin)	3:00 PM-5:00PM	19
306	486 DX 33 computers; Windows based; 4 Mg of RAM; 120 Mg Hard Drive; 1 3.5 disk drive; and 1 5.25 disk drive; SVGA monitors; Dot Matrix printers (24 pin)	2:00PM - 5:00PM	23

Note: *When you type more text than fits within the width of the cell, Word wraps the text and starts a new line in the same cell. Later in this chapter, you learn to adjust the column width. For now, let Word wrap your text as you type it. Do not be concerned if Word does not wrap your text exactly as shown in figure 8.6.*

Figure 8.6
The table with three records.

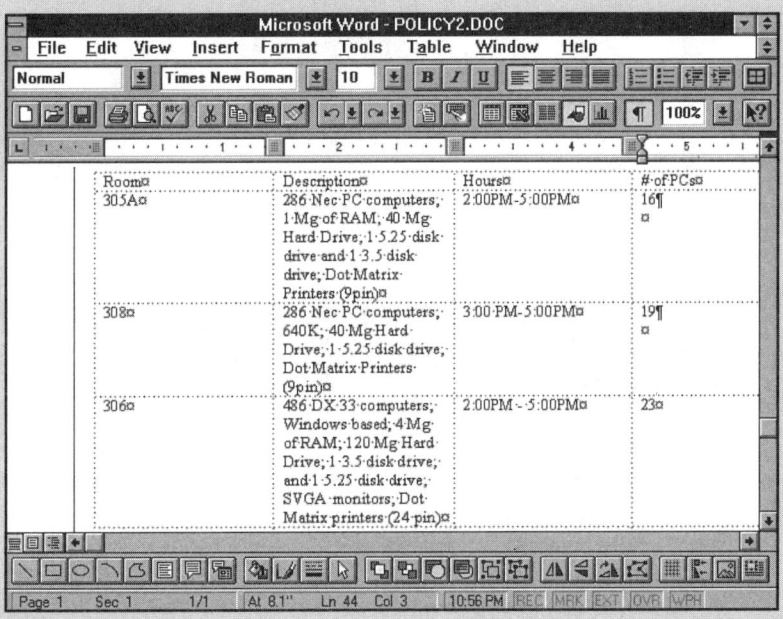

⑥ Close and save the document with the new table that you have created.

240 Designing Tables in a Document

Objective 4: Select Cells, Columns, and Rows

You must select the cells that you want to work with before you start an operation. In a table, you can select individual cells, one or more rows, one or more columns, or the entire table, to perform formatting or other functions. Word regards the contents of a cell as a paragraph.

Selecting a Cell and a Group of Cells

To practice selecting a cell and a group of cells within a table, follow these steps:

① Open the document POLICY2.DOC, and position the insertion point in the second cell of the first row of your table.

② Move the mouse pointer to the left edge of the cell until the pointer changes to an arrow pointing up and angled to the right.

③ Click the mouse to select this cell (see figure 8.7).

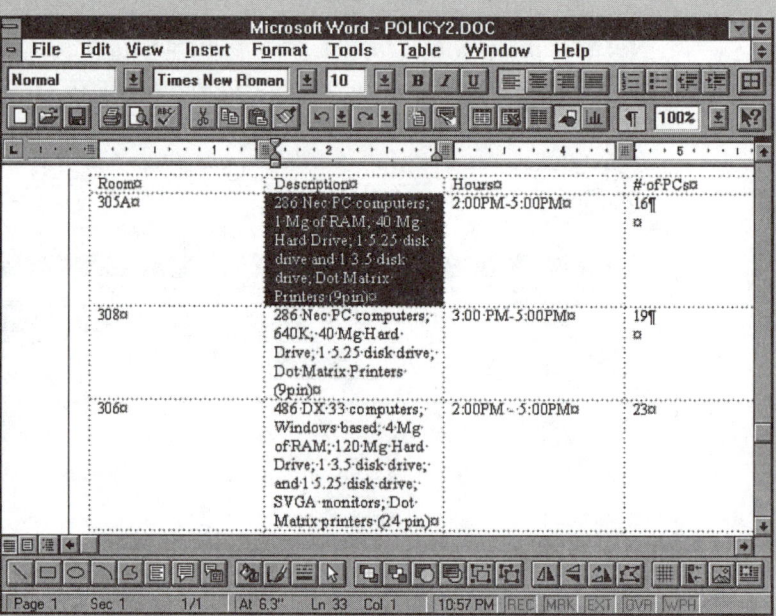

Figure 8.7
A selected cell within a table.

④ Move the mouse pointer to the right until it becomes an arrow pointing up and to the left. Click the mouse button, deselecting the cell.

⑤ To select the group of cells from the second cell in the second row to the third cell in the third row, select the second cell in the second row. Then drag the mouse pointer to the right until the group of cells is selected (from the second cell in the second row to the third cell in the third row).

⑥ To deselect this group of cells, simply position the mouse and click an insertion point in another location.

⑦ Keep the document open.

Select Cells, Columns, and Rows   241

You can also select a column, a row, or an entire table. For example, to change the typeface of an entire row or column, you must first select the column or row in your table.

Selecting a Column and a Row

To select both a column and a row in the open POLICY2.DOC, follow these steps:

1 To select the first column, point to the horizontal gridline at the top of this column and click.

When you have the pointer in the correct location, the pointer changes to a down arrow shown in figure 8.8.

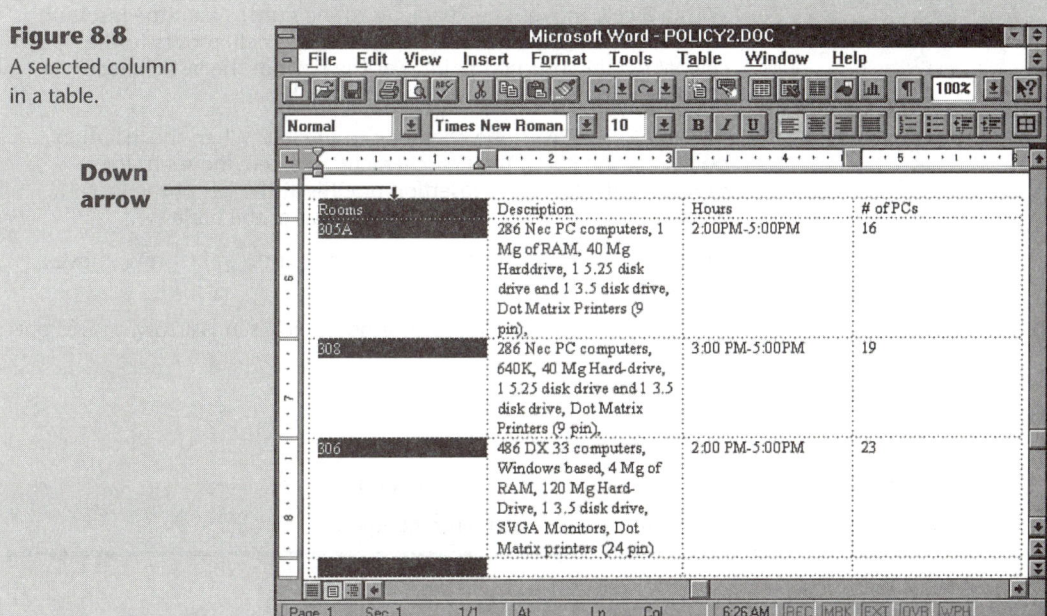

Figure 8.8
A selected column in a table.

Down arrow

Note: *To select two or more adjacent columns, point at the top of the first column, click and drag to the right or left to include more columns. You cannot select nonadjacent columns.*

2 To select the first row, point to the left of the row and click.

Note: *To select two or more adjacent rows, point at the first row, click and drag up or down to include more rows. You cannot select nonadjacent rows.*

3 To select the entire table, press Shift+Alt+5 (use 5 on the numeric keypad with NumLock turned on).

4 Keep the document open.

Objective 5: Move between Cells

When you are working within a table, you need to move from one cell to another, and Word provides shortcut keys for doing this (see table 8.1).

Table 8.1 Table Shortcut Keys

Shortcut	Action
Tab	Moves to the next cell to the right. If already at right end of a row, moves to the first cell in the next row. If at right end of bottom row, creates new row and moves to the first cell.
Shift+Tab	Moves to the next cell to the left. If already at left end of row, moves to the last cell in the preceding row. No effect if at first cell of first row.
→	Within a cell, moves one character to the right. When the insertion point is at the right of the last character in a cell, moves to the next cell. When the insertion point is at the right of the last character in the lower right cell, it moves out of the table.
←	Within a cell, moves one character to the left. When the insertion point is at the left of the first character in a cell, moves to the previous cell. When the insertion point is at the left of the first character in the upper left cell, moves out of the table.
↑	Moves up one row. When the insertion point is in first row, moves out of table.
↓	Moves down one row. When insertion point is in last row, moves out of table.
Alt+Home	Moves to first cell in current row.
Alt+End	Moves to last cell in current row.
Alt+PgUp	Moves to top cell in current column.
Alt+PgDn	Moves to bottom cell in current column.

Objective 6: Change Column Widths and Row Heights

You can change column widths quickly by dragging gridlines or the column markers, or you can use a dialog box to set column widths precisely. You also can change the space between columns and set row heights. When you change the width of columns, Word adjusts any word wrap within cells to suit the new column widths.

Changing Column Widths

To change a column width in POLICY2.DOC, follow these steps:

❶ Point to the gridline on the right of the second column. The mouse pointer changes to a double-headed arrow, as shown in figure 8.9.

Figure 8.9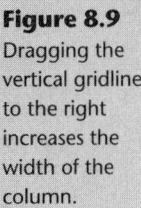
Dragging the vertical gridline to the right increases the width of the column.

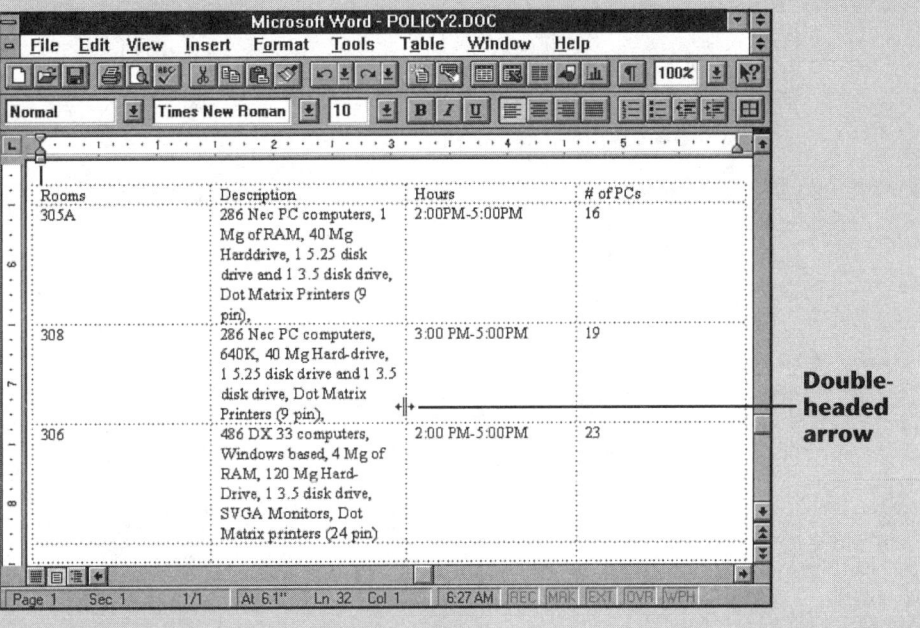

Double-headed arrow

❷ Click and drag to the right to increase the width of this column.

❸ Keep the document open.

When you drag a vertical gridline or drag in the horizontal ruler, the overall width of the table remains the same. When you change the width of one column, columns to the right are automatically resized in proportion to their original widths.

You can modify the way Word changes column widths by using any of the following:

- Press and hold down `Shift` while you drag. Only the immediate columns on each side of the gridline are affected. As one becomes wider, the other becomes narrower.

- Press and hold down `Ctrl` while you drag. All columns to the right of the selected gridline become equal in width.

- Press and hold down `Ctrl`+`Shift` while you drag. Only the column to the left of the selected gridline changes width. The overall width of the table changes.

To display the width of columns, point to any vertical gridline, press and hold down `Alt` while you click the mouse button.

Setting Precisely Column Widths

You can also change the column width to a precise value. To change the width of a column in POLICY2.DOC, follow these steps:

1 Place the insertion point in column two.

2 Choose **T**able, Cell Height and **W**idth.

3 If necessary, click the **C**olumn tab to display the **C**olumn section of the dialog box (see figure 8.10).

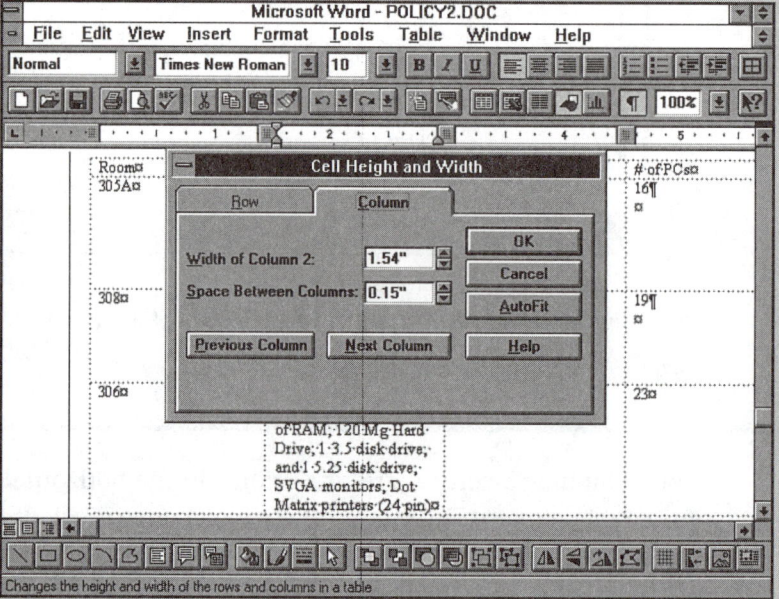

Figure 8.10
The Cell Height and Width dialog box shows the width of the column that currently contains the insertion point.

4 In the **W**idth of Column 4 text box, enter **1**.

Click the **N**ext Column or **P**revious Column button to show the width of another column.

5 To change the amount of space between columns, change the value in the **S**pace Between Columns text box to **.1**. The value you set affects the space between all columns.

When you change the space between columns, the overall width of the table changes.

6 Choose OK to redisplay the table with the new column widths.

7 Save the file, but keep it open.

Note: *If you click* **A***utoFit, Word adjusts column widths automatically according to the contents of the cells.*

Changing Row Heights

By default, Word automatically adjusts row heights to accommodate the text in the cells in each row, but you can also change the row height. You can change the height of rows, individually or for the entire table. For example, you may want to make Row 1 higher than the other rows to emphasize the headings.

To change the height of a row, you use the Cell Height and Width dialog box. From the Height of Row drop-down list, you can choose one of the following options:

- Auto. Word automatically determines the height of each selected row.

- At Least. Word sets each selected row to a specific height or more if the text requires more space.

- Exactly. Word sets each selected row to a specific height, even if this height does not provide enough space for all the text.

Changing Row Heights

To change row height in POLICY2.DOC, follow these steps:

1. Select Row 1.

2. From the Table menu, choose Cell Height and Width to display the Cell Height and Width dialog box.

3. If necessary, click the Row tab to display that section of the dialog box (see figure 8.11).

Figure 8.11
You can change row height in the Row section of the Cell Height and Width dialog box.

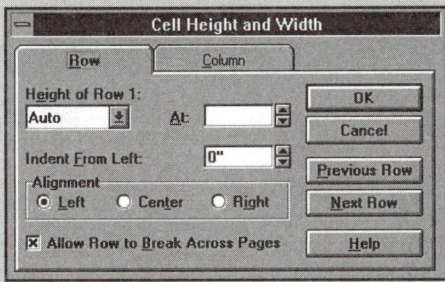

4. From the Height of Rows drop-down list, choose At Least.

5. In the At text box, enter 20.

   Note: *If you choose Auto in the Height of Rows drop-down list, the At text box is not used.*

6. If you want to set the height for another row, click the Next Row or Previous Row button, and repeat steps 4 and 5.

(continues)

Changing Row Heights (continued)

➐ Choose OK to set the rows in the table to the new heights.

➑ Save your changes, but keep the document open.

You also can click buttons under Alignment in the **R**ow section of the Cell Height and Width dialog box to align individual rows on the page. Click the **L**eft button, the default, to align selected rows at the left page margin; the Cen**t**er button to center selected rows on the page; or the Ri**g**ht button to align selected rows at the right page margin. By default, text in a row breaks across pages when the row contains two or more lines. To prevent this from happening, click the Allow Rows to **B**reak across Pages check box to remove the check mark.

Objective 7: Insert and Delete Columns, Rows, and Cells

When creating a table, you must make a preliminary choice regarding the number of columns and number of rows you would like to have in your table. You can subsequently change the number of columns and rows, however. You can insert and delete columns, rows, and cells of a table using the Standard toolbar or the T**a**ble menu.

Inserting Rows

To insert rows into a table in POLICY2.DOC, follow these steps:

➊ Select Row 2 because this is the row above which you want to insert a new row.

➋ Click the Insert Rows button on the Standard toolbar,

or

From the T**a**ble menu, choose **I**nsert Rows. Word inserts the new row.

Note: *If you select two or more rows, Word inserts that number of rows when you click the Insert Rows button.*

➌ Keep the document open.

All inserted rows have the same format as the row before which the insertion is made.

To add a new row to the bottom of the table, place the insertion point in the lower right cell and press Tab. This row has the formatting of the previous last row.

Inserting Columns

To insert columns into a table in POLICY2.DOC, follow these steps:

① Select Column 4 of your table. This is the column before which you want to make the insertion.

 ② Click the Insert Columns button on the Standard toolbar.

or

Choose Table, Insert Columns. Word inserts the new column.

③ Keep the document open.

All the inserted columns have the same format, including width, as the column preceding the insertion.

To add a column to the right side of the table, select all the end-of-row marks at the right side of the table; then click the Insert Columns button on the Standard toolbar.

Inserting Cells

To insert cells into a table in POLICY2.DOC, follow these steps:

① Select the first cell in the table.

Note: *When you select two or more cells, Word inserts as many cells as you have selected.*

 ② Click the Insert Cell button on the Standard toolbar.

or

Choose Table, Insert Cells. Word displays the Insert Cells dialog box (see figure 8.12).

(continues)

Inserting Cells (continued)

Figure 8.12
You can use the Insert Cells dialog to insert one cell, or a whole row or column of cells.

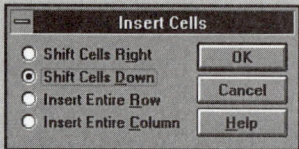

❸ Choose Shift Cells Right to insert one cell to the left of the selected cell.

❹ Choose OK.

❺ Save your changes, but keep the document open.

Other options in the Insert Cells dialog box include the following:

- Shift Cells Down. The cells below the insertion point are shifted down to make room for the insertion. Other columns are not affected.

- Insert Entire Row. The row that contains the selected cell, along with all rows below it, is shifted down to make room for the insertion. All columns are affected.

- Insert Entire Column. The column that contains the selected cell, along with all columns to the right, is shifted to the right to make room for the insertion. All columns are affected.

Note: *If you choose Shift Cells Right, cells that were in one column are no longer in the same column. If you choose Shift Cells Down, cells that were in one row are no longer in the same row.*

Deleting Columns, Rows, and Cells

Deleting columns, rows, and cells is similar to the way you insert. First, select the columns, rows, or cells to be deleted. Choose the Cut button on the Standard toolbar to remove a column or row from the table or to remove the contents of individual cells (not the cells themselves). The deleted items are placed in the Clipboard. This method deletes only the contents of the cells, not the cells.

Alternatively, after selecting columns, rows, or cells to be deleted, you can open the T**a**ble menu and choose **D**elete Columns, **D**elete Rows, or **D**elete Cells (the menu item changes according to what is selected in the table). If you are deleting cells, Word displays a dialog box, similar to the one for inserting cells, in which you choose what happens to the cells below or to the right of the deleted cells.

Deleting Columns, Rows, and Cells

To use the Table menu to delete the column, row, and cell that you inserted in the previous tutorials, follow these steps:

1 Select the cell that you inserted in the preceding tutorial. Choose T**a**ble, **D**elete Cells to delete the blank cell. Choose the Shift Cells **L**eft command to delete the additional cell.

2 Select the column that you inserted in a previous tutorial. Choose T**a**ble, **D**elete Columns to delete the blank column.

3 Select the row that you inserted. Choose T**a**ble, **D**elete cells Delete **E**ntire Row.

4 Save your changes, but keep the document open.

Objective 8: Move Columns, Rows, and Cells

You can move columns, rows, or cells, from one location in a table to another, by dragging them, or by using the Cu**t** and **P**aste commands.

Note: *Do not confuse moving rows and columns with moving text within a table. When you move text within a table, you move the contents of a cell. When you move rows and columns, you move both the cells and their contents.*

Moving a Column by Dragging

To move rows, columns, or cells by dragging them to their new location in POLICY2.DOC, follow these steps:

1 Select Column 3.

Note: *When moving a row or column, be sure to select the entire row or column. When moving cells, include the end-of-cell marks; otherwise, Word moves only the contents of the cells.*

2 Point to the selected column. Press the mouse button until the pointer changes to the drag shape.

3 Drag the mouse pointer to column 4, and release the mouse button. Your table should be similar to the one in figure 8.13.

(continues)

Moving a Column by Dragging (continued)

Figure 8.13
The column in your table that was previously column 3 is now column 4.

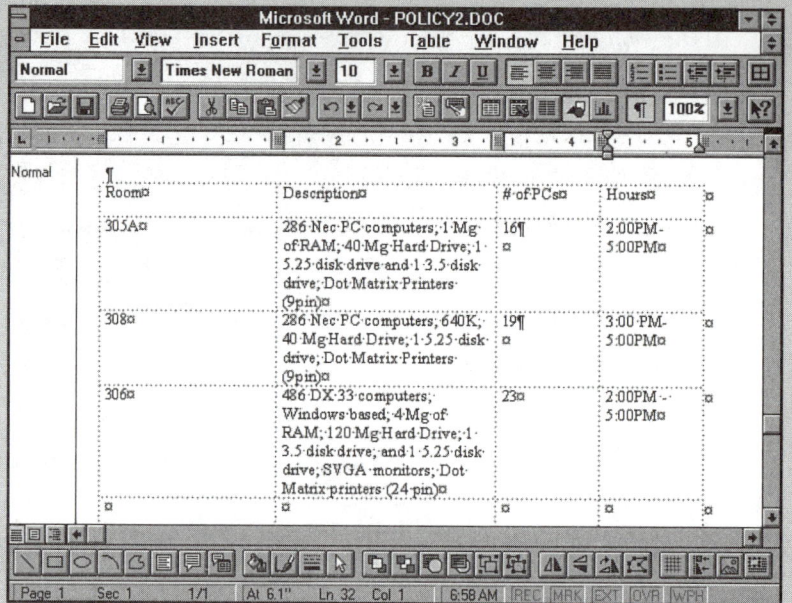

④ Save your document, but keep it open.

Note: *Use the same steps to move a row(s) or cell(s) by dragging. You also can copy columns, rows, and cells by holding down* Ctrl *while you drag.*

You also can move an columns, cells, and an entire row of cells, including the contents of those cells, by cutting and pasting.

Moving a Row by Cutting and Pasting

To move a row using the Cut and Paste commands in POLICY2.DOC, follow hese steps:

① Select the row for Room 306. Be sure to select the entire row, including any end-of-text or end-of-row marks.

② Choose the Cut button on the Standard toolbar.

or

From the Edit menu, choose Cut.

Word removes the entire row from the table.

③ Position the pointer in the TOTAL row to paste the cut row immediately above it. The area must match the shape and size of the cells you selected in step 1.

❹ Choose the Paste button on the Standard toolbar.

or

From the Edit menu, choose Paste.

Word places the cut cells back into the table in their new position (see figure 8.14).

Figure 8.14
Row 3 is now in Row 4.

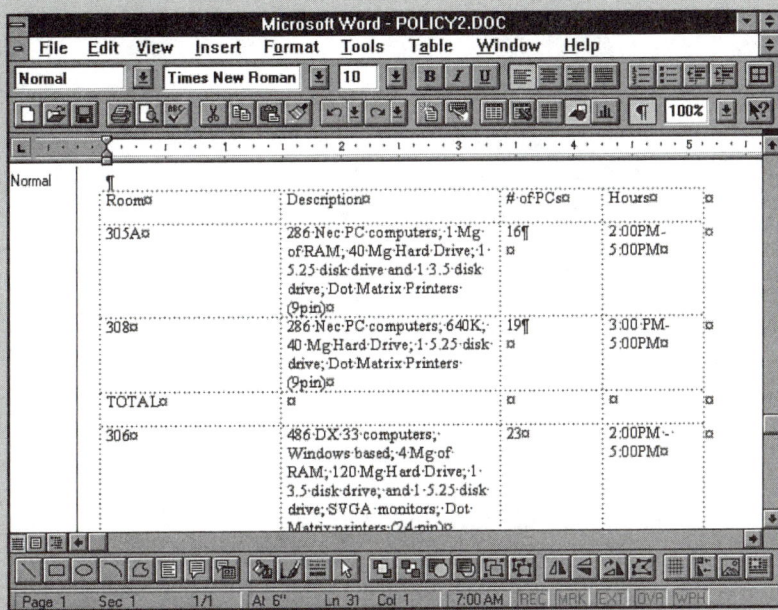

❺ Save the document, but keep it open.

Note: *You can move an entire table from one location in a document to another by cutting and pasting. Simply select the entire table, and then cut and paste as usual.*

Objective 9: Edit Text in a Table

Within a table, you can insert, delete, move, copy, and format text just as you do in normal paragraphs. To insert text in a cell, place the insertion point where you want to make the insertion; then type the text.

You can delete characters within a table by using `Backspace` and `Del`, just as you do outside a table. If you select an entire row or column, pressing `Backspace` deletes only the text in the first cell of the row or column, leaving the first cell blank. Pressing `Del` deletes all text in the row or column, leaving all the cells empty.

To move text within a table, you can open the Edit menu and use Cut and Paste, or you can use the Cut and Paste buttons on the Standard toolbar.

Moving Text

To move text in POLICY2.DOC, follow these steps:

1 Select *306* as the text to move to another cell.

Note: *If you want to move all the text in the cell, be sure that you select only the text. Do not include the end-of-cell mark in the selection.*

2 Choose the Cut button on the Standard toolbar.

or

From the **E**dit menu, choose Cu**t**.

Word removes the selected text from the cell.

3 Position the insertion point where you want to insert the text in the cell already containing *308*.

4 Choose the Paste button on the Standard toolbar.

or

From the **E**dit menu, choose **P**aste.

Word inserts the text at the insertion point.

5 Save your changes, but keep the document open.

You can copy a cell or a number of cells so that the same text appears in more than one place in the table. Copying text from one cell to another is similar to moving text, except that rather than using the Cut button or command, you use the Copy button or command.

Copying Text

To copy text from one cell to another in POLICY2.DOC, follow these steps:

1 Select *305A* as the text to copy. Be sure to include the end-of-cell marks.

2 Click the Copy button on the Standard toolbar.

or

From the **E**dit menu, choose **C**opy.

3 Position the insertion point in the blank cell (the destination cell).

4 Choose the Paste button on the Standard toolbar

or

From the **E**dit menu, choose **P**aste.

Word adds the copied cell to the destination cell.

> **Note:** *You can create tables in which some rows are longer than others. Suppose that you are working in a 4-by-4 table. If you copy cells A2 and B2 and then choose D2 as the first destination cell, you create cell E2. Row 2 is the only row with a fifth column. You cannot create a table in which some columns are longer than others.*
>
> **5** Close the document without saving your changes.

Objective 10: Add Borders and Shading

Gridlines
Nonprinting dotted lines between columns or rows in a table.

Table *gridlines* appear as dotted lines on-screen but do not appear in printed documents. You can, however, convert gridlines to printable lines. You also can add shading to emphasize sections of a table or to make a table easier to read.

You may want to print a table with lines that represent the gridlines, and you may want to shade certain sections of a table to call the reader's attention to those cells. The simplest way to add attractive borders and shading to a table is to have Word do it automatically. If you are not satisfied with the automatic borders and shading, you can modify what Word does or create your own borders and shading.

Adding Borders and Shading Automatically

Word can apply 34 different combinations of borders and shading to any table. Three of these combinations provide three-dimensional effects. Using automatic formatting can save you a great deal of time. To apply automatic borders and shading to the table in POLICY2.DOC, follow these steps:

1 Open POLICY2.DOC.

2 Place the insertion point anywhere in column two.

3 From the T**a**ble menu, choose Table Auto**F**ormat to display the Table AutoFormat dialog box (see figure 8.15).

Figure 8.15
You can choose among 34 combinations of borders and shading in the Table AutoFormat dialog box.

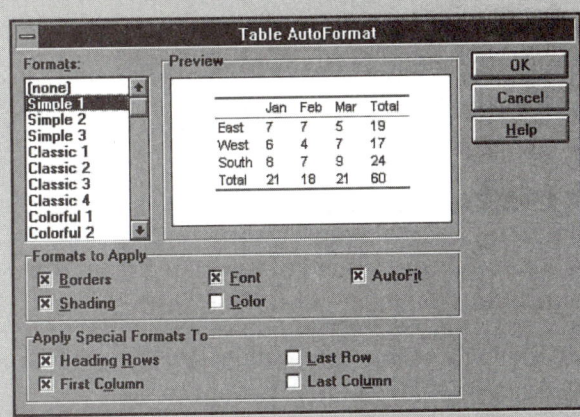

(continues)

> ### Adding Borders and Shading Automatically (continued)
>
> **4** Choose Classic 1 from the Formats list box. You can preview the format in the Preview box.
>
> **5** In the Formats to Apply area, choose the check boxes next to Borders, Shading, Font, and AutoFit. In the Apply Special Formats To area, choose the check boxes next to Heading Rows and First Column.
>
> **6** Choose OK to format your table according to the model.
>
> **Note:** *If you have access to a color printer, try some of the table formats with color enabled. You will probably be pleased with the results.*
>
> **7** Save your changes, but keep the document open.

Adding Borders and Shading Manually

To add borders and shading manually to a table, select all or part of a table. Then, choose **B**orders and Shading from the F**o**rmat menu to open the Table Borders and Shading dialog box (see figure 8.16). Chapter 6 provides information about using this dialog box.

To shade specific cells, select those cells in the table. Then open the Table Borders

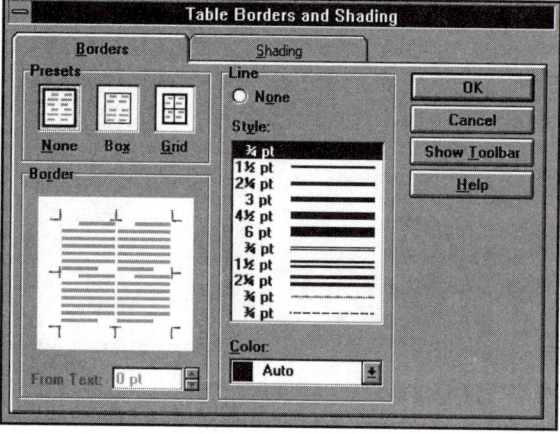

Figure 8.16
Use the Table borders and Shading dialog box to draw printable borders for tables.

and Shading dialog box, and click the **S**hading tab. Refer to Chapter 6 for more information on shading.

Objective 11: Calculate Values

Some tables contain numbers that are calculated from other numbers in the table. You can deal with these calculated numbers in three ways:

- Calculate the values manually, or with a calculator, and place them into cells just as you place other numbers in cells.

- Prepare the table separately in a spreadsheet application such as Microsoft Excel, and then import the table into your Word document or link the table to the document.

- Perform the calculations within the Word table.

When you are working with a small table and the calculations are fairly simple, you can probably use the first method. The second method is the only practical choice for large tables and complex calculations. The third method is a good choice when you have an average-size table, especially if it contains more than a few calculations. This section explains how to use the third method.

Formulas
An expression that performs mathematical operations on data in cells in a table.

With Word, you can calculate values in a table. Word uses *formulas* to add, subtract, multiply, and divide numbers. It also can calculate averages and percentages and find minimum and maximum values. As an introduction to calculations in tables, suppose that you need to know the number of computers in all rooms (see figure 8.17).

Figure 8.17
A short list of room information, with the quantity of each.

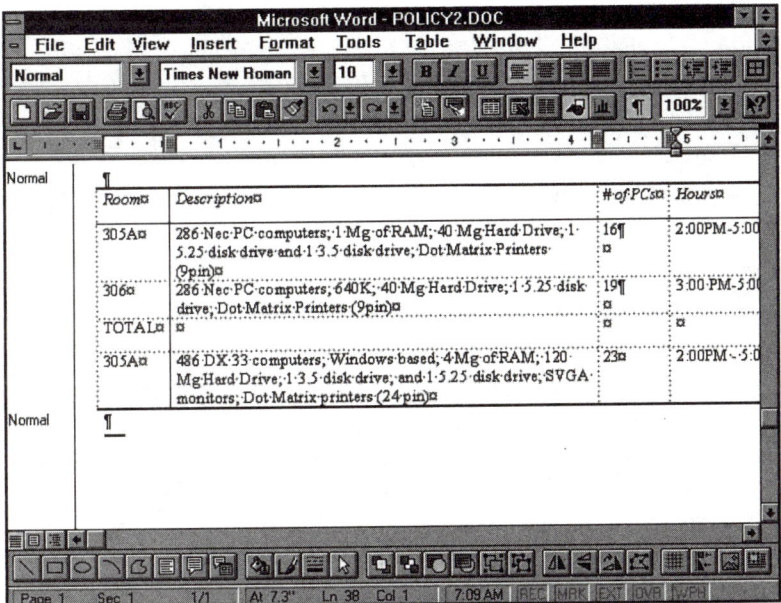

Note: *If you are familiar with a spreadsheet application such as Lotus 1-2-3, Microsoft Excel, or Borland Quattro Pro, you already know how to perform calculations within a Word table.*

Adding Numbers

To add numbers in a column in POLICY2.DOC, follow these steps:

1 Place the insertion point in the empty cell at the bottom of the fourth column.

2 Add the word **TOTAL** to the bottom of the first column.

3 From the T**a**ble menu, choose F**o**rmula to display the Formula dialog box (see figure 8.18).

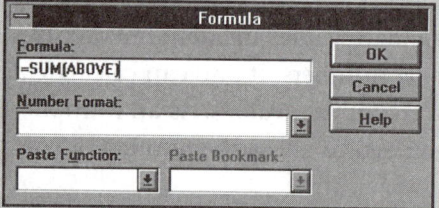

Figure 8.18
Use the Formula dialog box to define the calculation.

The formula dialog box appears with a suggested formula for a calculation in the Formula text box. Word guesses that you want to sum (add) numbers because this is the most common type of calculation. Word also guesses that you want to sum the numbers above the selected cell. You can, of course, select other types of calculations and other numbers on which to base the calculation.

4 Choose OK to accept the calculation. The calculated number appears in the selected cell (see figure 8.19).

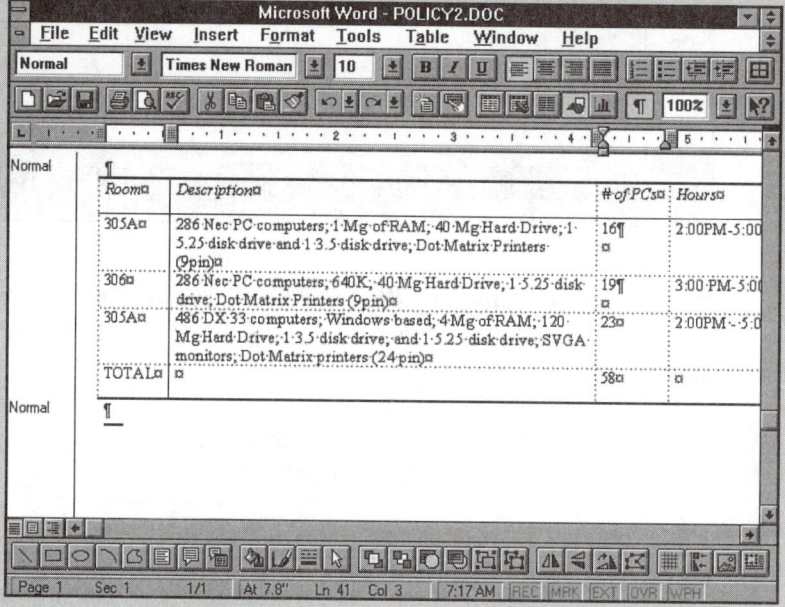

Figure 8.19
This table shows the TOTAL line.

> **Note:** *Although the calculated number looks like any other number in the table, it is actually a field. You cannot change the digits in this value because it depends on the numbers from which it is calculated. If you change any number from which the value is calculated, however, and then press* F9 *(Update), the calculated number is updated to show the new correct total.*
>
> **5** Save your changes, but keep the document open.

Multiplying Numbers

Adding numbers in a table is quite simple; multiplying numbers is a little more difficult because you must refer to cells in terms of their positions in the table. Word names columns alphabetically from left to right—the first column is *A*, the second *B*, and so on. Rows are named numerically from top to bottom—the first row is *1*, the second *2*, and so on. Individual cells are named in terms of the column and row that contain them—the upper left cell is *A1*, the cell in the second column and second row is *B2*, and so on.

Multiplying Numbers in a Table

To multiply numbers in a table in POLICY2.DOC, follow these steps:

1 Add a row to the table by pressing Tab in the last cell.

2 In the cell B6, type **Maintenance Fee**.

3 Place the insertion point in the empty cell, C5, where you want to have the result of the multiplication. Be sure that this is a blank cell.

4 From the **T**able menu, choose **F**ormula to display the Formula dialog box. When the dialog box opens, the insertion point is to the right of the text in the Formula text box.

5 Press Backspace 10 times to delete all but = from the text box. You must leave = there.

6 Type the formula **C5*100.00** to define the calculation (see figure 8.20).

(continues)

Multiplying Numbers in a Table (continued)

Figure 8.20
Write the formula to multiply the content of cell C5 by the value 100.00.

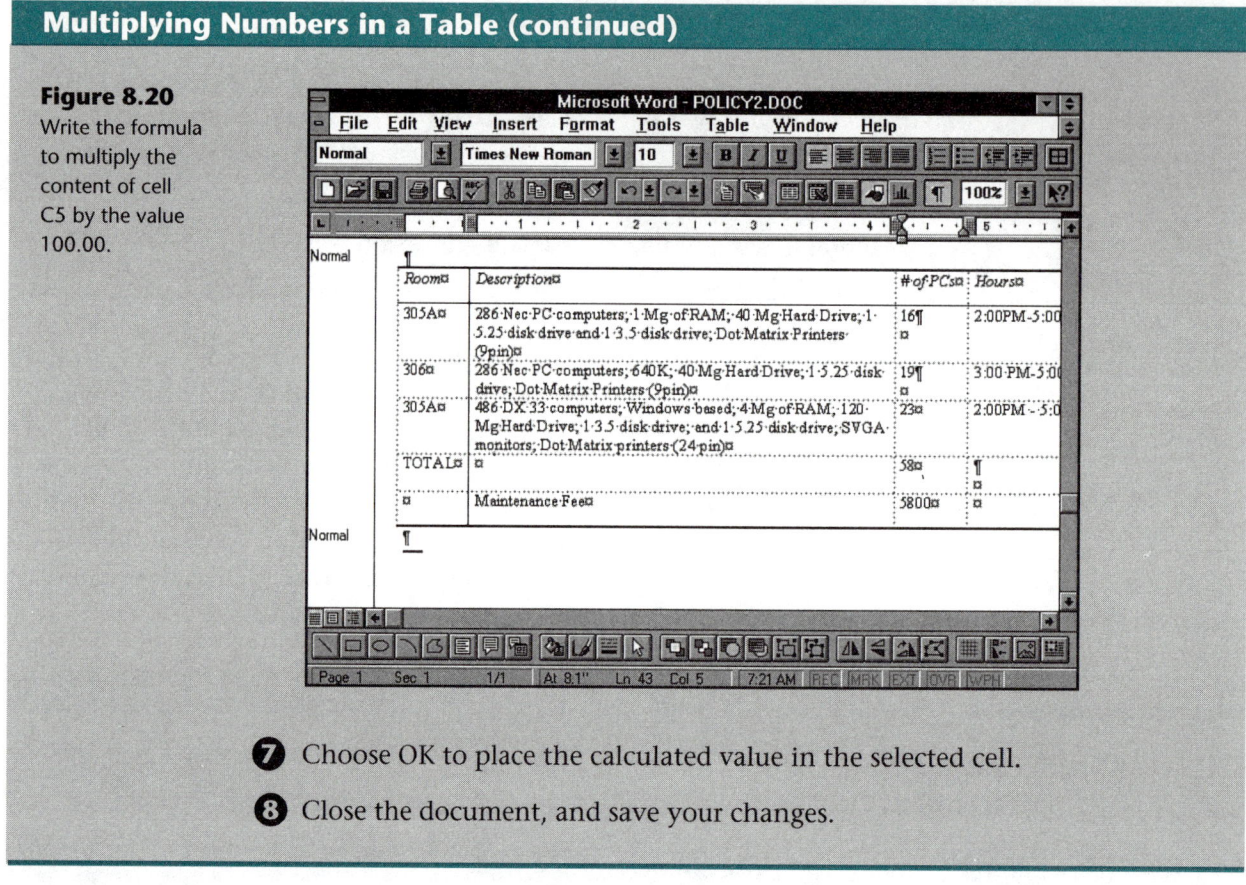

7 Choose OK to place the calculated value in the selected cell.

8 Close the document, and save your changes.

Chapter Summary

In this chapter, you learned to work with tables. You learned how to create tables within documents. You also learned how to edit and format tables. In the next chapter, you learn another time saving skill—how to merge form letters, envelopes, and labels to produce customized mass mailings.

Checking Your Skills

True/False Questions

For each of the following statements, circle *T* or *F* to indicate whether the statement is true or false.

T F **1.** The dotted lines displayed after selecting the rows and columns of a table are gridlines that show the size and position of the cells in the table.

T F **2.** In a table, you enter data into cells, which contain text, numbers or graphics.

T F **3.** When you move text within a table, you move only the contents and not the end-of-text mark.

T F **4.** Copying text from one cell to another deletes the cell from the current location and displays it in the new location.

T F **5.** Gridlines appear as dotted lines on-screen and appear in printed documents.

T F **6.** When you type more text than fits within the width of the cell, Word truncates the text.

T F **7.** You must select the cells that you want to work with before you start an operation.

T F **8.** Dragging the vertical gridline to the left increases the width of the column.

T F **9.** If you are not satisfied with the automatic borders and shading, you can modify what Word does or create your own borders and shading.

T F **10.** Word uses functions to add, subtract, multiply, and divide numbers.

Multiple-Choice Questions

In the blank provided, write the letter of the correct answer for each of the following questions.

____ **1.** To move to the next cell to the right within a table, press _____.

   a. Shift+Tab

   b. Tab

   c. Ctrl+Tab

   d. Alt+Tab

   e. Spacebar

____ **2.** You can format text in each cell, just as you format any other text, _____.

   a. by choosing buttons on the Standard toolbar or using menu commands

   b. by choosing buttons on the Formatting toolbar

   c. by using menu commands

   d. by choosing buttons on the Font toolbar

   e. both b and c

____ **3.** To change the heights of rows individually or for the entire table from the cell height and width dialog box, choose _____.

   a. At Least or Exactly

   b. Auto

   c. Alignment

   d. Allow Rows to Break

   e. Default

____ 4. If you select an entire row or column to delete, _____ to delete all text in the row or column.

    a. press [Spacebar]

    b. press [Ctrl]+[Tab]

    c. choose the Cut button

    d. press [Del]

    e. either c or d

____ 5. To calculate the extended price of an item using cell B8 containing the price and cell C8 containing the quantity, the formula would be _____.

    a. +D8XC8

    b. +D8*C8

    c. =D8*C8

    d. =B8XC8

    e. =D8timesC8

____ 6. If you want to use a spreadsheet program to set up a table and then use the data in Word, you would _____.

    a. create a drawing or chart within the cell

    b. import from another application

    c. retype the data from the other application

    d. copy the contents of the file within the document

    e. find that Word cannot import data from the spreadsheet program

____ 7. When the insertion point is in the last cell of a row, pressing [Tab] _____.

    a. moves the insertion down one cell

    b. creates a new row

    c. moves to the first cell in a new row

    d. moves the insertion point to the left

    e. does both b and c

____ 8. When you drag a vertical gridline or drag in the horizontal ruler, the overall width of the table _____.

    a. doubles in size

    b. reduces to half its size

    c. remains the same

d. exceeds its limit

e. increases to 1.5 times its size

____ 9. You can insert and delete columns, rows, and cells in a table using the _____ toolbar.

 a. Formatting

 b. Borders

 c. Drawing

 d. Standard

 e. Table

____ 10. To add a column to the right side of the table, select all the end-of-row marks at the right side of the table, and click _____ from the Standard toolbar.

 a. Insert Rows

 b. Insert Columns

 c. Add Rows

 d. Add columns

 e. Move columns

Fill-in-the-Blank Questions

In the blank provided, write the correct answer for each of the following questions.

1. The intersection of a row and a column in a table is a(n)_____.

2. To select an entire cell, click at the _____ end of the cell contents.

3. If you click _____, Word adjusts column widths automatically according to the contents of the cells.

4. You can _____ characters within a table by pressing [◆Backspace] or [Del], just as you do outside a table.

5. You can _____ a cell or cells so that the same text appears in more than one place in the table.

6. If any text is selected before you press the _____ Table button to create a table, Word attempts to convert that text into a table.

7. Click the _____ button on the Standard toolbar to switch between displaying and hiding nonprinting characters.

8. When you change the _____ of one column, columns to the right are automatically resized in proportion to their original widths.

9. You can move columns, rows, or cells, from one location in a table to another, by dragging them or by using the _____ and _____ commands.

10. If you change any number from which the value is calculated and then press _____, the calculated number is updated to show the new correct total.

Applying Your Skills

Review Exercises

Exercise 1: Creating a Two-Column Table
In the following exercise, you create a table.

1. Open a new document.

2. Create a table containing three business-related terms with corresponding definitions. Two examples follow:

Purchase Order	Form prepared by the Accounts Payable Department; prepared daily.
Destination Charge	Charge attached to various shipments.

3. Save the file to your data disk as **TERMS.DOC**.

Exercise 2: Creating a Three-Column Table
In the following exercise, you create a three-column table.

1. Open a new document.

2. Type the following text and create a table itemizing each item purchased:

    Newfield Company

    1890 Kelly Drive

    Sayerville, NJ 08871

    Enclosed you will find the itemized list requested, with a total for the order.

Item	Description	Price
A45	Camera Batteries for Cannon X25 Model	56.95
F89	Tapes (available only until April, 1994)	24.95
Total		81.90

3. Save the file to your data disk as **INVOICE.DOC**.

Exercise 3: Inserting a Table in MEDICAL.DOC
In the following exercise, you insert a table into MEDICAL.DOC

1. Open MEDICAL.DOC.

2. Add a table containing a schedule of fees to the end of the document.

Visit	Diagnosis	Fee
Routine	Physical, including Cardiogram, blood tests, and chest x-rays	135.00
Emergency	Broken Arm, able to x-ray and cast at the clinic	110.00

3. Save the file to your data disk as **MEDICAL.DOC**.

Exercise 4: Inserting a Table in FONTS.DOC

In the following exercise, you insert a table into FONTS.DOC.

2. Open FONTS.DOC, and move the insertion point to the end of the document.

3. Create a table with three rows and two columns.

4. Add the following information to the table:

Font	Points
Times Roman	12
Courier	14

5. Save the file to your data disk as **FONTS.DOC**.

Exercise 5: Inserting a Table into GUIDELINE.DOC

In the following exercise, you insert a table into GUIDELINE.DOC.

1. Open GUIDELINE.DOC, and add the visitation schedule for the evaluation.

2. Create a table with five rows and two columns.

3. Enter the following dates and times of visits.

Date	Time
August 11	9:00AM
July 15	10:00AM
August 14	2:00PM
July 7	11:00AM

4. Move the row containing July 7 to before August 14.

5. Save the file to your data disk as **TABGUIDE.DOC.**

Continuing Projects

Project 1: Practice in Using Word

In this exercise, you practice inserting a table into a document.

1. Open SCHEDULE.DOC.

2. Add a table to the middle of the document listing each contributor, the contributor's identification number, and the amount given with a total.

3. Enter the following text:

Contributor	Id#	Amount
James Allen 35 Chite Drive Roseville, CA 95661	42	100.00
Clyde Temper Simone Road Carmel, IN 46032	65	200.00
Susan Kempter Gale Court Norcross, GA 30093	33	125.00
Total		425.00

4. Move column 2 to column 1.

5. Be sure to use the calculating feature to add the column of numbers.

6. Save the file to your data disk as **SCHEDULE.DOC**.

Project 2: Federal Department Store

Continue your work on the catalog for the Federal Department Store by following these steps:

1. Open the OUTFIT.DOC.

2. Create a table at the end of the document listing the name of the product and a price.

3. Calculate the total in the price column.

4 Insert two rows in the second row position.

5. Save the file to your data disk as **OUTFIT.DOC**.

Project 3: Real Entertainment Corporation

After reviewing the newsletter, you decide that a table describing each product, as well as the fee, should be listed. Follow these steps:

1. Open the document REC.DOC.

2. Move the insertion point to the Marketing Department paragraph.

3. Create a new section after the paragraph, using continuous type.

4. Change the three-column structure to a one-column one, and begin entering the table.

Description	Fee
Casino Games including: black jack, wheel, chug-a-lug, and roulette tables.	1000.00
Videos, including children, young adult, and adult films, as well as providing all equipment.	750.00
Comedy Shows, including a crew from REC who involve the audience in the comedy routines; also tape individual comedy acts.	1500.00

5. Save the file to your data disk as **REC.DOC**.

CHAPTER 9
Merging Files

Merge
The process of combining information from one document with sets of information from another document.

Merging is one of the most important features in word processing tasks that organizations use. The *merge* feature is a very powerful and time-saving tool. Merging documents gives the capability to link a document file with a type of database file (list of names). The new Mail Merge Helper in Word guides users through the process so that anyone who needs to merge documents can.

Nearly every organization has a mailing that needs to be sent to all its contacts, but most do not have the manpower to enter thousands of personal letters for a marketing promotion. By using the Word merge feature, however, anyone can use one document to print a personalized letter for every contact.

Objectives

By the time you finish this chapter, you will have learned to

1. Understand the Basic Merge Procedure
2. Create a Main Document
3. Create or Open a Data Source
4. Insert Merge Fields in the Main Document
5. Merge the Data and Document
6. Use Other Merging Features

Objective 1: Understand the Basic Merge Procedure

Main document
A file containing the information you want to repeat in every copy of the document.

The basic procedure for *merging* is very consistent, whether you are printing form letters or address labels. You follow these general steps, which correspond to the steps in the Word Mail Merge Helper:

1. Create a *main document*.

    This file contains the information that will be identical in each document and the fields used to merge information.

Data source
The file containing the information that changes from one copy of the document to another.

Merge field
The name of a field in the data source.

2. Select a *data source*.

   This file contains the information, such as names and addresses, that will vary from document to document. You organize a data source so that Word can identify what fields each record contains and where each record ends.

3. Add *merge fields* to the main document.

   The merge fields determine which pieces of information from the data source are inserted in the document, and where.

4. Merge the data and document.

   The resulting multiple letters, labels, or envelopes can be printed directly. They also can be edited and saved as one long document with a section for each record in the data source.

Objective 2: Create a Main Document

The main document contains the information that is identical in each merged item. The main document for a form letter probably includes the date, the body of the letter, the closing, any formatting, and a few spaces and punctuation marks (for example, a comma between the city and state names). The main document for an envelope usually contains a return address and formatting such as the page size. For address labels, only the formatting usually remains the same in each merged item.

In each case, you open the Mail Merge Helper by choosing Mail Merge from the **T**ools menu and then create the appropriate kind of main document.

Creating a Main Document for a Form Letter

Creating a form letter is similar to creating any other letter except that you must leave placeholders (asterisks in this case) where information from the data source will go.

Creating a Form Letter Main Document

To create a main document for a form letter, follow these steps:

① From the **F**ile menu, choose **N**ew.

② Type the following letter.

   To: ****************

   ****

   ********, ** *****

   From: Information Systems Department

   This is a follow-up memo of the policy document. Each department has followed the suggested procedures, and we are now operating all current versions of software.

******, you have been selected for your excellence in the area of ********. A ceremony will be held on Tuesday, May 10th at 7:00 PM, to present the awards.

We congratulate you on your accomplishments and look forward to your continued support.

❸ From the Tools menu, choose Mail Merge. The Mail Merge Helper dialog box appears (see figure 9.1).

Figure 9.1
Use the Mail Merge Helper to guide you through the steps of the basic merge types.

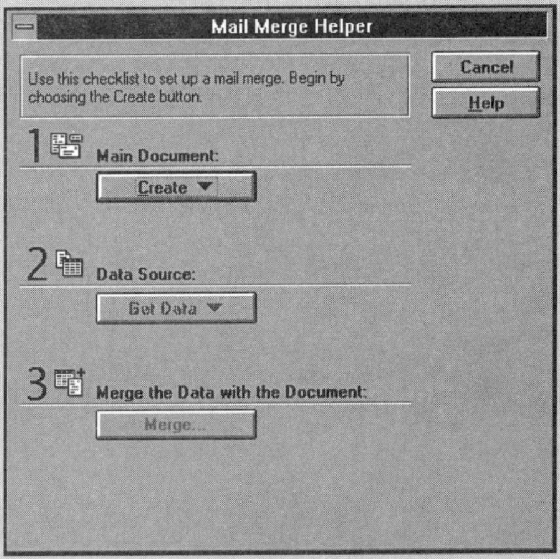

❹ From the Create drop-down list, select Form Letters. A dialog box prompts you to use the active document or create a new one.

Figure 9.2
When you create a main document, you can use the document you opened before starting the merge.

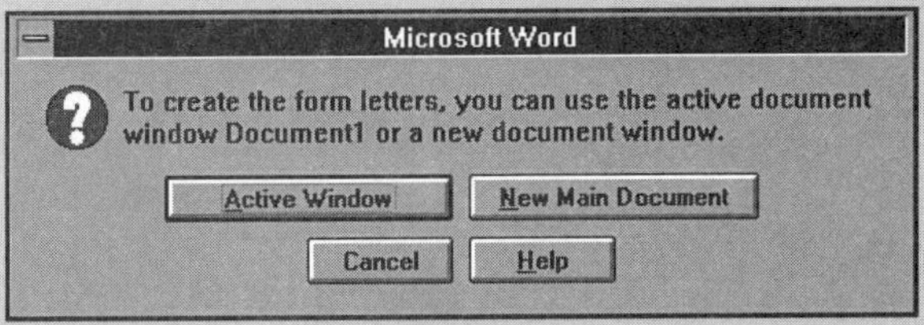

❺ Choose the Active Window button in the dialog box.

This step converts the document from step 1 into a main document for merging. If you change your mind, you can make the main document a normal document by selecting Restore to Normal Word Document from the Create drop-down list in the Mail Merge Helper dialog box.

❻ Press [Esc] to close the dialog box.

❼ Save your new document as **MAIN.DOC**.

270 Merging Files

You are now ready to set up a data source for the form letter.

Creating an Envelope Main Document

When you set up a main document for an envelope merge, Word automates most of the details. You specify the merge type for envelopes. To create a main document for envelopes, follow these steps:

❶ From the **T**ools menu, choose Mail Me**r**ge. The Mail Merge Helper dialog box appears.

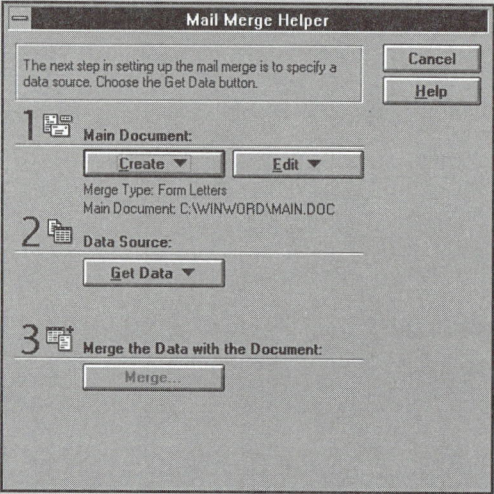

Figure 9.3
Use the Mail Merge Helper preset guides to set up envelope merges.

❷ From the **C**reate drop-down list, select **E**nvelopes. A dialog box prompts you to use the active document or to create a new one.

❸ Choose the **N**ew Main Document button.

This creates an empty main document for the envelope merge. After you specify the data source, you set up the main document by selecting an envelope size.

❹ Press Esc to remove the dialog box.

❺ Save your new envelope document as **ENVELOP.DOC**.

You are now ready to set up a data source for the envelope addresses.

Creating a Main Document for Labels

When you set up a main document for a label merge, Word handles the difficult details, including calculating the number of labels that will fit on a page. You specify the merge type for mailing labels.

Creating a Mailing Label Main Document

To create a main document for mailing labels, follow these steps:

1 From the **T**ools menu, choose Mail Me**r**ge. The Mail Merge Helper dialog box appears.

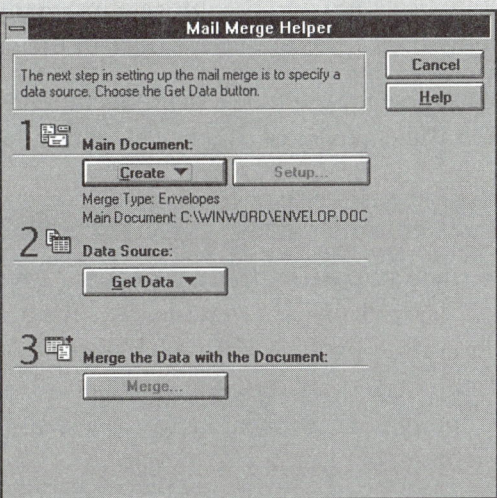

Figure 9.4
Use the Mail Merge Helper to preset forms for label merges.

2 From the **C**reate drop-down list, select **M**ailing Labels. A dialog box prompts you to use the active document or create a new one.

3 Choose the **N**ew Main Document button.

This step creates a blank main document for the label merge. After you specify the data source, you can select a standard label size.

4 Press « to remove the dialog box.

5 Save your new document as **LABELS.DOC**.

You are now ready to set up a data source for the label addresses.

Objective 3: Create or Open a Data Source

Record
All the information related to one set of fields—for example, all the information on one patient.

After you create a main document, you specify a data source. If the data source already exists (for example, if you are using an existing mailing list), you just open the file in the Mail Merge Helper. If you need to create a new file, Word helps you set up the fields and enter information in each *record*. For example, Word displays a screen with fields such as Name, Address, and so on, which can be changed, and then you type in the data.

When you open an existing data source or create a new one, the data source is attached to the main document. When you exit and save your documents, the data source is still attached when you open the main document later.

Creating a New Data Source

Field
One category of information—for example, the ZIP code in an address.

If you don't have an existing table or database of information to use as a data source, you can define *fields* and add the information manually. Word makes suggestions for commonly used fields and keeps track of the data records you enter.

To create a new data source for use in the main document, you define the categories of information in the data source (the fields), and then enter the actual data.

Defining Fields for the New Data Source

Before you add information to a data source, you need to name the categories of information you will be entering—the various elements of an address and any other categories you want to include. The field names, up to 40 characters long, can include letters, numbers, or underscore characters (_) and must begin with a letter. You can use capital letters to separate words visually in a field name, as in *FirstName*. To define the fields, follow these steps:

1. Determine which categories of information you have available and want to include in the merged documents. The categories needed in your form letter are Title, FirstName, LastName, Address, City, State, PostalCode, and Software.

2. Open MAIN.DOC, using the Mail Merge Helper.

3. Choose the **G**et Data. The drop-down list appears (see figure 9.5).

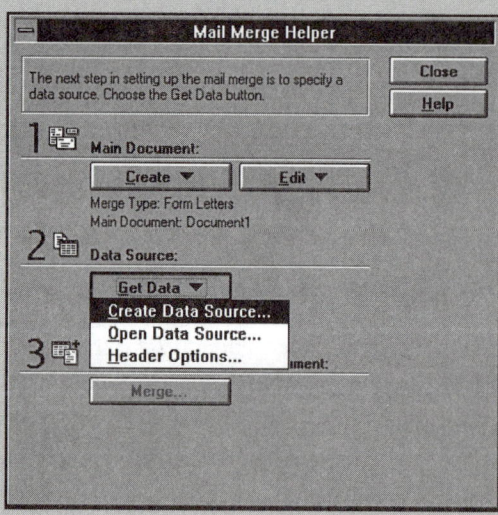

Figure 9.5
Use the drop-down list to create a data source or to open an existing one.

4. Choose **C**reate Data Source. The Create Data Source dialog box appears, showing a list of fields you can include in your data source.

Header record
A record that contains the names of each field in a data source.

5 From the Field **N**ames in Header Row list box, select a field you *don't* need in your data source *header record*, and choose the **R**emove Field Name button, repeating as necessary.

For example, you do not need the JobTitle, Company, and Country fields. If any unusual entries might need the extra fields, leave them in the list in case you want to add that information to your data source later.

6 You need a field that isn't in the list—Software. Type **Software** in the **F**ield Name box, and choose the **A**dd Field Name button. (This button becomes available when you type text in the **A**dd Field Name box.)

7 Enter the fields in the order given in the Data Form dialog box. To change the order of fields in the Field **N**ames in Header Row list, select a field name, and choose the up- or down-arrow Move button on the right.

The order of fields in your data source doesn't matter for the form letter, but entering data is more convenient if the fields are in the same order as the material you're entering. If you copy information from a stack of business cards, for example, they may tend to show the company name first, then first and last name, and so on.

8 After setting up the fields, choose OK. The Save Data Source dialog box appears.

9 Specify the drive containing your data disk as the location and name for the file, **AWARD.DOC**.

10 Choose OK. A dialog box appears, indicating that the data source now contains fields but no actual data (see figure 9.6).

Figure 9.6
Word prompts you to edit the data source to add records or set up the main document.

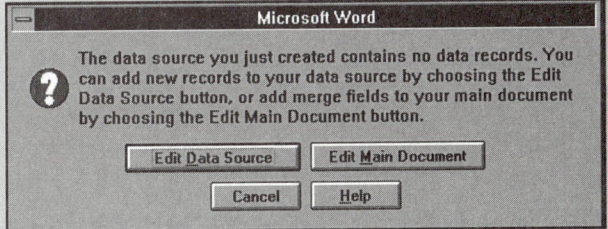

11 Choose the Edit **D**ata Source button from the dialog box.

If you choose the **S**et Up Main Document button instead, Word displays either the main document (form letters) or setup options (envelopes and labels).

Now that the fields are set up in your data source, you can enter the data.

Entering Data in the Data Source

When you finish creating fields in the Create Data Source dialog box, Word prompts you to edit the data source. If you went through these steps in a different order, however, you can still enter data from the Mail Merge Helper. Follow these steps to enter the data in AWARD.DOC.

1 If the Data Form dialog box is not already open, choose AWARDS.DOC from the **Ed**it drop-down list in the Data Source section of the Mail Merge Helper. The Data Form dialog box appears (see figure 9.7).

Figure 9.7
Use the Data Form to fill in each field of your data source.

2 Enter the data in each category of the first record, pressing Tab or Enter to move to the next field.

Title:	Mr.
FirstName:	Jack
LastName:	Frost
Address:	10 Summer Lane
City:	Marietta
State:	GA
PostalCode:	30066
Software:	Microsoft Word 6

Figure 9.8 shows the Data Form dialog box with the data for the first record entered.

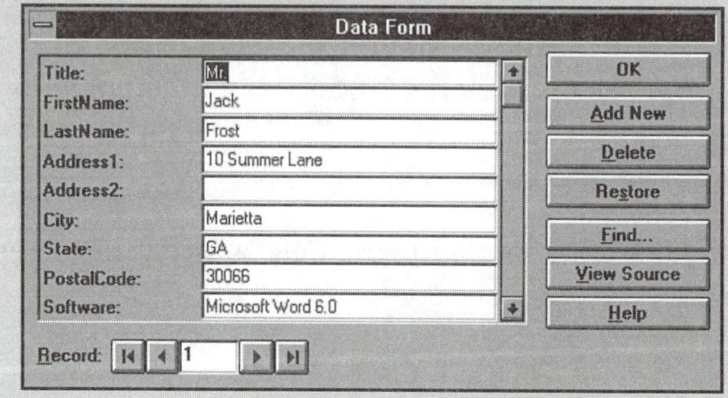

Figure 9.8
The data for the first record has been entered.

❸ Choose the **A**dd New button to insert a new record in the data source.

❹ To change a record already entered, type the record number in the **R**ecord box and press ⏎Enter .

You can also browse through the records one at a time. The arrow buttons (from left to right) display the first, previous, next, and last records in the data source.

❺ Repeat steps 2 through 4 until you have entered all the following data, and then choose OK.

Title:	Ms.
FirstName:	Jennifer
LastName:	Kayhill
Address:	890 Time Road
City:	Orem
State:	UT
PostalCode :	84057
Software:	Paradox for Windows
Title:	Mrs.
FirstName:	Alice
LastName:	Seymour
Address:	243 South Drive
City:	Chicago
State:	IL
PostalCode :	60604
Software:	Excel For Windows

Word displays the main document.

❻ Save the file to your data disk as **AWARD.DOC**.

Behind the scenes, Word creates a table to hold your data, using a column for each field you defined. Each cell in the first row (the *header row*) contains a field name. The other rows hold the data you enter in the Data Source dialog box, one row for each record you add.

You are now ready to prepare your main document and insert merge fields. If you want to edit the contents of the selected data source first, see the next section.

Editing a Data Source

You can edit a data source—for example, to add or update records. To edit AWARDS.DOC, follow these steps:

1. If you have closed MAIN.DOC, the document that uses the data source you want to edit, open this document. The Mail Merge toolbar appears when you open a main document.

2. Click the Edit Data Source button on the far right of the Mail Merge toolbar.

   The Data Form dialog box appears.

   Note: *Another way to open this dialog box is to choose Mail Merge from the Tools menu, and select the data source from the Edit drop-down list in the Mail Merge Helper.*

3. Edit the information in the data source, adding the following record:

Title:	Mr.
FirstName:	Sean
LastName:	O'Malley
Address:	457 Times Road
City:	Sayersville
State:	NJ
PostalCode :	08871
Software:	Borland C++

   Use the techniques described in the preceding tutorial, "Entering Data in the Data Source," to edit the data.

4. After you make all your changes, choose OK.

   Note: *To see the data as a table in a normal document, choose the View Source button in the Data Form dialog box. You can then add paragraph marks within a field (which you cannot do from the Data Form dialog box) and save the data source document for safety. To return to the dialog box, click the Data Form button on the Database toolbar.*

5. Save the file to your data disk as **MAIN.DOC**.

Create or Open a Data Source   277

You are now ready to prepare your main document and insert merge fields.

Opening an Existing Data Source

Conversion filter
A program that makes data entered in other applications compatible with Word.

The simplest way to store merge data is in a Word table. You also can take advantage of data created in other programs if you installed the corresponding *conversion filter* in Word. If you installed all the Word converters, you can open data created by the following applications:

- Microsoft Word 1.0–6.x, Word for Macintosh 3.x–5.x, and Word for MS-DOS 3.0–6.0.
- WordPerfect for Windows or DOS, Version 5.x
- Microsoft Excel (any version)
- Lotus 1-2-3 Release 2.x–3.x
- Microsoft FoxPro, Borland dBASE, and compatible applications
- Microsoft Access
- Borland Paradox

You can easily use the same data with more than one main document. If you created a name and address file to use with a form letter to solicit new business, for example, you can use the same names and addresses to print the envelopes.

Opening a Data Source for Use in the Main Document

To use MAIN.DOC and AWARD.DOC, follow these steps:

❶ Open MAIN.DOC, using the Mail Merge Helper (see figure 9.9).

Figure 9.9
To specify a data source, you can open an existing file or create a new one.

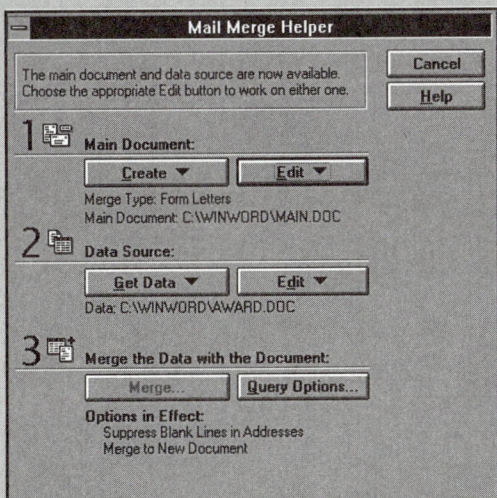

❷ From the **G**et Data drop-down list, select **O**pen Data Source. The Open Data Source dialog box appears, showing available files.

(continues)

> **Opening a Data Source for Use in the Main Document (continued)**
>
> ❸ From the List Files of **T**ype list box, select All Files (*.*).
>
> ❹ Open the drive and directory containing your data disk.
>
> ❺ Select AWARD.DOC in the File **N**ame list box, and choose OK.
>
> **Note:** *If you open a data source from another application, such as a spreadsheet, and are prompted to specify a range of data, enter the range you want to use—for example, cells B1:H20 in an Excel worksheet.*
>
> *After the file is opened and converted (if necessary), Word prompts you to edit or set up your main document. If the file was created by a Microsoft application that supports DDE (dynamic data exchange), Windows opens that application as well. If you need to edit the data source later, you can then do so in its original application.*
>
> ❻ Choose the Edit **M**ain Document button (form letters).
>
> or
>
> Click the **S**et Up Main Document button (envelopes and labels) from the Mail Merge Helper.
>
> Depending on the type of merge, you can now edit the form letter or set up the size and appearance of envelopes or labels.

You are now ready to prepare your main document and insert merge fields.

Objective 4: Insert Merge Fields in the Main Document

When you created a main document, you initially left empty lines or placeholders to identify the places in the document where you wanted to insert merge fields. Then, in a data source, you named and filled in those fields or imported the information. Now you can replace the blanks or placeholders in the main document with merge fields. (If you are merging envelopes or labels, set up the envelope or label options and then add merge fields.)

When you merge a data source with the main document, Word replaces merge fields in the main document with the information in the corresponding field of the data source. The formatting (such as bold or italic) you apply to the merge fields and any other text will appear in the final document.

The steps that follow vary depending on whether you are merging form letters, envelopes, or labels.

Inserting Merge Fields in a Form Letter

After you have specified a data source, you can insert merge fields in a form letter. To insert merge fields, you make the main document active and use the buttons on the Mail Merge toolbar. Follow these steps:

1. Open the MAIN.DOC document.

2. If the Data Form dialog box is open, choose OK. If the Mail Merge Helper is open, choose Cancel. If the data source document is active, choose the name of the main document from the **W**indow menu.

3. Place the insertion point after the colon following *To:*.

4. Click the Insert Merge Field button on the Mail Merge toolbar, and select Title.

5. Delete the asterisks.

6. Move the insertion point to the beginning of the next line.

7. Click the Insert Merge Field button again, and select the FirstName field on the first line after the title (see figure 9.10).

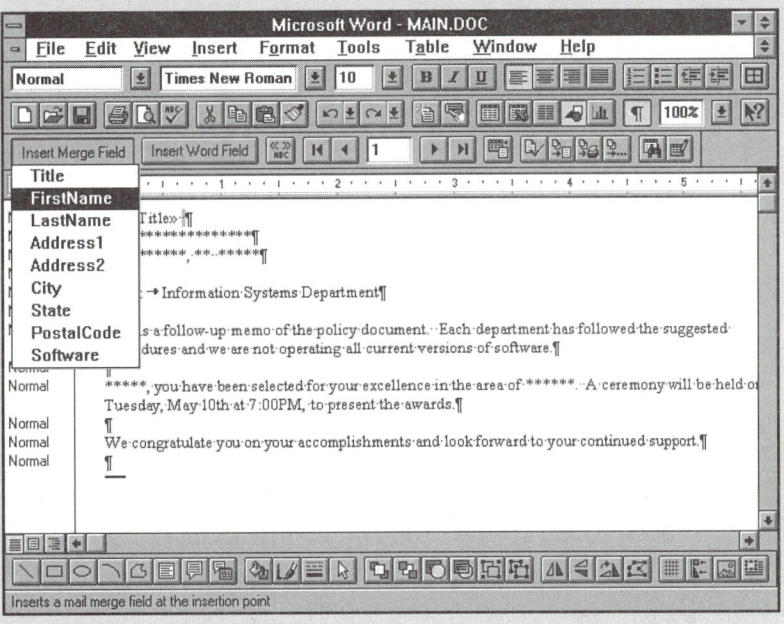

Figure 9.10
The Insert Merge Field button on the Mail Merge toolbar shows the merge fields from your data source.

If you want to remove a merge field you inserted, select the merge field you want to replace (click in it and then press Ctrl+Shift+F9) and press Del.

8. Repeat steps 6 and 7 to insert merge fields in all the locations where you want information from the data source, typing punctuation and new paragraphs where needed.

 9. To see the form letter as it will appear with the data merged, click the View Merged Data button on the Mail Merge toolbar.

(continues)

Inserting Merge Fields in a Form Letter (continued)

You can return to viewing merge fields by clicking the button again. The merge fields appear either as field names enclosed in chevrons (<<Last Name>>) or as actual data (1295 Tobler Lane). The appearance of the merge fields has no effect on the merging process.

10 To see a letter merged with any individual record, type a record number in the Go to Record box in the center of the Mail Merge toolbar and press `Enter`.

Click the View Merged Data button, if necessary, to see the data. You can use the arrow buttons in the toolbar to display the first, previous, next, or last record in the data source.

11 Do any final editing necessary to prepare the document to print.

Editing is best done while displaying merge fields rather than actual merged data. If you display merged data, it is gray when selected. Make sure that you edit only the text in the main document, not the contents of merge fields. To format a merge field but not the surrounding text, position the insertion point in the field and press `Ctrl`+`Shift`+`F9` before applying font formatting.

12 Save the main document to your data disk as **MAIN.DOC**.

You are now ready to merge the form letters you have set up.

Inserting Merge Fields for Envelopes

To insert merge fields for envelopes in the main document, you set up the envelopes in the Envelope Options dialog box and let Word do most of the work. Using the data source AWARDS.DOC, choose the **S**et Up Main Document button, and then the Envelope Options dialog box is already open.

Setting Up Envelopes before Inserting Merge Fields

In this tutorial, you use the names and addresses in the data source in AWARD.DOC to set up your envelopes.

1 Open the ENVELOPE.DOC and AWARD.DOC from the Mail Merge Helper.

2 Click Cancel to return to Mail Merge Helper.

3 Choose the **S**etup button under Main Document in the Mail Merge Helper.

4 Select the **E**nvelope Options tab. The dialog box appears (see figure 9.11).

Figure 9.11
Use the **E**nvelope Options section to preview your envelope size and formatting selections.

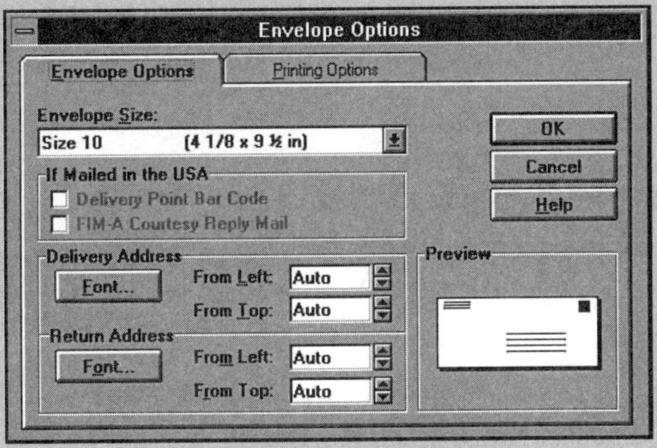

5. From the Envelope **S**ize list box, accept the default for the size of your envelopes. (If you select Custom Size, you can enter the envelope measurements in a dialog box.)

6. Accept the default fonts.

   To change fonts, choose the **F**ont button under Delivery Address or the **F**ont button under Return Address to change the font formatting of either part of the envelope.

7. Enter **Auto** to use the default measurements for any envelope size. Under Preview, you can see how the addresses will be positioned.

   In the From **L**eft and From **T**op boxes under Delivery Address or the Fro**m** Left and F**r**om Top boxes under Return Address, you can enter a custom distance you want to position the addresses from the corner of the envelope.

8. Select the **P**rinting Options tab (see figure 9.12).

Figure 9.12
The **P**rinting Options section has preset feed options for the active printer.

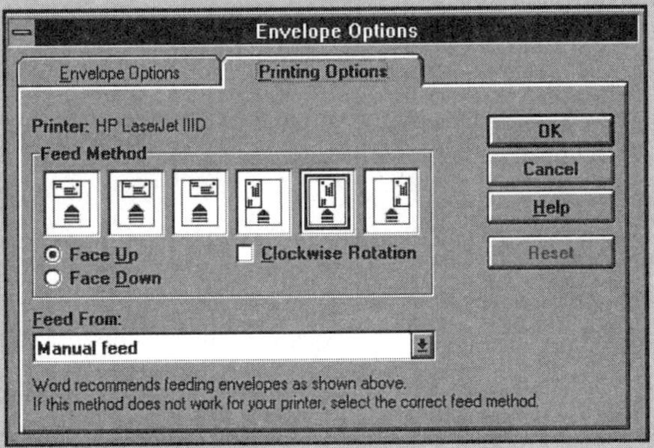

9. Select the Feed Method and **F**eed From options that work best for your printer.

(continues)

> **Setting Up Envelopes before Inserting Merge Fields (continued)**
>
> It's best to use the default settings for common printers. Select the picture most like the way you feed envelopes. Face **U**p or Face **D**own should match whichever side of the manually fed paper your printer prints on. To use side-fed envelopes, select **C**lockwise Rotation to rotate the printing by 180 degrees. Many printers work best with manual feed, but if your printer has an envelope feed, that may be the best option. Choose **R**eset to restore all these options to the defaults for the active printer.
>
> **10** Choose OK. The Envelope Address dialog box appears (see figure 9.13).
>
>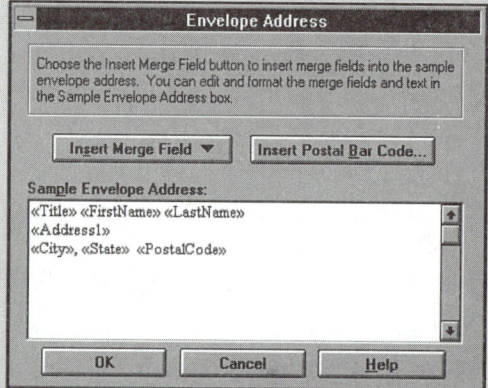
>
> **Figure 9.13**
> In the Envelope Address dialog box, you insert merge fields for the delivery address.
>
> **11** Choose the In**s**ert Merge Field button, and select the fields to insert in the delivery address, typing punctuation and new paragraphs where needed.
>
> For example, you will probably need a space between first and last names, a comma and a space between city and state, a space or two before the postal code, and a new paragraph before each line.
>
> **12** Select the data source fields that contain the PostalCode and the actual street address (for example, *295 Elm* rather than *Suite 200*) and choose OK.
>
> **13** When the Sam**p**le Envelope Address box contains all the information you need, choose OK.
>
> Word prepares a main document with the appropriate settings for the envelopes and displays it in Page Layout view.
>
> **14** Choose the Close button in the Mail Merge Helper to see the main document.
>
> **15** To see the envelopes as they will appear with the data merged, click the View Merged Data button on the Mail Merge toolbar (see figure 9.14).

Figure 9.14
You can see the envelopes with their merge fields in Page Layout view.

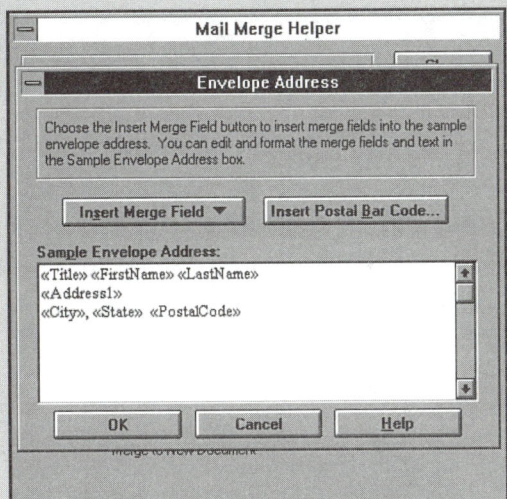

You can return to viewing merge fields by clicking the button again.

16 To see an envelope merged with an individual address record, type the record number **2** in the Go to Record box in the center of the Mail Merge toolbar and press ⏎Enter.

Click the View Merged Data button, if necessary, to see the data. You can use the arrow buttons in the toolbar to display the first, previous, next, or last record in the data source.

17 Do any final editing necessary to prepare the envelopes to print.

For example, you may want to change the return address, which is taken from the User Info tab of the **O**ptions dialog box (choose **O**ptions from the **T**ools menu). Or you could place a picture of your company logo somewhere on the envelope. Because the delivery address is in a frame, you can drag the frame's edge to reposition the block of text.

18 Save the main document to your data disk as **ENVELOP.DOC**.

You are now ready to merge the envelopes you have set up.

A similar process is used to set up labels, using the data source AWARDS.DOC.

Inserting Merge Fields for Labels

The fields to be used in the label need to set up before labels can be produced. To design the label, follow these steps:

❶ Open the Label Options dialog box (see figure 9.15).

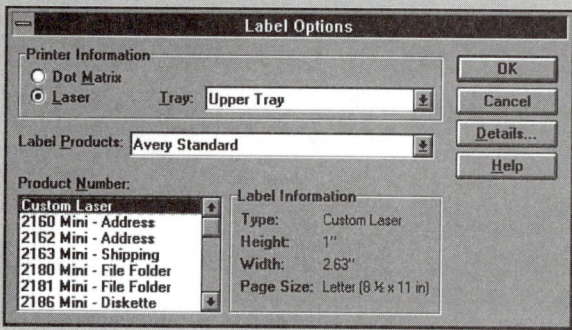

Figure 9.15
Use the Label Options dialog box to select from standard types of label sheets.

If the dialog box is not already open, make the main document active, choose Mail Me**r**ge from the **T**ools menu, and choose the **S**etup button under Main Document.

❷ Select your printer type (Dot **M**atrix or **L**aser) and a **T**ray option to specify where the labels will go.

These options are preset according to the active printer. The printer type is important because dot-matrix and laser printers use different label stock.

❸ From the Label **P**roducts list, select a brand name.

Most U.S. label producers are compatible with Avery products. A few other companies' products appear when you select Other.

❹ From the Product **N**umber list, select the product you are using, or one with the same dimensions shown under Label Information.

❺ To see or customize the specific measurements of your labels, choose the **D**etails button. The Custom Laser Information dialog box appears (see figure 9.16).

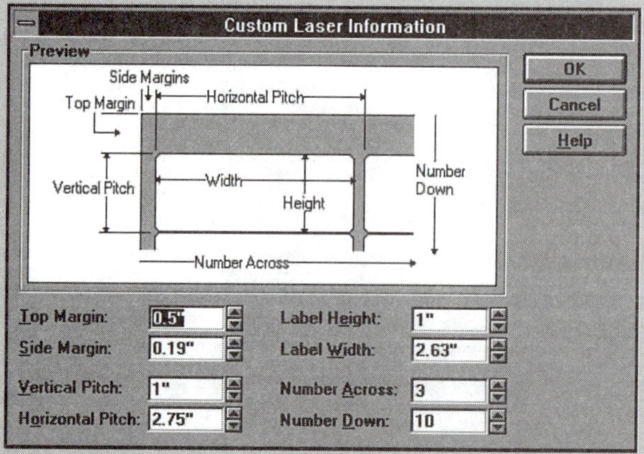

Figure 9.16
Use the Custom Laser Information dialog box to adjust measurements for nonstandard label sizes.

If you have labels that differ from the preset size, enter the appropriate measurements in the Label Options dialog box, and choose OK.

6 When you have selected the label options you need, choose OK. The Create Labels dialog box appears (see figure 9.17).

Figure 9.17
Use the Create Labels dialog box to insert merge fields for the label contents.

7 Choose the Insert Merge Field button, and select the fields to insert in the delivery address, typing punctuation and new paragraphs where needed.

For address labels, you will probably need a space between first and last names, a comma and space between city and state, a space or two before the postal code, and a new paragraph before each line.

8 Select all fields for the label including the city, state, and ZIP code.

9 When the Sample Label box contains the information you need, choose OK.

Word prepares a main document with the appropriate settings for the labels and displays it in Page Layout view.

10 Choose the Close button in the Mail Merge Helper to see the main document.

11 To see the labels as they will appear with the data merged, click the View Merged Data button on the Mail Merge toolbar. Your document should look similar to figure 9.18.

(continues)

Inserting Merge Fields for Labels (continued)

Figure 9.18
You can see the labels with merged data in Page Layout view.

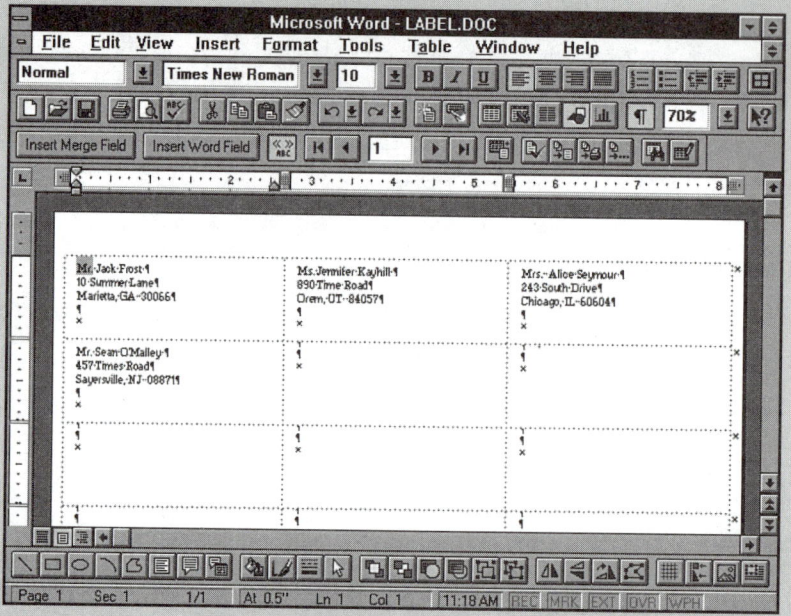

You can return to viewing merge fields by clicking the button again.

12 To see a label merged with an individual address record, type the record number **3** in the Go to Record box in the center of the Mail Merge toolbar and press ⏎Enter.

Click the View Merged Data button if you need to see the data. You can use the arrow buttons in the toolbar to display the first, previous, next, or last record in the data source.

13 Do any final editing necessary to prepare the labels to print. You may want to insert and position a logo or other information.

14 Save the main document to your data disk as **LABEL.DOC**.

You are now ready to merge the labels you have set up.

Objective 5: Merge the Data and Document

After you create a main document, specify a data source, and prepare the main document by inserting merge fields, you can merge the main document with the data source. Depending on your needs, you can merge directly to the printer or save the documents for later editing and printing.

If you merge to a document, Word creates one long document with section breaks between the documents for each record. You can then edit these, adding other individual notes or information, before printing. If you merge with a data source containing many records, you save disk space by merging directly to the printer.

Before performing the merge, you can have Word check the merge to identify potential problems. You can also sort the data source so that Word produces the merged documents in a certain order (for example, by ZIP code or alphabetically by last name). Several other options enable you to customize the merge.

Merging Form Letters, Envelopes, or Labels

You can perform a merge and send the results to a printer or to a new document by using either a Mail Merge toolbar button or the Mail Merge Helper. Most mail merges are sent to the printer for letters. Merging to a file occupies disk space, which can be used for other files. The only advantage in saving a merge to a file is when someone needs to print the file weekly and it contains few letters or labels. In either case, the main document should be active. The Mail Merge toolbar appears when the main document is active.

Merging from the Mail Merge Helper

To merge from the Mail Merge Helper, follow these steps:

1 If the Mail Merge Helper is not open, choose the Mail Merge command from the Tools menu.

2 Choose the Merge button under Merge the Data with the Document. The Merge dialog box appears (see figure 9.19).

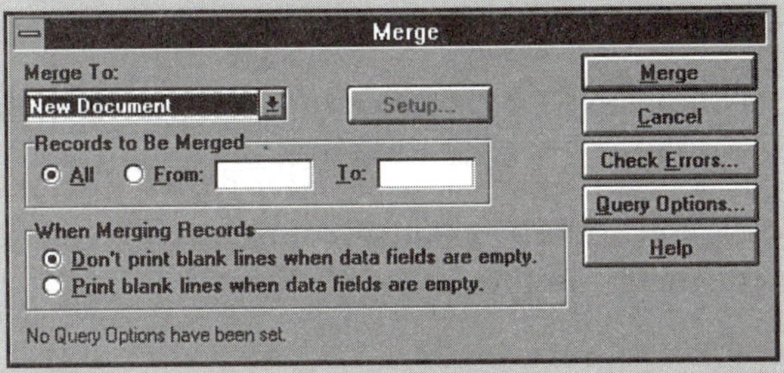

Figure 9.19
Use the Merge dialog box to specify options for the final merge.

3 From the Merge To list box, select the merge destination to the screen.

Select New Document to merge the data source and main document, creating a new document with section breaks separating each letter, envelope, or page of labels. Select Printer to merge the data source and main document and print the resulting documents.

(continues)

> **Merging from the Mail Merge Helper (continued)**
>
> ❹ To merge a group of records at a time, enter record number **1** in the **F**rom and **4** in the **T**o boxes.
>
> You also can use this option to check the printer output by printing just a few merged documents.
>
> ❺ Select the **D**on't Print Blank Lines option for normal merges.
>
> With this option selected, blank lines caused by an empty field in a record are not printed. If the Address2 field is empty (as it will be for many records in a mailing list), for example, blank lines do not appear in the middle of an address. If you are printing the contents of records for your own information, you may want to select the **P**rint Blank Lines check box to see which fields are unused in each record.
>
> ❻ Choose the **M**erge button.
>
> Word begins the merging process, creating new merged documents or sending the result to the active printer or the screen.

Merging with Toolbar Shortcuts

When the main document is active, the Mail Merge toolbar appears. You can click toolbar buttons to perform several of the merging tasks available in the Mail Merge Helper.

- Click the Mail Merge button on the Mail Merge toolbar to select options in the Merge dialog box.

- Click the Merge to New Document button on the Mail Merge toolbar to combine the results of the merge in a new document.

- Click the Merge to Printer button on the Mail Merge toolbar to print the results of the merge on the active printer.

Objective 6: Use Other Merging Features

Word offers powerful features for customizing merges to fit your needs. This section covers checking for errors, filtering the data source to print only certain records, and sorting the data source.

Checking the Merge for Errors

Before merging the data source and main document, Word can check the merge for potential problems. Error-checking catches some common problems. If you change the name of a field in the data source after inserting merge fields in the main document, for example, the two names might not match. If your data source contains a record containing only blank fields, the check catches the error. You can check for errors in advance, without merging, or have Word run the check while creating the final merged documents.

Checking for Errors

After merging the main document and the data source, you may display unexpected results. If this occurs, you may need to review the merge codes and data source document.

1 Open the main document window, and open the Mail Merge Helper by choosing Mail Merge from the **T**ools menu.

2 Choose the **M**erge button. The Merge dialog box appears.

3 Choose the Check **E**rrors button. The Checking and Reporting Errors dialog box appears (see figure 9.20).

Figure 9.20
You can check for nonexistent fields or blank records before or during a merge.

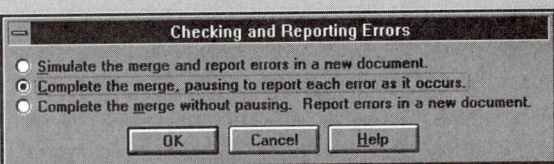

4 Select an error-checking option, and choose OK.

You can simulate the merge to check each record and field for errors without performing the merge. You can complete the merge, pausing for errors, if you want to interrupt the process when errors are found. You also can complete the merge without pausing, which merges the documents without interruption and afterwards lists any errors in a new document window.

If you choose to complete the merge, Word uses the current merge options.

You can use a shortcut to check for errors from the main document. Click the Check for Errors button on the Mail Merge toolbar.

Word notifies you if it finds errors in the merge. If the error is a nonexistent field name, a dialog box prompts you to delete the offending field or replace it with a merge field from the data source.

Merging Only Certain Records

To limit which records Word includes in the merge, you can filter records to test for one or more conditions, or rules. Using these rules, you can merge to create only the documents you really need. Remember that any rule assumes that the data was entered consistently—for example, that all records use two-letter abbreviations for state names.

To merge only records with a New York address, you could include records where the State field is NY. You could merge only records with ZIP codes beginning with 8 by specifying that the PostalCode field be greater than or equal to 80000 *and* less than 90000.

Filtering Data to Merge Only Certain Records

If the data source contains a large number of records and you need only specific records, you can set up a filter to merge only selected records. Follow these steps:

1. From the Mail Merge Helper or Merge dialog box, choose the Query Options button. The Query Options dialog box appears.

2. Select the Filter Records tab (see figure 9.21).

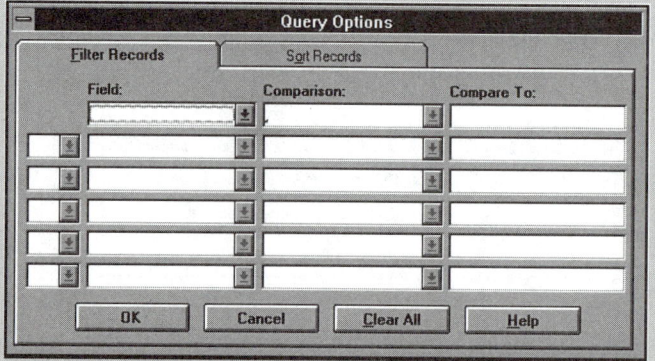

Figure 9.21 Use the filter options to merge only records that meet the conditions you set.

The Field list box contains merge field names from the data source. The Comparison list box contains the operators you can use to test a field's contents. In the Compare To box, you supply the value to check against the field. Together, the three boxes constitute a rule such as State Equal to UT.

3. Enter the appropriate values in the first row of boxes. **Title Equal to Mr.**

   You can add another rule, by selecting And or Or from the first box in the next row and filling in values for that row.

4. When you have defined your filter options, choose OK and begin the merge.

   To remove all rules in this dialog box, choose the Clear All button.

If you want to apply complicated combinations of filters, see the *Microsoft Word User's Guide* for instructions about multiple rules. For simpler rules, remember that using AND *limits* the possible number of matching records, whereas OR *increases* the possible number of matching records. Consider the following examples:

LastName Less than H

This selects records in which the last name begins with A through G.

LastName Greater than or Equal J AND Title Equal to President

This selects records in which the last name begins with J through Z and the title is President. Notice that AND excludes people who have the appropriate last name but a different title. If you used OR in this example, you would include every record with last name J–Z (no matter what title) as well as every record with the title President (no matter what last name).

Sorting Data before Merging

Before you merge the data source and the main document, you can sort the data source by field to produce documents in a particular order. To print form letters for a bulk mailing, for example, you may want to sort the data source by ZIP code, and then by last name within each ZIP code.

Sorting the Information in a Data Source

The records in the data source have been entered as the names were received, but there are times when the records need to be in a sorted order. To sort the data source, follow these steps:

1. From the Mail Merge Helper or Merge dialog box, choose the Query Options button. The Query Options dialog box appears.

2. Select the Sort Records tab (see figure 9.22).

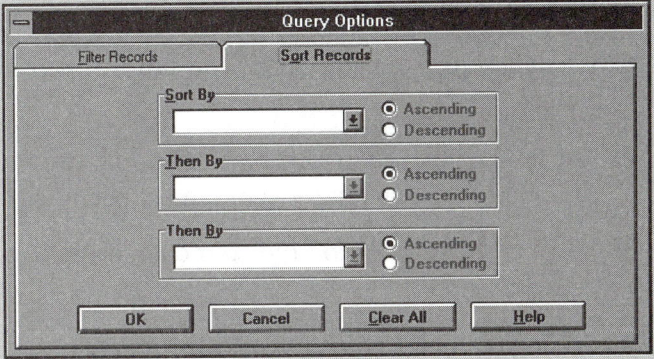

Figure 9.22
With sorting, you can merge records in a particular order.

The Sort By, Then By, and Then By list boxes contain merge field names from the data source.

3. Select the field LastName in the Sort by list box. The data source will be sorted according to the contents of this field.

4. Select the Ascending (A–Z, 1–9) or Descending (Z–A, 9–1) option.

5. To sort further levels, select options in one or both of the remaining boxes.

6. Choose OK.

When you merge the documents, they appear in the order you specified.

Chapter Summary

In this chapter, you learned how to set up a merge in Word. You learned about fields and records and about the factors to consider when planning a merge file. You can see that using the merge can save time and increase productivity in an organization. In the next chapter, you learn how to use Word features to automate your work.

Checking Your Skills

True/False Questions

For each of the following statements, circle *T* or *F* to indicate whether the statement is true or false.

T F **1.** The main document contains the information that is identical in each merged item.

T F **2.** When you open an existing data source or create a new one, the data source is attached to the main document.

T F **3.** The simplest way to store merge data is in a Word array.

T F **4.** To create a new data source for use in the main document, define the categories of information in the actual data.

T F **5.** The formatting you apply to the merge fields and any other text appears in the final document.

T F **6.** If a data source already exists, you simply open the file in the Mail Merge Helper.

T F **7.** The field names, up to 30 characters long, can include letters, numbers, or underscore characters (_) and must begin with a letter.

T F **8.** Word creates a table to hold your data, using a column for each field defined.

T F **9.** When you merge a document with the main document, Word replaces merge fields in the main document with information in the corresponding field of the data source.

T F **10.** Word prepares a main document with the appropriate settings for the labels and displays it in page layout view.

Multiple-Choice Questions

In the blank provided, write the letter of the correct answer for each of the following questions.

____ **1.** Which step is **NOT** used in the Word Mail Merge Helper?

    a. Create a main document.

    b. Select a data source.

    c. Add merge fields to the main document.

    d. Merge the data and the document.

    e. Select your printer.

____ **2.** A valid field name is _____.

    a. Field Name

    b. Last

        c. NewName

        d. Address

        e. Sam Jones

____ 3. You can replace the blanks or placeholder in the main document with _____.

        a. asterisks

        b. merge fields

        c. field names

        d. field sizes

        e. plus signs

____ 4. After you create a main document, specify a data source, and prepare the main document by inserting merge fields, you can merge the main document with the _____.

        a. data source

        b. field names

        c. table data

        d. select data

        e. database

____ 5. To select specific records, you can filter records to test for one or more _____.

        a. fields

        b. conditions

        c. records

        d. characters

        e. guidelines

____ 6. To insert merge fields, you make the main document active and use the buttons on the _____ toolbar.

        a. Standard

        b. Formatting

        c. Table

        d. Mail Merge

        e. Forms

____ 7. After the merge is complete, the merge fields appear with actual data or _____.

   a. as field names enclosed in asterisks

   b. as field names enclosed in chevrons (<< >>)

   c. as blank fields

   d. as field names with extra spaces

   e. as field names with the actual data

____ 8. If you merge with a data source containing many records, you save disk space by merging directly to _____.

   a. a floppy disk

   b. the screen

   c. the printer

   d. a file

   e. both a file and a printer

____ 9. To combine the results of the merge in a new document from the Mail Merge toolbar, _____.

   a. click Merge to New Document

   b. click the Merge to Printer button

   c. click Mail Merge

   d. click Mail Merge to Printer

   e. click Mail Merge to File

____ 10. Before you merge the data source and the main document, you may want to produce documents in a particular order, using the _____ feature.

   a. Search

   b. Find

   c. Sort

   d. Arrange

   e. Selecting

Fill-in-the-Blank Questions

In the blank provided, write the correct answer for each of the following questions.

1. The process of combining information from one document with sets of information from another document is known as _____.

2. The Data Form provides an easy way to fill in each _____ of your data source.

3. Word replaces _____ fields in the main document with information in the corresponding field of the data source.

4. If you merge to a document, Word creates one long document with _____ breaks between the documents for each record.

5. You can simulate the merge to check each record and field errors without performing the _____.

6. To create a new data source for use in the main document, you define the _____ of information in the data source, and then enter the data.

7. The _____ you apply to enhance the merge fields and any other text will appear in the final document.

8. The _____ toolbar appears when the main document is active.

9. Word begins the _____ process, creating a new merged document or sending the result to the active printer or the screen.

10. To limit which records Word includes in the merge, you can _____ records to test for one or more conditions.

Applying Your Skills

Review Exercises

Exercise 1: Creating a Main Document

Create a letter, as your main document, to be sent to all employees to announce the new choices in medical insurance offered as of June 1. Follow these steps:

1. Create the main document with merge fields for Employee name, department, and present insurance.

    May 1, 1994

    To: **********

    From: Accounting Department

    Re: New Choices in Medical Insurance

    You are presently enrolled in ********* insurance. The new insurance groups are Blue Cross, MD Heath Plan, and Connecticare. Please stop by the office for the paperwork. The change must be completed by June 1.

2. Save the file to your data disk as **INSURE.DOC**.

Exercise 2: Creating a Data Source

Create a data source containing five employees. The fields to be used are the following:

Employee name:

Department:

Insurance:

Save the file to your data disk as **EMP.DOC**.

Exercise 3: Merging

Perform a merge of the main document, INSURE.DOC, and the data source, **EMP.DOC**.

Exercise 4: Create a Main Label Document

Create a label design using EMP.DOC. Save the file to your data disk as **EMPLAB.DOC**.

Exercise 5: Merging

Perform a merge on the main label document, EMPLAB.DOC, and the data source, EMP.DOC.

Continuing Projects

Project 1: Preparing a Mail Merge

In Chapter 7, you created a flyer announcing a new real estate listing. Prepare a target mailing for this flyer by following these steps:

1. Create a Labels main document.

2. Create a data source containing 10 contacts.

3. Print the labels.

4. Save the main document as **LABNEW.DOC** and the data source as **CONTACTS.DOC** to your data disk.

Project 2: Federal Department Store

To prepare a mail merge with a filter, follow these steps:

1. Create a labels main document.

2. Create a data source containing 10 customers.

3. Print the labels of only the individuals from one city. (Be sure to have more than one record from the same city.)

4. Save the main document as **CATLAB.DOC** and the data source as **CUST.DOC** to your data disk.

Project 3: Real Entertainment Corporation

To create a mail merge for Real Entertainment Corporation, follow these steps:

1. Create a form letter, describing your service and product. Use the following text:

    <<Title>> <<Name>> <<LName>>

    <<Address>>

    <<City>>, <<State>> <<Zip>>

    Dear <<Name>>

    We hope you have enjoyed our newsletter. We are planning a special promotion during the month of August for <<highschool name>>.

We know many schools begin fund-raising events in the fall of the school year. One great event is for the students to plan a variety show for the public, and we will assist your production needs. The package price is $1500.00 to produce a variety show at your school. Our projection is that you can make $1500.00 on the event.

Please contact us if this interests your school. Call
1-800-CALL-REC.

Sincerely,

Elliot Clowns

2. Save the file to your data disk as **RECMAIN.DOC**.

3. Create envelopes to send to your contacts. Enter at least 10 records.

4. Save the data source to your data disk as **RECENV.DOC**.

5. Merge the document and envelopes to the printer.

CHAPTER 10
Increasing Your Productivity

AutoText
A Word feature that you can use to store and recreate text or data that you frequently insert into documents.

Word has several features you can use to automate the repetitive aspects of your work. In Chapter 3, you learned about AutoCorrect, Word's feature that automatically corrects the mistakes you make repeatedly. In this chapter, you learn about the Word *AutoText* feature that enables you to use the same text or pictures and to store that data to be used again. You also learn to customize Word to make the time you spend at your computer more efficient and productive. You learn how to work with styles and style sheets, AutoFormat, wizards, and macros.

Objectives

By the time you finish this chapter, you will have learned to

1. Work with Styles and Style Sheets
2. Use AutoFormat
3. Use Wizards
4. Use AutoText
5. Install Word Macros
6. Record Macros
7. Run Macros
8. Rename and Delete Macros

Overview of Templates, Styles, and Style Sheets

Style
A combination of character and paragraph formatting that you save in a style sheet.

Word's *styles* and *style sheets* save you time and effort because you eliminate many of the repetitive tasks associated with the content of the files. Although you can create any type of document without using styles and style sheets, you can produce better quality work in less time by using them.

In most cases, a document consists of headings, subheadings, paragraphs, and perhaps other parts—each having different formats. In a short document, it is not particularly difficult to format each part separately. In a longer document, however, formatting each part is time-consuming and tedious, and users often make mistakes.

Suppose that you gave the name *HEAD* to all the character and paragraph formatting details of headers, and you give the name *SUBHEAD* to all the formatting details of subheads. After doing this, you could label every heading with the name HEAD, which would apply that type of character and paragraph formatting to the headings.

If you could do that, every heading would be formatted exactly the same, every subheading exactly the same, and all ordinary paragraphs exactly the same. Also, if you decide to change the formatting of headings, for example, all you have to do is to change the contents of HEAD, and all headings in your document would change accordingly.

In Word, you can define HEAD, SUBHEAD, and PARA. Word calls each of these a style. When you collect these separate styles together to use them with a document, Word calls the collection a style sheet. A style sheet can contain many styles.

You probably work with several different types of documents such as letters, memos, reports, and so on. Each type of document is formatted differently and requires different styles. With Word, you can create any number of style sheets (collections of styles) so that you can easily apply the correct styles to each type of document.

All documents of a particular type, such as letters, usually have more than character and paragraph formatting in common. For example, all letters share specific page formatting characteristics such as margins, orientation, date, return address, and so on, in exactly the same location on the page.

Template
An empty document in which Word stores a particular style sheet and particular character, paragraph, and page settings.

A *template* is a framework on which you create a document. A template defines specific page formatting characteristics and contains a style sheet. Word comes with a number of built-in templates; you simply select the one you want to use when you create a new document.

You have used the Normal template in the preceding chapters of this textbook. If none of Word's built-in templates meets your needs, you can create a new one or modify the built-in templates to suit your needs.

After you have created a template for letters, you can use that template for all subsequent letters that you write. Without any effort on your part, all your letters will look the same. If several people in your organization write letters, they can all use the same template so that all letters have the same appearance.

A template defines the overall appearance of a document. It contains text and graphics that appear in every document based on that template. It also contains a style sheet that in turn contains styles that can be applied to the various parts of documents.

Note: *As Word has evolved, some terms have taken on different meanings in different contexts. One of these terms is* normal, *which is used in three contexts. As you have already learned, you can see a document in various views, one of which is Normal. When you open a new document, Word asks you to assign a template to it; the default template is named Normal. The Normal template contains several styles, one of which is named Normal. When the word Normal appears, make sure that you understand whether it is referring to a view, a template, or a style.*

Objective 1: Work with Styles and Style Sheets

A style is a description of how text appears. In Word, you can use character styles and paragraph styles. By using character styles, you can control the appearance of one or more characters. You can control the appearance of complete paragraphs by using paragraph styles.

As already discussed, styles are grouped in style sheets. Each style sheet is a component of a template. Word's default template is called NORMAL.DOT. NORMAL.DOT automatically loads when you load a file without attaching a different template.

Using Styles in the Normal Template

To use styles in the Normal template, follow these steps:

1. From the **F**ile menu, choose **N**ew to open the New dialog box.
2. Choose OK to use the Normal template file, the default document template.
3. Enter these four short lines of text:

    Work with Styles and Style Sheets

    Use Automatic Formatting

    Use Wizard

    Use AutoText

4. Save the file to your data disk as **STYLES.DOC**, but keep the file open.

Applying Styles in a Normal Template

Normal style
The style Word automatically uses unless you specify a different one.

In figure 10.1, notice that the style box on the far left of the Formatting toolbar contains the word Normal. This word indicates that you are using the *Normal style*. Whenever the Formatting toolbar is displayed, the Style box tells you which style is currently applied to the paragraph containing the insertion point. Word uses the Normal style as the default.

Figure 10.1
The Style list box shows the basic styles available in the Normal template. Normal is highlighted because that is the style of the paragraph that contains the insertion point. Bold style names in the list box are paragraph styles; others are character styles.

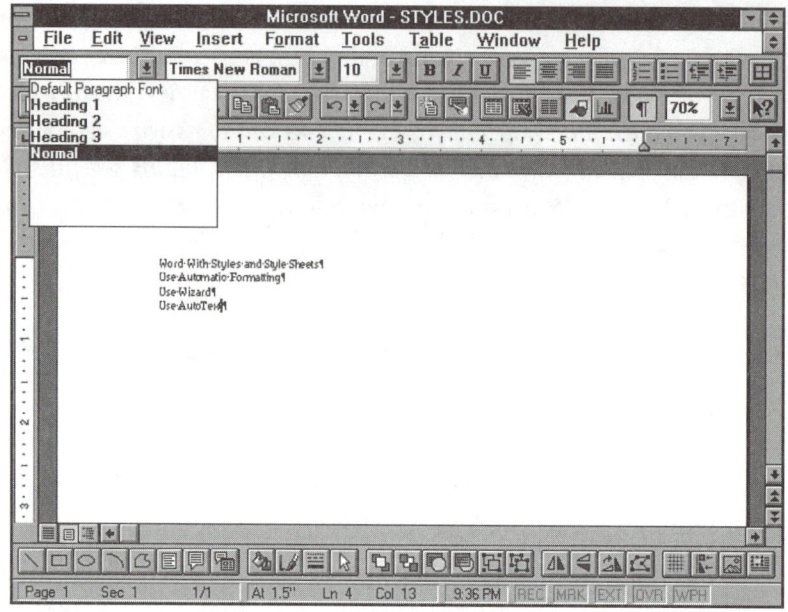

To see some of the styles available in the Normal template, click the down arrow next to the Style list box on the Formatting toolbar (refer to figure 10.1).

Applying a Style

When you apply a paragraph style to a paragraph, Word formats all the text in the paragraph according to that style. These formats include the font and font size for characters; line spacing within, before, and after paragraphs; tab settings; indents; and so on.

You can select a style and then type the paragraphs that are to have that style, or you can type paragraphs and then apply a style to them.

Applying a Style to an Existing Paragraph

To apply a style to an existing paragraph, follow these steps:

1. Using the STYLES.DOC that you created in the preceding exercise, click the first line to place the insertion point within it.

2. Open the Style list box, and choose **Heading 1**.

3. Move the insertion point to the second line, and choose **Heading 2** from the Style list box.

4. Move the insertion point to the third line, and choose **Heading 3** from the Style list box (see figure 10.2).

Figure 10.2
These four lines each have different styles.

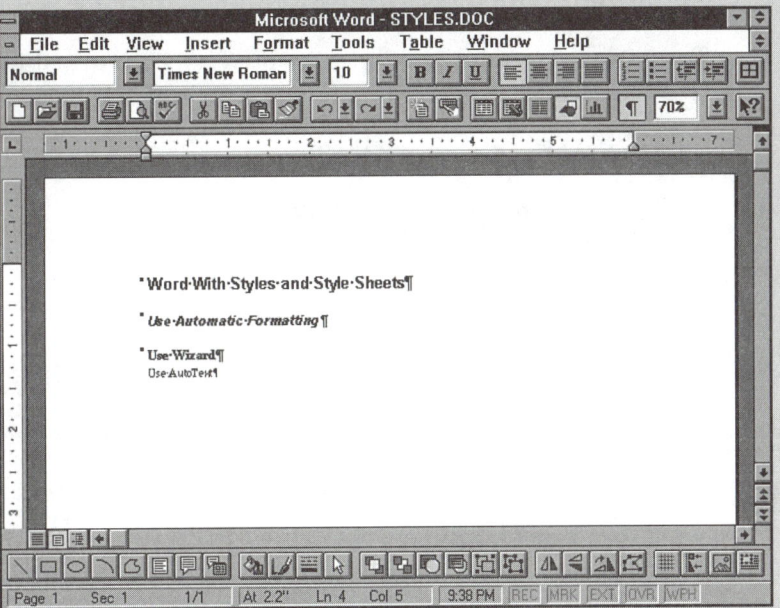

Note: *Word defines several heading styles, and each has a special purpose. You should use these styles only for headings in your documents.*

5 Save your changes, but keep the file open.

You can apply a style to several paragraphs at one time by selecting those paragraphs and then applying the style.

To apply a character style to only specific characters within a paragraph, select the characters, open the Style list box, and select the name of the character style or size you want to use. If you have a paragraph with Times New Roman 14 and you want one word to be Times New Roman 10, for example, you can override the larger font size with the smaller size. The selected style overrides any other style or size assigned to that paragraph.

As an alternative to using the Formatting toolbar to apply styles to paragraphs, you can use keyboard shortcuts for certain styles. First, place the insertion point within the paragraph to be formatted or select one or more paragraphs to be formatted. Next, apply the style that you want, using the following keyboard shortcuts:

Shortcut Keys	Style
Ctrl+Shift+N	Normal
Alt+Ctrl+1	Heading 1
Alt+Ctrl+2	Heading 2
Alt+Ctrl+3	Heading 3
Ctrl+Shift+L	List Bullet

Using the Style Command in the Format Menu to Apply a Style

To apply a style using the Style command in the Format menu, follow these steps:

1. In STYLES.DOC, select the fourth line of text.

2. From the Format menu, choose Style to display the Style dialog box (see figure 10.3).

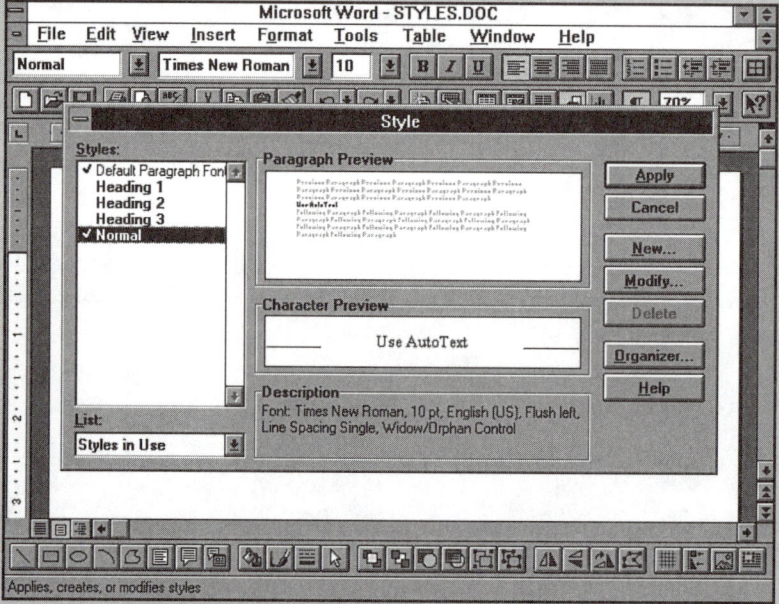

Figure 10.3
The left side of the Style dialog box lists the basic styles and checks those currently in use.

In the Styles list box of the Style dialog box, the style currently applied to the selected paragraph is highlighted. The Paragraph Preview box shows what the paragraph formatting of the selected style looks like, and the Character Preview box shows the character formatting.

3. In the Styles list box, choose Normal to apply the style to the selected text.

4. Choose the Apply button to apply that style.

5. Close the Style dialog box, and return to the document.

6. Save your changes, but keep the file open.

Note: *A quicker method of applying the same style to several paragraphs is to apply the style to one paragraph and then place the insertion point in another paragraph and press* Ctrl+Y. *Continue placing the insertion point in different paragraphs and pressing* Ctrl+Y *to apply the style to each paragraph.*

Expanding the List of Style Names

When you open the list of styles from the Style list box on the Formatting toolbar, you see only the first three heading styles, the Normal style, and any other styles that are currently used within the active document. To see an expanded list of styles, press and hold down ⇧Shift while clicking the arrow at the right of the Style box (see figure 10.4).

Figure 10.4
Use the greatly expanded list of paragraph and character styles to select styles.

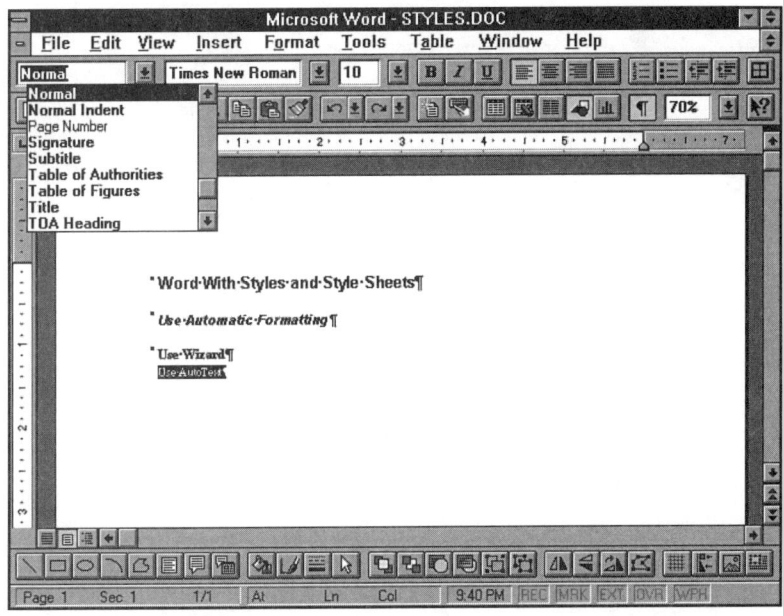

You can use the scroll bar in the Style list box to scroll down through the list and select the style you want to use.

Similarly, when you open the Style dialog box, you see only the principal styles and any others currently in use. Open the **L**ist drop-down list box at the bottom of the dialog box to choose other styles (see figure 10.5).

Figure 10.5
You can choose to see the styles currently in use, all styles, or the styles you defined.

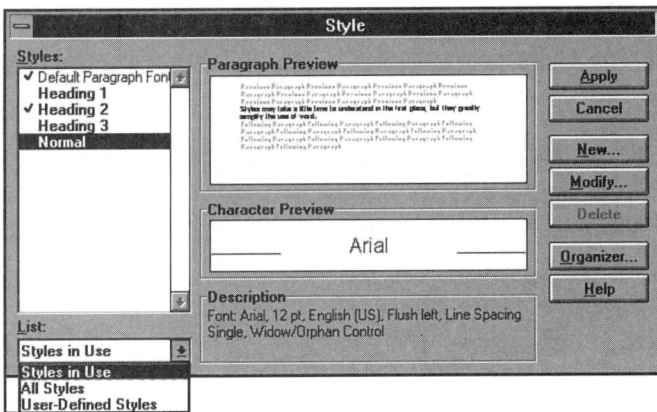

Select All Styles to see the complete list of styles in the Styles list box. After you have defined styles yourself, you can see only those by clicking User-Defined Styles. To see a list of shortcut keys defined in Word, open the **H**elp menu and choose the **S**earch For Help On command. Then, in the Search dialog box, choose the subject titled Shortcut Keys, Lists of.

Displaying Style Names

You often need to know which style is applied to each paragraph if you intend to apply the style to other paragraphs using the AutoText feature. To display the style names in STYLES.DOC, follow these steps:

1. From the **T**ools menu, choose **O**ptions to display the Options dialog box.

2. If necessary, click the View tab to display the View section of the dialog box (see figure 10.6).

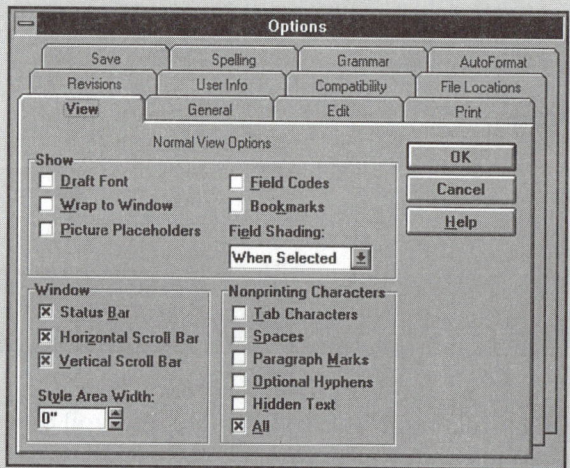

Figure 10.6
The bottom left corner of the dialog box contains the Style Area Width text box in the Normal view. When the box contains 0", no space is provided for style names.

3. Change the Style Area Width to **0.6**, and then choose OK.

The document reappears with a column for style names at the left (see figure 10.7).

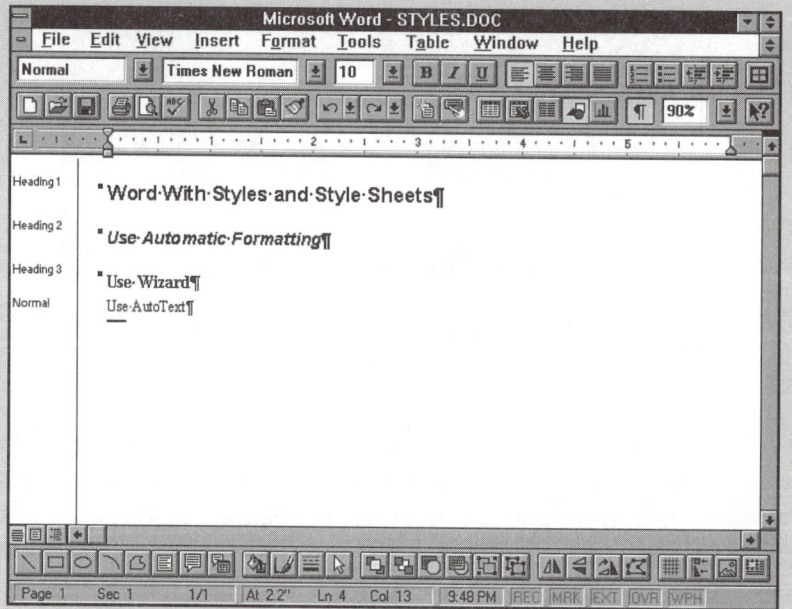

Figure 10.7
Each line in the document is marked with a style name.

Note: *You can easily change the width of the column in which style names are displayed. Point to the vertical line that separates style names from the text and drag to the left or right.*

④ Save your changes, and close the file.

In a typical document, a few styles are used often. Rather than choosing these styles from a list, you can apply them using shortcut keys.

Assigning Shortcut Keys to Styles

You can create shortcut keys for applying styles. To assign shortcut keys to styles, follow these steps:

① From the Format menu, choose Style.

② Select Normal as the style to assign a shortcut key.

③ Choose the Modify button at the right side of the dialog box to display the Modify Style dialog box (see figure 10.8).

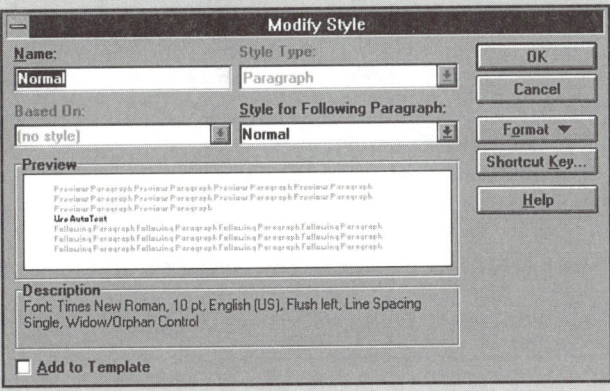

Figure 10.8
Use the Modify Style dialog box to change a style as well as to assign a shortcut key to it.

④ Choose the Shortcut Key button to display the Customize dialog box (see figure 10.9).

Figure 10.9
Use the Customize dialog box to specify the shortcut key to use for the selected style.

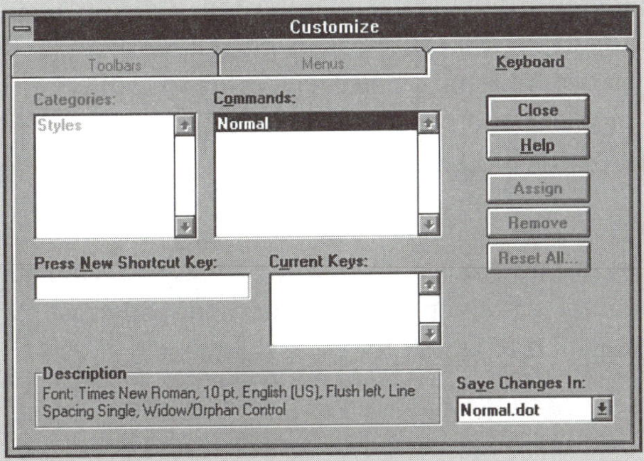

(continues)

Assigning Shortcut Keys to Styles (continued)

5 Press `Alt` + `N` as the shortcut key to use. That key combination appears in the Press **N**ew Shortcut Key text box. At the same time, the words `Currently Assigned To` appear under the text box.

Note: *If the shortcut key you selected is already assigned, Word tells you to what it is assigned; otherwise, Word displays the message* `[unassigned]`.

If the shortcut key you have chosen is already assigned and you do not want to replace that assignment, press `Backspace` *to delete your choice and try another shortcut key.*

6 Choose the **A**ssign button.

The C**u**rrent Keys list box now displays the currently assigned key and the C**o**mmands list box displays the style to which the shortcut key is assigned. The Description box at the bottom of the dialog box describes what happens when you press that shortcut key.

Note: *The text box at the lower right of the Customize dialog box tells you that any changes will be saved in the Normal template. If you are working with a document based on a different template, you have the choice of saving the change in that template or in the Normal template.*

7 Choose the Close button to close the Customize dialog box and to return to the Modify Style dialog box.

8 Choose OK to close the Modify Style dialog box and to return to the Style dialog box.

9 Choose Close to close the Style dialog box and to return to your document.

10 Close the document, and save your changes.

After assigning shortcut keys to a style, you can select a paragraph in your document and press the newly assigned shortcut keys to apply the style to that paragraph.

When you assign shortcut keys, avoid using `Ctrl` and `Ctrl`+`Shift` combinations because many of these are already assigned within Word. You can use `Ctrl`+`Enter` combinations, however, without conflicting with standard shortcut keys. Also, it is always a good idea to use a character that will help you remember what the shortcut key does.

Examining Styles

There are several methods of examining styles to decide whether the style can be used again in the document. In each method, you must place the insertion point within a paragraph to which the style is attached.

You can see a great deal about the style just by looking at the paragraph. To get more information, however, look at the Formatting toolbar, which displays the font name, size, and style. You can tell which alignment options are specified in the style by looking to see which alignment buttons on the toolbar are pressed.

To see even more detailed style information, from the F**o**rmat menu choose **F**ont to display the Font dialog box. Click the Cha**r**acter Spacing tab to see details about character spacing that you cannot judge by just looking at the paragraph and that are not shown in the Formatting toolbar. Open the F**o**rmat menu, and choose **P**aragraph to see the Paragraph dialog box; you can see such details as the exact indentation and line spacing and which of the text flow options are selected. Open the F**o**rmat menu, and choose **T**abs to see the exact positions and alignments of tabs.

Note: *If you apply a style to a paragraph and then use commands in the F**o**rmat menu to make changes to any individual character or paragraph formatting, the preview box will show the modified format.*

Another way to find out what is defined with a style is to open the F**o**rmat menu and choose **S**tyle to display the Style dialog box (see figure 10.10).

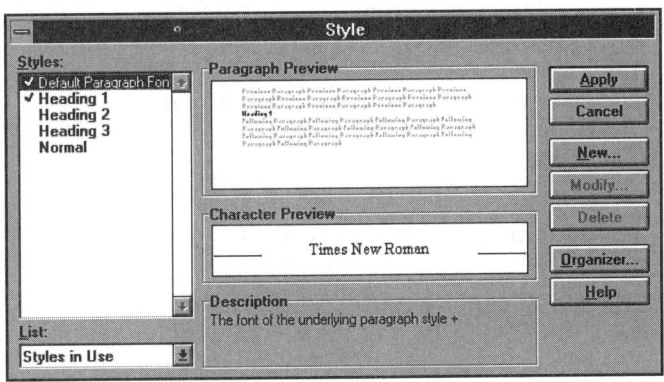

Figure 10.10
The Description box at the bottom of the Style dialog box contains a description of the style of the currently selected paragraph.

The Style dialog box shows the style of the currently selected paragraph highlighted in the Styles list box and a description of that style in the Description box.

To see an example of how one style can be dependent on another, use the scroll bar in the Style list box to find the Heading 1 style, and click to select it. The description now gives details about this style (see figure 10.11).

Figure 10.11
The description at the bottom of the Style dialog box starts with Normal +, indicating that the Heading 1 style is dependent on the Normal style. The remaining description indicates the differences between the Heading 1 style and the Normal style.

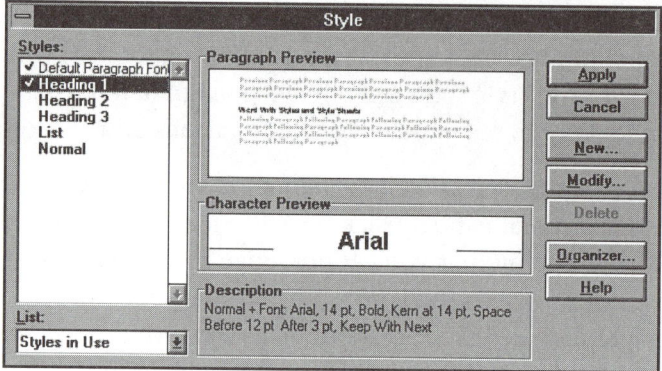

When one style is dependent on another style, the description in the Style dialog box does not completely define the selected style. It only details the differences between the selected style and the style on which it is dependent. You may therefore find it more convenient to use the Font and Paragraph dialog boxes to see a style's complete definition.

Note: *You may be thinking that it would be better if one style were not dependent on another because you would be able to see all about it in the Description box of the Style dialog box. When you read later about defining and modifying styles, you will see that it can be very advantageous for one style to depend on another.*

Modifying a Style

Because any style in the Normal template may be used in documents based on any template, you should follow these two recommendations:

- Do not modify styles in the Normal template. If you do, you may have some unpleasant surprises later when you open a document based on another template.

- If you need to create a style and are likely to use it in documents based on several templates, add that style to the Normal template.

To modify a style, you can open a new or existing document based on a template that contains that style, or you can open the template itself. You would do this, for example, if you wanted to modify the Body Text style in the Memo2 template.

Modifying the Body Text Style in a Template

To modify the Body Text style in a template, follow these steps:

❶ From the File menu, choose New to open the New dialog box.

❷ Select Memo2 as the template to modify, and then choose OK to open a new document based on the Memo2 template (see figure 10.12).

Figure 10.12
A copy of the Memo2 template appears on-screen with the style names listed.

❸ Move the insertion point to the location where you type the text of the memo.

❹ From the Format menu, choose Style to display the Style dialog box with the style (Body Text) of the selected text in the document highlighted.

❺ Choose the Modify button to display the Modify Style dialog box (see figure 10.13).

Figure 10.13
Use the Add to Template check box in the Modify Style dialog box to add a style to the template.

❻ Choose the Format button to display a list of style components you can modify (see figure 10.14).

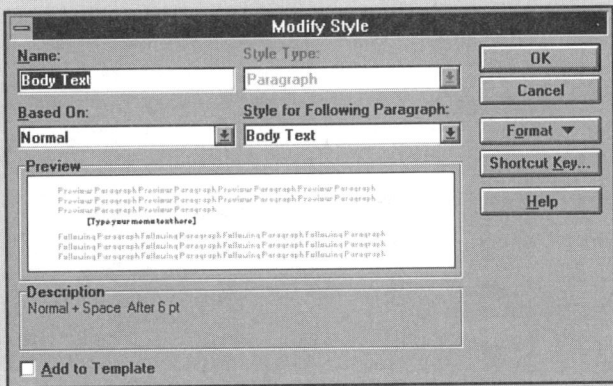

Figure 10.14
Use the list of style components to modify the font defined within the style, as well as other components of the style.

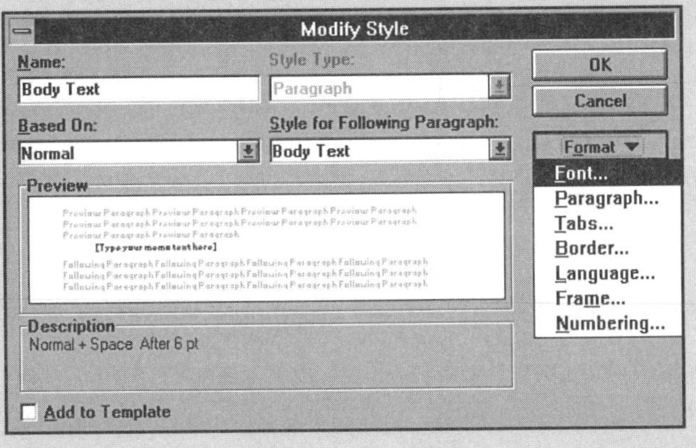

(continues)

Modifying the Body Text Style in a Template (continued)

7 Choose **F**ont to open the Font dialog box (see figure 10.15).

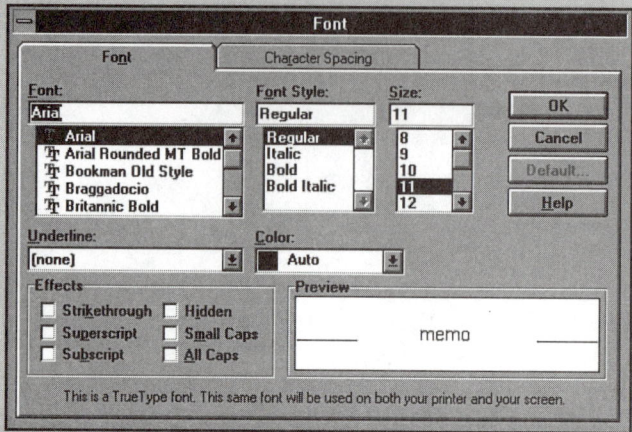

Figure 10.15
You can use the Font dialog box to modify any character formatting.

8 In the **S**ize list box, choose 14. Choose OK to accept the changes and to return to the Modify Style dialog box.

*Note: You can, of course, change any other component of character formatting in the Fo**nt** section or Cha**r**acter Spacing section of the Font dialog box.*

9 Click the F**o**rmat button, and choose **P**aragraph to open the Paragraph dialog box (see figure 10.16).

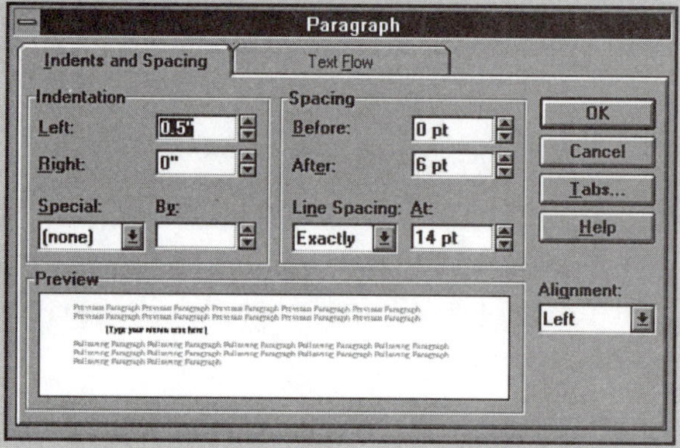

Figure 10.16
The Paragraph dialog box shows that the indentation for this style is set to 0.5".

10 To change the indentation, enter **0.75** in the **L**eft text box. Choose OK to accept the changes and to return to the Modify Style dialog box.

*Note: You can change any other component of paragraph formatting in the **I**ndents and Spacing or Text **F**low sections of the Character dialog box.*

11 Choose the **A**dd to Template check box in the Modify Style dialog box.

Note: If you omit this important step, only the formatting of the current document changes; the style does not permanently change.

12 Choose OK to return to the Style dialog box.

13 Choose Close to return to the document.

The style is now modified for use in the current document but not for future documents.

14 Move the insertion point to the text to which the Body Text style is applied so that you can see the effect of the changed style in the Formatting toolbar and in the ruler.

To save the changes to disk, continue with the following steps:

15 From the **F**ile menu, choose **C**lose. Word displays a message asking whether you want to save the changes you made to your document (see figure 10.17).

Figure 10.17
Word displays this message asking whether you want to save the document changes, not the style changes.

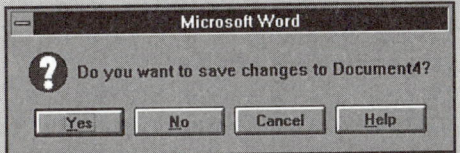

16 Choose **N**o. Word now displays a message asking whether you want to save changes to the template (see figure 10.18).

Figure 10.18
Word displays this message asking whether you want to save changes you made to the template.

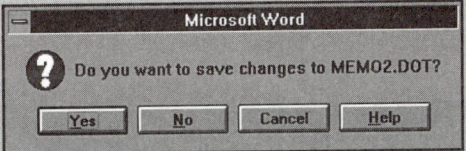

17 Choose **Y**es because the template contains the style that you modified and you want to save the changed style.

The next time that you use the Memo2 template to create a new document, your new settings for the Body Text style will apply.

Every time you open a document that you have previously created using the Memo2 template, all text to which the Body Text style is applied will be displayed and printed according to the new settings for that style.

If you open a new or existing document based on any template other than Memo2, any text to which the Body Text style is applied is unaffected by the changes you have just made to the Body Text style within the Memo2 template.

Specifying the Style for a Following Paragraph

When you create or modify a style, you can specify a style for the paragraph that follows it. If you do this properly, you can save yourself work when you create documents.

In a typical document, a heading is usually followed by body text. Also, one paragraph of body text is often followed by another paragraph of body text. Suppose that you use a style called HEADING for headings and a style called BODY for body text. Suppose also that the HEADING and BODY style definitions both include BODY as the style for the paragraph that follows.

When you create a new document based on a template that contains these styles, start by applying the HEADING style to the empty first line. As you type the heading, it appears in the style you defined. At the end of the heading, press `Enter` to end the paragraph. Automatically, the next paragraph opens in the BODY style. This is because the HEADING style contains the information that the next paragraph is in BODY style.

Likewise, after you complete each paragraph of the body, the next paragraph opens in the BODY style. Again, this is because the BODY style contains the information to format the next paragraph in the same style.

What you are doing is making Word automatically provide the styles you are likely to need each time you end a paragraph. Of course, there may be occasions when you want to apply the HEADING style to a line after a paragraph in BODY style. In those cases, you must select the appropriate style from the drop-down styles list box. However, rather than selecting a style for every paragraph, you only have to occasionally select a style.

Deleting a Style from a Template

After you delete a style from a template, documents you create cannot use that style. However, you do not affect documents you have already created based on that template because a copy of the template is saved with each document.

In this exercise, you learn how to delete a style from a template. These steps are provided for your information. **Do not complete this exercise** unless your instructor asks you to delete a specific style.

1. Open a new or existing document based on the template from which you want to delete a style, or open the template itself.

2. From the **F**ormat menu, choose **S**tyle to display the Style dialog box.

3. Highlight the name of the style you want to delete.

4. Choose the **D**elete button at the right side of the dialog box. Word asks you to confirm that you want to delete the style.

5. Choose **Y**es to delete the style.

6. Choose Close to return to the document or template.

After you have added or deleted styles from a template, you may want to have a list of the available styles in a template.

Printing a Style Sheet

You can print a list of all the styles in the selected template. Your list will be in alphabetical order, with a brief description similar to the descriptions that appear in the Style dialog box's Description box. To print the styles available in a template, follow these steps:

1. From the File menu, choose New to display the New dialog box.

2. From the list box on the New dialog box, choose the Normal template, and then choose OK to open the template.

   Note: *Make certain that you select the Document button, not the Template button.*

3. From the File menu, choose Print to display the Print dialog box.

4. Open the Print What drop-down list box (see figure 10.19).

Figure 10.19
Styles is one of the items you can choose from the Print What drop-down list box.

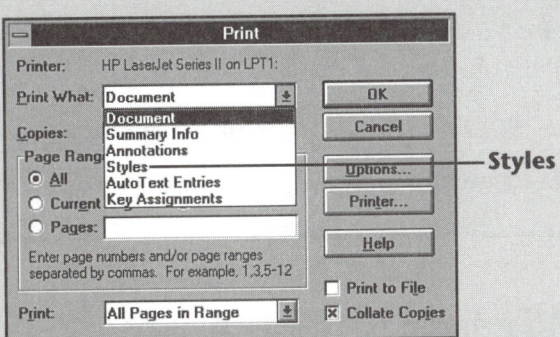

5. Select Styles, and choose OK to print a list of styles.

Objective 2: Use AutoFormat

If you need to format a document in a hurry, using AutoFormat may enhance the quality of your work. Because it is automatic, however, the feature does not make the formatting choices you would probably choose for yourself.

In addition to applying styles to your text, AutoFormat can also make some minor changes to improve your document's appearance. If you typed (c) to represent the copyright symbol, for example, AutoFormat can change this to ©.

Applying Formatting to Your Document

To apply automatic formatting to a document, follow these steps:

1. Open the document POLICY2.DOC—a document based on the Normal template and one in which all paragraphs have the Normal style.

2. From the F**o**rmat menu, choose **A**utoFormat. Word displays the AutoFormat dialog box that briefly explains what AutoFormat does.

3. Choose the **O**ptions button to display the AutoFormat section of the Options dialog box.

4. Make sure that no × appears in the Preserve Previously Applied Styles check box, and then choose OK to return to the AutoFormat dialog box.

5. Choose OK to enable Word to proceed with AutoFormat. When AutoFormat is complete, the AutoFormat dialog box appears, providing you with the following options.

    To review the changes AutoFormat made to your text, choose the Review **C**hanges button.

    To see a quick preview of the formatted document, click the **S**tyle Gallery button.

    To accept the automatically formatted document, choose **A**ccept.

6. Close the document, and save your changes.

Objective 3: Use Wizards

Wizard
An automated template that leads you step-by-step through the process of creating a document.

Wizards, new to this version of Word, are an extension of templates. Wizards are helpful in creating specific kinds of documents—such as agendas, fax cover sheets, newsletters, resumes, and so on— and can save you a great deal of time, providing that you are prepared to accept the built-in formats Word provides. You will probably want to use wizards at first, but you will soon want to use your own creativity—something wizards don't allow.

Figure 10.20 shows an agenda created using wizards. Refer to this figure to complete the steps in the following exercise.

Figure 10.20
An example of an agenda created with the help of wizards.

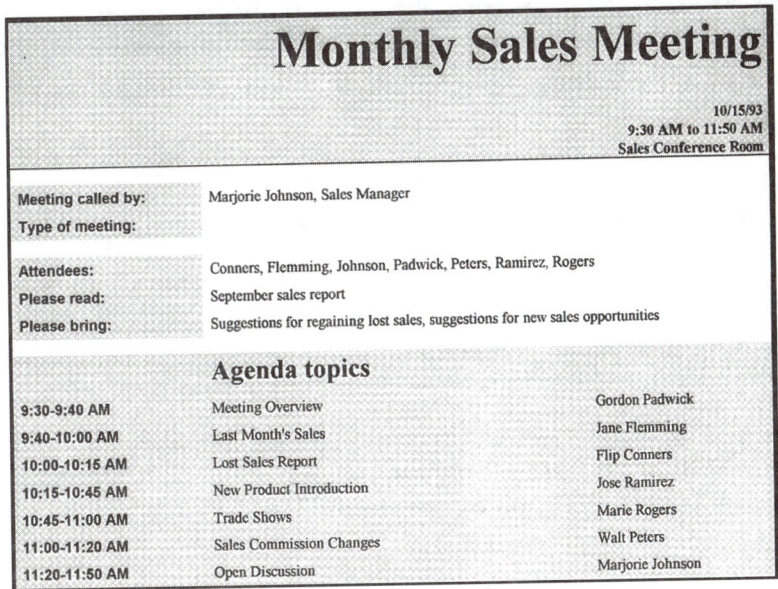

Use the Agenda Wizard

To use the Agenda Wizard, follow these steps:

1. From the File menu, choose New to display the New dialog box.

   The Template list box in the New dialog box shows the names of wizards as well as templates.

2. Choose Agenda Wizard, and choose OK. After a few seconds, the Agenda Wizard dialog box appears (see figure 10.21).

Figure 10.21
When the Agenda Wizard dialog box first appears, it offers a choice of styles for your agenda.

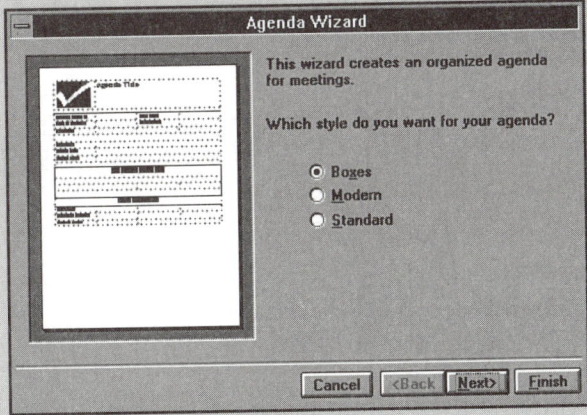

3. Using the information provided in figure 10.20, answer the questions in the dialog box by choosing options and typing text. Choose Next to display the next dialog box.

(continues)

Use the Agenda Wizard (continued)

4 Continue choosing options and answering questions until you have completed all the dialog boxes.

5 Choose Finish in the last dialog box.

6 Word creates the document, using the information you provide, and displays it on-screen. Your document should look similar to figure 10.20.

7 Save the file to your data disk as **AGENDA.DOC**.

The agenda you created in the preceding exercise may not have the layout you would choose if you took the time to plan and design it yourself, but it's much better than one you could create in the same amount of time without the help of wizards. Another great feature of wizards is that it prompts you for items you may otherwise forget.

It is a good idea to become familiar with all that wizards can do so that when you need to create a document in a hurry you are prepared.

Objective 4: Use AutoText

 You can use AutoText to save words, phrases, or graphics that you use regularly. When you want to use an item you saved as an AutoText entry, you don't have to type it or select it again. Instead, you only type a shortcut to insert that AutoText entry. If you use the following standard complimentary closing for all your letters, for example, you can store the whole selection in an AutoText entry named *close*. Then whenever you need to end a letter, simply type **close** and press F3, or choose the AutoText button on the Standard toolbar. Word inserts the stored information in the letter.

Sincerely yours,

JT Reilly

JT Reilly

Director of Information Systems

JGR:cb

You can also store graphics or text with formatting, such as italic text or special line spacing. When you insert an AutoText entry, you can choose whether to include formatting.

The AutoCorrect feature provides the same features except that Word automatically expands the abbreviated name as you type without requiring you to press F3.

Creating an AutoText Entry

When you create an AutoText entry, you assign it a short name to indicate the contents of the entry. Then whenever you want to use the AutoText entry, type the short name and press F3 or choose the AutoText button on the Standard toolbar. The name you assign should be long enough to identify the entry but short enough to type quickly. To create an AutoText entry, follow these steps:

1. Open a new document.

2. Insert the picture COMPUTER.WMF by choosing **I**nsert, **P**icture.

3. Type and format the entry **Computer Information Bulletin Board** (font size 16) that you want to store.

4. Select the text and graphics.

5. From the **E**dit menu, choose the AutoTe**x**t command or click the AutoText button on the Standard toolbar. The AutoText dialog box appears.

6. In the **N**ame text box, type **LETHEAD** as the name to assign to the AutoText entry (see figure 10.22).

Figure 10.22
The AutoText dialog box previews the selection to which you are assigning shortcut text.

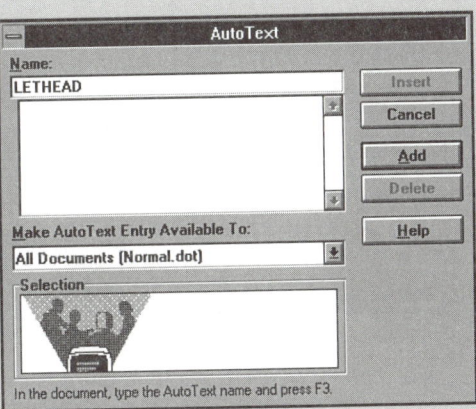

7. Choose **A**dd. (This button is not available unless you have selected text in the document and typed a name.)

8. Keep the file open.

You can store many AutoText entries in a document template. When you add an AutoText entry, you can decide which active template to save it in. The easiest method is to save AutoText entries in the NORMAL.DOT template, making them available to all documents.

Specifying Where to Store an AutoText Entry

To specify where to store your AutoText entry, follow these steps:

1 In the AutoText dialog box, select a template from the **M**ake AutoText Entry Available To list box (see figure 10.23).

Select All Documents (Normal.dot) to be able to use the AutoText entry in any Word document. If your document is based on another template, it also appears in the list. Select Documents Based on *Template* to use the AutoText entry only in documents based on that template.

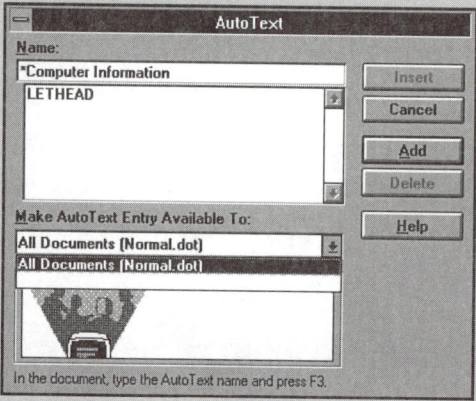

Figure 10.23
You can make AutoText entries available in all documents or just in documents based on the active template.

2 Choose OK.

By default, Word automatically saves templates when you exit. To save the template and its AutoText entries immediately, choose the Save A**l**l command from the **F**ile menu.

Inserting an AutoText Entry

You can insert an AutoText entry by using any of the following methods:

- Type the name of the entry and press F3.

- From the **E**dit menu, choose the AutoTe**x**t command.

- Type the name of the entry, and choose the AutoText button on the Standard toolbar.

If you use the keyboard method, Word inserts the AutoText entry exactly as you created it. If you use the AutoText command, you can choose whether to include any formatting.

Inserting an AutoText Entry by Name

To insert an AutoText entry by name, follow these steps:

1. Open a new document, and position the insertion point at the top of the document where you want the AutoText entry to appear.

2. Type the AutoText entry name **LETHEAD** (see figure 10.24).

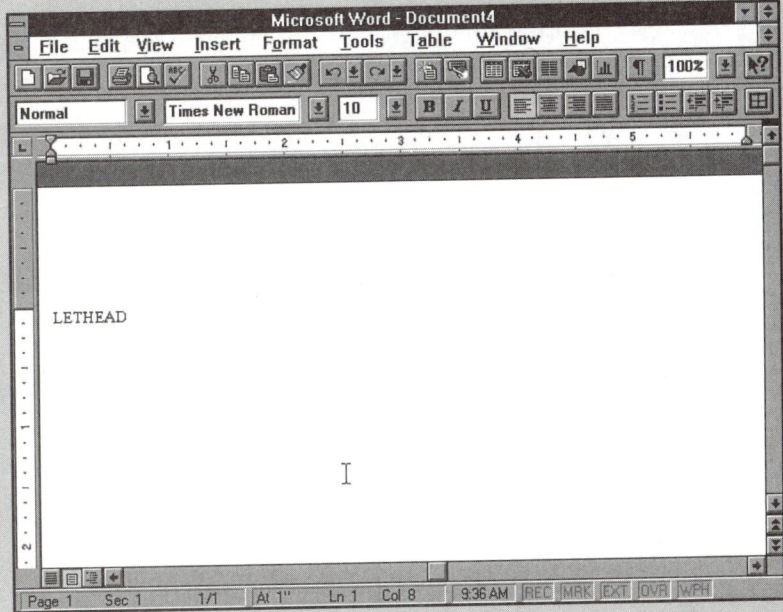

Figure 10.24
Type LETHEAD, the AutoText shortcut.

3. Press F3. Word inserts the AutoText entry with any formatting you applied when you created the entry (see figure 10.25).

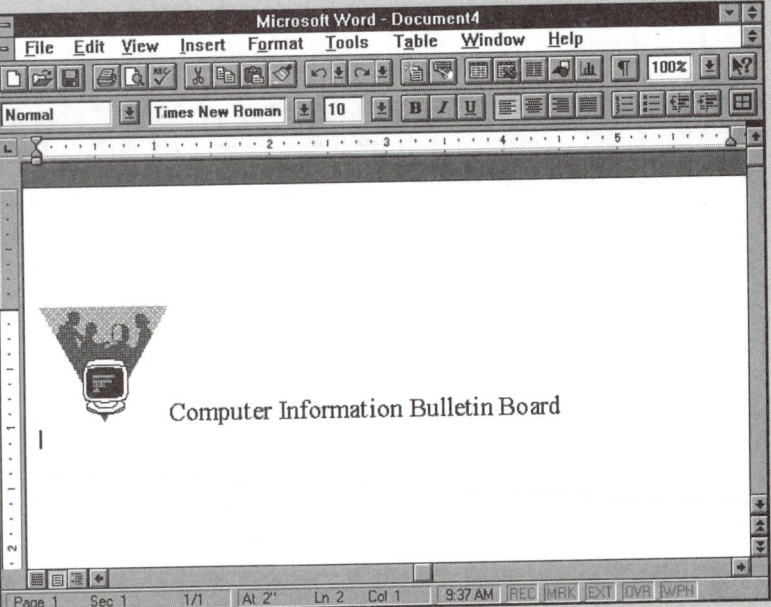

Figure 10.25
The AutoText entry replaces the shortcut text.

4. Do not close the document. You use it in the next exercise.

The quickest method of inserting an AutoText entry is to press F3; however, you may not remember the shortcut name you assigned.

Inserting an AutoText Entry When You Cannot Remember Its Name

To insert an AutoText entry when you cannot remember its name, follow these steps:

1. Insert a page break in the document that you created in the preceding exercise. Position the insertion point at the top of the second page, where you want the AutoText entry to appear.

2. From the **E**dit menu, choose the AutoTe**x**t command. (If you have not created any AutoText entries, the AutoText command is not available.)

    The AutoText dialog box appears.

3. From the **N**ame list box, choose LETHEAD as the AutoText entry you want to insert.

4. To insert the AutoText entry without any formatting, choose the **P**lain Text option.

    The Preview box shows the entry as it will be inserted.

5. Choose the Insert button.

    Now you have two letterheads in the document.

6. Save the file to your data disk as **LETHEAD.DOC**, but keep it open.

If you realize that an AutoText entry contains a spelling error or needs to be updated, you can quickly change the contents of the entry. In the AutoText dialog box, the Preview area shows you what the selected entry looks like.

Editing and Deleting an AutoText Entry

To edit and delete an AutoText entry, follow these steps:

1. Select the AutoText entry on the second page of LETHEAD.DOC.

2. Change the word *Board* in the document to **Boards**.

3. With the edited entry selected, choose the AutoText button on the toolbar.

4. Choose the **A**dd button. A dialog box asks whether you want to redefine the AutoText entry.

5. Choose **Y**es to redefine the entry, and close the dialog box.

❻ To delete the AutoText entry that you just changed, select it, delete it, and delete the page break.

❼ Keep the file open for the next exercise.

After you have an AutoText entry the way you want it, you may choose to make slight variations for other documents. You may want to rename the AutoText entry to distinguish it from the original.

Renaming an AutoText Entry

When you first create an AutoText entry, the default name that Word proposes is simply the first few words of the entry. If you use that name, you may notice later that it is too long to type. At any time, you can assign an entry a name that is shorter or easier to remember. To rename your LETHEAD AutoText entry, follow these steps:

❶ Select the LETHEAD AutoText entry in your document.

❷ From the Edit menu, choose the AutoText command or click the AutoText button on the Standard toolbar.

❸ From the Name list box, choose LETHEAD as the AutoText entry to rename.

❹ Choose the Delete button.

❺ In the Name text box, type NEWHEAD as the new name for the AutoText entry.

❻ Choose Add.

❼ Save the file to your data disk as **NEWHEAD.DOC**.

Creating, editing, deleting, and renaming AutoText entries are simple procedures. Eventually, you may build up quite a collection of entries.

Printing AutoText Entries

To see exactly what entries you have so that you can delete the obsolete ones, you can print a list of AutoText entries. To print the contents of your AutoText entries, follow these steps:

❶ Open a document based on the template that contains the AutoText entries you want to print (usually the NORMAL.DOT template).

❷ From the File menu, choose the Print command.

The Print dialog box appears. The Print What list box contains an AutoText Entries option (see figure 10.26).

(continues)

Printing AutoText Entries (continued)

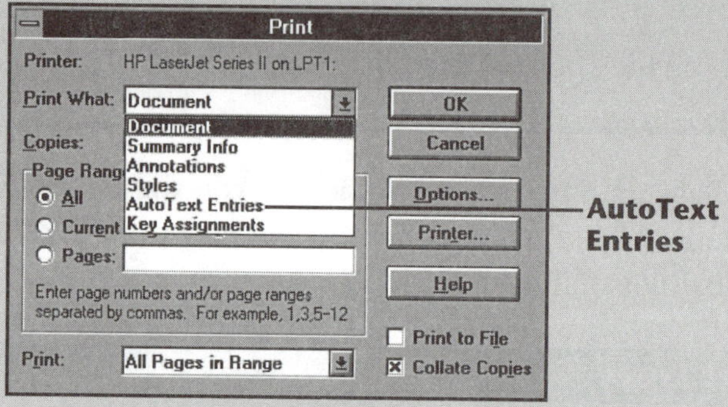

Figure 10.26
You can print a list of AutoText entries and names.

③ From the **P**rint list box, choose AutoText Entries.

④ Choose OK. Word prints each AutoText entry name and its contents, separated by blank lines.

Objective 5: Install Word Macros

Macro
A series of actions that you record and play back to accomplish specific tasks.

Word comes with a built-in collection of *macros* ready for you to use, and you also can record your own. Most of the built-in macros are useful for performing repetitive tasks. Word also provides examples of macros that you can study as you write your own.

You can use macros to perform repetitive tasks such as changing directories or inserting a frequently used symbol by simply pressing a key or clicking a button. In Word, you can assign a macro to a key combination, a menu, or a button on the toolbar.

The macros that come with Word are stored in the MACRO60.DOT file in the C:\WINWORD\MACROS subdirectory. This file is installed when you perform a complete installation of Word (or during a custom installation if you open the Wizards, Templates and Letters option and select the Macro Templates component). Before you can use these macros, you must make them available for use in other documents. You can use Setup at any time to install the Word's built-in macros.

Using Word's Built-In Macros

To use Word's built-in macros, follow these steps:

① From the **F**ile menu, choose the **T**emplate command. The Templates and Add-ins dialog box appears (see figure 10.27).

Figure 10.27
The Templates and Add-ins dialog box.

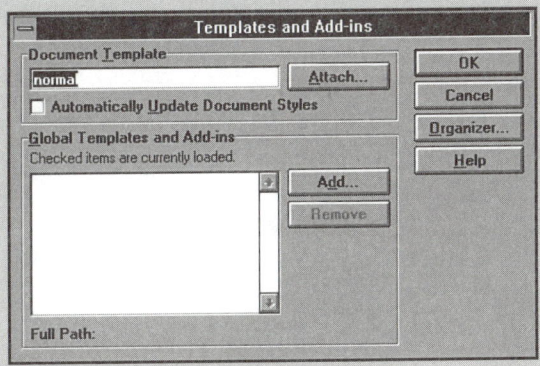

② Choose the **Ad**d button. The Add Template dialog box appears (see figure 10.28).

Figure 10.28
The Add Template dialog box.

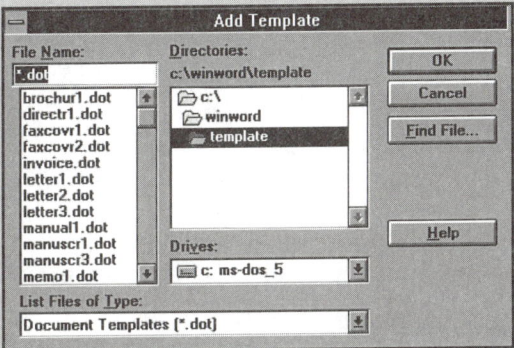

③ From the List Files of **T**ype list box, choose Document Templates (*.DOT).

④ From the **D**irectories list box, choose `C:\WINWORD\MACROS`.

⑤ From the File **N**ame list box, choose `MACRO60.DOT`.

⑥ Choose OK to return to the Templates and Add-ins dialog box. The MACRO60.DOT template appears in the **G**lobal Templates and Add-ins list box.

⑦ Choose OK.

The macros in MACRO60.DOT are now available in any of your documents through the Macro dialog box.

The MACRO60.DOT file contains several sample macros that can add useful features to Word for Windows. With one set of macros, for example, you can create a custom set of tips to display when you start Word. With another set of macros, you can search for symbol characters. In this section, you learn how to run a simple macro that creates a list of all printable characters in the font you specify. This procedure is a convenient way to see a sample sheet of the fonts included with Word.

Running a Prerecorded Macro

To run the RunWizard macro, follow these steps:

1 From the **T**ools menu, choose the **M**acro command to open the Macro dialog box (see figure 10.29).

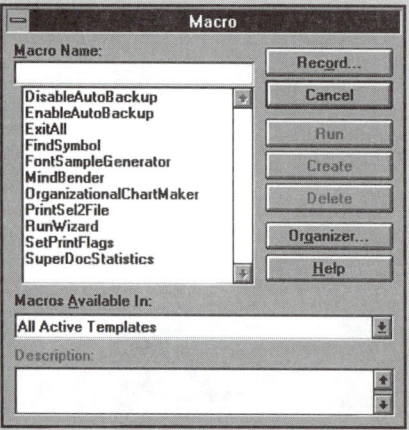

Figure 10.29
Use the Macro dialog box to run macros.

2 From the **M**acro Name list box, choose RunWizard.

The Description box displays a brief explanation of what the macro does. You can choose other macros to see their descriptions as well.

3 Choose the **R**un button.

The macro creates a dialog box that prompts you to select a wizard. The macro then creates a new document containing the specifications of the new wizard selected. To complete the document, choose **N**ext and **F**inish. If you want to, you can save your new file for later use.

Objective 6: Record Macros

You are not limited to Word's built-in macros—you can record your own. Although you can use the WordBasic macro programming language to write and edit macros, the easiest method of creating a macro is to have Word record and store your actions. All you have to do is start the macro recorder, perform the actions you want to record, and then stop the recorder.

Recording a Macro

To record your own macro, follow these steps:

1 Open a new document.

2 From the **T**ools menu, choose the **M**acro command.

3 Choose the Re**co**rd button. The **R**ecord Macro dialog box appears (see figure 10.30).

Figure 10.30
Use the Record Macro dialog box to record macros as you perform the actions you want it to complete.

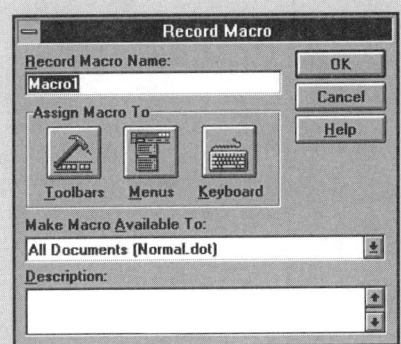

④ Type **Character** as the name for your macro. (You can accept the suggested name, but it is better to use a descriptive name). You cannot include spaces in the name, but you can use uppercase letters to indicate the beginning of each word (for example, InsertDate).

⑤ Choose OK. The Macro Record toolbar appears, REC turns bold on the status bar, and a small cassette tape appears next to the mouse pointer until you turn off the recorder (see figure 10.31).

Figure 10.31
While recording a macro, you can click the Stop Recording or Pause buttons on the Macro Record toolbar.

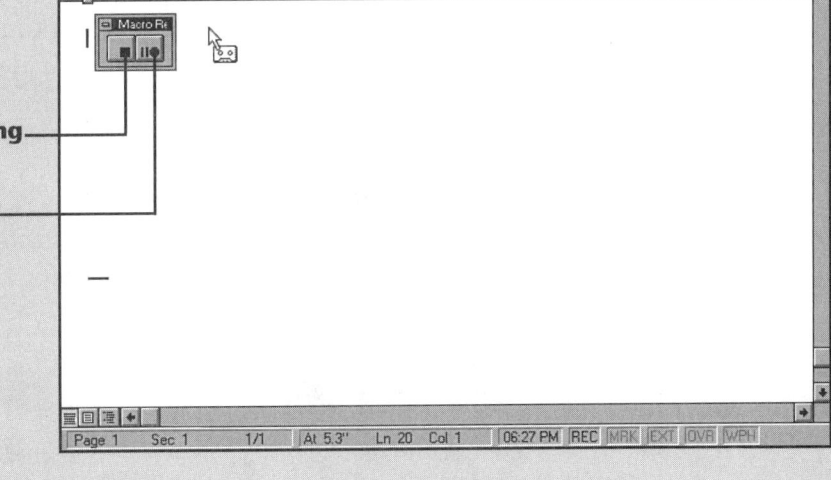

⑥ Choose the Font command on the Format menu.

⑦ Choose Helvetica, bold, 16, then choose OK.

⑧ Click the Center icon on the Formatting toolbar.

Note: *While recording a macro, you can use the mouse for menu commands and dialog boxes but not to directly manipulate text in the document.*

(continues)

Recording a Macro (continued)

 ❾ Choose the Stop button on the Macro Record toolbar to indicate that you have completed your recording.

Word stores the macro in the template, REC appears dimmed on the status bar, and the small cassette icon disappears from the mouse pointer.

By default, Word saves changes to the NORMAL.DOT template when you exit.

Tip

You can also double-click the REC box on the status bar at the bottom of the window to begin recording a macro.

If you want to use WordBasic to write macros, previous experience with macro languages or some programming background is very useful. If you do not have this kind of experience, consider buying the Microsoft Word Developer's Kit from Microsoft. Describing how to use the WordBasic programming language is beyond the scope of this book.

Objective 7: Run Macros

Word provides you with quick access to macros so that you can work as efficiently as possible. In addition to running a macro from the Macro dialog box, you also can assign the macro to a shortcut key combination, a toolbar button, or even a new menu command.

Running Macros from the Macro Dialog Box

If you do not use a macro very often, running it from the Macro dialog box may be sufficient for your needs. Running a macro from the dialog box requires no customizing after the macro has been recorded.

Running a Macro

In the preceding exercise, you created a macro named Character. To run your new macro, follow these steps:

❶ Type your name and address in a new document, and then select them.

❷ From the **T**ools menu, choose the **M**acro command. The Macro dialog box appears.

❸ From the Macros **A**vailable In list box, choose All Active Templates. Word displays a list of all macros available to you from the active templates.

④ From the **M**acro Name list box, choose Character.

⑤ Choose the **R**un button. Your name and address should appear in Helvetica 16 point, boldfaced, and centered.

The Macro dialog box also enables you to edit, delete, record macros, and open the Organizer to copy macros between templates.

> **Tip**
>
> You can execute any Word menu command from the Macro dialog box. This may be necessary if you delete a command from a menu and it is unavailable. Choose Word Commands from the Macros **A**vailable In list box, select a command from the **M**acro Name list box, and choose **R**un. Word runs the command as if you had chosen it from a menu.

Assigning Macros to Shortcut Keys

You should assign a macro that you want to run more frequently to a shortcut key combination, a menu, or a toolbar button to make it easily available. You can choose the method you find easiest to use.

In the Record Macro dialog box, you can specify a macro name, a description, and alternate ways of running the macro before actually recording it. To assign a shortcut key combination, choose the **K**eyboard button and press a shortcut key.

If you didn't assign a shortcut key combination when you first created the macro, you can do so by using the Customize dialog box.

Specifying Shortcut Key Combinations for Macros

To assign a key combination to your new macro, follow these steps:

① From the **T**ools menu, choose the **C**ustomize command. The Customize dialog box appears.

② Click the **K**eyboard tab to display the **K**eyboard section.

③ From the **C**ategories list box, choose Macros. The Macr**o**s list box displays a list of available macros.

④ From the Macr**o**s list box, choose Character.

Note: *If the macro is currently assigned to a key combination, that key combination appears in the C*u*rrent Keys list box. (You can assign a macro to more than one key combination, but it is best to save the key combination for another macro or command.)*

(continues)

Specifying Shortcut Key Combinations for Macros (continued)

5 Position the insertion point in the Press **N**ew Shortcut Key text box, and press Alt + C as the key combination to assign. Word displays the shortcut keys in the box.

Check below the Shortcut Key box to see whether that key combination is currently assigned.

6 Choose **A**ssign to assign the keystrokes you entered as the new shortcut keys for the selected command.

7 Repeat steps 3 through 6 to assign key combinations to other macros.

8 Choose Close.

You can remove a shortcut key combination by selecting the macro (in the Macros list box) and the key combination (in the C**u**rrent Keys list box). After you select both items, you can choose the **R**emove button. Note that you are removing only the shortcut key combination, not deleting the macro itself.

Assigning Macros to a Toolbar

If you use some of the same macros frequently, you may want to assign toolbar buttons for these macros. To do so, follow these steps:

1 From the **V**iew menu, choose **T**oolbars. The Toolbars dialog box appears.

2 Choose the toolbar to which you want to add the macro, and choose OK.

3 From the **T**ools menu, choose the **C**ustomize command. The Customize dialog box appears.

4 Click the **T**oolbars tab. The Customize dialog box displays toolbar options (see figure 10.32).

Figure 10.32
Use the Toolbars section of the Customize dialog box to add and remove buttons by dragging and dropping.

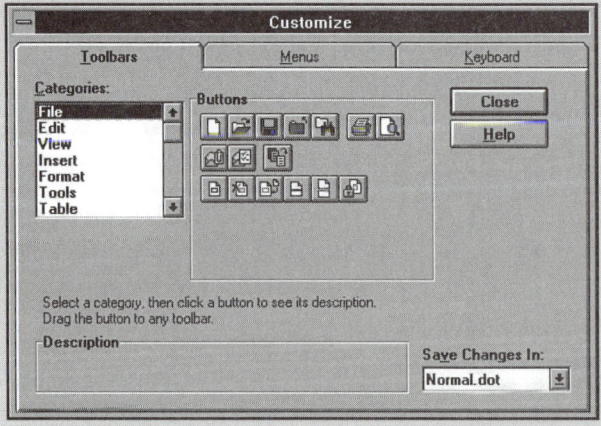

Run Macros   331

5 From the **C**ategories list box, choose Macros.

Note: *If the toolbar is full, drag a seldom used button above or below the toolbar and release the mouse button to remove it.*

6 Drag a macro from the Macros list box to a location on the toolbar on-screen, and release the mouse button. The Custom button dialog box appears.

7 Choose a button picture for your macro button, and choose **A**ssign. When you are finished, a ToolTip banner displays the macro name whenever the mouse pointer is over the macro button.

8 Repeat steps 5 through 7 to assign other macros to the toolbar.

9 Choose the Close button.

Note: *You can easily reset a toolbar to its original configuration. To remove any changes, choose the **T**oolbars command from the **V**iew menu, use the arrow keys to select the toolbar from the **T**oolbars list box, choose the **R**eset button, and choose OK. Then choose the Close button to close the Toolbars dialog box.*

You can also assign macros to Word menu commands for easy access without having to remember a keyboard combination or display a toolbar.

Assigning Macros to Menus

To assign macros to menus, follow these steps:

1 From the **T**ools menu, choose **C**ustomize. The Customize dialog box appears.

2 Click the **M**enus tab (see figure 10.33).

Figure 10.33
Use the Customize dialog box to choose options for adding and editing menu items.

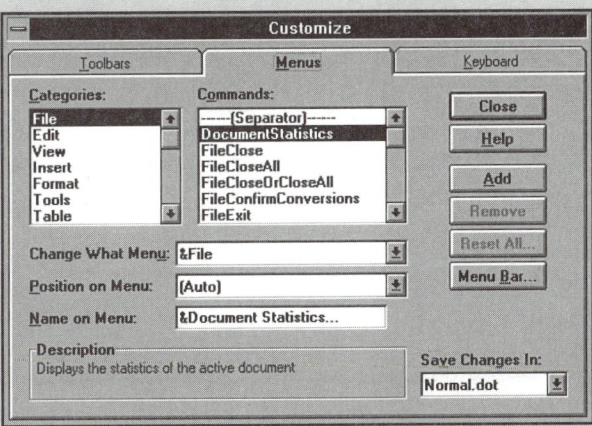

(continues)

Assigning Macros to Menus (continued)

3 From the **C**ategories list box, choose Macros.

4 From the Change What Men**u** list box, choose F&ormat.

5 From the Macr**o**s list box, choose Character.

The **N**ame on Menu text box displays the macro name that will appear in the specified menu. Notice that Word automatically inserts spaces into the name and adds an ampersand (&) before the letter that will be underlined in the modified menu.

6 If you want to change the name or underlined letter, edit the **N**ame on Menu text box.

In this exercise, F&ormat represents the F**o**rmat menu, and you press F to run the character macro from the F**o**rmat menu.

7 In the **P**osition on Menu list box, select (At Top) as the location to insert the new command on the menu.

8 Choose **A**dd to add the macro command to the menu.

9 Repeat steps 5 through 9 to assign other macros to menus.

10 Choose Close.

You can delete a menu item, such as a macro you added earlier, by selecting the menu (in the Change What Men**u** list box) and the menu item (in the **N**ame on Menu list box) you want to delete. After you select both items, choose the **Re**move button. You are deleting the *appearance* of that item on the macro, not the menu itself. To remove any changes you have made to the menus since installing Word, choose the Re**s**et All button.

Removing a Macro from a Menu

To remove the macro you added in the preceding exercise, follow these steps:

1 Press Alt+Ctrl+- (-, not the minus on the numeric keypad).

2 Choose the macro command from its menu. The command you choose disappears from the menu.

You are deleting the *appearance* of that item on the menu, not the macro itself. To remove any changes made to the menus since you installed Word, choose the Re**s**et All button.

Objective 8: Rename and Delete Macros

Using the Macro dialog box and the Organizer, you can delete macros you no longer use or rename macros to identify them more accurately.

Renaming a Macro

To rename the Character macro, follow these steps:

① From the **T**ools menu, choose the **M**acro command. The Macro dialog box appears.

② Choose the Or**g**anizer button. The Organizer dialog box appears with the **M**acros tab selected (see figure 10.34).

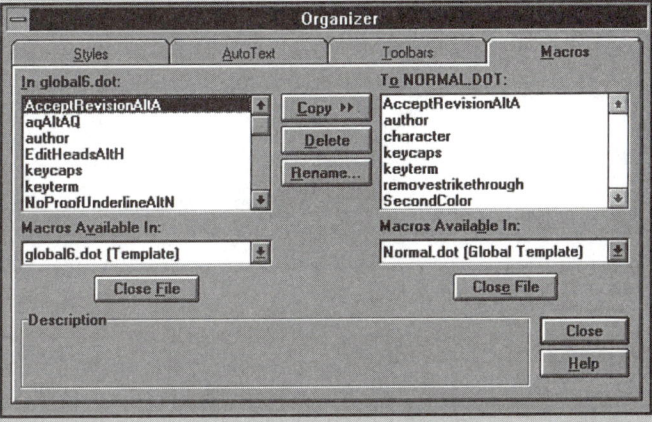

Figure 10.34
Use the Organizer to delete or rename macros in any template.

③ From the Macros A**v**ailable In list box, choose the template in which your macro is stored. Choose Character from the list.

If the template is not listed, choose the Close **F**ile button, then choose the Open **F**ile button, and open the template.

④ In the **I**n NORMAL.DOT (or your template name) list box, choose Character as the macro you want to rename.

⑤ Choose the **R**ename button. The Rename dialog box appears.

⑥ Type **CharCenter** in the New **N**ame text box and choose OK.

⑦ Choose the Close button.

Caution
You cannot undelete a macro.

Many macros have similar steps and, rather than creating a macro from the beginning, you can rename the macro, and then make changes. When the macro created is no longer useful, you can delete it.

Deleting a Macro

To delete a macro, follow these steps:

1. From the **T**ools menu, choose the **M**acro command.

   The Macro dialog box appears.

2. From the Macros **A**vailable In list box, select All Active Templates.

   If the macro does not appear, you must first open the template in which the macro is stored.

3. From the **M**acro Name list box, choose CharCenter as the macro to delete.

4. Choose the **D**elete button.

5. Choose **Y**es when prompted to delete the macro.

6. Choose the Close button.

Chapter Summary

In this chapter, you worked with Styles, AutoFormat, wizards, AutoText, and simple macros to automate your work and save you time. You learned that AutoText entries store text or pictures and that macros store instructions for executing Word commands.

Checking Your Skills

True/False Questions

For each of the following statements, circle *T* or *F* to indicate whether the statement is true or false.

T F 1. By using paragraph styles, you can control the appearance of one or more characters.

T F 2. The Paragraph Preview box shows what the paragraph formatting of the selected style looks like.

T F 3. Each template is a component of a style sheet.

T F 4. AutoText saves words, phrases, or graphics that you use regularly.

T F 5. To create a macro, you must start the recorder and record the actions.

T F **6.** When you apply a paragraph style to a paragraph, Word formats all the text in the paragraph according to that style.

T F **7.** When you create or modify a style, you can specify a style for the paragraph that follows it.

T F **8.** After you delete a style from a template, documents you create can still use that style.

T F **9.** A wizard is an automated template that leads you step by step through the process of creating a document.

T F **10.** You can store many AutoText entries in a document style.

Multiple-Choice Questions

In the blank provided, write the letter of the correct answer for each of the following questions.

____ **1.** When you apply a paragraph style to a paragraph, Word formats to that style all the _____.

    a. text in the paragraph

    b. text in the section

    c. characters in each line

    d. text on the page

    e. text in the document

____ **2.** Some of the ways to examine styles are _____.

    a. to place the insertion point into a paragraph

    b. to look at the Formatting toolbar

    c. to choose **F**ont from the **F**ormat menu

    d. to choose **P**aragraph from the **F**ormat menu

    e. all of these answers

____ **3.** Whenever you want to use the AutoText entry, type the short name and _____.

    a. press F2

    b. press F3

    c. click the AutoText button on the Standard toolbar

    d. press F4

    e. both b and c

____ 4. Which of the following steps is *not* used in creating a macro?

    a. start the macro recorder

    b. perform actions

    c. write a program for the action

    d. stop the recorder

    e. display actions

____ 5. To edit, delete, or record macros, or to open the Organizer to copy macros between templates, use the _____ dialog box.

    a. Edit

    b. Copy

    c. Record

    d. Macro

    e. Wizard

____ 6. The style that controls the appearance of one or more characters is _____.

    a. paragraph

    b. font

    c. character

    d. word

    e. page

____ 7. To see a list of shortcut keys defined in Word, open the Help menu and choose the _____ command.

    a. Contents for Help On

    b. Search for Help On

    c. Index for Help On

    d. Topics for Help On

    e. Commands for Help On

____ 8. Wizards are helpful in creating specific kinds of documents—such as agendas, fax cover sheets, and newsletters—and are an extension of _____.

    a. styles

    b. formats

c. templates

d. customs

e. frames

____ 9. If you create an AutoText entry and want to use it for another function but it needs to be changed, you can _____ the entry.

    a. rename

    b. copy

    c. delete

    d. re-enter

    e. modify the entry

____ 10. You can delete macros you no longer use or rename macros to identify them more accurately by using the _____.

    a. Organizer

    b. Macro dialog box

    c. AutoCorrect

    d. AutoFormat

    e. both a and b.

Fill-in-the-Blank Questions

In the blank provided, write the correct answer for each of the following questions.

1. A _____ is a skeleton for a document, a framework on which you create a document.

2. You can use _____ to save words, phrases, or graphics that you use regularly.

3. By default, Word automatically saves _____ when you exit.

4. To create a _____, start the recorder, perform the actions you want to record, and stop the recorder.

5. _____ automatically loads when you load a file without attaching a different template.

6. To see an expanded list of styles, press and hold down _____ while clicking the arrow at the right of the style box.

7. When you create an _____ entry, you assign it a short name to indicate the contents of the entry.

8. The _____ enables you to delete or rename macros in any template.

9. The _____ feature automatically expands the abbreviated name as you type without requiring you to press F3.

10. In the AutoText dialog box, the _____ area shows you what the selected entry looks like.

Applying Your Skills

Review Exercises

Exercise 1: Applying Styles

Open FIRST.DOC and apply the Header style to one paragraph and the Normal style to the other paragraphs. Save the file to your data disk as **FIRST.DOC**

Exercise 2: Using AutoFormat and AutoText

Using SCHEDULE.DOC, follow these steps in using AutoFormat and AutoText:

1. Apply Header Styles to the dates.

2. Use AutoFormat to format the first paragraph as double-spaced.

3. Using AutoText, format the other paragraphs with the double-space format.

4. Save the file to your data disk as **SCHEDULE.DOC**

Exercise 3: Using the Calendar Wizard

Open the Calendar Wizard, and modify it to reflect a schedule for the month of June. Save the file to your data disk as **CALENDAR.DOC**

Exercise 4: Using Agenda Wizard

Open the Agenda Wizard, and modify it to reflect the schedule for the evaluation of each employee. Refer to GUIDELINE.DOC for procedures. Save the file to your data disk as **EMPAGEN.DOC**

Exercise 5: Using AutoFormat

Using AutoFormat, format the STEPS.DOC as follows:

1. Make the first step italic text, font size 14, indented from both the left and the right.

2. Apply the same format to the second paragraph.

3. Save the file to your data disk as **STEPS.DOC**

Continuing Projects

Project 1: Practice Using Word

In the following exercise, you practice formatting in Word.

1. Open MEDICAL.DOC.

2. Format the first paragraph as double-spaced, Times Roman font, and font size 14.

3. Store the repetitive phrase *new office* in AutoText.

4. Store the graphic MEDSTAFF.WMF in AutoText.

5. Apply the Header Style to the salutation of the letter.

6. Insert the graphics MEDSTAFF.WMF at the end of the document.

7. Save the file to your data disk as **MEDICAL.DOC**.

Project 2: Federal Department Store

Complete your work on the brochure by following these steps:

1. Open OUTFIT.DOC.

2. From the Style list box, apply styles to each paragraph item description in the catalog.

3. Create a macro to apply Courier, font size 14, and center the text. Name the macro Newform.

4. Run the macro on each item name.

5. Insert the graphic JET.WMF at the end of the document.

6. Add the following text:

     Hurry for the Sale items

7. Create an AutoText entry for the graphic and text, and name it **JET.DOC**.

8. Insert the AutoText entry at the bottom of each page.

9. Save the file to your data disk as **OUTFIT.DOC**.

Project 3: Real Entertainment Corporation

Continue working on the newsletter by following these steps:

1. Open REC.DOC.

2. Create macros for the following functions:

    a. Apply paragraph styles to each Department—for example, Accounting, Marketing.

    b. Run the RunWizard macro for an agenda for the document. Save the macro as **AGENREC**.

    c. Create a customized macro menu, and include macros to print and to save.

3. Save as your changes, and close the document.

Appendix A
Working with Windows

Graphical user interface
An easy-to-use method of combining graphics, menus, and plain English commands so that the user communicates with the computer.

Microsoft Windows is a powerful operating environment that enables you to access the power of DOS without memorizing DOS commands and syntax. Windows uses a *graphical user interface* (GUI) so that you can easily see on-screen the tools you need to complete specific file and program management tasks.

This appendix, an overview of the Windows environment, is designed to help you learn the basics of Windows.

By the time you finish this appendix, you will have learned to

1. Start Windows
2. Use a Mouse in Windows
3. Understand the Windows Desktop
4. Understand the Program Manager
5. Get Help
6. Get Comfortable with Windows
7. Exit Windows

Objective 1: Start Windows

Window
A rectangular area on-screen in which you view program icons, applications, or documents.

Many computers are set to open in Windows. If your computer does not automatically open in Windows, however, you can easily access the program.

Starting Windows
To start Windows from the DOS command prompt, follow these steps:

1. Type **WIN**.
2. Press **Enter**. Windows begins loading. When it is loaded, you see the Program Manager window open on-screen.

Icon
A picture that represents a group window, an application, a document, or other element in a GUI-based program.

The Program Manager *window* includes many different elements, such as the menu bar, title bar, and icons. (You open windows, start applications, and select items by selecting the appropriate *icon*.) Your Program Manager window may look different from the window used in this book's illustrations. For example, you may have different program group icons across the bottom of the Program Manager window (see figure A.1).

Figure A.1
The first time you start Windows, a group window may be open on the desktop.

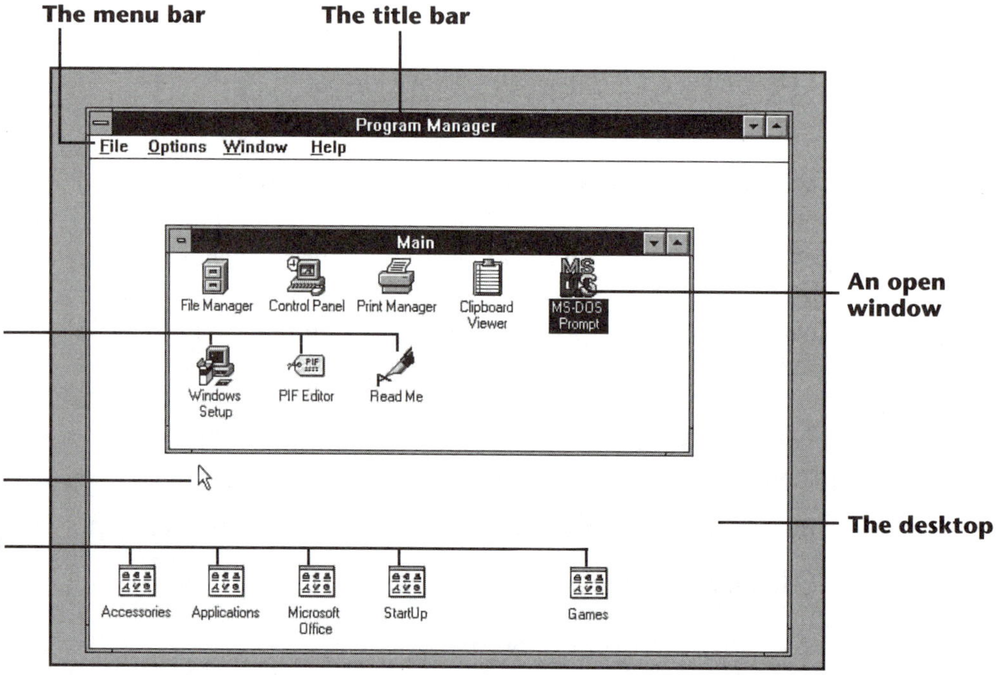

[Figure A.1: Screenshot of Program Manager window with labels pointing to: The menu bar, The title bar, An open window, The desktop, Program icons, The mouse pointer, Program group icons. The Main window shows icons for File Manager, Control Panel, Print Manager, Clipboard Viewer, MS-DOS Prompt, Windows Setup, PIF Editor, and Read Me. Program group icons at bottom: Accessories, Applications, Microsoft Office, StartUp, Games.]

Objective 2: Use a Mouse in Windows

Mouse
A pointing device used in many programs to make choices, select data, and otherwise communicate with the computer.

Windows is designed for use with a *mouse*. Although you can get by with just a keyboard, using a mouse is much easier. This book assumes that you are using a mouse.

In the Windows desktop, you can use a mouse to

- Open windows
- Close windows
- Open menus
- Choose menu commands

Mouse pointer
A symbol that appears on-screen to indicate the current location of the mouse.

- Rearrange on-screen items, such as icons and windows

The position of the mouse is indicated on-screen by a *mouse pointer*. Usually, the mouse pointer is an arrow, but it sometimes changes shape depending on the current action.

Mouse pad
A pad that provides a uniform surface for a mouse to slide on.

On-screen the mouse pointer moves according to the movements of the mouse on your desk or on a *mouse pad*. To move the mouse pointer, simply move the mouse.

There are three basic mouse actions:

- *Click*. To point to an item and press and release quickly the left mouse button. You click to select an item, such as an option on a menu. To cancel a selection, click an empty area of the desktop.

- *Double-click*. To point to an item and then press and release the left mouse button twice, as quickly as possible. You double-click to open or close windows and to start applications from icons.

- *Drag*. To point to an item, press and hold down the left mouse button as you move the pointer to another location, and then release the mouse button. You drag to resize windows, move icons, and scroll.

Note: *Unless otherwise specified, the left mouse button is used for all mouse actions.*

If you have problems... If you try to double-click but nothing happens, you may not be clicking fast enough. Try again.

Objective 3: Understand the Windows Desktop

Your screen provides a *desktop*, the background for Windows. On the desktop, each application is displayed in its own window (hence the name Windows). All windows have the same set of controls that enable you to move, resize, and manipulate the window.

If you have multiple windows open, they may overlap on the desktop, just as papers on your desk can be stacked one on top of the other. You may have one or more windows open when you start Windows.

The Title Bar

Across the top of each window is its title bar. At the right side of the title bar are the Minimize button for reducing windows to icons and the Maximize button for expanding windows to fill the desktop. At the left side of the title bar is the Control menu icon, a box with a small hyphen in it. The Control icon activates a window's Control menu (see figure A.2).

344 Working with Windows

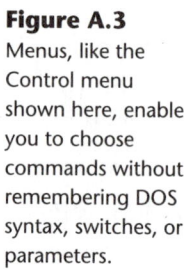

Figure A.2
Every open window has a title bar, used to identify the contents of the window.

The Main group window title bar

Menus

Menus enable you to select options to perform functions or carry out commands (see figure A.3). The Control menu enables you to control the size and position of its window, for example.

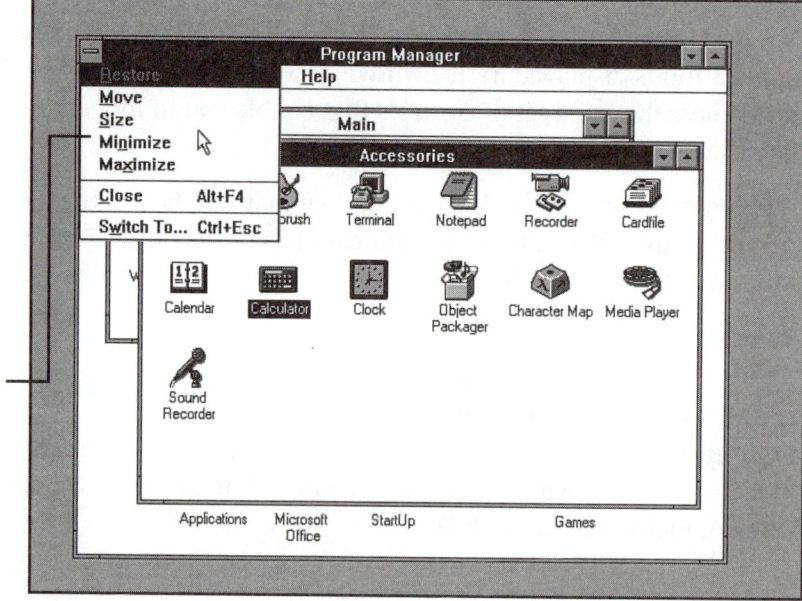

Figure A.3
Menus, like the Control menu shown here, enable you to choose commands without remembering DOS syntax, switches, or parameters.

Choose a menu command here

Dialog Boxes

Dialog box
A window that opens on-screen to provide information or to ask the user to enter additional information.

Some menu options require you to enter additional information. When you select one of these options, a *dialog box* opens (see figure A.4). You either type the additional information into a text box, select from a list of options, or select a button.

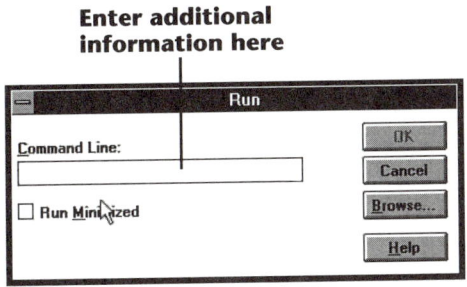

Figure A.4
In a dialog box, you provide additional information that Windows needs to complete the command.

Buttons

Buttons are areas on the screen with which you select actions or commands. Most dialog boxes have at least a Cancel button, which stops the current activity and returns to the previous screen; an OK button, which accepts the current activity; and a Help button, which opens a Help window (see figure A.5).

Figure A.5
By using buttons, you can set options or choose commands.

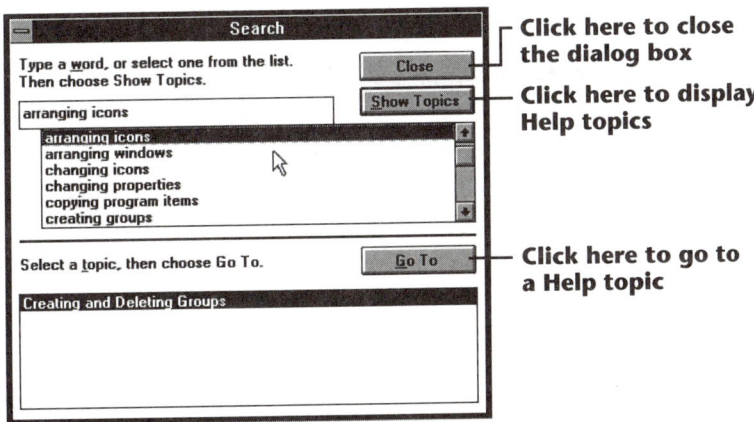

Objective 4: Understand the Program Manager

The Program Manager is the central Microsoft Windows program. When you start Microsoft Windows, the Program Manager starts automatically. When you exit Microsoft Windows, you exit the Program Manager. You cannot run Microsoft Windows if you are not running the Program Manager.

Program group
Application programs organized into a set which can be accessed through a program group window.

The Program Manager does what its name implies—it manages programs. You use the Program Manager to organize programs into groups called *program groups*. Usually, programs in a group are related, either by functionality (such as a group of accessories) or by usage (such as a group of programs used to compile a monthly newsletter).

Each program group is represented by a program group icon (see figure A.6).

Figure A.6
When you double-click a program group icon, a group window opens on-screen.

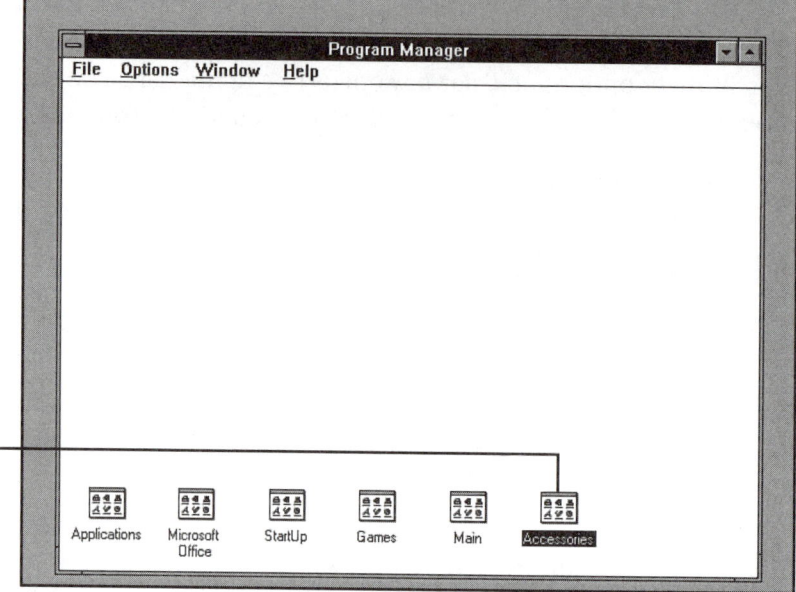

Double-click to open the Accessories group window

In each program group window, you see the icons for each individual program item in the group (see figure A.7).

Figure A.7
When you double-click a program icon, the program starts.

Double-click to start Windows Paintbrush

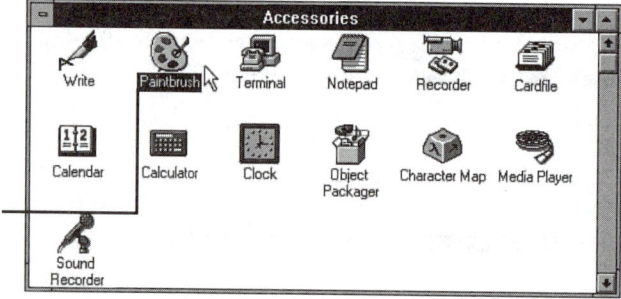

Objective 5: Get Help

Almost every Windows application has a Help menu. From the Help menu, you can start a Help program to display information about many aspects of the program.

To display Help information, take one of the following actions:

Context-sensitive
Pertaining to the current action.

- Press [F1]. The Help program starts, and a *context-sensitive* Help window opens on-screen.

- Choose **H**elp from the menu bar, and choose one of the Help menu commands.

    Note: *To choose a menu item, point to it with the mouse; then click the left mouse button.*

Displaying Help for a Topic

To display Help for a particular topic, follow these steps:

1. Choose **H**elp from the menu bar.

2. Choose **C**ontents from the Help menu. A Help Window opens; it displays the main topics for which Help is available (see figure A.8).

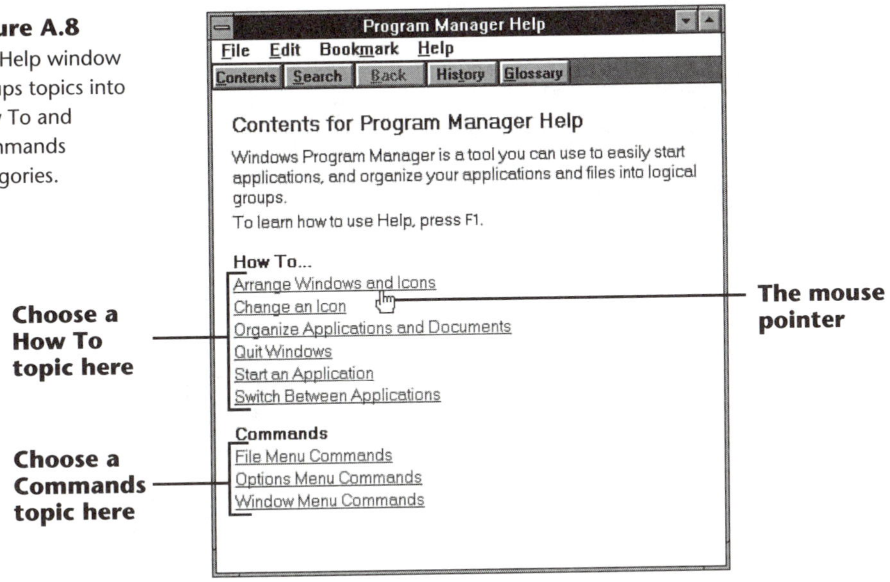

Figure A.8
The Help window groups topics into How To and Commands categories.

Choose a How To topic here

Choose a Commands topic here

The mouse pointer

3. Choose the topic for which you want additional information. Windows displays the Help information.

Closing the Help Window

To close the Help window, take one of the following actions:

- Choose **C**lose from the Help window's Control menu.
- Choose E**x**it from the Help window's File menu.
- Double-click the Control menu button.

If you have problems... To open the Control menu, click the Control menu button at the far left end of the window's title bar.

Objective 6: Get Comfortable with Windows

To be comfortable using Windows, you need to know how to control your Windows desktop, which in large part means controlling the windows themselves.

All the windows that appear in Windows, including the Program Manager, can be opened, closed, moved, and resized.

Opening a Window

To open a window, double-click the appropriate icon (see figure A.9). When you double-click a program group icon, you open a group window. When you double-click a program icon, you start that program.

> **If you have problems...** If a Control menu opens instead of a window, you are not double-clicking fast enough. Try again, or choose **R**estore from the Control menu.

Figure A.9
You can continue opening windows until the desktop is full or until you run out of memory.

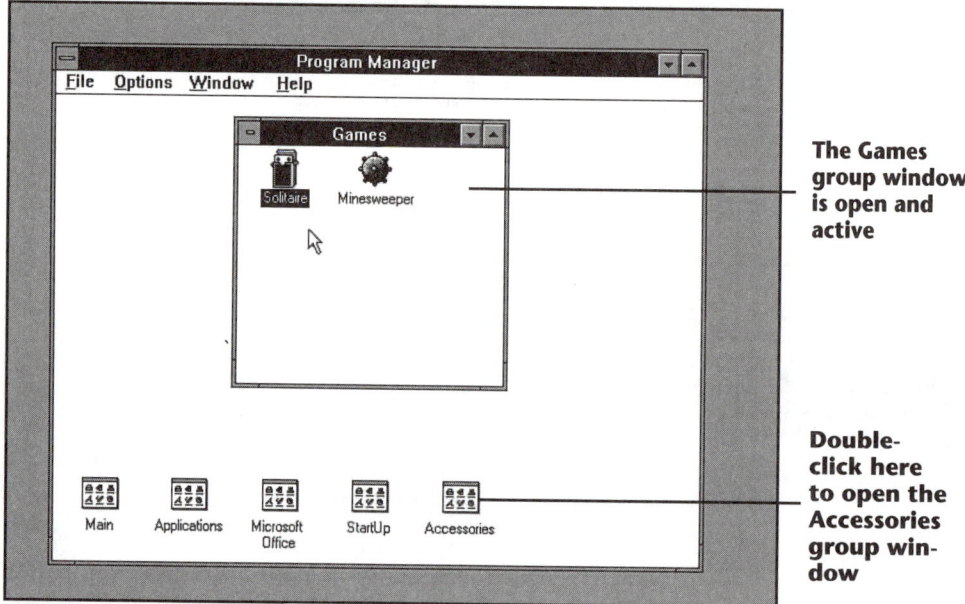

The Games group window is open and active

Double-click here to open the Accessories group window

Don't worry if your screen looks different from the screens used to illustrate this book. Your desktop may be organized differently. You still can perform all the same tasks.

Note: *You also can use the Control menu to open a window. Click the icon once to display the Control menu. Then click* **R***estore.*

Changing the Active Window

Active window
The window in which you are currently working.

No matter how many windows are open on the desktop, you can work only in the *active window*.

You can tell which window is active in two ways:

- The active window is on the top of other open windows on the desktop.
- The title bar of the active window is highlighted (see figure A.10).

Figure A.10
Four windows are open. The Games group window is the active window.

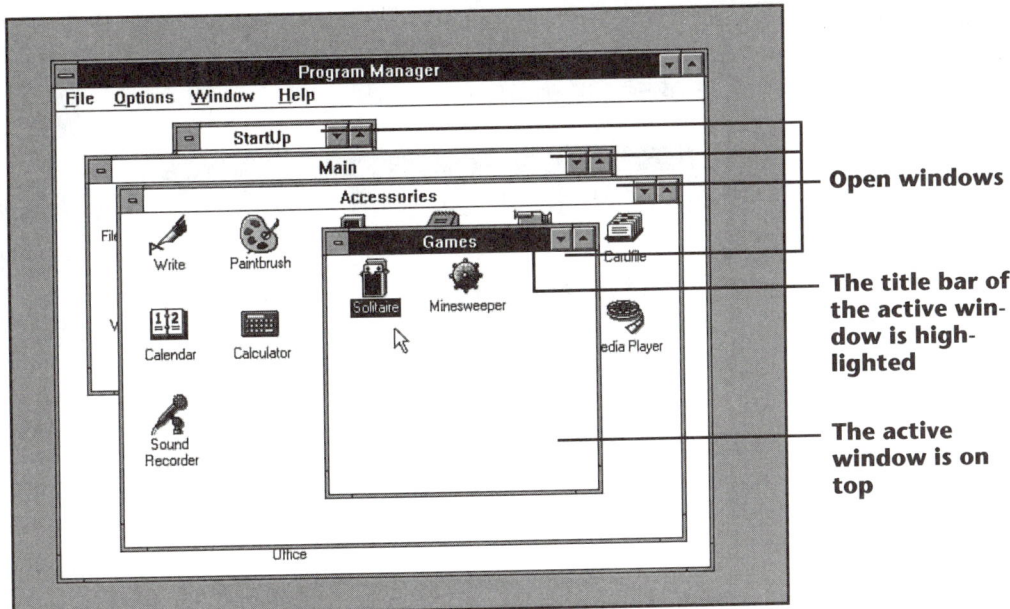

- Open windows
- The title bar of the active window is highlighted
- The active window is on top

To make a window active, click anywhere in it. The window moves to the top of the desktop, and its title bar appears in a different color or shade.

> **If you have problems...** If the window you want to make active is hidden behind another window, click **W**indow on the menu bar to open the Window menu. From the list of available windows, choose the one you want to make active.

Resizing a Window

You can change the size of any open window by dragging its borders with the mouse.

To resize a window, follow these steps:

1. Point to the border you want to move.

   Note: *When you are pointing to the border, the mouse pointer changes shape to a double-headed arrow.*

2. Press and hold down the left mouse button, and drag the border to its new location. As you drag, you see the border move along with the mouse pointer.

3. Release the mouse button. The window adjusts to the new size (see figure A.11).

   Note: *To change the height and width of the window simultaneously, drag one of the window's corners.*

Figure A.11
To resize a window, drag one of its borders.

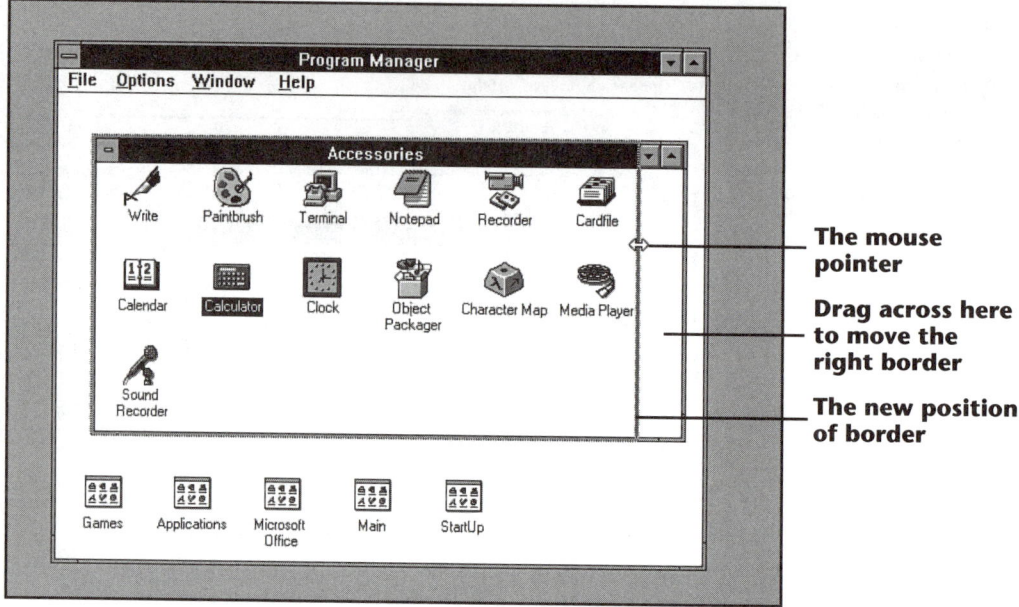

> **If you have problems...** If nothing happens when you try to change a window size, you probably are not pointing at a border. Make sure that the mouse pointer changes shape to a double-headed arrow before you drag the border.

Moving a Window

You can move a window to a different location on the screen by dragging it with the mouse.

To move a window, follow these steps:

1. Point to the window's title bar.

2. Press and hold down the left mouse button, and drag the window to the new location. You see the borders of the window move with the mouse pointer (see figure A.12).

3. Release the mouse button.

> **If you have problems...** If nothing happens when you try to move a window, you are probably not pointing to the window's title bar. Make sure that the mouse pointer is within the title bar before you drag the window.

Get Comfortable with Windows   **351**

Figure A.12
You can move a window to any location on the desktop.

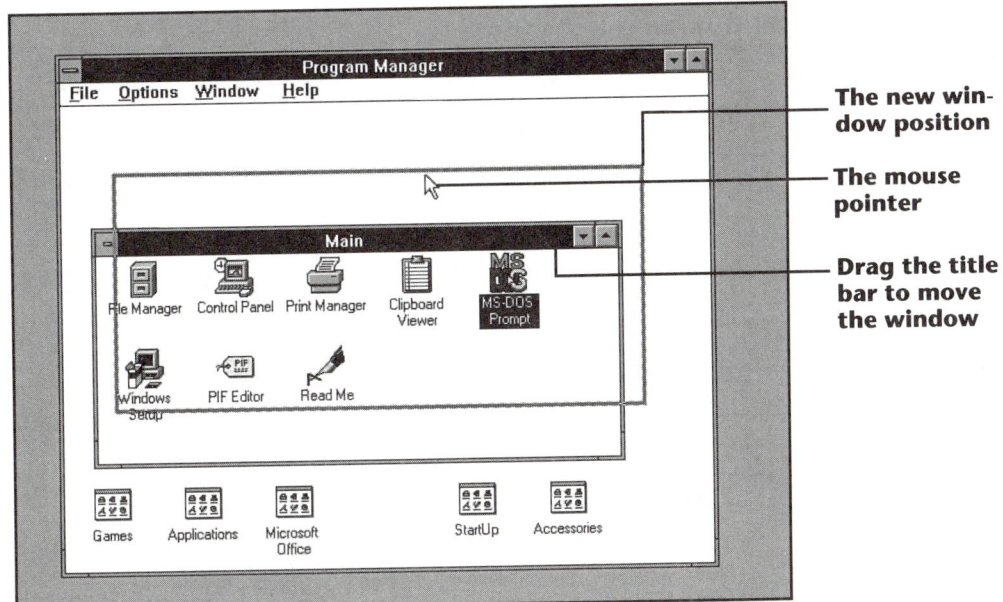

Maximizing a Window

Maximize
To increase the size of a window until it covers the desktop.

You can *maximize* a window to fill the entire desktop. Maximizing a window gives you more space in which to work.

To maximize a window, do one of the following:

- Click the Maximize button at the far right of the window's title bar. This button has an arrowhead pointing up.

- Choose **M**aximize from the window's Control menu (see figure A.13).

Figure A.13
Each window has a Maximize button at the right end of its title bar.

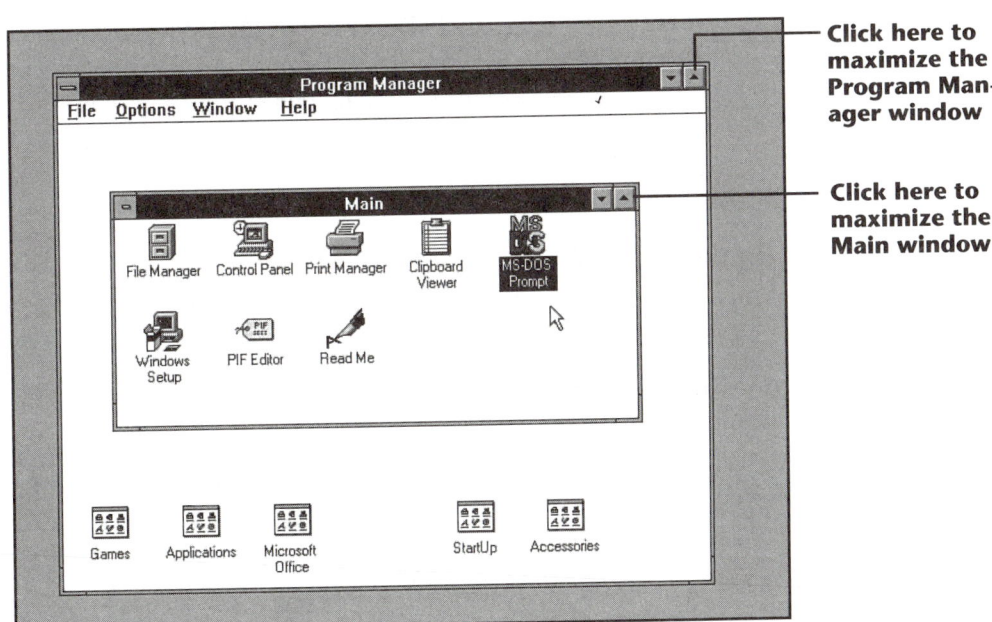

Minimizing a Window

Minimize
To reduce to an icon.

You can *minimize* a window that you are not currently using.

To minimize a window, take one of the following actions:

- Click the Minimize button on the title bar. This button has an arrowhead pointing down.

- Choose Mi**n**imize from the window's Control menu (see figure A.14).

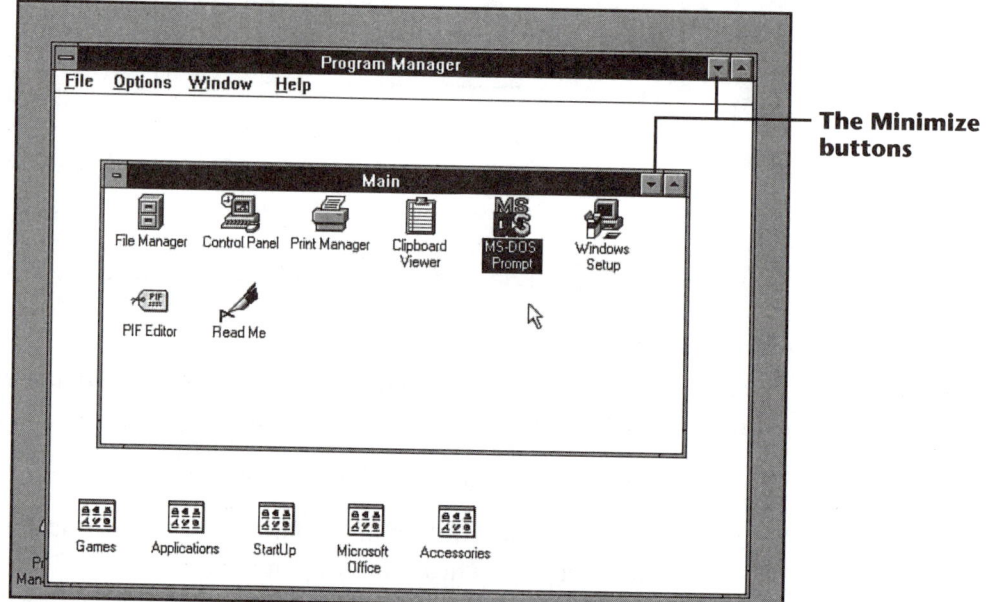

Figure A.14
Each window has a Minimize button that you can use to minimize the window to an icon.

Note: *Program group windows, such as the Main group, are reduced to program group icons at the bottom of the Program Manager. Application, utility, or document icons are positioned at the bottom of the desktop, behind any active windows. The application that has been minimized is still active; it is just out of the way.*

Restoring a Window

Restore
To return a window to its most recent size and position on the desktop.

You can *restore* a window that has been maximized or minimized to its most recent size and location.

To restore a window to its previous size, take one of the following actions:

- Click the Restore button, which replaces the Maximize button on the title bar. The Restore button has arrowheads pointing up and down.

- Choose **R**estore from the window's Control menu (see figure A.15).

Figure A.15
When you maximize a window, the Restore button appears at the left end of the title bar in place of the Maximize button.

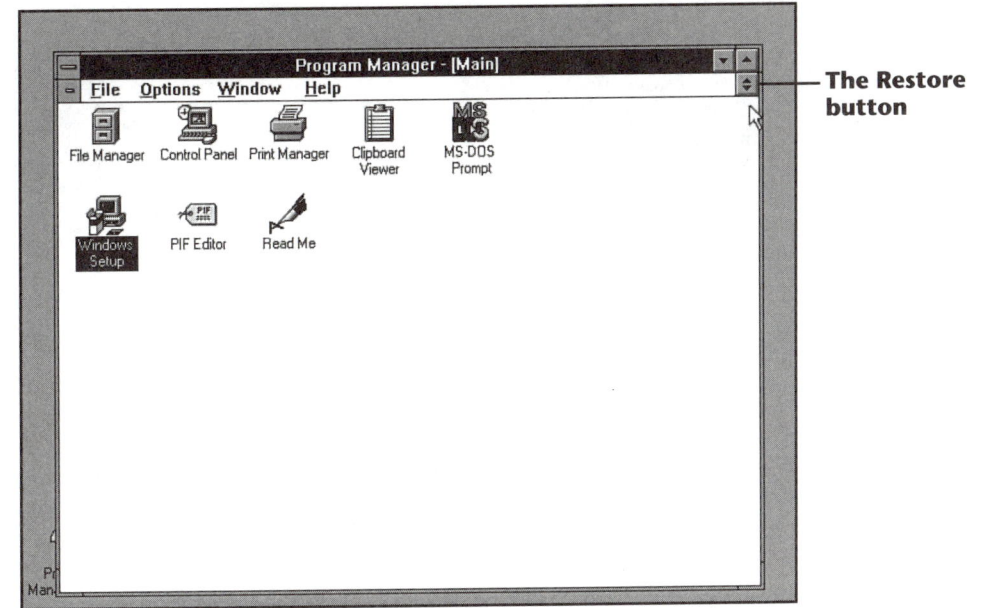

If you have problems... If you try to restore the window but nothing happens, the window has not been maximized or minimized. You cannot restore a window unless it has been maximized or minimized first.

Arranging the Windows on Your Desktop

Sometimes a desktop becomes so cluttered with open windows that you cannot tell what you are using. When that happens, you can choose either to *tile* or to *cascade* the open windows on-screen so that you can see them all.

To arrange the windows on the desktop, follow these steps:

1. Choose **W**indow from the menu bar to drop down the Window menu.

2. Choose one of the following:

    - **T**ile, to arrange the windows on-screen so that none are overlapping (see figure A.16).

    - **C**ascade, to arrange the windows on-screen so that they overlap (see figure A.17).

Tile
To arrange open windows on the desktop so that they do not overlap.

Cascade
To arrange open windows on the desktop so that they overlap, but at least a portion of each window is displayed.

Figure A.16
The windows are tiled on the desktop.

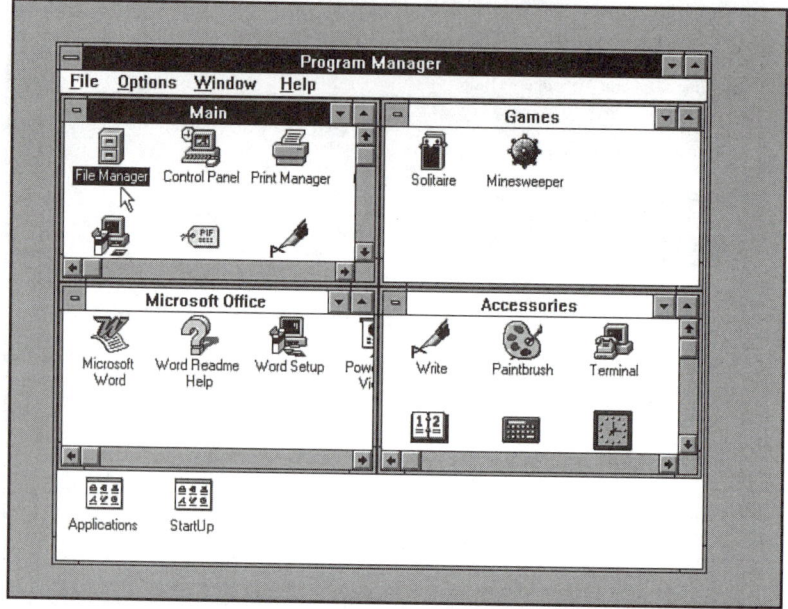

Figure A.17
The windows are cascaded on the desktop.

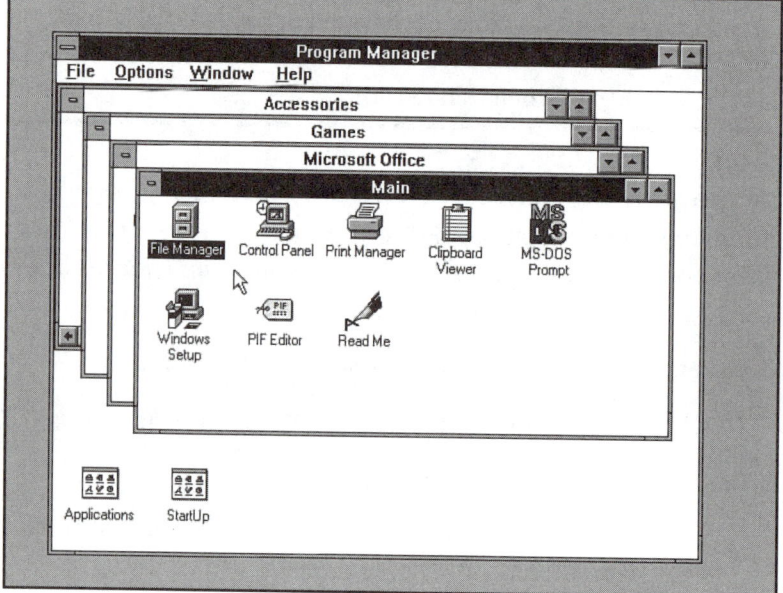

Closing a Window

To close a window, take one of the following actions:

- Choose **C**lose from the window's Control menu.

- Choose **C**lose from the window's File menu.

- Double-click the Control menu button. (To open the Control menu, click the Control menu button at the far left end of the window's title bar.)

> **If you have problems...** If the Exit Windows dialog box appears, you clicked the Control menu box for the Program Manager rather than the Control menu box for the window you want to close. Click Cancel.

Objective 7: Exit Windows

You should always exit Windows before turning off your computer. To exit Windows and return to the DOS command prompt, follow these steps:

1. Close all open windows and applications.
2. Point to File in the menu bar, and click the left mouse button.
3. Point to Exit Windows, and click the left mouse button. Windows asks you to confirm that you want to exit.
4. Point to OK, and click the left mouse button. Windows closes, and the DOS command prompt is displayed on-screen.

Note: *As a shortcut, simply double-click the Control menu button at the far left of the Program Manager title bar. Windows asks you to confirm that you want to exit. Click OK.*

Index

A

active window, changing, 348-349
Add Template dialog box, 325
adding numbers in tables, 256-257
additive search criteria, 106
Advanced Search button dialog box, 106
Agenda Wizard, 317-318
Align Left button (Formatting toolbar), 162
Align Right button (Formatting toolbar), 162
aligning paragraphs, 161-163
all caps character style, 129
alternating headers and footers, 207
Annotations option (printing), 113
applying styles, 302-304
Arrange All command (Window menu), 62
arranging windows, 353
assigning macros to toolbars, 330-331
Author text box (Summary Info dialog box), 102
AutoCorrect, 41-43
AutoCorrect command (Tools menu), 42
AutoCorrect dialog box, 42
AutoFormat, 315-316
AutoFormat button (Standard toolbar), 15
AutoFormat command (Format menu), 316
AutoFormat dialog box, 316
automatic hyphenation, 164-167
automatic kerning, 135
AutoText, 318
    creating entries, 319
    deleting and editing entries, 322-323
    inserting entries
        by name, 321
        from a list, 322
    printing entries, 323-324
    renaming entries, 323
    storing entries, 320
AutoText button (Standard toolbar), 318-319
AutoText command (Edit menu), 319
AutoText dialog box, 319

B

Background Printing option, 113
background repagination, turning off, 204-205
balancing column lengths, 220
Bar alignment option (tabs), 154
blank lines, 44-45
blocks of text
    deleting, 50
    selecting, 48
Body Text style (templates), 310-313
bold (character style), 129, 132
borders, 253-254
    paragraphs, 172-174
    Shading toolbar, 175-176
Borders and Shading command (Format menu), 172, 254
Borders in the Toolbars dialog box, 175
Bormuth Grade Level (Readability Statistics dialog box), 88
Break command (Insert menu), 213, 217, 220
Break dialog box, 203, 213, 217
built-in macros, 324-325
bulleted lists, 176-178
Bullets button (Formatting toolbar), 177

C

calculating values for tables, 254-258
capitalization, 132
Cascade command (Window menu), 353
cascading windows, 353
Cell Height and Width command (Table menu), 244-245
Cell Height and Width dialog box, 244-245
cells, 237
    deleting, 248-249
    inserting, 247-248
    moving between, 242
    selecting, 240
Center button (Formatting toolbar), 162
center-aligned tabs, 152
Change All button, 79
Change button, 79
characters, 122
    all caps style, 129
    bold style, 129
    color style, 129
    default formats, 136-137
    deleting, 51
    formatting, 121-145
        copying, 138-139
        methods, 122
        removing, 138
    hidden style, 129
    italic style, 129
    kerning (spacing), 134
    nonprinting characters, 147
    regular style, 129
    replacing, 51
    single underline style, 129
    small caps style, 129
    spacing, 133-135
    spacing with Font dialog box, 133-135
    strikethrough style, 129
    styles, 303
    styling, 129
    subscript style, 129
    superscript style, 129
    underline styles, 129
    words only underline style, 129
Check Errors button (Merge dialog box), 289
Check for Errors button (Mail Merge toolbar), 289
Checking and Reporting Errors dialog box, 289
clicking mouse, 343
Clipboard, 52-58
Close button (Header and Footer toolbar), 210
Close command
    Control menu, 347, 354
    File menu, 313, 354
closing
    Help window, 347
    windows, 354-355
    Word, 27
Coleman-Liau Grade Level (Readability Statistics dialog box), 88
collapsing headings, 184-185
Collate Copies option (printing documents), 112
color (character style), 129
columns, 215-220
    balancing lengths, 220
    deleting, 248-249
    dragging, 249-250
    equal width columns, 216-217
    formatting, 216-218
    inserting, 247
    inserting breaks, 220
    placing lines between, 220
    section breaks, 216
    selecting, 241
    separation lines, 220
    side-by-side, 234-237
    spacing, changing, 219
    titles, 237-238
    unequal width columns, 217-218
    width, 219, 242-244

Columns button (Standard toolbar), 15, 216
Columns command (Format menu), 214, 219
Columns dialog box, 219
commands
    Control menu
        Close, 347, 354
        Maximize, 351
        Minimize, 352
        Restore, 348, 352
    Edit menu
        AutoText, 319
        Copy, 55, 62, 252
        Cut, 54, 62, 250, 252
        Find, 88
        Paste, 54, 62, 251, 252
        Redo, 60
        Repeat, 60
        Repeat Paragraph, 172
        Replace, 93
        Undo, 60, 93
    File menu
        Close, 313, 354
        Exit, 21, 27, 347
        Find File, 104
        New, 17, 268, 301, 310, 317
        Open, 36
        Page Setup, 199, 201, 215
        Print, 22, 110, 315, 323
        Print Preview, 21, 66, 198
        Save, 20-21
        Save All, 20, 320
        Save As, 20-21
        Summary Info, 102
        Template, 324
    Format menu
        AutoFormat, 316
        Borders and Shading, 172, 254
        Columns, 214, 219
        Font, 127, 131, 133, 136, 327
        Heading Numbering, 188
        Page Setup, 214
        Paragraph, 160, 167-168
        Style, 304, 307, 309, 311, 314
        Tabs, 153
    Help information, 26
    Help menu, 23, 347
    Insert menu
        Break, 213, 217, 220
        Footnote, 214
        Object, 224
        Page Numbers, 206, 214
        Picture, 221
    Table menu
        Cell Height and Width, 244-245
        Delete Cells, 249
        Delete Columns, 249
        Delete Rows, 248
        Formula, 256
        Gridlines, 236
        Insert Cells, 247
        Insert Columns, 247
        Insert Rows, 246
        Insert Table, 236
        Table AutoFormat, 253
    Tools menu
        AutoCorrect, 42
        Customize, 329-331
        Grammar, 85
        Hyphenation, 165
        Macro, 326
        Mail Merge, 268-269, 287
        Options, 38, 80, 149, 204, 306
        Revisions, 107
        Spelling, 9, 78, 83
        Thesaurus, 84
    View menu
        Header and Footer, 208, 214, 223
        Outline, 179
        Page Layout, 159
        Ruler, 152
        Toolbars, 123, 175, 330
        WIN, 341
    Window menu
        Arrange All, 62
        Cascade, 353
        Tile, 353
Commands button (Find File dialog box), 105
Comments text box (Summary Info dialog box), 102-103
Compare Versions dialog box, 107
comparing documents, 107-108
confirming selections, 6
Contents command (Help menu), 23, 347
context-sensitive Help, 26, 346
Control menu commands
    Close, 347, 354
    Maximize, 351
    Minimize, 352
    Restore, 348, 352
Copy button (Standard toolbar), 15, 53, 62, 252
Copy command (Edit menu), 55, 62, 252
copy key, 55-56
copying
    documents, 105
    formatting, 138-139
    formatting with keyboard, 139
    text, 51
        between documents, 62
        in tables, 252-253
        with toolbars, 53
correcting with AutoCorrect, 41-43
Create Custom Dictionary dialog box, 80
Create Data Source dialog box, 272
Create Labels dialog box, 285
creating
    AutoText entries, 319
    custom dictionaries, 80-81
    data sources, 272-277
    documents, 16-20
    footers, 208-209
    headers, 208-209
    main document (merges), 268-271
    outlines, 179-180
    side-by-side columns, 234-237
    subheadings (outlines), 180-182
    summary information, 102-103
    tables, 234-237
    tables with Insert Table command, 236-237
Custom Button dialog box, 331
custom dictionaries, 78-83
Custom Laser Information dialog box, 284
custom tabs, 151-154
Customize command (Tools menu), 329-331
Customize dialog box, 308, 329-331
cut and paste operation, 250-251
Cut button (Standard toolbar), 15, 52, 62, 250, 252
Cut command (Edit menu), 54, 62, 250, 252

D

data
    entering in tables, 237-239
    filtering for selective merging, 290
    merging with document, 286-288
    ranges (merges), 278
    sorting before merging, 291
Data Form dialog box, 274, 276
data sources (merges), 271-278
    creating, 272-277
    data, entering, 274-275
    editing, 276
    fields
        defining, 272-273
        ordering, 273
    opening, 277-278
Date button, 208, 210
DDE (dynamic data exchange), 278
decimal-aligned tabs, 152
default character formatting, 135-137
default template (NORMAL.DOT), 301
defining fields for data sources, 272-273
Delete button, 79
Delete Cells command (Table menu), 249
Delete Columns command (Table menu), 249
Delete Rows command (Table menu), 248
deleting
    AutoText entries, 322-323
    cells, 248-249
    characters, 51
    columns, 248-249
    custom tabs, 153-154
    documents, 105
    hard page breaks, 204
    macros, 334
    macros from menus, 332
    rows, 248-249
    section breaks, 214
    styles from templates, 314
    text, 51
    with shortcut keys, 50
Demote button (Outline toolbar), 181
demoting headings, 183
deselecting text, 48
desktop, 343-345
dialog boxes, 345
    Add Template, 325
    Advanced Search button, 106
    AutoCorrect, 42
    AutoFormat, 316
    AutoText, 319
    Borders in the Toolbars, 175
    Break, 203, 213, 217
    Cell Height and Width, 244-245
    Checking and Reporting Errors, 289
    Columns, 219
    Compare Versions, 107
    Create Custom Dictionary, 80
    Create Data Source, 272
    Create Labels, 285

Custom button, 331
Custom Laser Information, 284
Customize, 308, 329-331
Data Form, 274
Document Statistics, 104
Envelope Address, 282
Envelope Options, 280
Find, 88
Find File, 104
Font, 122, 127, 131, 133, 136, 312
Formula, 256
Go To, 40-41
Grammar, 86
Heading Numbering, 188
Help information, 27
Hyphenation, 165
Insert Cells, 247
Insert Picture, 221
Insert Table, 236
Label Options, 284-285
Macro, 325-326
Mail Merge Helper, 269
Merge, 287
Modify Style, 307, 311
New, 17, 301, 310, 317
Object, 224
Open, 36
Open Data Source, 277
Options, 38, 149, 306
Organizer, 333
Page Number Format, 206
Page Numbers, 206
Page Setup, 199-201, 215
Paragraph, 160-161, 168, 312
Print, 22, 105, 110, 323
Print Setup, 111
Query Options, 290-291
Readability Statistics, 87
Record Macro, 326
Replace, 93
Revisions, 107
Save As, 21
Save Data Source, 273
Search, 104
Search for Help On, 24-26
Spelling, 78
Spelling Options, 80
Style, 304, 309, 311, 314
Summary Info, 21, 102, 105
Table AutoFormat, 253
Table Borders and Shading, 254
Tabs, 153-154
Templates and Add-ins, 324
Thesaurus, 84
Toolbars, 12, 123, 330
dictionaries, 78-83
directories
    saving documents to, 21
    searching, 104
displaying
    Formatting toolbar, 123-124
    Help, 347
    nonprinting characters, 45-46
    printers, 110
    style names, 306-307
    toolbars, 13-14
document statistics, 103-104
Document Statistics dialog box, 104
Document1, as initial document, 7
documents
    blank lines, 44-45
    comparing, 107-108
    copying, 105

    creating, 16-20
    deleting, 105
    displaying different views, 64
    editing, 35-75, 77-99
    files, inserting, 108-109
    formatting, 121-145, 197-232
    main document (merges), 268-271
    maximizing, 63
    merging with data, 286-288
    multiple, 61-68
    navigating, 37-41
    opening, 35-37
    orientation, 201
    pagination control, 203-207
    printing, 21-22, 109-114
    repaginating, 204-205
    saving, 20-21
    scrolling, 39
    searching part of, 89
    section breaks, 212-215
    sections (outlines), 187-188
    selecting with mouse, 48
    sequential numbering, 7
    sizing pages, 201
    sorting, 105
    Spelling Checker, 78-79
    splitting into two panes, 63-64
    summary information, 101-104
    tables, 233-265
    templates, 300
    text, entering, 19-20
    text, inserting, 44
    text, moving or copying between, 62
    text searches, 88-89
    Undo feature, 59
Don't Hyphenate option (Text Flow), 171
DOS, 104
dotted underline character style, 129
double underline character style, 129
double-clicking (mouse), 343
Draft Output option (printing), 112
dragging
    columns, 249-250
    indentation markers, 158-159
    mouse, 343
    text, 57
Drawing button (Standard toolbar), 16, 223
Drawing Objects option (printing), 113
drives, 21
dynamic data exchange (DDE), 278

E

Edit Data Source button
    (Mail Merge toolbar), 276
    (Save Data Source dialog box), 273
Edit menu commands, 54
    AutoText, 319
    Copy, 55, 62, 252
    Cut, 54, 62, 250, 252
    Find, 88
    Paste, 54, 62, 251-252
    Redo, 60
    Repeat, 60
    Repeat Paragraph, 172
    Replace, 93
    Undo, 60, 93

editing
    AutoText entries, 322-323
    data sources, 276
    documents, 35-75, 77-99
    footers, 212
    headers, 212
    text in tables, 251-253
enhancing text, 121-145
entering
    column titles, 237-238
    data in data sources, 274-275
    data in tables, 237-239
    records in tables, 238-239
    summary information, 103
    text, 19-20
Envelope Address dialog box, 282
Envelope Options dialog box, 280
envelopes
    main document, 270
    merge fields, inserting, 280-283
    merging, 287-288
    printer selection, 282
equal width columns, 216-217
error checking (merges), 288-289
errors (AutoCorrect), 43
Excel Worksheet button (Standard toolbar), 15
Exit command (File menu), 21, 27, 347
exiting Windows, 355
expanding
    headings, 184-185
    style names, 304-308
Explain button, 86
EXT (Extend A Selection) button, 9
extending selections, 49-50
extensions (file names), 105

F

Field Codes option (printing), 113
fields
    defining for data sources, 272-273
    merge fields, 278-286
    ordering in data sources, 273
File menu commands
    Close, 313, 354
    Exit, 21, 27, 347
    Find File, 104
    New, 17, 268, 301, 310, 317
    Open, 36
    Page Setup, 199, 201, 215
    Print, 22, 110, 315, 323
    Print Preview, 21, 66, 198
    Save, 20-21
    Save All, 20, 320
    Save As, 20-21
    Summary Info, 102
    Template, 324
files
    extensions, 105
    finding, 104-107
    inserting, 108-109
    merging, 267-297
    paths, 104
    printing to, 114
    summary information, 101-106
filtering data for selective merging, 290
Find command (Edit menu), 88
Find dialog box, 88

Find File command (File menu), 104, 114
Find File dialog box, 104-105
Find Next button, 89-90
Find Whole Words Only option (searches), 90
finding
    files, 104-107
    special characters, 91-92
finding and replacing text, 88-94
first page headers/footers, 211-212
Flesch Reading Ease (Readability Statistics dialog box), 88
Flesch-Kincaid Grade Level (Readability Statistics dialog box), 88
Font command (Format menu), 127, 131, 133, 136, 327
Font dialog box, 127, 131, 133, 136, 312
    changing and sizing fonts, 127-128
    character spacing, 133-135
    font styling, 131
    formatting documents, 122
fonts
    Font dialog box to change fonts, 127-128
    formatting, 122-129
    Formatting toolbar, 125-126
    points, 123
    Roman fonts, 123
    scalability, 123
    Script fonts, 123
    shortcut keys, changing and sizing with, 128-129
    styling, 130-132
    TrueType fonts, 122
    typefaces, 122
footers
    alternating, 207
    creating, 208-209
    differentiating for specific pages, 210-211
    editing, 212
    first page footers, 211-212
    numbering pages, 207
    positioning, 200
    tabs, 207
Footnote command (Insert menu), 214
form letters
    main document, 268-269
    merge fields, inserting, 279-280
    merging, 287-288
Format button, 311
Format menu commands
    AutoFormat, 316
    Borders and Shading, 172, 254
    Columns, 214, 219
    Font, 127, 131, 133, 136, 327
    Heading Numbering, 188
    Page Setup, 214
    Paragraph, 160, 167-168
    Style, 304, 307, 309, 311, 314
    Tabs, 153
Format Painter button (Standard toolbar), 15, 138-139
formatting
    alignment, 161-163
    AutoFormat, 315-316
    borders, 172-174
    bulleted lists, 176-178
    buttons, 130
    character spacing, 133-135

characters, 122
columns, 216-218
copying, 138-139
defaults, 135-137
fonts, 122-129
hyphenation, 164-167
indentation, 155-161
line spacing, 168-171
measurement unit setting, 149-150
mouse, 148
numbered lists, 176-178
outlines, 178-189
pages, 197-232
paragraphs, 147-196
printer selection, 121
printers, 149
removing, 138
removing and repeating, 171-172
ruler, 148
sections, 214-215
Tabs dialog box, 148
tabs, setting, 151-154
text, 121-145
Formatting toolbar, 122
    Align Left button, 162
    Align Right button, 162
    Bullets button, 177
    Center button, 162
    displaying, 123-124
    font styling, 130
    fonts, changing, 125
    fonts, sizing, 126
    Indentation buttons, 155-156
    Justify button, 162
    Numbering button, 178
    paragraph formatting, 149, 155-156, 162-163
Formula command (Table menu), 256
Formula dialog box, 256
Full Screen view, 64, 67-68

G

Go To dialog box, 40-41
Grammar Checker, 85-88
Grammar command (Tools menu), 85
Grammar dialog box, 86
graphical user interface (GUI), 341
gridlines, 253
Gridlines command (Table menu), 236
GUI (graphical user interface), 341
gutter spacing, 200

H

hanging indents, 157-158, 161
hard page breaks, 203-204
Header and Footer command (View menu), 208, 214, 223
Header and Footer toolbar, 208, 210
headers, 207-212
    alternating, 207
    creating, 208-209
    differentiating for specific pages, 210-211
    editing, 212
    first page headers, 211-212
    insertion point, 207

numbering pages, 207
positioning, 200
tabs, 207
see also footers
Heading Numbering command (Format menu), 188
Heading Numbering dialog box, 188
headings (outlines)
    changing, 183-189
    collapsing and expanding, 184-185
    demoting, 183
    numbering, 188-189
    ordering, 184
    promoting, 183
height adjustments (rows), 245-246
Help, 22-27
    command information, 26
    context-sensitive Help, 26
    context-sensitivity, 346
    dialog box information, 27
    displaying, 347
    general Help, 23
    Search for Help On dialog box, 24-26
    Windows, 346-347
    Word Help Contents, 23
Help button (Standard toolbar), 16
Help menu commands
    Contents, 23, 347
    Index, 26
Help window, 347
hidden text, 129, 132
Hidden Text option (printing), 113
horizontal ruler, 7
hyphenation, 164-167
Hyphenation command (Tools menu), 165
Hyphenation dialog box, 165

I

icons, 342
Ignore All button, 79
Ignore button, 79
Ignore Rule button, 86
ignoring Grammar Checker suggestions, 86
importing pictures, 220-222
Indentation buttons (Formatting toolbar), 155-156
indentation
    first lines to right, 161
    Formatting toolbar, 155-156
    hanging indents, 157-158, 161
    markers, 158-159
    mouse, 158-159
    normal indents, 156-157
    Paragraph dialog box, 160-161
    paragraphs, 155-161
    ruler, 158-159
Index (Help menu), 26
Insert AutoText button (Standard toolbar), 15
Insert Cell button (Standard toolbar), 247
Insert Cells command (Table menu), 247
Insert Cells dialog box, 247
Insert Chart button (Standard toolbar), 16
Insert Columns button (Standard toolbar), 247

Insert Columns command (Table menu), 247
Insert menu commands
　　Break, 213, 217, 220
　　Footnote, 214
　　Object, 224
　　Page Numbers, 206, 214
　　Picture, 221
Insert Merge Field button (Mail Merge toolbar), 279
Insert Microsoft button (Standard toolbar), 15
Insert mode, 44
Insert Picture dialog box, 221
Insert Rows button (Standard toolbar), 246
Insert Rows command (Table menu), 246
Insert Symbol button, 225
Insert Table button (Standard toolbar), 15, 234
Insert Table command (Table menu), 236-237
Insert Table dialog box, 236
inserting
　　AutoCorrect error entries, 43
　　AutoText entries, 321-322
　　blank lines, 44-45
　　cells, 247-248
　　column breaks, 220
　　columns, 247
　　files, 108-109
　　hard page breaks, 203-204
　　merge fields
　　　　envelopes, 280-283
　　　　form letters, 279-280
　　　　labels, 284-286
　　　　main document, 278-286
　　rows, 246-247
　　second-level subheadings (outlines), 183
　　section breaks, 213-214
　　text, 44
　　words in custom dictionaries, 82-83
insertion point, 7-8, 18
　　headers, 207
　　moving, 37-40
installing macros, 324-326
italic (character style), 129, 132

J-K

Justify button (Formatting toolbar), 162

Keep Lines Together option (Text Flow), 171
Keep With Next option (Text Flow), 171
kerning, 134-135
keyboard
　　alignment, 163
　　applying styles, 303
　　extending selections, 50
　　font styling, 132
　　formatting documents, 122, 139, 149
　　indents, 156-159
　　line spacing, 168-169
　　moving insertion point, 39-40
　　selecting text, 48-49
Keywords text box (Summary Info dialog box), 102-103

L

Label Options dialog box, 284-285
labels
　　main document, 270-271
　　merge fields, inserting, 284-286
　　merging, 287-288
Landscape orientation, 201
left-aligned tabs, 152
line spacing, 168-171
lines, selecting with mouse, 48
linking picture files, 222
Look Up button, 85

M

Macro command (Tools menu), 326
Macro dialog box, 325-326, 328-329
Macro Record toolbar, 327-328
macros
　　assigning to toolbars, 330-331
　　built-in macros, 324-325
　　deleting, 334
　　installing, 324-326
　　recording, 326-328
　　removing from menus, 332
　　renaming, 333
　　running, 326, 328-332
　　shortcut keys, 329-330
Mail Merge button (Mail Merge toolbar), 288
Mail Merge command (Tools menu), 268-269, 287
Mail Merge Helper, 267, 287-288
Mail Merge Helper dialog box, 269
Mail Merge toolbar, 276
　　Check for Errors button, 289
　　Edit Data Source button, 276
　　Insert Merge Field button, 279
　　Mail Merge button, 288
　　Merge to New Document button, 288
　　Merge to Printer button, 288
　　View Merged Data button, 279
mailing labels, 271
main dictionary, 79
main document (merges), 268-271
　　data sources, opening, 277-278
　　envelopes, 270
　　form letters, 268-269
　　labels, 270-271
　　merge fields, inserting, 278-286
manual hyphenation, 166-167
margins, 198-200
Match Case option
　　Replace command, 93
　　searches, 90
Maximize button, 63, 351
Maximize command (Control menu), 351
maximizing windows, 63, 351
measurement units, 149-150
Merge dialog box, 287-289
merge fields
　　envelopes, 280-283
　　form letters, 279-280
　　labels, 284-286
　　main document, 278-286
Merge to New Document button (Mail Merge toolbar), 288
Merge to Printer button (Mail Merge toolbar), 288
merges
　　data and document, 286-288
　　data sources, 271-278
　　envelopes, 287-288
　　error checking, 288-289
　　files, 267-297
　　form letters, 287-288
　　from Mail Merge Helper, 287-288
　　labels, 287-288
　　Mail Merge Helper, 267
　　main document, creating, 268-271
　　selective merging, 289-290
　　sorting data, 291
　　toolbar shortcuts, 288
Minimize button, 352
Minimize command (Control menu), 352
minimizing windows, 352
Mirror Margins option (Page Setup dialog box), 200
Modify button, 311
Modify Style dialog box, 307, 311
modifying
　　Body Text style in templates, 310-313
　　Standard toolbar, 10-11
　　styles, 310-313
　　see also editing
mouse
　　clicking, 343
　　double-clicking, 343
　　dragging, 343
　　formatting, 148
　　indents, 158-159
　　moving insertion point, 37-39
　　selecting items, 47-48
　　setting tabs, 152
　　splitting documents into two panes, 63-64
　　Windows, 342-343
mouse pad, 343
mouse pointer, 342
Move Down button (Outline toolbar), 184, 188
move key, 55-56
Move Up button (Outline toolbar), 184
moving
　　between cells, 242
　　columns by dragging, 249-250
　　custom tabs, 153
　　document sections (outlines), 187-188
　　in documents, 37-41
　　insertion point, 37-40
　　rows with cut and paste operation, 250-251
　　text, 51
　　　　between documents, 62
　　　　Edit menu, 54
　　　　Spike, 58
　　　　tables, 252
　　　　toolbars, 52
　　to specific document locations, 40-41
　　windows, 350
MRK (mark revisions) button, 9
Multiple Pages button (Print Preview toolbar), 67
multiplying numbers in tables, 257-258

N

naming
    AutoText entries, 323
    macros, 333
New button (Standard toolbar), 15, 18
New command (File menu), 17, 268, 301, 310, 317
New dialog box, 17, 301, 310, 317
New File button, 61
Next Sentence button, 86
nonbreaking hyphens, 164
nonprinting characters, 45-46, 91, 147
normal hyphens, 164
normal indents, 156-157
Normal style, 301
Normal template, 16-17, 301, 310
Normal view, 8, 64-65, 67, 186-187, 301
NORMAL.DOT (default template), 301
numbered lists, 176-178
numbering
    documents, 7
    headings, 188-189
    pages, 205-207
Numbering button (Formatting toolbar), 178
numbers (tables), 256-258
numerals in words, ignoring (Spelling Checker), 83

O

Object command (Insert menu), 224
Object dialog box, 224
Open button (Standard toolbar), 15, 36
Open command (File menu), 36
Open Data Source dialog box, 277
Open dialog box, 36
Open Read Only option (Find File dialog box), 105
opening
    data sources, 277-278
    documents, 35-37
    Tabs dialog box, 154
    windows, 348
optional hyphens, 164
Options command (Tools menu), 38, 80, 149, 204, 306
Options dialog box, 38, 149, 306
ordering
    fields in data sources, 273
    headings, 184
Organizer dialog box, 333
orientation, 201
Outline command (View menu), 179
Outline toolbar, 179
    Demote button, 181
    Move Down button, 184, 188
    Move Up button, 184
    Promote button, 183, 186
Outline view, 8, 64, 66, 179, 186-187
outlines (paragraph formatting)
    creating, 179-180
    document sections, moving, 187-188

headings
    changing, 183-189
    collapsing and expanding, 184-185
    numbering, 188-189
    ordering, 184
    second-level, 183
    subheadings, 180-182
Overtype mode, 44
OVR (Overtype mode) button, 9

P

Page Break Before option (Text Flow), 171
page breaks
    hard and soft breaks compared, 203
    setting, 203-204
Page Layout command (View menu), 159
Page Layout view, 8, 64, 66, 198
Page Number button, 209
Page Number Format dialog box, 206
Page Numbers button (Header and Footer toolbar), 210
Page Numbers command (Insert menu), 206, 214
Page Numbers dialog box, 206
Page Setup button (Header and Footer toolbar), 210
Page Setup command
    File menu, 199, 201, 215
    Format menu, 214
Page Setup dialog box, 199-201, 215
pages
    formatting, 197-232
    numbering, 205-207
    printing, 111-112
    size and orientation, 201
pagination, 203-207
panes (windows), 61-64
paper sources (printers), 202
Paragraph command (Format menu), 160, 167-168
Paragraph dialog box, 168, 312
    alignment, 163
    formatting, 149
    indentation, 160-161
    line spacing, 168-169
    Text Flow options, 170-171
paragraph marks, 47, 147-148
Paste button (Standard toolbar), 15, 52, 62, 251-252
Paste command (Edit menu), 54, 62, 251-252
Pattern Matching option (searches), 90
picas (measurement), 150
Picture command (Insert menu), 221
points (font sizes), 123, 150
POLICY.DOC file, 66-67
positioning
    footers, 200
    headers, 200
    toolbars, 10-11
Print button (Standard toolbar), 15, 22
Print command (File menu), 22, 110, 315, 323
Print dialog box, 22, 105, 110-112, 323
Print Preview, 15, 21, 64, 66-67, 198
Print Setup dialog box, 111

printers
    displaying, 110
    envelopes (merges), 282
    paragraph formatting, 149
    selecting, 110-111, 121
printing
    annotations, 113
    AutoText entries, 323-324
    background, 113
    collating, 112
    documents, 21-22, 109-114
    draft, 112
    drawing objects, 11
    field codes, 113
    Find File command, 114
    hidden text, 113
    multiple documents, 114
    pages, 111-112
    reverse order, 112
    special information, 113
    style sheets, 315
    Summary Info, 113
    to files, 114
    unopened documents, 114
Program Manager (Windows), 342, 345-346
Promote button (Outline toolbar), 183, 186
promoting headings (outlines), 183

Q–R

Query Options dialog box, 290-291
ranges (data) in merges, 278
Readability Statistics dialog box, 87-88
REC (macro recorder) button, 9
Record Macro dialog box, 326
recording macros, 326-328
records in tables, 238-239
Redo button (Standard toolbar), 15-16, 58-75
Redo command (Edit menu), 60
regular character style, 129
removing
    formatting, 138
    macros from menus, 332
    paragraph formatting, 171-172
    see also deleting
renaming
    AutoText entries, 323
    macros, 333
repagination, 204-205
Repeat command (Edit menu), 60
Repeat Paragraph command (Edit menu), 172
repeating paragraph formatting, 171-172
Replace button, 92
Replace command (Edit menu), 93
Replace dialog box, 93
replacing
    characters, 51
    text, 88-94
resizing windows, 349-350
Restore button, 352
Restore command (Control menu), 348, 352
restoring
    default character formats, 136-137
    windows, 352-353
Reverse Print Order option, 112

Revisions command (Tools menu), 107
Revisions dialog box, 107
right-aligned tabs, 152
Roman fonts, 123
rows
    cutting and pasting, 250-251
    deleting, 248-249
    height adjustments, 245-246
    inserting, 246-247
    selecting, 241
ruler
    margin setting, 198-199
    paragraph formatting, 148, 158-159
    tabs, setting, 152
Ruler command (View menu), 152
running macros, 326, 328-332

S

Same as Previous button (Header and Footer toolbar), 210
Save All command (File menu), 20, 320
Save As command (File menu), 20-21
Save As dialog box, 21
Save button (Standard toolbar), 15, 20-21
Save command (File menu), 20-21
Save Data Source dialog box, 273
saving documents, 20-21
scalable fonts, 123
Script fonts, 123
scroll bars, 7-8, 39
search criteria as additive, 106
Search dialog box, 104
Search for Help On dialog box, 24-26
searches, 89-91
searching
    directories, 104
    document parts, 89
    files with summary information, 106
    for files, 104-107
    for synonyms, 85
    for text, 88-89
second-level subheadings (outlines), 183
section breaks (outlines), 212-215
selecting
    cells, 240
    columns, 241
    confirming selections, 6
    extending selections, 49-50
    paper sources, 202
    printers, 110-111
    rows, 241
    Standard toolbar, 15-16
    text, 46-50
selective merging, 289-290
Send Behind Text button, 223
separation lines (columns), 220
sequential numbering of documents, 7
Set Up Main Document button (Save Data Source dialog box), 273
setting
    default character formats, 136
    margins, 198-200
    measurement unit, 149-150
    page breaks, 203-204
    tabs, 151-154

shading, 175-176, 253-254
Shading toolbar, 175-176
shaping toolbars, 10-11
Shortcut Key button, 307
shortcut keys
    changing fonts, 128-129
    deleting text, 50
    macros, 329-330
    moving between cells, 242
    sizing fonts, 128-129
    styles
        applying, 303
        assigning, 307-308
        fonts, 132-133
Show Between button (Header and Footer toolbar), 210
Show Next button (Header and Footer toolbar), 210
Show Previous button (Header and Footer toolbar), 210
Show/Hide button
    Header and Footer toolbar, 210
    Standard toolbar, 16, 45, 148
side-by-side columns, 234-237
single underline character style, 129
sizing
    fonts
        Font dialog box, 127-128
        Formatting toolbar, 126
        shortcut keys, 128-129
    pages, 201
    panes, 64
    toolbar buttons, 12-13
    windows, 349-350
small caps (character style), 129
soft page breaks, 203
sorting
    data before merging, 291
    documents, 105
Sounds Like option (searches), 90
spacing
    between paragraphs, 169-170
    characters, 133-135
    characters with Font dialog box, 133-135
    columns, 219
    gutters, 200
    replacement text strings, 94
Special button, 91
special characters, 91-92
special text effects, 222-226
Spelling button (Standard toolbar), 15, 78
Spelling Checker, 9-20, 77-83
Spike, 58
split box (scroll bars), 8
splitting documents into two panes, 63-64
Standard toolbar, 7, 9-20
    AutoText button, 318-319
    Copy button, 53, 62, 252
    Cut button, 52, 62, 250, 252
    Format Painter, 138-139
    Insert Cell button, 247
    Insert Columns button, 247
    Insert Rows button, 246
    Insert Table button, 234
    modifying, 10-11
    Open button, 36
    Paste button, 52, 62, 251-252
    Print Preview button, 66
    Redo button, 58-75, 59
    selecting from, 15-16
    Show/Hide button, 45, 148

    Undo button, 58-60
starting
    Spelling Checker, 78
    Windows, 341-342
    Word, 6
statistics, 103-104
status bar, 8-9
Stop button (Macro Record toolbar), 328
storing AutoText entries, 320
strikethrough character style, 129
style area, 9
Style command (Format menu), 304, 307, 309, 311, 314
Style dialog box, 304, 309, 311, 314
style sheets, 300-315
styles, 300-315
    applying, 302-304
    characters, 129, 303
    deleting from templates, 314
    displaying names, 306-307
    expanding lists, 304-308
    fonts, 130-132
    modifying, 310-313
    Normal template, 301
    shortcut key assignments, 307-308
    templates, 310-313
subheadings (outlines), 180-183
Subject text box (Summary Info dialog box), 102-103
subscript (character style), 129
Summary Information, 21, 101-106, 113
superscript character style, 129
Suppress Line Numbers option (Text Flow), 171
Switch from Header to Footer button, 208
switching between views, 64-65
switching measurement units, 149-150
synonyms (Spell Checker), 85

T

Table AutoFormat command (Table menu), 253
Table AutoFormat dialog box, 253
Table Borders and Shading dialog box, 254
Table menu commands
    Cell Height and Width, 244-245
    Delete Cells, 249
    Delete Columns, 249
    Delete Rows, 248
    Formula, 256
    Gridlines, 236
    Insert Cells, 247
    Insert Columns, 247
    Insert Rows, 246
    Insert Table, 236
    Table AutoFormat, 253
tables, 233-265
    adding numbers, 256-257
    borders, 253-254
    calculating values, 254-258
    cells, 237, 247-248
    columns
        inserting, 247
        moving, 249-250
        width, 242-244
    creating, 234-237

364 tables

tables (continued)
- data entry, 237-239
- gridlines, 253
- multiplying numbers, 257-258
- record entry, 238-239
- rows
  - height, 245-246
  - inserting, 246-247
  - moving, 250-251
- shading, 253-254
- text
  - copying, 252-253
  - editing, 251-253
  - moving, 252

tabs
- bar alignment, 154
- center-aligned, 152
- custom, 151
- decimal-aligned, 152
- default, 151
- headers and footers, 207
- left-aligned, 152
- right-aligned, 152
- setting, 151-154

Tabs command (Format menu), 153
Tabs dialog box, 148, 153-154
Template command (File menu), 324
templates, 300
- Body Text style, 310-313
- Normal template, 16-17, 301, 310
- NORMAL.DOT, 301
- styles, deleting, 314

Templates and Add-ins dialog box, 324
text
- copying, 51
  - between documents, 62
  - in tables, 252-253
  - with toolbars, 53
- deleting, 50-51
- deselecting, 48
- dragging, 57
- entering in documents, 19-20
- Find and Replace operation, 88-94
- formatting, 121-145
- inserting, 44
- insertion point, 7
- moving, 51
  - between documents, 62
  - in tables, 252
  - with Edit menu, 54
  - with the Spike, 58
  - with toolbars, 52
- paragraph marks, 47
- replacing, 93
- searching for, 88-89
- selecting, 46-50
- special effects, 222-226
- tables, 251-253

text area, 7, 18
Text Flow options (Paragraph dialog box), 170-171
Thesaurus, 83-85
Thesaurus command (Tools menu), 84
Thesaurus dialog box, 84
Tile command (Window menu), 353
tiling windows, 353
Time button (Header and Footer toolbar), 208, 210
time of day, 8
title bar, 343
Title text box (Summary Info dialog

box), 102-103
titles in columns, 237-238
toolbars, 9-16
- assign macros, 330-331
- copying text, 53
- displaying, 13-14
- Formatting toolbar, 122, 155-156
- Header and Footer, 208
- Macro Record, 327
- Mail Merge, 276
- merging shortcuts, 288
- Outline, 179
- positioning, 10-11
- Print Preview, 67
- Shading, 175-176
- shaping, 10-11
- sizing buttons, 12-13
- Standard toolbar, 7, 9-20

Toolbars command (View menu), 123, 175, 330
Toolbars dialog box, 12, 123, 330
Tools menu commands
- AutoCorrect, 42
- Customize, 329-331
- Grammar, 85
- Hyphenation, 165
- Macro, 326
- Mail Merge, 268-269, 287
- Options, 38, 80, 149, 204, 306
- Revisions, 107
- Spelling, 9, 78, 83
- Thesaurus, 84

ToolTips, 9
TrueType fonts, 122
typefaces (fonts), 122
typing text, 19-20

U

underlining, 132
Undo button (Standard toolbar), 15-16, 58-60
Undo command (Edit menu), 60, 93
Undo feature, 58
Undo Last button, 79
undoing spelling changes, 79
Update Display button, 225
Update Fields option (printing), 112
Update Links option (printing), 113
uppercase lettering, (Spelling Checker), 83
Use Pattern Matching option (searches), 90

V

value calculation for tables, 254-258
View menu commands
- Header and Footer, 208, 214, 223
- Outline, 179
- Page Layout, 159
- Ruler, 152
- Toolbars, 123, 175, 330

View Merged Data button (Mail Merge toolbar), 279
View Source button (Data Form dialog box), 276
viewing document statistics, 103-104
views

- document view, 8
- displaying documents, 64
- Full Screen, 64, 67-68
- Normal, 8, 64-65, 186-187, 301
- Outline, 8, 64, 66, 179
- Page Layout, 8, 64, 66
- Print Preview, 64
- switching between, 64-65

W–Z

watermarks, 223-224
Widow/Orphan Control option (Text Flow), 171
widths (columns), 219, 242-244
wild-card characters, 90-91, 104
WIN command, 341
Window menu commands
- Arrange All, 62
- Cascade, 353
- Tile, 353

Windows, 341-355
- buttons, 345
- desktop, 343-345
- dialog boxes, 345
- exiting, 355
- GUI (graphical user interface), 341
- Help information, 346-347
- menus, 344
- mouse, 342-343
- Program Manager, 345-346
- starting, 341-342
- title bar, 343

windows
- active window, 348-349
- arranging, 353
- cascading, 353
- closing, 354-355
- maximizing, 351
- minimizing, 352
- moving, 350
- multiple documents, 61-68
- opening, 348
- panes, 61
- Program Manager, 342
- restoring, 352-353
- sizing, 349-350
- tiling, 353

wizards, 316-318
Word
- closing, 27
- starting, 6

Word Help Contents, 23-24
word wrap, 18-19
WordArt, 224-226
WPH (help message) button, 9

Zoom Control button (Standard toolbar), 16